BANTAM BOOKS

NEW YORK   TORONTO   LONDON   SYDNEY   AUCKLAND

Super
Casino

INSIDE THE
"NEW"
LAS VEGAS

Pete Earley

This edition contains the complete text of the
original hardcover edition.
NOT ONE WORD HAS BEEN OMITTED.

SUPER CASINO

A Bantam Book

PUBLISHING HISTORY

Bantam hardcover edition published January 2000
Bantam paperback edition / January 2001

Library of Congress catalog card number 99-35774

ISBN 0-553-57349-7

Published simultaneously in the United States and Canada

Bantam Books are published by Bantam Books, a division of Random House,
Inc. Its trademark, consisting of the words "Bantam Books" and the portrayal
of a rooster, is Registered in U.S. Patent and Trademark Office and in other
countries. Marca Registrada. Bantam Books, 1540 Broadway, New York, New
York 10036.

PRINTED IN THE UNITED STATES OF AMERICA

OPM 10 9 8 7 6 5 4 3 2 1

**FOR
KATHERINE MARIE EARLEY**

Luck: a combination of circumstances, events, etc., operating by chance to bring good or ill to a person.

—The Random House Dictionary of the English Language

CONTENTS

....

COUNTING CARDS

....

The blackjack player slid a stack of black chips, each worth $100, across the green felt. Keith Uptain couldn't be certain how many chips were being bet because he was standing about fifty feet away, but as he hurried toward the table he estimated it was about twenty-five. It was not the *amount* of the wager that concerned him. Uptain had seen much larger bets. Once he had watched a "whale"—casino jargon for the world's biggest gamblers—bet $200,000 per hand, over and over again for several hours, in a baccarat game in Atlantic City. No, it was the *timing* of this bet that had caught the veteran casino shift manager's eye. Until this moment, the blackjack player had bet the table minimum of $100 per hand. It had not mattered whether he had won or lost. He had bet one black chip and only one. Until now. Why had he bumped up his wager to twenty-five times his norm? Uptain suspected that he knew, and he didn't like it.

The game of twenty-one, commonly called blackjack, is the most popular casino table game in the country. It is easy to play and offers skilled gamblers a better chance of winning than most other casino games. Every game is designed to give the house a mathematical advantage, called the "edge." Roulette has one of the highest edges—a 5.26 percent statistical advantage for the house. Blackjack has one of the lowest edges: 2.0 percent if played flawlessly. If a gambler bets $100 per spin on a roulette table for one hour (fifty spins), he will theoretically lose $263. If a gambler bets $100 per hand at blackjack for one hour (sixty hands), his theoretical loss will be $120. Obviously, if he is lucky, he might win some of the casino's money, but over time, the casino will grind out its 2.0 percent edge no matter how smart the player is—and if he happens to make a few mistakes, the casino will whittle down his stack of chips even more quickly. "Players depend on luck," a common saying goes. "Casinos depend on math. That is why casinos always win." But despite the casino's edge, it is possible for a knowledgeable blackjack player to actually tip the odds in his favor for short periods. This is what Uptain suspected the player now wagering $2,500 was doing, and it was Uptain's job to stop him.

At the Luxor, all cards are dealt faceup to players, and when Uptain reached the table, he saw that the gambler had been dealt the king of hearts and queen of clubs. One of the dealer's cards was turned facedown—this was his "hole" card—and his other was dealt faceup. It was the six of clubs. In blackjack, all the cards in a regular poker deck are given a numerical value. Face cards—the king, queen, and jack—are worth ten points each. The ace can be worth eleven points or one point—the player chooses. All the other cards are worth their face value. (A six of clubs is worth six, for example.) The object is to get twenty-one points, or as close to twenty-one points as possible, without "busting" by going over. The player who is closest wins.

The gambler's two cards added up to twenty points, which meant the dealer would have to get twenty-one points to win. That seemed unlikely because he had dealt himself one of the worst possible cards in blackjack: the six. Whenever a dealer has a six showing, veteran players assume that he is going to exceed twenty-one points—with good reason. In blackjack, a dealer must continue to draw cards until he reaches seventeen or more points. At that moment, he must "stand." He cannot draw any more cards. When a dealer has a six showing, unless his hole card is an ace (eleven points), the most that he can have is a total of sixteen points—a face card plus his six—and that means he will have to draw a third card. The odds of his drawing a card worth five points or less are not as good as the odds of his drawing a card that will put him over the twenty-one-point limit. From Uptain's vantage point, it appeared certain that the gambler was about to win his $2,500 bet. All he had to do was stand at twenty and wait for the dealer to take a third card and bust.

But this was not what the gambler did. Instead, he slid another $2,500 in chips across the table. He was making a move that most blackjack experts warn players *never* to do. He was "splitting" the king and queen into two separate hands. A player could do this whenever he was dealt a numerically matching pair of cards as long as he also doubled his bet. But experts warn against it when a player has twenty points because he is taking a winning hand and possibly turning it into two mediocre hands. The gambler's decision was so unorthodox that the dealer asked him about it.

"Are you splitting your cards?"

"Yes," he replied.

As Uptain watched, the dealer picked up the queen and moved it beside the king so that the two cards were now side by side rather than one above the other. The Luxor did not permit players to touch their own cards because it didn't want cheaters to switch or otherwise tamper with them. The dealer then dealt the gambler a new card from the "shoe"—a plastic container that held six decks. It was the nine of hearts, which gave the player nineteen points. The dealer placed this new card on the top corner of the king, indicating that the two cards belonged together. The gambler waved his right hand above the two cards—a hand signal that meant he did not want any more cards added to them. He pointed toward the queen of clubs and tapped the table with his forefinger. This meant he was ready for a "hit"—another card to go with his queen. The dealer slid a card from the shoe. It was the ten of spades, giving him twenty points. The gambler swept his right hand over the two cards.

To someone unfamiliar with blackjack, the position of the cards on the table and the hand gestures might have seemed unnecessary. After all, the player was sitting right in front of the dealer and could easily talk to him. But the dealer was required to position the cards in a precise manner and the player was required by the casino to use hand signals. Initially this was done in Las Vegas to reduce talking between dealers and players because casino owners were afraid that they might be scheming together. But now it was required because of the "eye in the sky"—the nickname for the hundreds of cameras mounted in casino ceilings. These cameras were used by card experts in the Luxor's surveillance room to monitor the games. When the dealer put the player's two face cards side by side, the surveillance crew knew that the player was splitting his pair. When the player waved his hand over his cards, the crew knew he was finished drawing. Every move was carefully choreographed so the surveillance crew would know what was happening without ever hearing a word.

The player now had hands worth nineteen and twenty points and it was time for the dealer to turn over his hole card. It was the queen of spades, giving him sixteen points. He was required to draw another card and it was the ten of diamonds. He had busted with twenty-six.

Uptain glanced at the gambler. There was no huge grin. No delighted eyes. No shout of triumph. The dealer counted out five teal-colored chips, each worth $1,000, and spread them out on the table so that the eye in the sky could see that he was paying the player the correct amount. He then stacked them next to the gambler's bets. But rather than collecting his winnings, the gambler waved his hand, indicating that he was ready to be dealt another hand. He was letting his winnings "ride," which meant he was now betting a total of $10,000—his original bet plus his winnings—the maximum that he could make at this particular blackjack table.

Uptain knew the gambler's name even though they had not been introduced. One of the Luxor's casino "hosts" had welcomed the player when he entered the high-limit gaming area and had asked his name. The host then had tipped off Uptain.

"I got a customer named Gary Brown playing BJ in pit one," the host had said. "He's got a twenty-five-thousand credit line with us."

While the dealer got ready to deal a new hand, Uptain typed Brown's name into a nearby computer terminal. Most of the information that flashed on the screen had been supplied by Brown himself during a visit two weeks earlier, when he had applied for a credit line at the Luxor. The computer identified him as a resident of a wealthy enclave near Boston, where he owned a string of fast-food restaurants. During his last visit, the gambler had played blackjack for thirty-two hours, betting an average of $100 each hand. He had lost $8,150. The casino had invited him back as its guest and arranged for him to fly free round-trip, stay in a complimentary suite for high rollers, and eat without charge inside the Luxor. These "comps," or complimentary inducements, would cost the casino about $3,500, but based on Brown's computer profile, the Luxor expected him to lose twice that. This calculation was based on the amount of time that Brown had previously played blackjack, the average size of his bet, and his skill at playing, as determined by a pit boss who had "rated" Brown by watching him during his initial visit.

With $10,000 now at risk, Brown was dealt a ten of clubs and the ace of spades. Blackjack! An automatic twenty-one points. While casinos pay "even money" when you win a normal hand, the payoff for getting a blackjack is one and a half times your bet. Brown had won $15,000 in less than thirty seconds. He now had $25,000 in chips stacked in front of him.

Winners automatically attract other gamblers. There is something magnetic about beating the house. Neither the dealer nor Brown had done anything to call attention to themselves, yet two more gamblers had gravitated to the table. Brown welcomed both as if they were old chums. He waved to Diane Spataro, the cocktail waitress in the high-roller pit, and ordered a bottle of water, tipping her $20 when she brought it. He then leaned forward and carefully collected all of his chips. He tossed two teal ones on the table as his next bet and the dealer began slipping cards out of the shoe. Brown's first was a queen. The two new players at the table were dealt a nine and a seven respectively. Brown got another queen, giving him twenty points. The other men drew kings, while the dealer had an eight of hearts showing.

Uptain was curious: Would Brown once again split his two face cards into separate hands? Without hesitating, Brown waved his right hand over his pair of queens. He was standing. Why hadn't he split his cards this time? The player seated next to Brown also stood, with a total of nineteen points. That left the third player, whose cards were worth seventeen points, to decide. He glanced at the dealer's eight of hearts and nervously chewed on his lower lip.

"I figure you got a ten hiding under there," he said, referring to the dealer's hole card. "And that would mean you got my seventeen beat." There was a chance, however, that the dealer had a card worth less than ten. Seconds dragged by.

"Okay, hit me," he finally declared. "Just make it a small one."

It wasn't. It was a seven and he busted.

"Damn!" he snapped, smacking the table with his palm so hard that his bottle of imported beer almost toppled over. "I knew I shouldn't have taken that card." The dealer removed the man's $500 bet from the table.

Brown looked at Uptain and smiled, and in that instant Uptain felt certain he knew exactly what Brown was thinking. The glance was one of those knowing exchanges that people make when they share the same thought. Anyone who understood basic blackjack strategy, commonly called BBS, knew that you never take a third card once you have seventeen points, because the odds are simply too great that you will bust. (BBS is a mathematical formula that tells players when they should or shouldn't ask for a third card.)

The dealer flipped over his hole card, revealing the five of diamonds. Added to his eight of hearts, it gave him thirteen points, and he was required to draw another card. It was the four of clubs, giving him seventeen points. He had to stand. The dealer's seventeen points lost to Brown's twenty points and the other player's nineteen, so the dealer paid both men. (Up to seven players can compete against the house. Brown left his $2,000 in winnings and his initial $2,000 bet on the table. In the last three hands, Brown had won $22,000. He was now risking another $4,000. Was he lucky, or was he doing what Uptain suspected: counting cards?

There is nothing illegal about card counting. Almost all skilled blackjack players do it because it can give them an advantage over the casino. Uptain himself was so proficient at counting cards that the Luxor used him to teach other employees how to do it so they could spot card-counting players. But even though it is not illegal, casinos routinely ban players who count cards. Casinos are able to do this because they are private businesses; they can bar anyone they wish. Part of Uptain's job was catching card counters. Only one week earlier, a team of five card counters had won $1.1 million at Caesars Palace before their tactics attracted attention and they fled.

Card counting was invented by a California mathematician, Edward O. Thorp, who published a book in 1962 titled *Beat the Dealer,* which is still considered the card counter's bible. Thorp was teaching at the University of California at Los Angeles in 1960 when a colleague showed him an article in the *Journal of the American Statistical Association* whose two authors claimed they had found a way to win at blackjack. During a school holiday, Thorp and his wife drove to Las Vegas, where he tested the article's theory by playing blackjack at a $1-minimum-per-hand table. He quickly lost $8 and quit. But when he got home, Thorp kept thinking about the article, and in what he later described as "a flash of mathematical insight," he realized where the authors had gone wrong. They had based their statistical calculations on the assumption that a dealer always used a deck of fifty-two cards, but that was not what had happened when Thorp had played blackjack. As soon as a card was dealt, the composition of the deck changed, and after six hands had been played, the deck was radically different from what it had been at the start of the game. Consider, for instance, what would happen if the first four cards dealt during a game were aces. It would be impossible for anyone using that same deck to get a blackjack from that moment on, because all the eleven-point cards would already have been dealt. Thorp's revelation quickly led him to another insight. If the composition of the deck changed, so did the odds. Depending on what cards were left in a deck, the mathematical edge could swing wildly back and forth between a dealer and a player.

It was at this juncture that Thorp made perhaps his most important discovery. Because of the rules in blackjack, a player could beat the house at specific times. How? The key was the rule that required dealers to continue taking cards until they reached seventeen or more points. Thorp discovered that this rule worked against the casino whenever there were more high-value cards left in a deck than low-value cards. Imagine, for instance, that there are six cards left in a deck and that all of them are either eights or sevens. A gambler could draw two cards and stand, but no matter what two cards a dealer drew, he would never have more than sixteen points. Consequently, he would be required to draw a third card and would bust. The "must stand on seventeen" rule was the casino's mathematical Achilles' heel.

Thorp now had all of the pieces of the puzzle—he knew that the composition of a deck changed with every hand and that a deck with more high cards gave the player an advantage. What was still missing, however, was a way for a player to recognize when this happened. Thorp turned to an IBM 704 computer for help and soon learned that there were thirty-four million different ways for cards to be dealt during blackjack from a single deck. With so many variables, it looked impossible to accurately predict what cards might be left in a deck as a game was being played. But Thorp kept experimenting. One computer program that he wrote took the computer seven hours to run. He soon began noticing patterns. When all the fives were removed from a deck, the player gained an edge of 3.3 percent because of the must stand on seventeen rule. If a deck was loaded with all of the sixteen cards that had a value of ten (the tens, jacks, queens, and kings), a player gained an advantage of as much as 10 percent over the casino. As he studied these patterns, Thorp finally devised a way to successfully track cards.

He began by dividing all fifty-two cards into three groups. He then assigned each group a value. The low cards—two through six—were given a value of +1. He gave the seven, eight, and nine a value of zero, and he assigned the ten through the ace a value of −1. By using these three groupings, a player could know at any given time how many high cards were still in a deck.

Let's say, for example, the blackjack player is dealt a ten of diamonds and an eight of clubs. Using Thorp's grouping method, a card counter would assign the ten of diamonds a value of −1 and the eight of clubs a value of zero. The "count" after these two numbers were added together would be −1, which simply means that there is one fewer high card in the deck than when the game began. Then, let's say the player's next two cards are the ace of spades and six of clubs. The ace, which is −1, and the six, which is +1, would cancel each other out. This means the count would remain −1. Another hand is dealt and this time the player receives a jack (−1) and a five (+1). Again these cards cancel each other out. A card counter would know after these three hands had been played that the running count of the deck was −1, giving the casino an advantage of 1 percent. (In this illustration, for simplicity's sake, the cards dealt to the dealer are not included.)

As Thorp worked on his charts and figures, he discovered that a player did not gain much of an advantage until there were at least two more high cards in the deck than there were low ones: a +2 count. With each +1 after that, the player's odds increased dramatically. If the count was +6, a player had a 5.4 statistical percentage edge over the casino. A +8 meant that a player had nearly a 9.8 percent edge. The trick to winning money would be to bet heaviest when the count was in the player's favor (+), and to reduce the size of the bets whenever a deck favored the house (−).

Because he was an academician and not a gambler, Thorp did not rush to a casino to test his findings. Instead, he presented a paper about his theory at the annual meeting of the American Mathematical Society in Washington, D.C. Word spread quickly and he was besieged with calls from gamblers, some offering to invest $100,000 in him if he would test his theory in Nevada. Meanwhile, casino owners scoffed. One belittled Thorp on a nationally televised newscast by suggesting that he was simply another egghead professor with a crackpot theory. "When a lamb goes to slaughter, the lamb might kill the butcher, but we always bet on the butcher," said the casino owner.

Thorp decided to test his theory. Late one night, he drove to a Reno casino and quietly began playing blackjack at a $1-minimum-per-hand table. He lost at first, partly because he kept losing track of the count. He also was not a proficient card player. But as the night moved toward morning, he began teaching himself how to use his own system. It was nearly dawn when he realized that he had found a deck with a high plus count. He bet $4, won, raised his bet to $8, won, and then bet the $16, winning that hand too. Satisfied, he left the casino as inconspicuously as he had arrived.

Two nights later, Thorp strutted into a casino in Lake Tahoe to much fanfare, ready to demonstrate his card-counting system to the world. With financial backing from a New York City millionaire, he began betting at the $100-per-hand blackjack table. Within thirty minutes, he had emptied the table's money rack, having won $17,000 worth of chips. A horrified dealer and pit boss accused Thorp of cheating. The dealer began shuffling the deck every few hands. Still, Thorp continued to win. The casino finally stopped him from playing.

As word spread, card counters flooded Nevada casinos. The losses were so high that the casinos announced they were changing the rules of blackjack to make it harder for a player to win, but gamblers rebelled and boycotted the game, and so many players stopped playing that blackjack dealers threatened to revolt too. "Casino employees, whose income depends in large part on the number of tips they receive, are screaming that the new blackjack rules are a bane to the industry," the *National Observer* reported. After three weeks, the casinos reluctantly restored the old rules, but they also began trying to discourage card counting by using six decks of cards when dealing and frequently mixing them. The casinos also announced that card counters would be banned from playing. Some card counters reacted by donning disguises. Others devised different ways to conceal that they were counting cards. Thorp's discovery had given birth to the longest-running cat-and-mouse game ever staged in Nevada.

Keith Uptain was the Luxor's chief card-counting cat. What was still unclear at this moment was whether he was watching a mouse or someone who was just lucky. Uptain began counting the cards as Brown played and noticed that whenever the count was in Brown's favor, he bet big. When it was in the casino's favor, he reduced his bet. It seemed obvious that Brown was a card counter but Uptain still couldn't be certain. What bothered him was how blatant Brown was being. Most card counters tried to keep from being noticed by betting small amounts. Brown was increasing his bets by thousands of dollars when the count was in his favor and dropping it wildly when it wasn't. These obvious plays made Uptain wonder: Was Brown bold, or was he clueless about card counting and one of those players who makes huge bets on a whim and pulls back because of a hunch?

Another reason why Uptain was unsure was because Brown frequently deviated from BBS. At one point, his cards added up to thirteen points, yet he asked for a third card even though the dealer had a five showing and the count indicated that there were more high cards left in the shoe than lower ones. This was something an experienced player just wouldn't have done. Predictably, Brown busted, losing $1,000. Still, Uptain knew that some card counters deliberately made foolish mistakes to confuse any casino employees who were watching them.

The more Uptain saw, the more suspicious he became. Brown had had only one drink in three hours, yet he was acting tipsy and began to joke that he couldn't concentrate. Uptain thought he was acting. At one point, one of the gamblers at the table told Brown a long joke. Each time Brown tried to concentrate on his cards, the man tapped him on the shoulder and continued talking. After the gambler finished his story, Brown asked the dealer for directions to the bathroom and excused himself.

Uptain turned to his assistant, Richard Woods, who was watching Brown too. "He's lost count," Uptain said. "He's going to wait in the bathroom until there's a new shoe because he doesn't know if the count is plus or minus."

Sure enough, Brown resurfaced just as the dealer finished shuffling the cards for a new shoe.

"I feel lucky," Brown declared, tossing out a $1,000 chip on the first hand.

That bet is what finally convinced Uptain that Brown was counting cards. Uptain knew that card counters often tried to hide what they were doing by making a big bet at the "top of the shoe." They did this to confuse suspicious casino employees. The employees would assume that a player must not be counting cards at the start of a shoe because there was no count yet. But Uptain knew that at the beginning of the deck the odds were about even, so a smart card counter really wasn't risking much by tossing out a large bet.

Banning a player from blackjack at the Luxor was a big decision. The casino had just started recruiting higher-end players—people at Brown's $100,000-plus annual income level. If Brown was counting cards, Uptain's bosses would not complain if he was barred. But if Brown was simply lucky, Uptain would be embarrassing a potentially lucrative customer. The casino already had invested $3,500 to bring him to Las Vegas.

Uptain had another worry as well. "I'm ready to bounce this guy right now," he whispered to his assistant, "but I don't want to upset Mr. Wallace." Uptain was referring to Jack Wallace, a multimillionaire from the Midwest who was sitting next to Brown. The two men had become friendly, especially after Brown offered Wallace some advice that had helped him win. Wallace needed all the help that he could get. He was now down $10,000, about one-third of what he usually lost during his monthly treks to Las Vegas. His wife, Martha, usually lost $5,000 per visit playing slot machines. The Wallaces were customers that the Luxor didn't want to offend, and if Brown was a card counter, he might make a scene if he was barred. Although casinos detested card counters, other blackjack players admired them. And why not? It took skill to count cards and daring to beat the house. Uptain decided to watch a bit longer. He could afford to. A number of hands had been dealt and the shoe had a minus count favoring the house. Besides, Brown was on a losing streak.

During the next several hands, Brown's bad luck continued and by the time the shoe was empty, he had lost $11,200. He rose from the table as the dealer mixed the cards and it looked as if he was going to leave. Instead, he simply stretched his legs. "My luck is bound to change," he announced, and he was right. The new shoe was a disaster for the casino. Brown won three hands and then lost two that, statistically, he should have won. Uptain was nervous. The count was approaching +6 and Brown had at least $14,000 in chips. Brown also seemed to sense that Uptain's patience was running thin. If he was going to make a big score, he had to do it now. As Uptain watched, Brown began counting out large stacks of chips in anticipation of the next hand.

It was at that moment that Martha Wallace waltzed into the high-roller area to ask Jack how he was doing. "I'm down a few grand," he informed her nonchalantly.

"Darling, I want to get something to eat. Aren't you hungry?" she asked.

Uptain moved quickly. "Mr. Wallace, we would love for you and Mrs. Wallace to be our guests at the Isis (the Luxor's finest restaurant). I promise that I will keep your cards warm for you, sir."

Wallace chuckled. "Taking a break will save me money," he quipped. "I'm not getting good cards tonight." He tipped the dealer a couple of $100 black chips and then stood to leave. Turning, he spoke to Brown: "Good luck, young man."

Brown was now all alone at the table. As soon as Wallace began walking out of the high-roller area, he immediately bet $10,000, and the dealer snapped out two cards before Uptain could intervene. Brown received the ten of clubs and an eight of hearts. Total: eighteen points. The dealer turned over his second card. It was a six of hearts. A six—the worst card possible for the dealer. Uptain noticed a slight smile form on Brown's lips. The shoe's +6 count meant that there were six more high cards in the deck than lower ones. There was a good chance that the dealer would have to draw a third card and bust. Brown quickly waved his hand over his two cards. He would take his chances with eighteen. The dealer flipped over his hole, revealing the four of spades. That gave him ten points. Brown grimaced as the dealer pulled a third card from the shoe: the ten of hearts. Twenty points for the dealer, who quickly collected Brown's $10,000 in chips. It had looked as if Brown was a sure winner. That was one of the maddening ironies of the game. A gambler could learn everything that he could about card counting, but there was no sure way to predict on any given hand who would get the best cards. "That," Uptain often repeated, "is why they call this gambling."

"Excuse me, Mr. Brown," Uptain said, slipping into the chair next to him. "I think your play is a bit too strong for us. I'm afraid that I have no choice but to bar you from playing blackjack here. But you are certainly welcome to try our other games."

Brown appeared shocked. "What do you mean—my play is too strong? I just lost!"

"I know exactly what your next move is going to be when I see your cards before you make it, and if I know, then you need to play elsewhere," Uptain replied.

"How do you know what my next move is going to be when I don't even know?" Brown protested.

"Oh, you know how I know and we both know why. Don't we?"

Brown lit a cigar, took a long puff, and then shoved the chips that he had remaining in front of him across the table to be counted. The dealer called out the total: $3,500. That was all that he had left. For several minutes, he sat at the table sipping from a plastic bottle of water, and then he gathered up his three teal chips and five black ones and went to the cashier's cage to convert them into cash.

Moments later a new player sat down at the black-jack table and pulled out $4,000 in $100 bills. He looked over at Uptain and nodded. He was ready to play.

Part One

IN THE BEGINNING

....

Four hundred years before Las Vegas happened, Spanish conquistadors kept trying to find it. They were sure that somewhere to the north and west, across the great deserts, would be a city of gold and light, incredible riches, eternal youth, exquisite pleasures—an intoxicating city of riches and dreams. Expedition after expedition failed to find it, yet they were sure. . . . They would never know how right they were—right that there was such a city, right that it lay in the great western desert. They were just wrong about when. The place itself was generating Vegas-vibe . . . but [it] would need 400 more years to generate an actual Las Vegas—a city of gold. . . .

—Michael Ventura,
Las Vegas: The Odds on Anything, 1993

PROLOGUE

....

The New Las Vegas

Forget the gangsters: Moe Sedway, Benjamin "Bugsy" Siegel, Tony "the Ant" Spilotro. Forget the Rat Pack: Frank, Dino, Sammy, Peter, and Joey. Forget the glamorous Sands hotel and casino where leggy showgirls suntanned alongside a swimming pool with a "floating" craps table built right in its center. Anyone who still thinks of Las Vegas as a holiday haven for pug-nosed mafiosos with bulges under their jackets and suitcases stuffed with cash, or as the scandalous desert playground of Hollywood's rich and raucous, is living in the past. The legendary Dunes hotel and casino, built in the 1950s with loans from the Teamster Union's Central States Pension Fund arranged by mobsters, was imploded in 1993 before two hundred thousand onlookers chanting "Blow it up!" Howard Hughes, the eccentric billionaire who once owned most of the big casinos in town, is now only a historical footnote. Liberace's trademark candelabra sits in a museum. Elvis has been gone so long that tourists often think his legions of impersonators look more like "the King" than he did.

The "old" Las Vegas is dead.

A "new" Las Vegas has risen.

While much of the rest of America was slumbering in an economic recession during the close of the 1980s, Las Vegas shed its gangster skin and reformed itself. It is now, in the words of its tireless promoters, "a world-class destination resort suitable for the entire family." Hype? Hoopla? Absolutely. Las Vegas has always thrived on superlatives. It's a town where even the corner 7-Eleven convenience store sports a flashing green-and-red neon marquee. It's an oasis for dreamers, get-rich-quick schemers, and charlatans. But for once the hucksters' claims may be, if anything, too modest. The "new" Las Vegas really has become a resort city like none other on the planet.

Consider the intersection of Tropicana Avenue and Las Vegas Boulevard, the southern tip of what is widely known as the Las Vegas Strip—a glittering four-mile stretch of hotels and casinos that have lured gamblers here since 1941. On the intersection's northwest corner, a replica of the Manhattan skyline rises from the desert sand. This is the New York New York hotel and casino, which opened in early 1997 with a facade that is a collage of twelve New York skyscrapers approximately one-third the size of the originals. The Brooklyn Bridge and the Empire State and Chrysler Buildings are here, as well as a 150-foot-tall Statue of Liberty that eagerly welcomes tourists to the casino's teeming shores. Across the street is the Excalibur, a hotel and casino built in the shape of a medieval castle, with a 265-foot-tall bell tower, red turrets, blue spires, gold domes, and a moat from which a mechanical dragon emerges periodically to menace bypassers being whisked on escalators across a concrete drawbridge. On the southeast corner of the intersection is the Tropicana, home of the Strip's most elaborate swimming pools—a sequence of lagoons and grottoes with waterfalls and fountains set in a lush South Seas decor. The MGM Grand lies on the intersection's fourth corner, guarded by a huge statue of a golden lion. It is the largest resort in the entire world, with 5,005 guest rooms, a 171,500-square-foot casino, a fifteen-store shopping mall, a one-mile-long monorail, ninety-three elevators, a 15,000-seat boxing arena, a 1,700-seat theater, and a 33-acre amusement park with seven major rides, all built within a 112-acre compound. The exterior of the MGM Grand is covered with emerald-tinted glass, which is supposed to make it resemble the fantasy city of Oz created by L. Frank Baum in his popular Dorothy and Oz books.

The Manhattan skyline, a medieval castle, a tropical lagoon, and Oz. Close to $2 billion worth of buildings, more than ten thousand hotel rooms. Slot machines—thirteen thousand of them—plus hundreds of blackjack games, roulette wheels, and craps tables. Roller coasters, magic shows, jugglers, and video arcades for the children. All this at one Las Vegas intersection!

Need more proof of the Strip's grandiosity? Then consider the stunning Bellagio, which cost $1.6 billion—that's right, billion—when it opened in late 1998, making it the most expensive hotel ever built. Surrounded by an 8.5-acre man-made lake that contains 1,400 hidden fountains, the Bellagio has a thirty-by-seventy-foot chandelier hanging in its lobby and its own art gallery with $300 million worth of Picassos, Mirós, and other notable works. Not to be outdone, the Strip's second billion-dollar resort, the rival Mandalay Bay, opened in early 1999, with a tropical jungle theme complete with fifty-foot-tall waterfalls, vine-covered cliffs, and an eleven-acre man-made "ocean" at the front of the resort that is capable of producing six-foot waves for surfing competitions.

Welcome to the new Las Vegas!

• In the early 1990s, the most expensive and innovative—some would say outrageous—buildings in the world were under construction in Las Vegas. Seventeen of the twenty largest hotels in the world were on the Strip. Besides those already mentioned, the Strip had its own pyramid, a huge circus tent, a Roman palace, a pirate hideaway, and replicas of the cities of Paris and Venice. The highest observation tower west of the Mississippi is on the Strip.

People noticed.

• In the 1990s, Las Vegas overtook Orlando's Walt Disney World as the most popular tourist destination in the United States. The city drew bigger crowds than all of the Florida-based theme parks combined. More people visited Las Vegas in the mid-1990s than visited the entire state of Hawaii.

Las Vegas thrived.

• In the 1990s, Las Vegas became the fastest-growing and most prosperous city in America. Its population doubled in less than ten years. By 1996, six thousand new residents were arriving each month. Studies that same year named Las Vegas as the number-one city in America for creating new jobs, the number one for growth in personal income. A slew of magazines trumpeted it as one of the best metropolitan areas in which to live. It was one of the few cities in the country where a hotel valet could earn enough to send his kids to college and still have money to buy a camper and fishing boat; where a newlywed couple could afford a three-bedroom house without having to hoard their money by living with their parents for several years.

How did Las Vegas become the boomtown of the 1990s?

The town's promoters were quick with reasons. Las Vegas features 320 days of sunshine. It has five hundred churches, eleven city libraries, nine acute-care hospitals, twenty-seven golf courses. There is no state income tax for individuals or corporations, and no inheritance, estate, or gift tax.

But none of these draws is behind the city's astronomical growth. The "new" Las Vegas is the spawn of two parents: a dramatic change in the public's attitude toward gambling and the creation of a new class of casino—the so-called entertainment superstores, commonly called "super casinos."

The first sign of what was to come appeared in November 1989 with the opening of the Mirage, the first hotel-casino built from scratch in Las Vegas in sixteen years. No one had ever seen anything like it. Conceived by Steve Wynn, a flamboyant casino operator with movie-star good looks, a much noted temper, and a passion for perfection, the Mirage was three million square feet in area and cost $600 million to construct. Its three hotel towers each rose twenty-three stories, were covered with shimmering gold-tinted glass, and together held 3,049 guest rooms. To make certain that no one slipped past the Mirage without ogling, Wynn constructed a fifty-four-foot-tall volcano between his hotel's entrance and the sidewalk on Las Vegas Boulevard. The volcano erupted every fifteen minutes, spewing steam, water, and fire into the hot desert air. He put a fifty-seven-foot-long aquarium behind the registration desk and filled it with twenty thousand gallons of water, pygmy sharks, and dazzling coral—a breathtaking sight framed by seven-inch-thick acrylic walls. The Mirage was a virtual city within itself. There was no need for guests to venture outside. Fine restaurants, exclusive retail shops, spectacular shows, spas, pools, and, of course, a massive casino lay within its boundaries.

Doubters expected Wynn's megacreation to go bust. How could anyone possibly fill a three-thousand-room hotel night after night? The timing of his resort also seemed out of sync. Las Vegas didn't have the draw that it once had—or so the naysayers claimed. Once upon a time, Nevada had held a monopoly on casino gambling, but in May 1978, Resorts International opened the first legalized casino in Atlantic City, New Jersey, and easterners no longer needed to fly west to satisfy their cravings for dice, cards, and one-armed bandits. Ten years later, Nevada took another hit when President Ronald Reagan signed the Indian Gaming Regulatory Act, which gave Native Americans permission to run casinos on reservation land. Almost overnight, 150 tribe-owned casinos opened. Jealous state legislators, fumbling for ways to raise revenues without increasing taxes, hurriedly passed their own "limited" gambling legislation. Casinos soon appeared in Colorado, Illinois, Indiana, Iowa, Louisiana, Mississippi, Missouri, and South Dakota. How could Wynn even think about building a super casino on the tired old Las Vegas Strip when gambling fever could be fed locally across the nation? Some critics compared him to the investors who had sunk millions into launching immense ocean liners at a time when transoceanic flights by airplane were first coming of age.

Wynn proved them wrong. It wasn't genius, he would later say. It was simple arithmetic. Wynn's Golden Nugget, an older hotel and casino in downtown Las Vegas, had been turning away hundreds of customers each night for months because it didn't have enough rooms. He recognized that the demand for gambling in Las Vegas outstripped supply. The opening of casinos in other parts of the country was only whetting tourists' appetites for the main entrée: Las Vegas. But if mathematical extrapolations showed Wynn the way, it was his moxie that gave him the vision to build the world's first super casino. From the morning it opened, the Mirage was hugely successful. During its first year, it reported more than $200 million in profits—one-third of what it had cost to build.

Wynn was not the only casino owner who saw what was happening. Circus Circus Enterprises, run by William G. Bennett and William N. Pennington, was in the midst of erecting its own super casino when the Mirage opened. Bennett and Pennington's creation, the Excalibur, was even bigger, almost a thousand more rooms, when it was unveiled on June 19, 1990. Yet it cost half as much—$300 million—and it was aimed at a much different customer from that of the upper-crust Mirage. The Excalibur targeted middle-class vacationers with children, taking Wynn's super casino concept into a new market. Dads in Bermuda shorts and moms wearing fanny packs took their children to see the Lipizzaner stallions perform at matinees. At night, there was King Arthur's Tournament, where the entire family ate roasted chicken with their fingers while rooting for knights who jousted in a cavernous arena. The cost for a four-course dinner and show: a mere twenty bucks. There were no gourmet restaurants inside the Excalibur. Instead, meals were served at Lance-A-Lotta-Pasta, Sir Galahad's Prime Rib House, and the Sherwood Forest Coffee Shop. Each featured a children's menu. There was no Gucci shop, no $80-per-ticket magic show by Siegfried and Roy, the Mirage's headliners.

The minivan crowd loved it. The first year the Excalibur opened, it became Circus Circus Enterprises' most profitable casino, earning $85 million before taxes and giving investors a 30 percent return. The staggering financial successes of the Mirage and the Excalibur launched a $12-billion construction rush on the Strip.

The race to build even more dazzling super casinos began. Three opened in 1993 alone. The biggest was the MGM Grand, which cost billionaire financier Kirk Kerkorian more than $800 million and had more amusement rides than any theme park in America except Walt Disney World. Wynn, who had decided to enter the family market too, unveiled Treasure Island, a 2,900-room resort with a pirate theme. On a man-made lake in front of the complex, Wynn choreographed daily battles between a full-scale replica of a British warship and a pirate ship named *Hispaniola*. The cannon fire, smoke, and swashbuckling eye-patched pirates drew sweltering sidewalk crowds, caused traffic along the Strip to slow to a crawl, and—because this was Las Vegas—always ended with the pirates winning. Circus Circus Enterprises reacted by opening the Luxor, a thirty-three-story hotel built in the shape of a pyramid with a ten-story-tall, laser-lighted sphinx outside its entrance.

Only 15 percent of Americans had ever visited Las Vegas before the Mirage and Excalibur opened. In 1995, only six years later, that figure had doubled to 30 percent. Pollsters determined that most came to see the super casinos. In its 1996 annual report, Circus Circus Enterprises explained its view of the future:

....

> The prosperous cohort of baby-boomers are now coming into middle age, prime years for discretionary spending. And our golden grays—the post-55 generation that owns close to half of the financial and real assets in the U.S.—have increasing time, mobility, and money on their hands. For them entertainment has become a lifestyle staple rather than a luxury . . . These underlying factors are behind the gaming boom. In an era when

social attitudes toward play, and the means
to afford it, have dramatically changed, so
has the role of the casino. In recent polls, 90
percent of American consumers have indicated that they consider gaming a "legitimate leisure activity" and 30 percent of
Americans have gambled in a casino.

Critics of gambling had only to look at casino profits to
see the truth in the company's boosterism. Across the
nation, gamblers lost $16.3 billion in casinos in 1995,
making gambling the most popular form of entertainment in the country based on consumer spending. For
the first time, gambling in America generated more "entertainment" income than Hollywood movies—and the
biggest share was being spent at Las Vegas super casinos. Six billion of that $16.3 billion was lost in Las Ve-
gas, by tourists who paid another $6 billion for hotel
accommodations, meals, and entertainment. Las Vegas
casino owners pocketed an average 22 percent profit on
their investments. By 1999, legalized gambling world-
wide was estimated to total $1 trillion. In the United
States, casinos collected $27.2 billion in revenues—
nearly $11 billion more than had been lost by gamblers
only four years earlier.

Seven companies dominated the Las Vegas scene in
the mid-1990s: Hilton Hotels, ITT's Caesars Palace,
Kerkorian's MGM Grand, Harrah's Entertainment,
Steve Wynn's Mirage Resorts, Bally Entertainment, and
Circus Circus Enterprises. At the height of the Las
Vegas boom, *Casino Executive,* the gaming industry's
magazine, chose Circus Circus Enterprises as its company of the year in 1996. The cover story quoted two
stock analysts' prediction that Circus Circus Enterprises
was destined to become the most powerful gaming
company in America by the year 2000. Only Steve

Wynn's Mirage Resorts was seen as a serious rival. One reason was Circus Circus Enterprises' track record of building super casinos faster and more cheaply than anyone else and running them more efficiently. The company was dubbed the McDonald's of the gambling business—the company most likely to put a casino in your neighborhood if gambling was ever legalized nationally.

"The super casino is to tourism what the Pentium chip is to technology," Circus Circus president Glenn Schaeffer said in a speech to his colleagues in late 1996. "It has revolutionized gaming. There are no natural wonders on this stretch of vast desert that we call Las Vegas. The environment here is entirely what we create, and the reason why tourists are flocking to the Strip is because we are building the most spectacular and unique buildings on this planet. We are building them so that the customers have to come see them. Historically, the theater has been a special place where you suspend your disbelief. An audience goes into the theater to depart from the ordinary. We have invented the equivalent of a new form of theater with our buildings. The super casinos are expressly designed for the purpose of gawking. In Las Vegas, we promote the sight and the sound and the spectacle that you can't find back home or anywhere else."

Outside the gaming industry, Schaeffer was not well known. If Americans put a face on gambling, it was either Steve Wynn or his East Coast rival, Donald Trump. But within gaming and on Wall Street, Schaeffer cast a big shadow. Back in 1989, Wynn had built the Mirage with junk bonds delivered by his friend Michael Milken, the high-flying junk bond king who eventually was sent to a federal prison because of financial hijinks unrelated to Wynn. Schaeffer had gotten Circus Circus Enterprises the millions in cash that it had needed from investment banks at a time when no respected financial institution outside Nevada had ever dared risk as much as a penny in casinos. Circus Circus Enterprises had been the first casino operator to obtain multimillion-dollar credit lines and low-interest loans, and Schaeffer had brought this about by convincing Wall Street that his company was a legitimate business not unlike any other blue chip corporation—save for one astonishing difference. Because of the nature of gambling, Circus Circus Enterprises could rake in extraordinary amounts of cash. Once Schaeffer had opened Wall Street's financial coffers, other casino owners were quick to follow. Casinos no longer had to turn to mob-controlled pension funds or the likes of Howard Hughes or Michael Milken for funding. Banks were now willing to fund casino construction projects and investors were eager to buy stock in "gaming companies." (Casino companies don't like to call it "gambling" because they believe the term has negative connotations.) The era of corporate ownership had begun.

In different ways, Steve Wynn and Glenn Schaeffer both played critical roles in the launching of the first super casinos and the Las Vegas boom. I approached both men in August 1996 about writing a book that would describe the new Las Vegas and the inner workings of a super casino. At the time, Wynn was in the midst of filing a multimillion-dollar libel suit against the publisher of an unflattering biography. Understandably, he was not in a mood to cooperate, although he did agree to be interviewed. I had a better outcome with Schaeffer, who introduced me to the chairman of Circus Circus Enterprises, Clyde Turner. They agreed to give me carte blanche at the Luxor, the company's pyramid-shaped super casino. I could attend any meeting I wished to and talk to anyone who agreed to be interviewed. I made it clear from the start that this was to be my book. Circus Circus Enterprises would not be allowed to censor or edit anything I wrote. The only concession

I made was to let both men read the manuscript before it was published so that they could react to it. Any changes, however, were totally up to me. Further, I insisted on paying my own way: I would not accept free rooms, complimentary meals, or any other amenities.

Schaeffer and Turner gave me several reasons why they agreed to cooperate. They were proud of Circus Circus Enterprises and eager to prove that the persisting image of casinos as mob-run was badly outdated. They were also concerned about current attempts in Congress to form a committee to investigate gambling. They feared it would be stacked with antigambling forces who would conjure up extreme examples in order to attack the industry as a whole. "We do not mind opening our doors to anyone who is going to be fair-minded," Turner said.

This book is in two parts. The first tells the history of Circus Circus Enterprises and Mirage Resorts, the two most powerful super casino operators in the nation. The second describes events I witnessed and people I met during the two years that I visited the Luxor. The names of a handful of persons have been changed at their request to preserve their privacy, and, in some cases, to protect them from criminal prosecution. But all the characters are real and the events are described exactly as they happened. As always, what follows should be read in context. The focus on the Luxor, considered by itself, gives readers a skewed view, because every super casino is different. But all super casinos have much in common. They are never-never lands in which those who come to Las Vegas can lose themselves for a few larger-than-life days.

I also have chosen to describe much of what I witnessed through the eyes of several recurring characters. Once again, while I made every effort to choose people who are illustrative of Las Vegas's many faces, no one individual can be totally representative. And because

Las Vegas has always welcomed outcasts and embraced the unconventional, figures from its seamy side are as valid a part of the city's mosaic as its movers and shakers. For this reason readers will meet one of them: Shawna Gray, a teenage prostitute. Hookers unabashedly hand out their business cards and make room calls, even though prostitution is illegal within the city and county.

Finally, because Las Vegas wears a thousand different faces and speaks in as many voices, interspersed among the chapters are first-person vignettes of people who talk about their lives and their work in the hotels and casinos. These "Inside the Casino" segments are meant to reveal some of those faces and voices.

Las Vegas is a chaotic and hectic place. The average visitor to the city stays three days and leaves. Events on the Strip often seem to happen in a fast-forward mode. In a twenty-four-hour period at one blackjack table inside the Luxor, a dozen dramas can unfold. Fortunes are bet, made, lost. Hearts are broken, dreams shattered. A cocky college student from Cal Tech experiments with a "foolproof" betting scheme that he insists will soon make him rich; a thick-necked cowboy tosses down a $1,000 bet to impress his rhinestone-encrusted date; a sixty-five-year-old homosexual from Omaha sits with his hand on the right knee of his hired twenty-something male escort; an intoxicated, newly divorced father asks if he can bet his gold wedding band.

Sights that would be scandalous back home barely merit a glance. Late one Saturday night at the Luxor, an attractive woman wearing an elegant evening gown began playing at a blackjack table where the minimum bet per hand was $25 and soon struck up a conversation with the dealer. The gambler was in her early forties, tanned and fit. She said she was an elementary-school physical education teacher from a tiny Colorado town. A gold necklace hung around her neck and disappeared into her décolletage. When the dealer complimented the woman on it and asked if there was a pendant attached, she replied: "No, just my nipples. I got both of them pierced and the chain goes through the nipple rings. It was my husband's idea. He said if my boobs ever started to droop, I could just shorten the chain."

During one of our first talks, Circus Circus chairman Clyde Turner told me why he believes Las Vegas is unique among cities. "Are you familiar with the word 'indeterminism'?" he asked. I wasn't, so I looked it up in my dictionary:

> **Indeterminism**—The doctrine that human actions, though influenced somewhat by pre-existing psychological and other conditions, are not entirely governed by them but retain a certain freedom and spontaneity.

Las Vegas is the world capital of indeterminism, Turner explained. Visitors do things in Las Vegas they would never do at home, take risks that they would shun in any other locale, and because this is a gambling mecca, fate seems to hover here. Tom Robinson, the Luxor's casino manager, told me: "No one can work on the Strip for very long without realizing the role that luck plays in all of our lives. No matter how you try to control your destiny, you can't—and there is no better place than Las Vegas to see how fate or luck or whatever you want to call it can change a person's life. I often ask our guests if they would bet on a horse race if there was only one horse running in it. Most laugh and say, 'Of course! It would be a sure thing.' But you know what, I wouldn't bet on a one-horse race. Why? Because the horse's jockey might fall off, the horse might stumble and break its leg—a thousand other mishaps could happen. The most common word you will hear being spoken in a casino is 'luck.' "

One gambler pulls a slot machine's handle and wins a million dollars after betting a single quarter. Another loses a fortune with the turn of a card. Why? Luck. Fate. Chance. The only "sure thing" in Las Vegas is that nothing in life is predetermined, nothing is certain except the moment. "That's what makes this town and the Strip so exciting," said Robinson. "No one knows for sure what will happen next here. No one."

Inside the Casino:
Poolside at the Luxor

Tammy and I came here from Tennessee on vacation because we decided it was time for one of those Thelma and Louise trips where we girls get away by ourselves. We're sisters, although no one would know it by looking at us. I'm thirty and Tammy here is twenty-eight. I got two kids and she has one, but people think we are much younger because we stay in really good shape. I mean, it's important to us. Neither of us ever wants to turn into one of those fat housewives who wear baggy sweats all day. My husband runs a landscaping business and Tammy's is an attorney. They're staying home with the kids. God, that's got to be a big mess by now.

So you asked why we were sunning ourselves topless—that's why you came over here, right—to get a better look at our titties? [Laughs.] Let me tell you first that this is not something Tammy or I ever would have done at home, okay? We are really conservative. I mean, my favorite radio show is G. Gordon Liddy, for godsakes, and we both are Republicans. Our husbands would freak out if they knew we were sitting by the pool with our boobs showing. They would just die. But last night we went to see the show Enter the Night down at the Stardust and it was topless, and we were sitting there thinking, "Hey, we got bodies as nice as these showgirls'." Anyway, we were sunbathing down here by the pool and suddenly Tammy says to me: "Wouldn't the guys back home just die if we came back without a tan line?" And I laughed and said, "Tammy, there's got to be five hundred people sitting around this pool. You really going to show them your tits?" And she said, "Let's go for it."

The funny thing is that when we took off our tops, it seemed like no one reacted, but Tammy and I have been watching and every guy down here has rolled over on his chaise lounge or re-arranged his chair or gotten up to get a towel or done something so that he could see us. And the pool boy has been by here three or four times to ask if we want drinks and now an author shows up and wants to talk to us for a book. I mean, it's like the second we take off our tops, we're celebrities! We had these two guys come over a few minutes ago and ask if they could buy us drinks. They started hitting on us and we just shut them down.

We're going home tomorrow and I can hardly wait to make love to my old man. I mean, this has been a real turn-on this afternoon. That's what I really like about this town. I mean, I would never have the nerve to do this anywhere else. You can really let your inhibitions go down here and have fun and then go home and no one will ever know how crazy you acted. I think we need cities like this.

My husband, Julius, and I first started coming to Las Vegas back in the 1940s. Of course it was much different then. We came out every year. We never went anywhere else but Las Vegas. We didn't have children, you know, so we never even went down to see the Grand Canyon. I'd play the slots and he'd play blackjack and we'd dress up at night and go to a show. He died eight years ago and I didn't come out that first year. I sat at home and then I said, "Gertrude, this is crazy. Jules— that's what I called him—would want you to go." So I have come out every year since then on the week of his death. I play blackjack because I like to meet the people. I play on the $2 table because people don't mind if you talk at that table. The bigger tables, they're trying to win and don't want to make friends. I've met some wonderful people and it gives me a chance to talk to strangers and find out about their lives and not just sit home in Miami playing bridge with the same ladies, talking about how our husbands are all dead and those that are still alive, how they are making their wives so miserable they wish they were dead! [Laughs.] I'm only joking, you know. I miss my Jules. He was such a good man! At least once during my trips here, I get all dressed up and I go out to dinner and then see a show and then I come back to my hotel room and I look out the window in the dark at the stars and I talk to Jules about the dinner and the show and I feel like he is right here with me in Vegas. Sometimes when I'm in Miami, I tell myself that he's not dead at all. He's out in Vegas playing blackjack and waiting for me to join him so we can go dancing again. I used to love that—when we went dancing.

—*Guests at the Luxor*

CHAPTER ONE

....

Las Vegas Bound!

Within minutes after the Delta flight lifts off from the Salt Lake City airport runway, the passenger in seat 22B lowers the plastic tray in front of him and opens a deck of cards.

"Blackjack?" he asks the woman next to him. "Just for fun. Might as well get started early!" She lowers her tray as he begins to deal.

"It's our first time," a honeymooner two rows back confides to the airline attendant taking drink orders. "My husband wants to play poker, but me, I'm going right for the slots. Do you know of any good places to eat?"

"The all-you-can-eat buffet at the Rio is the best!" the man sitting across the aisle volunteers.

"You really need to see the white tigers at the Mirage!" offers another.

"Don't play any of the slots at the airport," a nearby passenger warns. "They're the tightest in town!"

The flight attendant, whose badge identifies her as

Jasmine, explains that passengers en route to Las Vegas are usually a talkative bunch. "It's like when we have a Super Bowl flight and everyone shows up with their faces painted, hooting and hollering. We've had people trying to shoot craps down the aisles on these flights. At least when we are flying *into* Las Vegas, everyone is happy."

"I see it!" a boy announces less than an hour later. In the distance, Las Vegas appears in miniature, as if its Strip hotels are pieces on a Monopoly game board. It is a city that sprouts unexpectedly in a dead valley, encircled by gray mountains with slag surfaces of stone and gravel. After a flight over cracked riverbeds, wind-burned gulches, and the scorching, moonlike surface of the Mojave Desert, Las Vegas is splashes of color. From the air, green golf fairways come into focus, along with the intense blue shapes of resort and backyard swimming pools. As the plane descends there's more: black asphalt parking lots, gray concrete driveways, brown-necked palm trees, the red tile roofs of Spanish-style houses ringed by privacy walls made of pink adobe.

"Look, look! There they are!" a woman cries as the flight circles McCarran International Airport, at the southern edge of the city. All aboard have a clear view of the world-famous Strip as the woman begins identifying the casinos by name, as if they were friends. "There's Caesars Palace and the Mirage! Can you see the volcano? Oh, look—there's the Luxor and MGM and New York New York!"

Forty-seven percent of the tourists who visit Las Vegas each year arrive by air, making McCarran the tenth busiest airport in the nation. Every day, eighty-four thousand passengers arrive or depart. That's the equivalent of nearly one-tenth of the entire Las Vegas population moving through McCarran in a single day. On most afternoons, air traffic controllers can't keep up. They keep planes circling while waiting for runways to clear.

If a traveler was completely ignorant of Las Vegas's history and somehow missed seeing the outlandishly shaped super casinos on its Strip, he might be fooled into thinking as his flight circled the airport that he was about to land in a typical southwestern city. A handful of tall office buildings rise from the downtown area and, much like the rings on a tree stump, the urban sprawl rippling outward reflects how the city has grown and prospered. The farther from the city center, the bigger and newer the houses, until you reach the fringes where shopping malls sit next to planned communities with golf courses, tennis and swim clubs, and cul-de-sacs lined with homes. It could be Phoenix, Albuquerque, or El Paso.

But once a traveler enters the McCarran terminal, any notion that Las Vegas might be ordinary is quickly dispelled. The voice from the ceiling speakers telling travelers to stand to the right of the moving walkway is not some computer-generated drone. It's Joan Rivers. At the baggage claim area, banks of slot machines are tucked between the carousels.

Bells ring, coins tumble into chrome trays, but it is the continuous rhythm made by these slot machines' electronic spinning wheels that permeates the air. *Duh-duh-em-da-a-lop! Duh-duh-em-da-a-lop!* A hundred times each minute. A million times each hour. *Duh-duh-em-da-a-lop! Duh-duh-em-da-a-lop!* It is impossible to escape. *Duh-duh-em-da-a-lop! Duh-duh-em-da-a-lop!* In supermarkets, where slot machines are stationed near the cashiers so shoppers can rid themselves of change; in restaurants, where they are set up outside the rest rooms; in neighborhood pubs, where their twirling wheels are built into glass-topped tables; and in convenience stores, where they can be found near the soda machines, the games emit the same strain: *Duh-duh-em-da-a-lop!* Only one noise can challenge it, and that's the metallic snapping that issues from video poker machines dealing their picture-tube cards. *Snap, snap, snap, snap, snap! Duh-duh-em-da-a-lop! Snap, snap, snap, snap, snap! Duh-duh-em-da-a-lop!* Cruise the Strip with your car windows open and the radio switched off early any morning and the ringing of spinning wheels and snapping of electronic cards is all around you. It is the city's unofficial theme song.

The eyes are assaulted as intensely as the ears. During the short ride from McCarran Airport into the city, visitors are greeted by a second phenomenon: the Las Vegas glow. Electronic billboards define the city's skyline. The rainbow-colored neon tubing burns day and night. The lightbulb–re-created face of singer Tom Jones emanating from the fifty-foot electronic billboard outside the entrance of the MGM Grand catches the eye. A forty-billion-candlepower spotlight shoots a continuous beam of light ten miles into the desert blackness from dusk to dawn from the apex of the Luxor pyramid. Fifteen-foot-tall knights joust electronically outside the medieval Excalibur hotel and casino; showgirls kick high with strobe-light legs on the Stratosphere's sign. It is not just the colors of the fifteen thousand miles of lights that overwhelm onlookers. Throbbing, flickering, streaking, sparkling, twinkling, at night the entire city seems one enormous, pulsating neon billboard.

Has there ever been another destination like Las Vegas? There is nowhere gaudier, splashier, more electric. Call it what you will: Lost Wages, Pair-o-Dice, Never-Never Land. In a location that normally attracts only lizards and rattlesnakes, this is a nonstop temple to excess, where fantasies become true.

For most tourists, Las Vegas consists of two districts: the legendary Strip and Glitter Gulch, an avenue of casinos located in the center of the city. The downtown joints used to be much grittier than their upscale Strip rivals, largely because of their seedy location. Las Vegas was founded by the railroad. Consequently, there is an Amtrak station in the center of the city, next to railroad tracks that run north and south, cutting the town in half. The front doors of the station open onto Fremont Street, the city's de facto main street, which runs east to west and is where most of the early casinos took root. In the late 1940s, the four-block stretch between the train station and Fourth Street was nicknamed Glitter Gulch because there were so many neon signs outside its casinos that it looked to arriving train passengers as if they were disembarking into a gaudy ravine. One of the most memorable signs featured Vegas Vic, a skinny neon cowboy with a red-tipped cigarette dangling from his lips and a bent elbow and outstretched thumb that pointed toward the Pioneer Club. But the Gulch's glitter began to dim during the 1950s, when the Strip became the city's hottest gambling spot. Few downtown casinos could compete with its fancy resorts. Most lacked frills and class. They were dark, dirty, and dingy. By the 1960s, downtown was where the derelicts hung out begging for quarters that they hoped to turn through chance into enough for a bottle of whiskey. Even the casinos' names seemed shopworn: Horseshoe, Four Queens, Lady Luck, Golden Nugget. But during the booming 1980s and 1990s, Glitter Gulch got a face-lift. Nearly every club was remodeled. The bums were banished. The city helped out in 1995 by closing a portion of Fremont Street to traffic and turning it into a pedestrian mall covered with a four-block-long metal awning. Now Glitter Gulch is illuminated at night by 2.2 million bulbs hidden in the mall's awning. They flash in computer-choreographed patterns with such brilliance it is impossible to tell it is nighttime.

The Strip begins three miles south of Glitter Gulch

on Las Vegas Boulevard, which once was the main
north-south route for motorists coming into town. In
the 1940s, this was where the city limits ended, and
although the city has expanded its boundaries south-
ward, the Strip still starts where Las Vegas Boulevard
intersects with Sahara Avenue, so called because the
Sahara hotel and casino sits at the intersection's southeast corner.

Motorists riding those three miles south from
Glitter Gulch toward the Strip get to see a Las Vegas
never shown in glitzy ads. They pass through one of the
city's scroungier neighborhoods. Flat-roofed World War
II–era houses sit in disrepair along Las Vegas Boulevard,
iron bars protecting their windows. Pawnshops, wedding chapels, one-hour-photo booths, liquor stores,
1950s-era motels featuring X-rated movies, adult bookstores, topless bars, and used furniture stores line the
boulevard. But all these dives disappear at the Sahara
Avenue intersection. From this point on, motorists are
shaded by towering palm trees that rise from the land-
scaped median that divides the boulevard as it expands
from four to six lanes along the next four miles. The
Strip's oldest resorts are located close to Sahara Avenue,
on what is known as the "northern tip" of the Strip.
Most of them have familiar names: Circus Circus,
Stardust, Frontier, Desert Inn, Riviera. Although some
of their exteriors have been remodeled, they look much
as they did when they were first erected in the 1950s
and 1960s. The popularity of the northern tip has been
dropping over the years as tourists moved farther south
to newer and more elaborate casinos. In 1995, a renegade casino owner named Bob Stupak tried to reverse
this southern trend by erecting a super casino on the
northern tip. Located a short distance north of Sahara
Avenue, Stupak's Stratosphere Tower rises 119 stories
high, making it the tallest building in the West. Stupak
put a roller coaster on its roof and added a ride that

rockets thrill seekers along a metal antenna at the tower's peak even higher into the sky. But despite its daring rides, the Stratosphere has failed to draw crowds, largely because tourists feel uncomfortable walking through the seedy neighborhood at its base.

The biggest tourist attractions are found in the middle of the Strip, at an intersection that has two different names. Originally, the street that intersected with Las Vegas Boulevard here was called Flamingo Road because it is where Benjamin "Bugsy" Siegel built his famed Flamingo casino in 1946. At the time, the city thought it was a clever idea to name streets that crossed the Strip after whatever big casino was located at that intersection, leading to names such as Sahara Avenue and Tropicana Avenue. But this practice soon caused problems. When the Flamingo's popularity declined in the 1960s and the Dunes became the premier casino at the same intersection, its owners demanded that the avenue's name be changed. Naturally, the Flamingo's owners protested. Unsure what to do, the city agreed to keep the Flamingo street name from the Strip eastward, but changed the name to Dunes Road from the Strip westward. A few years later, when Caesars Palace opened at the same intersection, the city refused to change the name again, even after the Dunes closed.

The intersection of Dunes Road and Flamingo Road is now the heart of the Strip, and this midsection area is where the Strip's first super casino, the Mirage, was built. Other resorts located here include Treasure Island, Harrah's, Bally's, and Barbary Coast, as well as Caesars Palace and the Flamingo, now called the Flamingo Hilton. With their spraying fountains, flashing lights, and dramatic exteriors, they give the Strip the look of a movie studio backlot. Enter Caesars Palace and you are in ancient Rome. Choose Treasure Island and be greeted by an eye-patched pirate and his parrot. Most of the newest super casinos are located on the southern tip of the Strip. This is home to the Bellagio, Venetian, MGM Grand, Monte Carlo, New York New York, Excalibur, Luxor, Tropicana, and Mandalay Bay. Although Las Vegas Boulevard continues south for several more miles, for all practical purposes the Strip ends with Mandalay Bay, its last super casino complex.

There is much more to Las Vegas, of course, than its two gambling districts. At first glance, this "other" Las Vegas seems little different from any other city. It has the same shopping malls, fast-food eateries, Wal-Marts and Kmarts, as those found in Denver, San Diego, and Austin. There is a university, a large convention center, a chamber of commerce, and an elected mayor and city council. On any given Saturday, there are Little League baseball games and soccer matches where dads jog up and down the sidelines waving red flags whenever the ball goes out of bounds. Girl Scouts here recite the same pledges, churches deliver food to the needy, everyday life goes on. Still, behind these ordinary scenes are subtle reminders that even this "other" Las Vegas is different. More stores than usual stay open twenty-four hours; there are thriving Rolls-Royce and Ferrari dealerships; clerks don't flinch when a customer uses a hundred-dollar bill to buy a few dollars' worth of goods; billboards advertise the telephone numbers of the local Alcoholics Anonymous and Gamblers Anonymous chapters; the Yellow Pages contain twenty pages of ads placed by outcall services whose women and men employees dance nude for a price.

Some not-so-subtle reminders that you are in Las Vegas are the thousands of slot and video poker machines that are found everywhere. In a city of nearly one million men, women, and children, there is an average of one slot or video poker machine for every ten residents.

Because the most popular style of residential architecture in the city is a combination of southwestern and

Spanish, many of the city's homes are hidden behind tall adobe walls. This not only gives motorists the impression that they are traveling through a maze, but contributes to what some longtime residents claim is a breakdown in neighborliness. The walls also make it difficult for newcomers to tell what sort of neighborhood they are traveling in. Poor areas can be found only a block away from middle-class and upper-crust subdivisions in some sections of town. The most expensive houses, however, line the city's outer ring. Las Vegas has five times as many million-dollar homes as have other western cities its size, and nearly all of them are owned by gambling executives or entertainers. High walls, iron gates, and uniformed guards can be found outside these enclaves. Over the years, the huge salaries that casino moguls have earned have made their families frequent targets for kidnappers. Because of this, there are more private schools and private security companies in Las Vegas than in cities nearly double its size.

Antigambling forces have published reams of statistical studies since the city's early days that portray it as infested with social ills. They claim it has higher rates of divorce, crime, unemployment, bankruptcy, wife and child abuse, alcoholism, sexually transmitted diseases, and suicide than other comparable cities. The casino industry and city boosters have responded with their own data that show Las Vegas has either fewer such problems or just about the same number as cities of similar size. According to the Clark County sheriff, it is always outsiders, not the local citizens, who cause trouble.

Where's the truth? Common sense tells you that living in Las Vegas is not the same as living in Omaha. But for every cynic, there are scores of longtime residents who insist they live perfectly mundane lives in Sin City. "Obviously, this is a city of huge excesses," says a lawyer who reared his four children here, "and the only way you can survive is if you realize early on that no one can live their life as if they were on a vacation every day of the year. You can't gamble and drink free drinks every day. After you learn that, you really don't think about it much." Not think about it? The multimillion-dollar jackpots, the racy shows, the free drinks, all-you-can-eat buffets, hookers, slots, dice, cards? "That's right. You don't even think about it unless you have company from out of town who want you to show them around."

Perhaps this is true, but few who live outside Las Vegas seem willing to believe it. It smacks of blasphemy. Talk of the bland strips the city of its allure. "Tourists come in here every day and tell me that gangsters are still running this city," a casino manager chuckles. "After a while you think: Why disabuse them? They want to see a gangster behind every craps table, let them believe the lie."

There is one truth about Las Vegas that no one can dispute. It is quintessentially American. It is a city that is constantly reinventing itself, always looking for an edge to exploit, something new to sell. It is capitalism in the extreme. If you have enough money, everything is possible in Las Vegas. The history of the city is a story of stubbornness, ingenuity, greed, and sin. Smack in the middle of a boiling desert, Las Vegas had nothing to offer, no reason to be, until its residents came up with a justification that has allowed it not only to survive, but to thrive. In its exaggerated opulence, its energy, its grandiosity, its craziness, Las Vegas could have arisen nowhere else.

In the beginning, there was water. Locked underneath the concretelike surface, artesian aquifers filled with groundwater until the pressure finally caused the caliche rock to crack thousands of years ago and release a series of springs in the middle of the desert valley. Prehistoric Indians were the first to arrive, followed by the mysterious Anasazi, who left traces suggesting they lived near the springs nearly five hundred years before they vanished around 1500 A.D. Next came the Paiutes, known as "the desert people." Surveyor John C. Frémont described them in 1844 as "humanity in its lowest form," noting that they survived by growing sunflowers and pumpkins, and luring lizards out of holes to eat them. By 1851, Big Springs, as the area was known, had become such a regular watering hole for wagon trains traveling along the Mormon Trail between Utah and California that Brigham Young sent thirty missionaries into the valley to convert the Paiutes and erect a town. They stayed only long enough to build a fort before the 114-degree temperatures drove them home. White settlers remained scarce until 1859, when the Comstock Lode, rich in silver, was discovered in northern Nevada.

Octavius Decatur Gass was one of the early fortune seekers, but he put aside his prospector's pan in 1865 and instead began homesteading at Big Springs. Using logs from the old Mormon fort, he built a ranch house, planted crops, raised cattle, and got himself elected to the state legislature. In 1876, he borrowed $5,000 from Archibald Stewart, a skinflint businessman who charged him a 30-percent interest rate. When Gass defaulted two years later, Stewart seized Gass's eight-hundred-acre ranch at Big Springs. Other landowners shunned Stewart, but it didn't bother him because he spent much of his time up north operating his businesses. However, his twenty-nine-year-old wife, Helen, was lonely. Some accounts claim Helen fell under the spell of Schuyler Henry, a handsome cowboy from a nearby ranch. Others say the cowpoke harassed her to the point that she was forced to keep him away at gunpoint. Regardless of which version is accurate, when her jealous husband hurried home and confronted Henry, the cowboy promptly shot him dead. A jury ruled the killing self-defense and Helen, who was three months pregnant and had four other children to rear, quietly buried her husband as her suitor left town. This messy episode was the first reported killing in what later would become Las Vegas, and some historians would note that it somehow seemed a fitting start for the town.

Helen Stewart turned her husband's ranch at Big Springs into a campground for thirsty prospectors and other vagabonds traveling along the Mormon Trail. She correctly guessed that it would be only a matter of time before a railroad line would be built linking Salt Lake City and Los Angeles. Railroad engines couldn't run without water, so she began buying as much land as she could around the artesian wells, and when the railroad finally showed up in 1902, she owned nearly 1,800 acres. The railroad offered her $55,000, a hefty sum back then, but demanded that she first provide it with a land survey. The surveyor she hired, J. T. McWilliams, discovered that eighty acres west of Helen Stewart's ranch had never been titled, so he grabbed it for himself and began selling lots to land speculators who figured the arrival of the railroad was sure to send property values soaring. They were right. By the time the railroad finished laying track in January 1905 through the land it had bought from Stewart, a town of 1,500 residents had sprung up on McWilliams's eighty-acre parcel. It was called Ragtown, and it had a bank, a brickyard, a weekly newspaper, and an ice plant.

But the owners of the San Pedro–Los Angeles–Salt Lake Railroad Line were not about to let McWilliams profit from their investment, so they platted their own rival town a few miles down the tracks from Ragtown. It consisted of forty identical square blocks, with First through Fifth Streets running north and south, and nine streets with names such as Fremont, Lewis, and Clark running east and west. The railroad called it Las Vegas, which means "the meadows," the name that Spanish explorers had first given the valley. Advertising heavily in California and Utah, the railroad exaggerated the potential of its "new" city, and the outlandish claims sparked a frenzy of speculation. When it was over, the railroad had sold its seven hundred desert lots for $265,000—almost 500 percent more than Helen Stewart had been paid three years earlier.

The exuberance of the town's new residents didn't last long. The inhospitable climate drove many away, but it was the railroad's tyrannical control over the area's water supply that really kept Las Vegas from growing. Without water, farmers couldn't grow crops, ranchers' livestock couldn't survive, and no industry would risk moving into town. The railroad cut off Ragtown's water supply and turned it into a ghost town. Meanwhile, Las Vegas stagnated. The only businesses that flourished were the town's "social clubs" that railroad workers and cowboys frequented on "Block 16" of the town plat. Whiskey cost a dime per shot, cards were dealt around the clock, and whores operated openly in cribs out back.

Under pressure from the state's Mormon voters, mostly up north in Reno and Carson City, the Nevada legislature voted in 1910 to outlaw all gambling, and it was at this juncture that Las Vegas made a fateful choice. Afraid of losing their only thriving enterprises, the 1,400 citizens chose to completely ignore the new law. Block 16 grew even more raucous. When the railroad changed hands in 1921, it looked as if Las Vegas might get an economic reprieve, but the new owners proved even worse than the first. They fired most of the railway workers who lived in Las Vegas after the workers joined a nationwide railroad strike, and the town's shaky economy turned so bad that the entire community was near the brink of collapse by the mid-1920s.

Then, just as Las Vegas was about to become a

ghost town, Congress saved it by authorizing the construction of the Boulder Dam, later renamed the Hoover Dam, twenty-five miles south of town. The dam was the largest federal water project ever undertaken and was such an architectural marvel that it was being called "the Eighth Wonder of the World" when construction began in 1931. Las Vegas was the closest town and the only one with a railroad. By this time, Nevada had changed its mind about gambling. State legislators had made it legal once again, and that worried some Washington, D.C., politicians. Afraid that the five thousand dam workers might be corrupted, Congress decided to build its own city for them. With typical bureaucratic creativity, it was named Boulder City and was declared a government reservation under federal, not state, jurisdiction. It banned drinking, gambling, and sexual activities by single men—rules that only made Las Vegas more enticing. Dam workers poured into Block 16. New businesses opened, streets were paved, and Las Vegas was modernized with gambling profits. Before long, the city gained enough clout to force the railroad to relinquish its stranglehold on the area's water supply, and seemingly overnight, Las Vegas doubled in size and then doubled again, swelling to a population of 7,500.

After the dam was completed in 1936, the city's economy hiccupped. But three years later came the start of World War II, and the military needed critical minerals such as magnesium that were plentiful in the desert. Congress also gave Las Vegas another boost, this time by building Nellis Air Force Base at the city's outskirts. Military authorities liked the desert's dry weather because there were very few days when their pilots couldn't train, although several generals fretted about sending four thousand fresh recruits every six weeks for training right next to Las Vegas. Under pressure from the War Department, the city closed Block 16. But the move was merely a shell game. The prostitutes and casino operators simply relocated one block south along Fremont Street.

It is at this point—the early 1940s—that writers usually mention the arrival of Benjamin "Bugsy" Siegel, the ruthless New York City gangster who in recent movies has been portrayed as the visionary behind the Las Vegas Strip. The way Hollywood tells the story, Siegel paused one afternoon to urinate in the desert while driving into Las Vegas from Los Angeles. As he peed alongside Highway 91, Siegel was struck by a vision of colossal hotels and glittering casinos rising like a mirage before his eyes. Of course, this never happened. Siegel did not name the Strip, nor was he the first to build there. He did not even choose the spot along Highway 91, later renamed Las Vegas Boulevard, where the Flamingo hotel was built.

The real story behind the Strip starts in 1938, when Fletcher Brown was elected mayor of Los Angeles and began shutting down illegal gambling joints. One of the crooks who fled town was Guy McAfee, a captain in the Los Angeles Police Department's vice unit, who had been running several illegal gambling clubs of his own. McAfee relocated to Las Vegas, where he opened a club on Fremont Street and bought the Pair-o-Dice Club several miles south of town. McAfee spent so much time driving on Highway 91 between his downtown club and the Pair-o-Dice that he began referring to the route as "the Strip," after L.A.'s Sunset Strip. The name slowly caught on.

At about this same time, a man named Thomas Hull, who operated several California hotels, arrived in Las Vegas looking for a spot on which to build. Legend has it that Hull's car overheated a few miles south of town and while he was waiting for a mechanic, he began to count the cars zooming by. America was in the process of changing from a nation that traveled by train to one that went in automobiles, and Los Angeles was only seven hours away by car. Hull counted so many California license tags speeding into Las Vegas that he decided to build a hotel on Highway 91. When he approached Jessie Hunt, who owned much of the land next to the highway, she actually offered to *give* him the thirty-three acres he wanted because she thought them worthless and was tired of paying taxes on them. He paid her $150 per acre instead.

On April 3, 1941, Hull opened the El Rancho Vegas hotel at the southern edge of Las Vegas—the site of the present-day intersection of Sahara Avenue and Las Vegas Boulevard. He chose it because it was where the city limits ended, which meant that he didn't have to pay city taxes or seek a gambling license from city officials, whose strings were being pulled by Fremont Street club owners. The El Rancho Vegas had a single-story main lodge surrounded by sixty-four bungalows, all decorated in a western motif. It was not only the first Strip casino, but a prototype that others would copy for decades to come. Hull didn't want his guests gambling elsewhere, so he designed the El Rancho Vegas to be self-contained. It offered guests a steak house, retail shops, a swimming pool and sunbathing area, palm trees, and a show room separate from the casino. He cut deals with local ranchers for his lodgers to go horseback riding and sightseeing. Hull wanted to attract not only gamblers but also wealthy men and women seeking divorces. Nevada was a divorce haven. Other states had stiff residency requirements and stringent regulations governing divorce, but Nevada required applicants to live within its borders for only six weeks in order to qualify for the equivalent of a no-fault divorce. Reno was flourishing up north, in part because its hotels catered to the divorce crowd, and Hull hoped to steal its business. He wooed divorce-seekers by offering them a dude ranch setting where they could meet others seeking divorces while waiting out their six weeks.

El Rancho Vegas offered its guests something else that was revolutionizing Las Vegas. Air-conditioning, or refrigerated air, as it was called, made the desert's heat bearable. El Rancho Vegas was such a hit that two years later, another resort called the Last Frontier opened less than a mile farther south down Highway 91. Its owners tried to outdo Hull by sending stage-coaches to greet arriving guests at the train station or the city's fledgling airport. The Last Frontier's rooms were furnished with antiques from the homes of early pioneers. Zuni Indians sold handmade baskets in the lobby, and Sophie Tucker, the legendary "Last of the Red Hot Mamas," became the first stage and Hollywood screen star to perform at a Strip resort when the Last Frontier booked her in its theater. She rode from the downtown train station to the resort on a city fire truck with its siren wailing and a marching band playing behind it.

By the time Bugsy Siegel arrived in 1946, El Rancho Vegas and the Last Frontier were booming. Siegel had been sent west in the late 1930s by his gangster pal Meyer Lansky to seize control of the mob in Los Angeles and muscle in on the horse-race wires Las Vegas bookies used to send gambling odds across the country. As soon as he accomplished those tasks, Siegel tried to break into acting. He wanted to star in gangster movies, much like his friend actor George Raft, but he lacked talent. It was during a trip to Las Vegas to shake down the owner of a Fremont Street club that Siegel noticed the El Rancho Vegas and the Last Frontier and bragged to a pal, "I can do better." With $1 million borrowed from East Coast mobsters, Siegel bought a majority interest in a half-finished Strip hotel started by Los Angeles publisher Billy Wilkerson Jr. He promptly renamed it the Flamingo and set out to turn it into a playground for the Hollywood elite he desperately wanted to impress. During the coming months, Siegel got his mob backers to invest more and more cash until he had spent $5 million and the Flamingo still wasn't finished. Rumors spread that he was stealing the cash. Years later, the son of Billy Wilkerson Jr., Siegel's legitimate partner in the Flamingo, told the *Las Vegas Sun* that his father had received a late-night visit from Siegel. "Siegel told my dad, 'You're going to turn over your interest to me and if you don't give it to me, I'm going to kill you.'" His father quickly signed over his 48 percent of the unfinished hotel and fled to Paris. Siegel gave this share to his mob cronies to get them off his back.

The Flamingo's grand opening on the day after Christmas in 1946 made national headlines because Siegel chartered flights, filled them with Hollywood celebrities, and flew everyone into Las Vegas to watch comedian Jimmy Durante open the resort's theater. The casino dealers wore tuxedos, and male patrons were required to wear suits and ties. Women wore gloves. The Hollywood crowd partied for three days and then flew home, leaving the casino empty. Local gamblers and tourists were too intimidated to gamble there, and rumors spread that Siegel was pilfering what few profits there were. Fourteen days after it opened, the Flamingo closed, only to reopen two months later without the tuxedos and dress code. It soon showed a steady profit, but by then Siegel's fate had been sealed. On June 20, 1947, he was reading a newspaper in the living room of the Hollywood mansion that he had bought for his girlfriend, starlet Virginia Hill, when someone fired an army carbine nine times through the living room window. Siegel was killed instantly. Although the murder has never been solved, police quickly theorized that Siegel was killed by his mob investors. Gus Greenbaum, who had overseen the New York mob's bookmaking franchise in Phoenix, was introducing himself as the new boss of the Flamingo before the coroner had formally confirmed that Siegel was dead.

Even though Siegel wasn't the first to build on the Strip, he was the first to understand the importance that Hollywood would play in Las Vegas's development. His murder also marked the beginning of four decades of organized crime's control of the city. In 1948, Meyer Lansky sent his brother, Jake, to open another Strip resort, the Thunderbird. Meyer Lansky recognized that a Strip casino was the perfect business for a crook. The gambling revenues were in cash, which was easy to skim, and the casinos provided their owners with an easy way to launder money. Jake Lansky was followed by Cleveland mobster Moe Dalitz, who opened the Desert Inn in 1950, bringing the total number of mob-run Strip resorts to three. That same year, Tennessee Senator Estes Kefauver and his Senate Committee to Investigate Organized Crime launched a national probe of gambling. Kefauver hauled New York City mob bosses before his committee and then headed for Las Vegas, where he grilled Moe Sedway, one of the gangster owners of the Flamingo, and Moe Dalitz. With great fanfare, Kefauver announced that illegal gambling was rampant in most major cities and that organized crime was behind much of it. His highly sensationalized charges triggered a national hysteria. Vice squads in Miami, Boston, St. Louis, New Orleans, Dallas, and Seattle were pressured by voters into shutting down local betting parlors, and hundreds of small-time hoods fled to Nevada to avoid prosecution. This migration alarmed state officials, who quickly enacted laws to keep criminals from buying casinos. But while the new regulations looked foolproof, they were easy to foil with bribes. The Sands and the Sahara opened on the Strip in 1952, the Dunes and the Riviera in 1955, the Hacienda in 1956, the Tropicana in 1957, and the

Stardust in 1958. The FBI would later determine that
nearly all of them were controlled by the mob. The
Sands was run by a New Jersey mobster; the Riviera by
Chicago hoods. The Tropicana was secretly controlled
by Frank Costello, the boss of bosses in New York, and
the Stardust was the creation of Tony Cornero, a boot-
legger, smuggler, hijacker, and stock swindler who had
settled in Las Vegas. The Strip was simply too juicy for
any single gangster or crime syndicate to dominate it.
Instead, the various factions agreed that it would be
"open territory," which meant that crime families from
across the country were free to operate as long as they
left their competitors alone. Any mobster who could
raise $2 to $5 million—enough to build a casino, a theater, and the equivalent of a two-story hotel with a
swimming pool—could go into business. Land was
plentiful because the Strip began at the city limits and
there was nothing on either side of Highway 91 but
desert.

   If anything the gangsters' presence seemed to increase the city's lure. Nevada officials reported that
Las Vegas had taken in approximately $50 million in
gambling revenues in 1950. Ten years later, the figure
was close to $300 million, and that was just the money
the casinos reported, not the millions in cash being
skimmed. The city was drawing as many as eleven million visitors a year, 60 percent of them from California.
Historians would later declare the 1950s the city's
golden era. Just as Bugsy Siegel had envisioned, the
Strip had turned into a playground for Hollywood's
rich and famous. Its theaters had replaced vaudeville.
Singers Kay Starr and Rosemary Clooney were regulars
at the Flamingo. Other Strip performers included
Henny Youngman, Mae West, Betty Hutton, Tennessee
Ernie Ford, Mickey Rooney, Phil Silvers, Milton Berle,
Buddy Hackett, Marlene Dietrich, Peggy Lee, and
Connie Francis. The Mills Brothers were the first blacks

to perform on the Strip, although they had to stay across the tracks in the segregated city's "colored" section. They were followed by Pearl Bailey, Nat King Cole, Harry Belafonte, and Eartha Kitt. While the rest of the country fretted about the rise of communism and the "Red Scare," any mention of "Reds" on the Strip was a reference to Redd Foxx, Red Buttons, and Red Skelton.

Las Vegas developed its own local talents too, most notably a twenty-three-year-old pianist who had been jeered in 1945 because of his effeminate mannerisms when he started performing for $400 a week at the Last Frontier. By 1956, however, Liberace had become the Strip's premier entertainer, signing a three-year contract at Chicago gangster Sam Giancana's Riviera for $50,000 a week, a record at the time. Elvis Presley opened at the Last Frontier in April 1956, but bombed and was fired after only one week. Even Ronald Reagan appeared on a Strip stage briefly, as part of a comedy act with trained monkeys. And the stars weren't only onstage. Elizabeth Taylor, Eddie Fisher, Debbie Reynolds, Jerry Lewis, Dean Martin, Paul Newman, Joanne Woodward, Lauren Bacall, and Judy Garland were often spotted at the clubs.

There was such explosive growth in Las Vegas during the 1950s that the city experienced its first glut of hotel rooms. This led to price slashing. Rooms were marked down to $10 a night, and owners began wooing customers with all-you-can-eat buffets. Some put entertainers into their lounges, creating a new type of entertainment—the lounge show. The Dunes introduced bare-breasted showgirls in 1957. The Stardust responded by offering totally nude acts. Prostitutes became so commonplace that the city's hookers were mentioned in the Broadway play *Guys and Dolls,* when Sky Masterson sang of returning from Las Vegas, "where all the girls have nice teeth and no last names."

Completely unnoticed among the celebrities, entertainers, tourists, gangsters, sightseers, and dreamers pouring into this self-proclaimed "entertainment capital of the world" was a grossly overweight, balding, unabashed womanizer who often acted more like a clown than a visionary. Yet this compulsive gambler was about to change the face of the Strip and help shape the future of Las Vegas.

His name was Jay Sarno.

Inside the Casino:
Blind Luck

I started out working in keno. A player gets a card that contains the numbers one through eighty. He picks up to twenty of the numbers. The casino then selects twenty numbers at random. If the player's numbers match those picked by the casino, he wins. It's as simple as that. The payout is based on how many numbers a person hits and how much he bets.

One day, this big fellow begins speaking to me in Russian and I don't understand a thing, but he slides a $25 casino chip over the counter and I figure he wants to make a bet. Since he hasn't filled out a card, I ask him if he wants to do what we call a "quick pick," which is when the computer actually picks the numbers for you. I ask him, "How many numbers?" He doesn't say anything so I say, "Six? Seven?" and he says, "Yes." So I take his chip and the computer picks seven spots for him and I slide the ticket back to him and he walks away. By gosh, that ticket hits six out of the seven numbers which means his ticket wins $8,000.

After a while, he comes back and he says something to me and I say, "You won! We owe you eight thousand dollars, but I need some sort of identification before I can pay you." Well, he doesn't understand a thing, so he goes off and gets a friend of his who speaks broken English and he comes back and I say, "Your friend just won eight thousand dollars, but I need his ID before I can pay him." This gentleman just about falls over. He tells me this guy has just gotten out of Russia and he thought that I was a cashier for the casino who made change. He was giving me his chip to cash in and leave the casino. He thought that the keno ticket that I gave him was some sort of receipt, and he had been wandering around the casino looking for someplace to turn it in so he could get his twenty-five bucks! Now I got customers who spend hours tracking numbers. Some follow their astrological charts. Others are into numerology. And this guy walks in and wins and he doesn't even know that he is playing keno.

—*Melinda Winn, Luxor keno manager*

CHAPTER TWO

....

Jay Sarno, Casino Clown

Jay Sarno was shooting dice at a craps table inside the Flamingo in 1961 when it dawned on him that the only person making money was the guy who owned the casino. Sarno lost about $5,000, but he didn't complain on his flight back to Atlanta. He was too busy designing a casino of his own in his head, and as soon as he got home, he woke up his wife, Joyce, and told her about it.

"I'm going to build a real palace on the Las Vegas Strip," he announced. "In fact, I'm going to call it the Desert Palace!"

Sarno had never built a casino. He had never built a Strip resort. He had never operated either one. He had been to Las Vegas only on gambling junkets. Yet he babbled about his scheme all night. Joyce wasn't the least surprised. During the four years that they had been married, she had become convinced that her husband was a genius, capable of achieving anything that he wished. She had also decided that he was often a complete lunatic, given to the most harebrained schemes. Whether or not this was one of them really didn't matter. Trying to talk Sarno out of an idea was impossible. She had never met anyone as bullheaded.

Born in 1921 in St. Joseph, Missouri, Sarno was the youngest of seven children and the one who was always a disappointment. His parents, who were Jewish immigrants from Poland, pushed their kids to do well, and each of them had become a teacher, a lawyer, or a doctor, except for Jay. After an undistinguished youth, he had spent World War II running dice games in the Air Force. His mother enrolled him in the University of Missouri after he was discharged, but Sarno spent most of his time playing poker at the Zeta Beta Tau fraternity house. His future best friend and business partner, Stanley Mallin, met Sarno there in 1946.

"I was walking into the fraternity house when this guy comes up and asks me if I want to make a few bucks," Mallin remembered. It was Jay Sarno.

"Sure," Mallin told him, so Sarno led him to a vacant lot near the university's football stadium, where a game was scheduled to kick off.

"Stand in the street and direct cars in to me," Sarno ordered. "We'll charge them a dollar to park here."

"Do you know who owns the lot?" Mallin asked.

"Don't worry," Sarno replied. "We'll be gone before anyone catches on."

The incident was pure Sarno. "Jay had more chutzpah than anyone I've ever met," Mallin said. Nearly every weekend, Sarno would entangle Mallin in some money-making scheme, but no matter how much they earned, Sarno was always broke. He lost it gambling on sports. Mallin had never met anyone so addicted to betting. One Sunday night, Mallin spotted Sarno packing his clothes into cardboard boxes. He was pawning them so he could pay his bookie.

After four years, Mallin graduated with a business degree, but Sarno had only completed about half the required courses. "Let's go to Miami Beach," Sarno suggested. "I've got a cousin working there who says he can get us into the tile business."

"Jay, we don't know anything about installing tile," Mallin protested.

"So what?" replied Sarno. "It beats hanging around here."

Within a week, they were bidding on tile jobs at Miami Beach hotels. They hired craftsmen to do the actual work and made their profit by tacking on a contractor's fee. The nation was still in the midst of the post–World War II building boom, and there was such a shortage of housing that the federal government was lending cash through an incentive program to any contractors willing to build apartments. Sarno and Mallin moved to Atlanta, where there was less competition, and built a thirty-unit apartment house, followed by an eighty-unit one. They were doing so well they decided to buy a truck. Sarno went shopping one morning while Mallin was busy elsewhere. He came back that afternoon with a bright red Cadillac convertible.

"Jay, this is totally impractical," Mallin protested.

"C'mon," Sarno replied. "Who wants to drive a truck when you can drive a Cadillac?"

They were the only contractors in Atlanta who delivered boxes of nails and two-by-fours in a Cadillac.

Sarno met Joyce while both were in Miami Beach in 1957 on family vacations. He was staying with his parents at the Fontainebleau Hotel, the fanciest resort in Miami. (Its owner later helped build the Tropicana on the Strip, and the Fontainebleau served as Steve Wynn's inspiration when he built the Mirage.) Joyce was leaving the hotel with her parents after lunch when Sarno burst into the lobby late for an appointment and accidentally crashed into her. In the course of apologizing, he learned their room numbers, and that night he sent her parents a note inviting them to dinner. He wanted permission to date their daughter, he wrote, but felt they should dine with him first so they could see that he was a reputable fellow. While that impressed Joyce's parents, she thought it odd, and when he called her later, she told him that she was busy.

"Cancel your date," Sarno said.

"If I do that, then what would keep me from doing it to you if someone better came along?" she asked.

"You wouldn't dare cancel a date with me," he replied.

"And why is that?"

"Because," he said, "I'm the man you are going to marry."

She was twenty-three years old. He was thirty-five. Both of them were being pressured by their mothers to get married. He arrived for the date carrying flowers and smothered her with compliments. Completely charmed, Joyce married him six weeks later and soon was pregnant. She was thrilled, but just before their baby was born, she discovered her new husband had a secret life. He was cheating on her with not one but several other women, and he was a compulsive gambler. Although she was heartbroken, Joyce didn't confront him. "I told myself, 'Once he has a family, he'll settle down.' I knew he loved me and I loved him. I really wanted our marriage to work."

When the government ended its generous loan program for apartment construction, Sarno and Mallin decided to build office buildings in Atlanta, but no banks would lend them money. An attorney whom Mallin knew introduced them to the head of the International Brotherhood of Teamsters local, and he, in turn, referred their loan application to regional officials who controlled the union's pension fund. The union gave them a high-interest loan, and Sarno and Mallin put up a small office building for doctors, then started work on another. It was at this point that Sarno came up with what proved to be a brilliant idea.

He had noticed that more and more businessmen were traveling by car rather than train, but that most downtown hotels didn't have parking garages. So he designed a "motor hotel," where guests could check in and have a valet park their car or drive around to the rear of the building and park it themselves. He called it a "motor cabana." He convinced the Teamsters to give him another loan and with Mallin's help built a cabana in Atlanta. The place was swamped, and it made so much money that they built another one in Dallas, and started on a third in Palo Alto. It was during a trip west to oversee construction there that Sarno stopped over to gamble in Las Vegas.

"I can beat myself to death building a chain of cabanas across the country," Sarno told Joyce, "and I still will never have the kind of money I can make if I can build a single casino." Joyce liked the idea of their making a fresh start. By this point, they had three children and would soon add a fourth. "I thought maybe if we got away from Atlanta, he would change his ways. Obviously, I was very naive."

Sarno and Mallin requested a meeting with Teamster president Jimmy Hoffa because they knew his union was the only source most casino operators had when it came to borrowing money. Hoffa had begun lending casino owners money in the late 1950s. It would later be learned that he was getting a kickback on nearly every loan. Sarno and Hoffa hit it off instantly. "Both were big, boisterous fellows," said Mallin. But Hoffa turned down Sarno's request for a $10 million construction loan because neither he nor Mallin had any experience as casino operators. Hoffa promised to reconsider, however, if they could find other investors as well.

As soon as Sarno returned home, he called his brother Herman, a New York City lawyer who had made several million dollars speculating in real estate. Herman Sarno introduced his brother and Mallin to several of his wealthy friends, including Nathan Jacobson, a multimillionaire insurance magnate from Baltimore. Jacobson joined them and they began recruiting other investors, including several Miami businessmen whose names were given to them by Hoffa. By late 1962, Sarno, Mallin, and Jacobson had enough financial backing to qualify for a Teamster loan. All they needed now was somewhere to build Sarno's desert palace.

By this time, the boundaries of the Las Vegas Strip were well established. The El Rancho Vegas had burned to the ground in June 1960, leaving the Sahara hotel as the farthest northern casino on the Strip. Some four miles away, the low-rent Hacienda Hotel marked the southern end, directly across from McCarran Airport. Between these two gambling bookends were eight hotel-casinos, each a separate entity surrounded by sand and built far enough away from the competition so there was plenty of room for parking lots and expansion. There were no sidewalks linking them. Although Las Vegas now had a population of sixty thousand, the Strip remained largely divorced from the rest of the city. It was much like an island, run by the casino kingpins who controlled its hotels.

Sarno wanted to buy a tract directly across the highway from the Flamingo, near the Dunes. This prime real estate was owned by Los Angeles entrepreneur Kirk Kerkorian, who had bought it less than one year earlier for $960,000, a bargain price for forty acres located in the very center of the Strip next door to two famous casinos. The tract had sold so cheaply because it was set back from the Strip and thought to be useless. Someone else owned the narrow slice of property in front of it, barring access to Las Vegas Boulevard. But shortly after Kerkorian bought the tract, he negotiated what local newspapers called a "brilliant" land swap with the frontage owner, giving him a much larger parcel at the far end of the property in exchange. The forty-five-year-old Kerkorian, the papers predicted, had a "bright future" as a businessman. Little did they know how bright. Kerkorian was on his way to becoming one of the richest men in America, with a net worth in the 1990s estimated at $3.7 billion.

Had Sarno approached Kerkorian at any other moment, it is unlikely that they would have struck a deal. Kerkorian had purchased the tract because he planned to build his own casino there. But in late 1962 he was having second thoughts.

The two businessmen were a study in contrasts. Both liked to gamble. Both were risk takers. Both were the youngest sons of hard-driving immigrants. But unlike Sarno, Kerkorian was practical and self-effacing. He had also had a much tougher upbringing. His Armenian parents had fled a Turkish massacre in their hometown by hiding in a cattle boat. After arriving in California's lush San Joaquin Valley in 1905, his nearly illiterate father managed to buy several fruit farms through hard work while at the same time establishing a reputation as a hot-tempered eccentric. He sported a handlebar mustache, carried a Colt revolver, and raced through watermelon patches in a big Stutz Bearcat automobile. But he overextended himself financially and the family lost everything when the 1921 recession hit. Kirk Kerkorian was four. Forced to move constantly to avoid bill collectors, the family eked out a living selling fruit to Los Angeles wholesalers, and Kerkorian quit school in the eighth grade to work at odd jobs. A friend taught him how to fly a Piper Cub airplane, and his older brother taught him how to box. He won all but four of his next thirty-three amateur fights, a good enough record to consider turning pro, but instead got a job as a civilian pilot when World War II began. He delivered

Canadian-made Mosquito bombers across the Atlantic Ocean to Scotland and England for the Royal Air Force. It was risky business. The bombers had been hurried into production and were unreliable—one-fourth of them crashed during delivery. Kerkorian survived several close calls, then returned to California with $5,000 in savings that he used to buy a surplus military cargo airplane. He reconditioned it, sold it at a profit, and reconditioned a second. Soon he was delivering reconditioned surplus planes as far away as South America.

Kerkorian earned enough to buy a small charter air service that operated out of Los Angeles Airport. It was the start of the 1950s boom on the Las Vegas Strip, and his charter service became profitable by ferrying Hollywood celebrities back and forth each weekend. He used his profits to expand his airline into an international charter service called Trans International Airlines (TIA). By 1955, he was earning $100,000 a year and gambling regularly on the Strip. He married a showgirl and lost $50,000 in a failed attempt to buy the Dunes with several other businessmen—a deal that to this day he refuses to discuss. In 1962, he sold TIA for $950,000 to the Studebaker company, which wanted to diversify, and used the money to buy his forty-acre tract on the Strip. Kerkorian began designing a casino, but decided to put it on hold when Studebaker's board of directors decided it didn't really want TIA after all and put the airline up for sale. Kerkorian still thought the airline had tremendous growth potential, but he didn't have enough cash to buy it back and go ahead with his casino. He would have to choose.

It was at this moment that Sarno knocked on Kerkorian's door. The two men quickly cut a deal. Kerkorian would rent the land to Sarno and his partners for $190,000 a year, plus 15 percent of the future casino's gross. As soon as that contract was signed, Kerkorian bought back his airline.

"I'm going to design a casino," an excited Sarno told Joyce the night he returned from Las Vegas, "with lots of columns and statues and fountains and tons of marble."

The most extravagant Strip resort at the time was the Tropicana, which had cost $15 million and had been nicknamed the "Tiffany's of the Strip." It had mahogany-paneled walls, Czechoslovakian crystal chandeliers, and a 150-foot curved glass wall built around its dining room. Most of the other Strip resorts were really glorified motels with casinos and theaters tacked on. The Stardust had bragged that its 1,032 hotel rooms made it the biggest resort in the world, but they were housed in five two-story buildings that jutted into the desert behind the casino much like military barracks. Sarno decreed that his Desert Palace would outclass them all.

It took nearly four years to build Sarno's creation and by then, he had renamed it. "I'm calling it Caesars Palace, and I'm *not* going to put an apostrophe before the 's' in Caesars," he told reporters, "because this is going to be a palace for all the Caesars—a palace for all the people. I'm going to create a feeling that everybody in the hotel is a Caesar. *That's* why I'm not going to make Caesars a possessive name!"

Caesars Palace truly was unlike anything anyone on the Strip had ever seen. Guests were supposed to feel as if they had stepped back into the glorious days of ancient Rome. Unlike other resorts, Caesars Palace was set back from the highway. Its crescent-shaped, fourteen-story tower contained 680 luxury suites. The 135-foot-long driveway was lined with imported Italian cypresses. Eighteen fountains sprayed 350,000 gallons of water per minute into the desert air. Inside were $150,000 worth of marble statuary imported from Florence, Brazilian rosewood and gold leaf, white marble panels, and black mosaics. The world's largest ceiling fixture, made of the finest German crystal, hung in the center of the Caesars Forum casino. Its swimming pool was in the shape of a Roman shield.

Two days before the grand opening on August 5, 1966, Sarno, Mallin, and Jacobson huddled in an emergency meeting. Sarno's extravagance had drained all the investors' funds. Rather than the planned $10 million, Caesars Palace had cost $25 million, much more than any other Strip resort. Sarno had gone back to Jimmy Hoffa so often that the Teamster Union now had $22 million in loans invested in the enterprise. Mallin and Jacobson were nervous because the casino didn't have enough cash on hand to cover its losses if several high rollers won right after it opened. If it couldn't pay its gambling debts, Caesars Palace would be forced to close down. Jacobson urged his partners to put limits on the casino's table games to prevent gamblers from wagering huge sums and to scale back Sarno's extravagant grand opening. But Sarno would have none of it. "If we want high rollers to gamble here, we have to look and act like a high-roller operation," he declared. Mallin reluctantly backed him up.

Sarno's grand opening party cost $1 million and lasted three days. Two tons of filet mignon, three hundred pounds of crabmeat, thirty thousand fresh eggs, fifty thousand glasses of champagne, and the largest single order of Alaskan king crab and Ukrainian caviar ever bought by a private company were devoured by the 1,800 invited celebrities and guests. Andy Williams, then the star of his own NBC television show, crooned in the eight-hundred-seat Circus Maximus theater. Harry Ritz, who along with his brother Jimmy set a record for lounge-act longevity in Las Vegas by playing in Nero's Nook at Caesars Palace for two years straight, later described the opening as "the biggest event I've ever seen—that anyone had ever seen. You absolutely couldn't get in to see us during that opening week."

During the second day of the festivities, Sarno, Mallin, and Jacobson gathered in another emergency session. Just as Jacobson had feared, several high rollers had been lucky in the casino, and they were now demanding to be paid close to $1 million in winnings. Without a quick input of cash, Caesars Palace was going to go belly-up even before Sarno's party ended. Sarno went to talk to Hoffa, who was staying in the hotel's finest suite.

"Are you kidding?" Hoffa replied when Sarno asked him for yet another loan. First he looked outraged, then he broke into laughter. He assured Sarno that the union would provide more money.

The public loved the place. The *Las Vegas Sun* enthusiastically reported that "Caesars Palace [had] established a new standard of elegance and luxury for the Nevada hotel industry and perhaps the world." By the end of its first month, Caesars Palace was earning money faster than anyone could count it. There was so much cash coming in that the casino began separating it by denomination and weighing it after each shift, rather than taking time just then to count it. A million dollars in hundred-dollar bills weighed a little over 20 pounds; a million in twenties 102 pounds; a million in fives 408 pounds. Because Sarno, Mallin, and Jacobson knew absolutely nothing about running a casino, they had hired Jerome Zarowitz as the financial manager of their operation, wooing him away from the Sands. He had been recommended to them by the Miami investors whose names had been supplied by Hoffa. Zarowitz assured them that the casino was running smoothly. All they had to do was sit back and spend the profits. Sarno did.

"The wives of hotel owners were members of our own little club and the hotel men had their little fraternity too," Joyce Sarno recalled. "Everyone knew everyone else and we all were going to parties every night . . . I was having all the caviar that I wanted and I was going to Caesars Palace back when people dressed like ladies and gentlemen. I never went out at night without my white gloves. It was magical."

The 1960s would later be described as the era when the Strip was at its most decadent. Frank Sinatra, Dean Martin, Sammy Davis Jr., Peter Lawford, and Joey Bishop were performing nightly at the Copa Room in the Sands, where their antics on and off the stage earned them the nickname of the Rat Pack. They had come to town in 1960 to film the movie *Ocean's 11*, about a Las Vegas heist. During the day, they worked on the movie set. At night, they performed in the Copa. Afterward, they gambled extravagantly and caroused with abandon. Sinatra had two of his teeth knocked out during one highly publicized brawl.

Jay Sarno spent his mornings playing golf, often betting as much as $15,000 on a single hole. At night, he bet $10,000 with each roll of the dice. Sarno's daughter, September Joy Sarno, so named because she was born in that month and was her parents' "pride and joy," would later recall having dinner with her family when she was eight years old in the exclusive Bacchanal restaurant at Caesars Palace. "My dad would excuse himself for fifteen minutes and walk over to a craps table. Then he would come back from winning with fifty thousand dollars in cash and say, 'Okay, who wants a present?' " September's younger sister, Heidi, remembered that "everything was an event." There were no limits, few rules. "We would go out and have a gourmet dinner and then stop at a fast-food place on the way home for a snack because my father loved to eat. His favorite saying was: 'When in doubt, eat, eat, eat.' "

Around the Strip, Sarno's hedonistic ways became legendary. He would press thousand-dollar chips into the hands of attractive women at Caesars Palace whom he wanted to bed. Once he gave a showgirl who caught his eye a ride home in his Rolls-Royce and then handed her the keys. A joke made the rounds: "Most men meet girls and buy them a drink. Jay Sarno meets them and buys them a mink." He bragged of having sex three or four times daily with different women.

The fact that the Sarnos frequently socialized with mobsters didn't bother either of them. "We all knew who was in the mob," Joyce Sarno recalled. "Our kids went to the same schools as theirs. No one thought anything of it . . . in fact, it made Las Vegas even more exciting." There was a belief that gangsters only killed one another or, as movie star Debbie Reynolds put it, "nobody ever got killed that wasn't supposed to." It was an attitude that dated back to the mid-1940s, when Del Webb, the Phoenix construction mogul who built the mob-backed Flamingo, became nervous about how Bugsy Siegel's partners were going to react to his lavish spending. Siegel reportedly reassured him by quipping: "We only kill each other."

Of course, that wasn't always true. Siegel's replacement at the Flamingo, Gus Greenbaum, had retired to Phoenix in the early 1950s after he had gotten the place running successfully for the mob. When he refused to return to the Strip to manage the Riviera, his gangster pals sent him a message. His sister-in-law was smothered to death in her Phoenix home. Greenbaum reported to work at the Riviera but was soon in trouble again. A compulsive gambler, he ran up a tab that exceeded $1 million. In December 1958, he and his wife were found dead in their bedroom. Their throats had been slashed.

Caesars Palace kept the Sarnos awash in cash, but neither was happy.

"Why do you have to humiliate me?" Joyce demanded one night after Sarno came home from bedding a showgirl.

"Joyce, these other women are just for amusement," he replied.

"I didn't know you could love someone and then do these other things," she snapped.

"What's the difference?" he asked.

Sarno reminded her that he always treated her best. If he gave one of his girlfriends a new Ford Mustang, he brought home a Cadillac for Joyce. If he gave a lover a Cadillac, he bought Joyce a Rolls-Royce. "You always get whatever is one step higher up," he assured her. He thought that she would be flattered, but she came to hate each gift. A frantic Joyce began cooking pork chops, his favorite dish, nearly every night. "At least I know if I cook pork chops, he will come home, rather than having dinner with some other woman," she confided to her best friend.

Sarno, meanwhile, had come to detest being Nathan Jacobson's partner. Both of them were quick-tempered and had massive egos. Sarno complained that Jacobson was taking credit for Caesars Palace. "They acted like a bunch of children running around fighting all the time," Joyce Sarno said. Sarno decided to build another casino that he and Mallin would run on their own. He bought a tract of land in 1967 on the northern end of the Strip across from the Riviera, but ran into trouble attracting investors. His reputation for wild spending made even the Teamsters reluctant to lend him money. He had no choice but to scale back his plans. He removed the hotel from his drawings and announced that he would build a stand-alone casino on the Strip in the shape of a huge pink-and-white circus tent.

" 'Circus' was the word that Romans used for 'theater,' and that's how I came up with the name for my new resort: a circus inside a Roman circus—or a Circus Circus," Sarno explained. He dropped the Roman theme when he decided to put his new casino on the northern tip of the Strip, but he kept the double name.

Sarno once again gave the Strip something it had never seen when he opened Circus Circus on October 17, 1968. Dressed as a big top ringmaster, he led two hundred invited celebrities and other VIPs through the entrance of the four-story concrete tent into a mezzanine, where he paused in front of a giant metal slide. The only way for his guests to enter the gaming area was by slipping down the slide to the basement, where the casino was located; there were no stairs. One by one, clad in their evening gowns and tuxedos, his guests slid down into monumental clutter and confusion. Mimes and clowns strolled between blackjack tables, often interrupting the gamblers with cornball tricks. Trapeze artists did midair somersaults above the craps tables. Sideshow barkers lured guests to gaudy midway attractions built along the inside walls of the massive tent. A fourteen-piece brass band blared out circus tunes nonstop. At least once each hour, a ringmaster climbed onto a perch in the center of the casino and held a "jam auction." Holding up an expensive watch or a piece of fine jewelry, he auctioned it off at a ridiculously low price. This was a "come-on" item, and it would be followed by cheap imitation goods that were hawked to excited bidders who didn't realize they were the victims of a bait-and-switch scam.

Sarno would later be mistakenly identified as the first Strip operator who had built a casino for adults and children. This was because his casino featured nonstop circus acts and carnival games. But Sarno never intended the place to be for children. His casino was for adults who wanted to act like kids. Customers threw balls at a target that, when hit, caused a blast of air to blow a sheet off a seminude woman who leaped from her chaise lounge and danced for several minutes. The Ooh-La-La Theater featured topless showgirls. Another midway attraction claimed to have a nude prehistoric woman sealed in a block of ice. Men who stepped behind a curtain got to ogle a naked woman lying inside a glass container with water sprinkled on top to make it look like melting ice. The billboards advertising Circus Circus showed a sexy redhead, who appeared to be nude, leering at motorists from behind a white billboard that simply said: "Circus Circus Ain't Kid Stuff."

Sarno reveled in the zaniness of his new creation. "He was like a big kid," according to Mallin. One morning, Sarno told newspaper reporters that Circus Circus had located an elephant that could actually fly, just like the Disney character Dumbo. It was a publicity stunt, of course. Sarno had installed a heavy-duty monorail system in the casino's ceiling and had ordered a leather harness especially made to fit a baby elephant named Tanya. He planned to use the device to raise Tanya a few inches off the ground and then sweep her through the casino on the monorail track. On the morning of the press conference, Sarno decided to preview the system. Tanya was hooked to the monorail, and as soon as her feet were raised off the floor, she panicked and began thrashing around. Her horrified trainer tried to calm her as Tanya kicked over slot machines and knocked down gaming tables. The harness finally snapped. At the press conference, Sarno announced that the "World's First Flying Elephant" had flown away, but he had found a replacement: Tanya, the World's First Gambling Elephant. As reporters watched, Sarno led Tanya to a slot machine where she pulled the lever—a trick that her trainer had hurriedly taught her. From that moment on, Tanya was given free rein to wander among guests in the casino pulling slot levers. Her trainer followed behind with a bucket.

At first, out-of-towners paid $4 to enter Circus Circus, but Sarno stopped charging admission after he counted several hundred people turning away one Friday night. Other adjustments also had to be made. A woman broke her ankle on the slide. A man had to have glass shards removed from his buttocks after he sped down and hit several shot glasses that a drunk had put there as a joke. One night, Sarno hired a man to dress like an Indian chief and leap from a ledge fifty feet above the casino floor into a giant airbag. When the acrobat hit the bag, there was a tremendous whoosh of air and the cards on nearby blackjack tables flew everywhere. Several outraged players claimed that their winning hands had been blown away and demanded compensation. Gonzo journalist Hunter S. Thompson described the craziness inside Sarno's casino with disdain. "Circus Circus is what the whole hep world would be doing on Saturday night," he wrote, "if the Nazis had won the war."

The FBI didn't even have an agent stationed in Las Vegas in 1957, but this changed in the 1960s. Director J. Edgar Hoover began dispatching dozens of G-men there to flush out mobsters, and U.S. Attorney General Robert Kennedy investigated Jimmy Hoffa and his handling of the Teamster Union's pension fund. The government's goal was to get the gangsters off the Strip, and although it would take several decades to accomplish this, the effects of the federal crackdown were soon evident. In 1964, Joseph "Doc" Stacher, the New Jersey mobster behind the Sands, pleaded guilty to two tax code violations and exiled himself to Israel. Chicago mobster Sam Giancana "voluntarily" gave up his shares in the Riviera and Stardust in 1966 under pressure from the Federal Organized Crime Task Force, a joint unit manned by FBI and IRS agents. That same year, Hoffa was forced to formally relinquish control of the pension fund, although for several years he would continue to secretly influence decisions on who received loans. Federal agents quickly developed a routine. They would concentrate on a single resort, identify the mobsters behind it, and either charge them with felonies or pressure the state to revoke their gaming licenses. Once they were satisfied, they moved to another resort.

The antigangster campaign caused unexpected problems on the Strip. Since society in general still looked down on gambling, who was going to buy and run the casinos after the mob was kicked out? The answer: billionaire Howard Hughes. Together with his cadre of Mormon advisers, Hughes rented the entire ninth floor of luxury suites at the Desert Inn in late 1966. He had just sold the airline TWA for a half-billion dollars in cash and had decided to relocate to Las Vegas so that he could "become a big frog in a small pond," as his spokesman, Bob Maheu, later put it. The fifty-one-year-old recluse had plenty of money. When he was twenty-one, he had inherited the $100 million Hughes Tool Company, which manufactured oil well drilling bits. At first, Hughes had amused himself by dabbling in movies and bedding Hollywood starlets. He then moved into aeronautics, setting both transcontinental and around-the-world speed records in airplanes that he designed. By the time he relocated to Las Vegas, he had expanded his holdings into electronics, increasing his estimated worth to $2 billion. What only a few knew at the time was that Hughes was suffering from an advanced case of syphilis and was slowly going mad. It was easy to keep this secret because he already had a reputation for eccentricity. He once ordered an airline mechanic to wait for him in a New York hotel and then forgot to send for him until one year later. He had hired a dozen promising starlets and sent them to acting classes for years, until they were past their prime and had no hope of appearing on-screen. His biographers would later note that Hughes wasn't necessarily cruel. He simply put people on shelves to use whenever it fit his fancy.

Like so many Las Vegas stories, the one about Hughes's purchase of the Desert Inn has been greatly embellished over time. The most popular version has the Desert Inn's owner, Moe Dalitz, thrilled when Hughes first checks in, but soon becoming disgusted with his wealthy guest. Dalitz earned his profits in the casino, not by renting out luxury suites, and neither Hughes nor his entourage gambled. After several weeks, Dalitz decided to evict them, but the billionaire didn't want to leave, so he simply pulled out his checkbook and bought the entire place. While the basics of the story are true, there is much more to it.

Because of Moe Dalitz's mob connections, the FBI was pressuring him to find a buyer for the resort, and Hughes was in need of a tax write-off. But the two men couldn't cut a deal because Hughes didn't want to appear at the public hearing that was required whenever individuals applied for a gambling license. An enterprising Las Vegas banker named E. Parry Thomas came to the rescue. Thomas was already well known in casino circles because his tiny Valley Bank of Nevada had given several high-interest loans to casinos—something no other respectable bank would do. Like Hughes's advisers, Thomas was also a Mormon and he had several political contacts, including a close friendship with the governor. Knowing that his bank could profit greatly if Hughes became one of its customers, Thomas lobbied the governor to change the laws that regulated casino ownership. In 1967, the state passed the Nevada Corporate Gaming Act, which allowed publicly traded corporations to acquire gambling licenses without the need to license every individual stockholder. Once that door was opened, Hughes was free to buy the Desert Inn through his Summa Corporation. He paid Dalitz $13.2 million, which was considered an outrageously inflated price, and went on a buying spree. He bought the mob-tainted Sands and Frontier and several smaller casinos. He was buying so many casinos that the federal government threatened to invoke antitrust statutes in

1968 when he made a bid for the mob-backed Stardust. By then, 17 percent of the state's tax revenues were coming directly from Hughes-owned casinos, and state officials were afraid that he was becoming too power-ful. Rebuffed, Hughes began gobbling up other ven-tures. He purchased a 518-acre ranch outside town, the Paradise Valley Country Club, a Las Vegas television station, the North Las Vegas Airport, and huge chunks of the best vacant lots in the city.

Hughes was not the only tycoon who saw a chance to profit from the government's drive to rid the Strip of mobsters. Kirk Kerkorian had turned his international airline into a publicly held company, giving him a net worth of $66.3 million, and he announced in 1967 that he was going to build the biggest hotel-casino in the world on an eighty-two-acre tract located one block east of the Strip on Paradise Road, which runs parallel to Las Vegas Boulevard. Kerkorian had wanted to buy land on the Strip but none was left; Hughes had bought all the vacant tracts. No one had ever built a successful casino on Paradise Road, although several developers had tried, but Kerkorian claimed his resort would be so grand it was certain to attract crowds. He called his thirty-story, triangle-shaped hotel the International. It was to have 1,512 guest rooms, a casino twice the size of any on the Strip, and a huge convention center. The cost: $60 million, all of which would come out of his own pocket.

Kerkorian's announcement outraged Hughes. He had already come up with a master plan for the city that called for turning it into the country's first space-age landing center, with airport runways long enough to accommodate futuristic supersonic jets and space shuttles. Las Vegas was his personal playground. The day after Kerkorian made his announcement, Hughes revealed in a press release that he was going to expand his Sands hotel-casino into a four-thousand-room resort, dwarfing Kerkorian's project.

Financial analysts urged Kerkorian to scale back his plans. The Strip could not support two giant hotels, and Kerkorian was sure to go bankrupt if he challenged the much wealthier Hughes. But Kerkorian refused to blink. Instead, he bought the Flamingo, which had fallen into disrepair, and began using it as a training school for the three thousand employees he would need at the International.

Hughes was bluffing. He had been trying to scare Kerkorian and had no intention of expanding the Sands. His own internal memos would later show that he considered a number of plans to undermine Kerkorian, including some that were illegal. But he eventually decided the best way to drive his rival out of town was by opening a casino directly across the street from the International. In January 1969, Hughes offered to buy the unfinished Landmark hotel-casino on Paradise Road. This time, federal officials didn't intervene by raising antitrust issues. The reason: Las Vegas had been desperately seeking someone willing to complete the $8.5 million Landmark, and they got Nevada's U.S. senators to hold the Justice Department at bay. Work on the Landmark had started in 1961 but its developer had run out of money. Patterned after the Space Needle at the Seattle world's fair, its incomplete, futuristic shell had been collecting tumbleweeds at its base for five years when Hughes announced that he would buy the eyesore for an inflated $17.3 million.

The race between Hughes and Kerkorian was on. Hughes ordered his staff to get the Landmark ready before the International's scheduled opening on July 3, 1969. Hordes of workers scrambled on both sides of Paradise Road, each mogul watching the other's progress to see who was ahead. Hughes pumped $3.2 million into the Landmark, and he won the race to open—by *one* day.

It proved to be a hollow victory. The Landmark's opening was met with a yawn. The International's caused a huge splash. Barbra Streisand performed in its packed 1,600-seat theater. Elvis came a month later, breaking every attendance record in a Las Vegas theater. In its first month, Kerkorian's resort posted $1.5 million in profit. Hughes's Landmark reported losses of $2 million in that same period.

Neither tycoon stayed around after their rival hotels opened. Hughes left Las Vegas permanently, fleeing by ambulance in the middle of the night to a waiting corporate jet that whisked him off to the Bahamas. His aides would later explain that he had decided to leave town because he was worried about the dangers from radiation released by atomic bomb testing at nearby Nellis Air Force Base. He had spent more than $300 million in Las Vegas and he was leaving six casinos behind, each losing money. Kerkorian went back to Los Angeles, where he launched a hostile takeover of Metro-Goldwyn-Mayer Studios. His bid for the failing Hollywood studio proved more costly than expected, and less than two years after the International opened, Kerkorian was forced to sell it and the Flamingo to the Hilton hotel chain.

The Federal Organized Crime Task Force bore down on Caesars Palace in 1969. It accused Jerome Zarowitz, the casino's financial manager, of having ties with Genovese crime family member Anthony "Fat Tony" Salerno and New England godfather Raymond Patriarca. Zarowitz had a criminal record, having spent two years in prison for trying to fix the 1946 National Football League championship game between the Chicago Bears and New York Giants; and one year before Jay Sarno, Stanley Mallin, and Nathan Jacobson hired him to help them run Caesars Palace, Zarowitz had been photographed attending what the FBI claimed was a "mob summit" in Palm Springs called by the heads of the country's top crime families. As part of their probe, federal agents seized Zarowitz's personal safety deposit box. When they cracked it open, they found $1 million in $100 bills. Investigators claimed it was proof that he had been skimming cash at Caesars Palace.

Despite these sensational accusations, the federal government was eventually forced to dismiss all its charges against Zarowitz for lack of evidence. But well before that happened, the task force began pressuring Sarno, Mallin, and Jacobson to sell Caesars Palace. It assumed the three partners had either willingly installed Zarowitz or had been duped into giving him a pivotal job by organized crime figures from Miami. Either way, the government wanted them out. "Our attorneys told us that Zarowitz was a real, real problem," Mallin said later. "We were told that if we didn't sell, the feds and the state would just keep after us until they found some way to shut us down. They were blunt about it."

In April 1969, the partners reluctantly sold Caesars Palace for $60 million to the Lums restaurant chain of Miami, operated by Clifford Perlman. There were several behind-the-scenes reasons why they didn't put up a fight. Not only did Sarno and Jacobson despise each other; Sarno and Mallin were busy trying to keep Circus Circus afloat.

From the day it opened, it had bled red ink. Serious gamblers avoided it, and Sarno's unchecked spending depleted the casino's meager revenues. There were legal hassles. State gaming officials accused Sarno of not fully disclosing the sources of several loans he had received to finance the casino. Only after he agreed to step down as Circus Circus's president and let Mallin take charge did the state decide not to prosecute. Although Sarno and Mallin were able to pump more money into Circus Circus after they sold Caesars Palace, by 1971 it was clear that they were going to have to close their casino unless they got another shot of capital. They decided to take a bold move that at first glance made little sense. They announced that Circus Circus was expanding.

"One of our big problems," Mallin said later, "was that we didn't have a hotel, so we weren't attracting high rollers." Most gamblers played in casinos where they were also staying as guests. This was especially true of high rollers, who demanded free luxury suites and other comps in return for their gambling action. Sarno and Mallin decided to build a four-hundred-room hotel adjacent to their casino. As Sarno had done so many times before, he turned to the Teamster Union for help. By now his old pal Jimmy Hoffa was in prison, serving a four-year sentence for fraud and jury tampering. But he had left Allen Dorfman in charge of the Central States Pension Fund and Dorfman agreed to give Sarno a $23 million construction loan in return for several favors. "Dorfman called and said he wanted Sarno to give the gift shop concession at Circus Circus to a friend of the Teamster Union," Mallin said later. "He told us the guy's name was Anthony Stuart. We didn't know anything about him." Nor did they ask. Instead, records show that Sarno doctored the books to make it appear as if Anthony Stuart had paid the casino $70,000 for the gift shop concession even though no money had changed hands. When Anthony Stuart showed up, Sarno handed him the keys to the gift shop.

It turned out that "Anthony Stuart" was an alias being used by Anthony "Tony the Ant" Spilotro, whose wife's maiden name was Stuart. Spilotro was a contract killer sent by the Chicago mob to oversee skimming operations at the Stardust, which had not yet come under the Federal Organized Crime Task Force's purview and was still gangster-run. Spilotro's exploits, and his close friendship with Frank "Lefty" Rosenthal, a famous Las Vegas oddsmaker, and Rosenthal's wife Gerri, would later be recounted in the 1995 national best-seller *Casino*, by Nicholas Pileggi, and made into a popular movie of the same name, starring Robert De Niro, Sharon Stone, and Joe Pesci. Sarno had welcomed into Circus Circus one of the most violent criminals ever to frequent the Strip.

Nor was he the only crook in the casino. Sarno had hired Carl Wesley Thomas, a former blackjack dealer with impeccable credentials, to oversee the casino's day-to-day operations. It would be several years before Thomas was exposed as perhaps the greatest casino skimmer of all time in Nevada. When FBI agents finally nabbed him, he was working at a different casino, but he would brag that he had been stealing as much as $100,000 per month from Circus Circus for various mob bosses while he worked there. It is little wonder that the casino was in dire financial trouble.

Sarno's personal life was in just as big a mess. Joyce announced in 1971 that she wanted a divorce, and Sarno launched a desperate campaign to keep her. He gave her a mink coat and offered her yet another Rolls-Royce. When that didn't work, he hired private detectives to look for evidence to use against her in a custody fight. He hoped this would scare her, but it didn't.

"I know people who can take you out in the desert and make you disappear," he threatened one night.

"Go ahead and call them," she replied. "I'm tired of being treated like hamburger meat."

In a state that prides itself on quickie divorces, Sarno was able to tangle up the process for nearly three years. When it seemed the divorce was imminent, Sarno sent his friends to plead his case, including then–Nevada governor Mike O'Callaghan. "The governor said to me, 'You really need to think before you sign those papers. Jay is not really a bad guy,' " Joyce Sarno recalled later. "I told him, 'Yes, Governor, Jay isn't a bad guy, but you aren't married to him.' " When the divorce became final, Sarno gave Joyce their house and moved into the newly completed Circus Circus hotel. Everything in his luxury suite was bright pink and white.

But Sarno's financial hijinks were catching up with him. The FBI tracked Tony Spilotro to the Circus Circus gift shop, which he was using as a place to get his messages. Curious, FBI auditors began poring over Circus Circus records looking for a reason why Sarno would lease a gift shop to a thug like Spilotro. They soon discovered the $23 million Teamster loan and suspected that Sarno had paid a hefty kickback to Dorfman in return for the money. After several months of examining the company's books, the Justice Department accused Sarno of several tax code violations. But when the case came to trial, a jury acquitted him. Angry prosecutors complained it was impossible to convict a casino owner of any crime in Nevada, especially one as well connected politically as Sarno, but a few months later, federal agents tried again. This time they accused him of trying to bribe an IRS agent. Again, Sarno won the case in court, but the legal battle cost him thousands of dollars in attorney fees and wasted months of time. Meanwhile, Circus Circus continued to hemorrhage.

By 1974, Sarno and Mallin decided they had no choice but to sell it. It was losing almost $400,000 per month and Sarno was being pressured by state gaming officials to get out of the casino business. Once again, both men were forced to sell their casino, this time to four investors for $25 million.

It was a tragic day for Sarno. He had designed and built the two most original casinos on the Strip—Caesars Palace and Circus Circus—and within eight years, he had lost them both. Despite all of his legal and financial troubles, however, Sarno was chipper when he met with the new buyers to close the sale. After the paperwork was signed, an attorney noticed that no one had ever specified who would pay $11,000 in closing costs. The new buyers suggested that this be split between the buyers and sellers, but Sarno offered another solution. "Let's play one hand of gin rummy," he suggested. "Losers pay." The new owners agreed and Sarno won. Pressing his luck, he told them that he wanted to continue living in his Circus Circus hotel suite for three more years free of charge. In return, he offered to use his political clout to get a traffic light installed directly in front of the casino. All the traffic on the Strip would be forced to stop at the Circus Circus entrance. The new owners accepted his offer and a few weeks later, a new traffic signal appeared. No one asked him how he had pulled it off.

In the coming years, Sarno would propose a dozen exotic projects, among them the Grandissimo, a six-thousand-room hotel and casino complex. But no one would invest in his schemes, not even his old pal, Stanley Mallin. "Jay told me that he needed one billion dollars to build Grandissimo and I said, 'Jay, *countries* can't even borrow one billion dollars!"

The Strip was changing and Sarno was being left behind. On January 20, 1983, Teamster pension fund manager Allen Dorfman was shot and killed as he walked out of a suburban Chicago restaurant. He had just been convicted of trying to bribe a Nevada senator. The badly beaten and tortured bodies of Tony Spilotro and his brother, Michael, were found a few months later buried in an Indiana cornfield south of Chicago. Spilotro had been facing separate trials for skimming at the Stardust and for the murder of a government witness. Control of the Teamster Union pension fund was taken away from the union and put into the hands of an independent money manager. The union would never make another loan to a casino.

"When he couldn't find investors, Jay became very depressed," Joyce Sarno recalled, "and whenever he was really depressed, he turned to his gambling even more than usual." By 1984, Sarno was losing as much as $20,000 a night at Caesars Palace. Joyce and his children urged him to attend Gamblers Anonymous. He tried it once, arriving in a Rolls-Royce, but he left a few minutes later, complaining that he couldn't relate to gamblers who thought betting $100 per hand was a big deal. Mallin urged him to leave Las Vegas and Sarno responded by trying to get Mallin to invest in his newest project. "I'm going to build a whorehouse in Mexico," he explained, "the finest anyone has ever seen. We can fly gamblers down there."

On July 21, 1984, Sarno played craps for a few hours at Caesars Palace and then checked into the Fantasy Suite with a woman in her early twenties. He had designed the Fantasy Suite himself and it was his favorite spot to have sex. After soaking in the hot tub, Sarno and his date moved onto the oversized bed. As they were making love, Sarno suffered a heart attack and died. He was sixty-two years old. The executors of his estate discovered that he was nearly broke. They estimated that he had lost as much as $20 million gambling since opening Caesars Palace—about $1.25 million a year. "My father built the first themed resort in Las Vegas," September Joy Sarno said, "and the Grandissimo was really the first super casino ever designed. He was clearly a man well ahead of his time."

In hindsight, few would argue with her view, but in 1974 when Sarno and Mallin had sold Circus Circus, Sarno was being described as a buffoon, not a visionary. Although Caesars Palace was clearly a groundbreaking casino, its success had been overshadowed by his failing pink-and-white circus tent. It was the laughingstock of the Strip, a financial fiasco, the oddball creation of a madman.

No one had a clue that it soon would become the foundation of the largest gambling empire in the world.

Inside the Casino:
A Dealer Remembers

I was dealing twenty-one at a table in the Castaways one night and who walks in but Frank Sinatra, Dean Martin, and Sammy Davis Jr. You got to understand that this is when they were really at the pinnacle of their success. Sinatra and his pals came to town in 1960 to film this movie, and they would shoot scenes during the day and at night perform in the Copa Room at the Sands. Each night, one of them would be the headliner but at some point, the other two would join him. Then Joey Bishop and Peter Lawford got into the act too and the "Rat Pack" started. I mean everyone wanted to see them. They really made the Strip come alive and they could do no wrong. They were like gods in Las Vegas. Now, Mr. Sinatra had been drinking when he came into the Castaways—in fact, he was smashed, and when he got drunk, he got mean, real mean. The rule in those days was if you had a dead game [no customers], you were supposed to stand facing straight ahead with your arms folded. You were not supposed to be looking side to side and you were not supposed to talk to anyone. You were just supposed to stand there. That was the rule. For one thing, they didn't want you talking to any customers because they figured if you did, then something might be going on between you. It was never assumed that you might be saying, "Come on— play!" It was a real fear that you might be trying to cheat the casino. Also, they were afraid that you might just say something wrong and offend someone. So it was better just to stand there and say nothing.

Sinatra, Sammy Davis, and Dean Martin sit down at the game next to mine and Sinatra starts losing and he is getting madder and madder and he looks over and sees me standing at this game next to his table and he says, "Hey, what are you staring at?" And I was in a real hard place because you're not supposed to talk to them, but he's getting offended. I was hoping the floor person would come over and smooth the situation, but he is nowhere to be seen, of course, and Sinatra is getting louder. "What the hell are you staring at?" he snaps. He looks like he is about to get up and come over and really get in my face. Well, the dealer helps me out by dealing Sinatra a card and asking him what he wants to do and then Dean Martin says, "Leave him alone, Frank. Why are you always bothering people?" They started talking and then they left the casino.

I ended up going to the Sands as a dealer not long after that. It really was the hot spot on the Strip and a great place to deal because of the tips, and what happens but here comes Frank Sinatra, and he sits down at a table adjacent to mine and I suddenly end up with a dead game. I'm standing there just hoping like crazy that he will not remember me or cause a stink because at the Castaways I had some juice [connections]. I knew the people there and they respected me and knew I would never do anything to irritate a customer so they would have helped me out at the Castaways, but at the Sands, whew, they didn't know me at all. I had no juice. All it would take for me to lose my job was for Sinatra to say, "I want him gone." That was it. He was that much of a big shot and he knew it. There were stories about him throwing his weight around, being a tough guy, throwing cards in dealers' faces, all that sort of stuff. Now he starts drinking and he looks over and I'm standing there staring straight ahead and he says, "Hey you," and I didn't respond. And he says, "Hey, I'm talking to you. Are you ignoring me, you cocky son of a bitch?" Now I'm glancing around and there is no one going to come to my aid, so I said, "No, Mr. S., I would never ignore you. We have a rule here that says we are not supposed to pay attention to anything but our own game." That wasn't good enough. He was getting angry and he says, "I'm going to come over there and kick your ass, you cocky son of a bitch," and he is starting to get off his chair and his bodyguard steps in and says, "Frank, leave him alone for christsake. He's not bothering you." And the dealer quickly gives him a card and he sits back down. All that night I stood there expecting to get fired. In those days, you lived in fear of your job. I mean, the first thing that went wrong, bingo, you were gone. Sinatra knew that. He intimidated a lot of people on the Strip in those days. You were at his mercy—all of those people like that ruled the Strip.

—*Alan Buchholz,*
Luxor director of casino marketing

CHAPTER THREE

························

A Casino for the Working Class

The word on the Strip in May 1974 was that the four new owners of Circus Circus wouldn't last ninety days before going belly-up. The casino was now losing $500,000 per month. Only two of the owners had actually sunk any money into the deal and they had borrowed heavily just to make the down payment. There were no cash reserves for them to fall back on. If the casino was to stay open, it would have to begin earning a profit soon—very soon.

The two men behind the purchase were William N. Pennington, a former oil lease speculator, and William G. Bennett, a former furniture salesman who had made a fortune while still in his early twenties but lost it all in bad business deals. They had been forced to take on two additional partners in order to close the $25 million buy. Mickey Briggs, a member of the wealthy Detroit family that founded the Briggs and Stratton Company, had been given a 10 percent share of their casino partnership because they needed his balance sheet to qualify for a loan. They also had given a 10 percent share to Angel Naves, a seasoned casino manager, because they were counting on his help to revive their faltering casino. Because of the way the sale was structured, however, Pennington and Bennett were the only two whose personal assets were at risk. Each owned 40 percent of the casino.

Behind the scenes, there was one other pivotal player. E. Parry Thomas, the Mormon banker who had helped change state gaming laws in 1967 so that Howard Hughes could begin buying casinos, had put the deal together. He had been the first to suggest to Pennington and Bennett that they buy Circus Circus and it was his Valley Bank of Nevada that had loaned them the money. What none of the new owners knew at the time was that Thomas suspected they were going to fail, and he had given them the loan because his bank was interested in getting control of a piece of collateral they had put up. If Circus Circus went under, Thomas could claim possession of Western Equities, a fledgling company that Pennington had founded.

The story behind the purchase of Circus Circus tells much about Pennington, Bennett, Nevada gambling, E. Parry Thomas, and how two close friends with only $1 million between them were able to buy a $25 million casino—albeit a failing one. It begins with William Pennington, a scrappy entrepreneur who was a man's man, tall, barrel-chested, with a weathered face, an oil-well driller's firm grip, a ready grin, and a colorful past. He was from America's heartland, having been born in 1924 in Smith Center, Kansas, where his grandfather was the county's wealthiest landowner. Pennington's father, William V. Pennington, had assumed that he would take over the extensive land holdings, but the winds and drought turned much of Kansas into a dust bowl during the 1930s and wiped out the family fortune. Disillusioned and bitter, William V. Pennington moved to California with his four children. "My father was born with a silver spoon in his mouth and he never could forget about what happened to my grandfather," Pennington said later. "He spent his entire life trying to get back what his father had lost."

The senior Pennington was forced to take a job selling washing machines at a Montgomery Ward store in Piedmont, California, a job he thought demeaning. The younger Pennington threw newspapers before high school and worked at odd jobs after class to save money for college. The family lived in a rented three-bedroom house next to a wealthy enclave. "I grew up thinking rich people were simply lucky—they weren't any smarter or better than me—just luckier." The senior Pennington would often borrow cash from his son to invest in get-rich-quick schemes and would never re-pay him.

Pennington was a good enough high school football player to earn a college scholarship, but when World War II erupted, he left school and enlisted in the Air Force, where he flew B-29 bombers. After the war, he returned home, married, and went to work as a salesman. He did well, but quit after his boss refused to pay him a bonus that he had earned. Pennington tried land development next, but the project went bust and his partner fled town at night, leaving him to pay angry creditors. He was divorced after seven years, and moved to Nevada to join his father in one of his schemes. The Penningtons searched for oil, but not by drilling wells. Instead, they shadowed other roughnecks who were drilling test wells for major oil companies. Whenever one of the wildcatters struck oil, the Penningtons would race to buy the oil leases on the nearby land. The oil companies would then have to pay them for the right to drill if they decided to expand into adjoining tracts. It was a living of sorts, but neither man was satisfied, so they began selling oil leases by mail. Their ads in national magazines were enticing: "Buy an oil lease in Nevada and strike it rich!" The price: $10 down and $10 a month for ten months. "We sold thousands of leases. I wouldn't buy any oil leases unless they were next to where Shell or Arco was already drilling and people liked that." The government didn't. In April 1966, the Securities and Exchange Commission filed suit against the Penningtons to force them to stop selling oil leases by mail. They complied.

By then, Pennington and his father had earned enough from their ads to drill a few test wells of their own, and four of their five wells hit oil. Using those wells as collateral, they borrowed enough to take an even chancier step. They bought the rights to an oil well owned by a major company and hired a crew to drill it deeper. The company's geologist had abandoned the well because he was convinced there was a thick layer of granite fifteen hundred feet under the surface that was too expensive to break through. But the Penningtons had spoken to an independent geologist who didn't believe the granite layer existed. They were risking everything they owned. If they hit granite, they would go bust. If the granite wasn't there, they felt confident they would find additional oil. The independent geologist was right. There was no granite and the Penningtons' "dry well" produced two million barrels of oil. They arranged for the crude to be delivered to a Utah refinery, but the owner refused to process it for fear major oil companies would retaliate against him. The Penningtons had to get a Nevada senator to put pressure on the owner to get their crude refined.

It was a newspaper article published in Reno that described how the Penningtons had risked everything and struck oil that prompted two inventors to knock on the front door of Bill Pennington's house late one night. They told him that they had designed a device called a random number generator that worked—at least on paper—and they had come to ask his help getting it marketed to casinos. They figured that if he was daring enough to stand up to the major oil companies, he would be shrewd enough to deal with casino owners and possibly the mob. Pennington didn't know much about gambling, but he knew enough to realize that a random number generator would be worth millions if it really worked.

Although slot machines were widely used in Nevada, no one had been able to make a machine that could pick numbers or deal card games completely at random. Every number-picking or card-dealing device had some sort of pattern programmed into it, and once a player figured out the formula, he could drain the machine of money. Worried that word of the invention might leak out if he used someone local, Pennington flew an engineer from Canada to Nevada to test a prototype. It worked, so Pennington quickly formed Raven Electronics with the two inventors as his equal partners, and used the random generator to build an electronic keno machine. Keno is a numbers game that pays off when a gambler correctly selects numbers picked at random by a casino, or in this case by a machine. After he collected all the necessary state licenses, Pennington persuaded the manager at Harrah's Club in Reno to put four of the keno machines in his casino for a three-month tryout. Harrah's would keep all the cash the machines made. Back then, a slot machine in Harrah's earned about $100 a week. The four keno machines averaged $218 per machine per week. Harrah's offered to buy all four, but Pennington refused to sell them. Instead, he offered the casino 60 percent of the machines' profits. He pocketed the rest. "I wouldn't even give anyone else a key to open my machines," Pennington said later, "because I didn't want them getting inside and seeing how they worked and I didn't want anyone opening them without me being there and taking out the money."

Raven Electronics was off to a profitable start, but Pennington and his partners soon began bickering, so he sold them his shares and left to start his own company, which he called Western Equities. He developed an improved random generator of his own that could deal cards for blackjack and poker as well as pick keno numbers. His former partners at Raven Electronics also developed an advanced generator, so the two companies began scrambling to see who could get their machines into Reno casinos first. Pennington took a shortcut. He had heard about a company that had manufactured several hundred faulty blackjack machines before state investigators shut it down. The machines were supposed to contain random generators, but actually had cheating devices built into them that made it impossible for players to win. Pennington found a hundred of the crooked machines in a warehouse outside Reno, where they had been abandoned. He bought them as scrap, had his engineers remove the cheating devices, and installed random generators in them. Because he didn't have to build his machines from scratch, Pennington was able to get them into Reno's casinos before his former partners. That gave him the edge that he needed to put his rivals out of business. He was soon earning $50,000 a month from Western Equities.

His blackjack machines were so successful in Reno that Pennington began negotiating to put them in Las Vegas. It was during a sales jaunt there that he met William G. Bennett, a failed businessman who was working as the general manager of the Mint casino, a downtown joint. The two quickly became friends. Both had been pilots during the war and were still avid fliers. Even more important, both were extremely ambitious. One night they sat up until dawn in Bennett's office talking about ways to make their fortunes, and it was during this conversation that Bennett first suggested that they buy a casino.

"It won't be long before someone will come along with a newer or better blackjack machine than what you're selling," Bennett warned. "The real money to be made in gambling is in owning a casino."

Bennett bragged that he could run a casino better than anyone in Nevada. All they had to do was find one to buy and they were sure to become rich. The more Bennett talked, the more confident Pennington became, and by the time the sun came up, Pennington had agreed to give Bennett 40 percent of Western Equities. In return, Bennett would quit his job at the Mint and take charge of Western Equities' Las Vegas operations. He would use his connections to get Pennington's blackjack machines onto the Strip and would handle all the repairs and collections so that Pennington could concentrate on the Reno market. At the same time, he would search for a casino to buy. "I promise that within five years after we buy a casino, we will have enough money for me to own a casino in Las Vegas and for you to own one in Reno," Bennett said. When they met a week later at a law office to sign a formal agreement, however, Bennett balked at getting only 40 percent of Western Equities. He insisted on being an equal partner; otherwise Pennington would be able to overrule anything he wanted to do. Pennington gave him half of his company.

It didn't take Bennett long to find a casino. He chose Howard Hughes's Landmark, the Space Needle–shaped casino that the billionaire had rushed to open in July 1969. It was not for sale, but Bennett knew it was losing money and he thought Hughes might want to unload it since he was now living in the Bahamas. Bennett and Pennington went to see E. Parry Thomas at Valley Bank because he was still Hughes's local banker.

Though neither of them knew Thomas well, both were aware that he was the most influential banker in Nevada when it came to buying and selling casinos.

Rail thin and deeply religious, Thomas had first arrived in Las Vegas from Salt Lake City in 1954 with $250,000 in start-up cash given to him by Mormon investors to open a bank. It didn't attract many customers so Thomas, who was then only twenty-nine years old, decided to take a risk no other bankers had dared. He agreed to lend money to Strip casinos whose owners needed cash to remodel. This was before Jimmy Hoffa began flooding the Strip with Teamster Union loans. "We were looked down upon," Thomas said later. "Other bankers said gambling was a sinful business and so forth." The "so forth" referred to doing business with mobsters, but Thomas managed to run his bank without getting into trouble, either with the mob or the federal government. By the late 1950s, nearly all the casinos on the Strip had started bypassing Thomas in favor of Teamster loans, but most of them still used Valley Bank for their legitimate business transactions, giving him steady income. He earned huge profits later by handling Howard Hughes's purchases and helped Hilton Hotels magnate William Barron Hilton buy the International and the Flamingo.

Bennett and Pennington told Thomas that they wanted him to find out if Hughes would sell them the Landmark, but the banker dismissed them quickly. Bennett's only tangible assets were his house and some savings, which added up to about $250,000. Pennington had about $700,000 in cash, mainly from profits earned by Western Equities. If they wanted to buy a casino from Hughes, Thomas told them, they were going to need a bigger balance sheet. Pennington approached several wealthy Los Angeles businessmen, but none took him seriously. "Everyone told us, 'You guys aren't in our league,' " Pennington recalled.

After they were rejected by Thomas, Bennett found them a cheaper casino to buy. The Four Queens was a Fremont Street club valued at half the price of the $21 million Landmark. Once again, Bennett and Pennington went to see Thomas, this time for a loan. Instead, he rejected their loan application and steered the sale of the Four Queens into the hands of a better-financed buyer.

A frustrated Pennington decided to have Western Equities appraised to see whether it would make their balance sheet look bigger. The appraiser's report stunned him. The company's potential worth was estimated at $14 million. Not long after that, Thomas called Pennington with a tip. State gaming officials were hounding Jay Sarno and Stan Mallin to sell Circus Circus. "Parry Thomas said to me, 'If you're willing to put your little company on the line as collateral, we might be able to arrange some financing for you,' " Pennington recalled later. The banker's sudden interest surprised him. After telling them they couldn't afford the $21 million Landmark, he was now suggesting they buy the $25 million Circus Circus. "It suddenly dawned on me why Parry had changed his tune," said Pennington. "He had found out about our appraisal." A few days after Valley Bank agreed to lend Pennington and Bennett the bulk of the money they needed to buy Circus Circus, Pennington discovered that Thomas already had a buyer waiting for Western Equities. "Thomas was playing all the angles," said Pennington. If the new owners defaulted, Thomas would take over Western Equities and sell it for a profit.

The actual purchase of Circus Circus had been negotiated by Pennington, but as soon as the deal was completed, Bennett took charge. He had been studying the place for months, walking through it at different hours, talking to its customers, watching its employees, and he was eager to get started. His legwork had convinced him that a large part of the casino's losses came from employee theft and bad management, so he fired all the top managers and replaced them in a single night with a crew that had been assembled by Angel Naves, the veteran casino manager who had been given a 10 percent share of Circus Circus in return for his expertise. It had been Bennett's idea to bring in Naves as the manager of their new casino, and it proved to be a brilliant move. The two men were close friends from the days when they had worked together in Lake Tahoe at the Sahara Tahoe casino. Naves had convinced twenty other seasoned employees at the Tahoe resort to move with him to Las Vegas and Circus Circus. This was the cadre of supervisors whom Bennett put in place. Two of them would later play key roles at Circus Circus. Mike Ensign, an enterprising bear of a man, had started his career by walking around a casino floor making change for people playing slot machines; Antonio "Tony" Alamo, a Cuban refugee, had begun as a porter cleaning toilets. Ensign was put in charge of running the casino during its busiest time at night. Alamo was his assistant.

Moving the entire crew into Circus Circus overnight produced immediate results. Bennett would later estimate that $100,000 had been saved during that first month simply because of the drop in employee theft. Bennett and Pennington also got rid of mafia hit man Tony Spilotro by giving him a promissory note for $400,000 to buy back the Circus Circus gift shop concession. It was a ridiculously high price, but it did the job. He grabbed it and left.

Bennett moved quickly to redesign the casino. "The problem is, people don't know what to expect when they walk in here," he told Pennington. He exiled Tanya, the slot-playing elephant, to a zoo, shut down the nude girlie attractions, and ended Sarno's bait-and-switch jam auctions. He had a ceiling built over the casino so gamblers no longer had trapeze acts flying over their heads. He kept the free circus acts, but moved the performers and the midway games onto the second floor, away from the gambling.

Pennington would fly down every weekend from Reno, where he was still running Western Equities, to see how Bennett was doing. "I would sit in the casino on weekends talking to Mike Ensign until two or three in the morning and he'd say, 'I think we are going to make it, boss. There is a good feel here, but it's going to be tight.' I'd look around and wonder how we could possibly make it, because the place seemed empty." Pennington worried that he and Bennett weren't going to be able to turn the place around fast enough.

But Bennett seemed confident as he continued making changes. He decided the midway attractions were boring, so he and Pennington went to see how the carnival attractions on the famed Santa Monica pier in California were being run. A carny expert there gave them several pointers. At Circus Circus, if a customer knocked over three milk bottles with a bean bag, he was given a coupon that he then had to take to another part of the casino to redeem for a prize. "You've got to hang your prizes on the walls at every game so people can see them right there," the carny said. Bennett and Pennington were so impressed by his tips that they offered him a percentage of the midway profits at Circus Circus if he would take charge of the attractions. He came and before long, Bennett noticed Circus Circus was attracting a different crowd of customers. Moms and dads were coming into the casino and sending their children to play in the midway. It was against the law in Nevada for minor children to loiter in a gaming area, but there was nothing wrong with kids congregating on another floor to watch circus acts and play carnival games while their parents gambled. Almost by accident, Circus Circus had become the first Strip casino to provide entertainment for the entire family. Some other casinos provided baby-sitters to high rollers, but no other resort on the Strip had games for kids to play. Bennett posted security guards at the doorway of the casino to make sure they didn't wander inside the gambling area, and he also put guards at the entrance of the midway to keep an eye on the children playing there. Word spread, and Circus Circus was soon being called "Nevada's baby-sitter."

While making Circus Circus kid-friendly proved to be an important first step, it was Bennett's next decision that ultimately saved the casino and set it down a golden path. Like every other casino owner on the Strip, Jay Sarno had tried to attract high rollers into Circus Circus, although few serious gamblers played there because the place was so tacky. Bennett decided that Sarno had been going after the wrong crowd. "There are a hell of a lot more working stiffs out there than high rollers," he told Pennington. "I want to switch this place over and begin catering to truck drivers and the guys who work in factories. Sure, they may come in here and only leave four hundred or five hundred bucks behind, but there's a lot of money to be made by going after their business rather than fighting with everyone else on the Strip for the big players."

At the time, such talk smacked of heresy. Ever since Bugsy Siegel had opened the Flamingo, Strip casinos had catered to the rich and famous. The seedy downtown clubs had been left to fight over the nickel-and-dime players. But Bennett had worked downtown at the Mint and had seen how much money could be won from these smaller gamblers. He was also perceptive and adroit at identifying popular trends, and during the 1960s, he had watched Ray Kroc turn his McDonald's fast-food chain into one of the most successful companies in America. Bennett had an interest in restaurants because he had operated two successful eateries earlier in his business career, and he admired Kroc's obsession with quality, service, cleanliness, and value—the four cornerstones of McDonald's. If Ray Kroc could sell millions of hamburgers to middle-class America, Bennett decided he could use those same four cornerstones to introduce baby boomers to gambling. "Our new motto," he declared, "is going to be that we will give our customers the best value for their dollar. . . . We will give them all the frills of a Strip casino without paying Strip prices."

Bennett stopped extending credit to the few high rollers who frequented Circus Circus. He closed the casino's baccarat pits—the game that big players favor because of its high stakes. He did away with comps for favored gamblers. He even ended the use of VIP passes, which were given to high rollers so they could strut ahead of others waiting in line to eat in the casino's restaurants. At Circus Circus, everyone was to be treated equally.

Once those changes were in place, Bennett began catering to his middle-class customers by giving them more of what they wanted, starting with slot machines. Initially, slot machines had been added to casinos to provide the wives and girlfriends of high rollers something to do. Even in the 1970s, some casinos still thought of them as distractions for women. But Bennett knew better. Novice customers were often afraid to play blackjack or other table games for fear they might make mistakes and look foolish. Slot machines were easy to play and highly profitable for a casino. At the time a slot machine cost less than $2 thousand. In one year, it would produce at least double that in profits. Better still, the machines worked around the clock, rarely needed repair, and never called in sick. Other Strip casinos were allocating 30 percent of their floor space to slot machines. Bennett covered 70 percent of his casino floor with them. At Circus Circus, they were tucked into every possible nook.

Bennett also calibrated his slot machines so that they paid jackpots more frequently than the machines at other casinos. Obviously, it is illegal for a casino owner to know in advance when a slot machine is going to pay a jackpot. But casino owners are allowed to determine how many jackpots are going to be paid at random within a given number of handle pulls. Bennett set his slots so they were the "loosest" in town, which meant they paid players more jackpots than other machines. This was a trick he had learned while working at the Sahara Tahoe casino.

"Our slots at the Sahara had a twenty-two percent box hold," he explained. "That means the machines were set so tight they kept twenty-two percent of all the coins dropped into them. The Sahara's two main competitors were Harrah's and Harvey's Club, and both of them were mobbed with slot players at night while our machines were doing lousy. I wanted to know what our competitors' box hold was, so one night I decided to play a dirty trick."

Bennett had become friendly with the casino manager at Harrah's Club, so he invited him to the Sahara for a drink after work. "I said to him, 'You know, we have the loosest slots in town, they are much looser here than at your place,' and this guy comes flying off the stool. He says, 'You're full of shit! Our slots are looser!' and I said, 'I'll bet you one hundred dollars that ours are looser.' Why, he jumps at the bet and then he says, 'How are we going to prove it?'" Bennett suggested that they exchange "reel strips," the tiny strips that casinos put in their slot machines to determine how many coins each machine will keep and how many will be paid as jackpots. "I told this guy, 'You write down on a reel strip how much each of your machines is holding and I'll do the same.' The next day, we swapped, and the strips showed that our slots were set four times tighter than the machines at Harrah's. That's why they were so busy and we weren't. We weren't competing at all. Now that information had cost me one hundred bucks—since I paid him the bet—but I got to see how Harrah's had its reel strips set for every nickel, dime, quarter, and dollar machine that it operated, and when I moved to Las Vegas and became general manager of the Mint, I put those exact same reel settings from Harrah's into our slot machines and guess what happened?"

According to Bennett, the Mint had lost $2.5 million the year before he took charge. After he began using Harrah's reel strips, it showed a $2 million profit in one year. Its profits hit $10 million the next year and $20 million the third, he said. "We were kicking the shit out of all of the other downtown joints and the main reason was because we were using Harrah's reel strips. It was our slot machines that were making that difference."

Bennett wasn't worried about paying out more jackpots than other Strip casinos because he knew from experience that very little of his customers' winnings would ever leave the casino. Most slot players simply feed the coins they win back into the machines. At one point, the slots at the Mint had been paying out $1 million in jackpots every day, yet less than $3,000 of those winnings ever left the building. Bennett set the reel strips on his slot machines at Circus Circus at 97.4 percent, which meant that over time nearly ninety-eight cents of every dollar put into a machine was paid out in a jackpot. No other Strip casino had that loose a hold.

Although Bennett was clearly in control of the casino, he didn't make any major changes without first talking by telephone to Pennington, who was busy in Reno running Western Equities. Because Pennington was still leasing keno and blackjack machines to other casinos, he was able to seek out the tricks that they were using to attract customers. One afternoon he flew to Las Vegas to tell Bennett about a new rage in Reno. A casino there had arranged eight slot machines in a circle and connected them electronically, so that gamblers playing them were competing for a single, combined jackpot. Rather than winning $1,000 from a single machine, they could win $8,000. Bennett liked the idea so much that he grouped eight machines together at Circus Circus. "They were dollar slot machines and they went over like gangbusters," Pennington recalled. "It took the rest of the Las Vegas Strip a long time to catch on. Meanwhile, we were making big profits from those machines."

Seven months after Bennett and Pennington took charge, Circus Circus earned its first profit, netting $700,000 in a single month. It was the first time that the casino had made money during its six-year history. Bennett was now more convinced than ever that his decision to target the working class was a smart one, and so were his top managers.

"If we want to bring more blue-collar workers in here," Angel Naves said to Bennett one afternoon, "why don't we lower our hotel room rates?" He told Bennett that once when occupancy at the Sahara Tahoe had slipped, the hotel manager there had asked for permission to raise room rates by five dollars a night to make up for the decline. But Naves had argued against it, stunning his colleagues by suggesting instead that the casino begin giving away hotel rooms for free to anyone who promised to gamble exclusively inside the Sahara. His reasoning was simple. Gambling was the way the casino made its money, not by charging expensive hotel rates. The Sahara's owners had balked at giving away free rooms, but decided to test Naves's suggestion by cutting the room rates. "Our occupancy rate shot up to ninety percent," Naves bragged, "and all of those guests gambled in our casino. It was the smartest thing we could have done."

Bennett liked Naves's idea. The average price of a hotel room on the Strip was $60 a night, so he lowered the price of a Circus Circus room to $18. During the first week, the hotel was so swamped with calls it had to begin turning away guests. Bennett didn't like sending customers elsewhere, so he came up with a novel solution. He contacted smaller hotels off the Strip that often had trouble filling their rooms since they didn't operate casinos, and offered them a deal. If they would agree to charge the same nightly rate as Circus Circus, he would deliver all his overflow to them. As part of the deal, Bennett would provide their guests with free transportation back and forth between his casino and their rooms. Several hotels signed on, and Bennett began advertising Circus Circus as the only casino in Las Vegas that guaranteed an $18-a-night room to everyone who called. Bennett posted his bargain prices on billboards in California. "Circus Circus—$18 per night. Guaranteed!" The hotel at Circus Circus had only four hundred rooms, but its reservation clerks were soon booking rooms for eight hundred or more guests per night. Just as Naves had predicted, casino revenues soared.

The increase in customers also created a demand for more food. In keeping with his philosophy of attracting the working class, Bennett installed an all-you-can-eat, forty-five-item buffet near the center of the Circus Circus casino and made it the cheapest in town. Breakfast cost 89¢, lunch was $1.25, and dinner was $1.90. Lines stretched out the door and, as Bennett had expected, most diners stuck around and gambled after they ate. On an average day, 8,500 people patronized the Circus Circus buffet, making it the second-largest meal server in the state, exceeded only by the dining hall at Nellis Air Force Base. The sheer volume of food being served enabled Circus Circus to buy its supplies in bulk, and shortly after it opened, the buffet began earning a profit despite its rock-bottom prices.

"Everyone on the Strip—all the other casino owners—thought we had gone crazy," said Pennington.

"We didn't charge for entertainment because our circus acts were free. We had the lowest-priced hotel rooms in town, the least expensive food, and the loosest slots. We didn't give a hoot about high rollers either. We didn't care if our customers came in shorts and tank tops and dragged their kids along because that is what Circus Circus was all about—entire families coming to Circus Circus to have fun. No one thought we could possibly be earning a profit, but they were wrong." In fact, Circus Circus's profits were climbing steadily each month.

Bennett kept looking for ways to bring in more gamblers. Whenever he rode in a limousine, he sat in the front seat so he could talk to the driver about what he liked and didn't like. When he traveled, he ate in truck stops and diners so he could see what sort of food was popular there. At most Strip casinos, dealers were prohibited from chatting with customers, but Bennett ordered his dealers to be friendly. They were required to ask gamblers their names and where they were from as soon as they sat down at a blackjack table. Bennett even told his dealers to offer players advice if they seemed unsure how to play a hand. He hired women as dealers, which wasn't widely done at the time. "I want Circus Circus to be known as the friendliest little casino on the Strip," he declared.

Many of the changes Bennett implemented seem routine now, but they weren't in the 1970s. He also took several business techniques that he had used when he operated restaurants and furniture stores in Phoenix and adapted them to the casino business. Many were innovations for casinos. One of them was a "daily financial sheet" that tracked how much money was spent, won, and lost during each shift. This report enabled Bennett to keep track of how his casino was doing financially every twenty-four hours. As soon as his shift managers became proficient at filling out these daily reports, Bennett began using the information to fine-tune his operation. He installed more of the popular table games, such as blackjack, and got rid of others. He had learned how important incentives could be when he sold furniture, and he carried that practice over to the casino. He paid managers hefty bonuses if they cut costs and increased profits. He was especially generous with his casino managers. In 1974, a casino shift manager on the Strip earned about $40,000 a year. Bennett began giving out yearly bonuses that were nearly twice that. "Bennett swore us all to secrecy," recalled one manager, "and it was maddening, because you'd stop at Caesars Palace for a drink and mention that you worked at Circus Circus and they'd laugh at you because it was such a grind joint and at that moment you'd think, 'Pal, if you only knew that I'm making three times what you make.' "

Bennett proved to be obsessive when it came to details. If he saw a cigarette butt on the carpet, he picked it up. Employees caught on quickly; if the owner was picking up trash, they'd better do the same. He ate lunch every day in the Pink Pony Café and if he didn't enjoy his meal, he quizzed the chef. If a candy bar in the gift shop cost more than it did across the street at the Riviera, Bennett wanted to know why. But he made it his policy to never chew out his low-level employees. Instead, he would call in his managers, who were being well paid to make certain the workers under them performed. It was their necks that were on the chopping block.

By the end of their first year in business, Bennett had put Circus Circus on such a sound financial footing that he and Pennington were able to expand. They added a fifteen-story hotel tower with 795 more rooms. From the day it opened, the tower was filled to capacity. Circus Circus was on its way to becoming known as the Kmart of the Las Vegas Strip.

In 1978, Bennett and Pennington felt confident enough to celebrate. They flew eighty guests, mostly Circus Circus managers and their wives, to New Orleans for Super Bowl XII, the first to be played in the Superdome. Midway through the game, Bennett and Pennington got bored and took off in the bus they had rented, leaving their guests stranded. They later joked that they had taken the bus, rather than a limousine, because the bus had a bigger bar in it. The day after the football game, the two men competed against each other to see who could hand out the most $100 bills to street musicians in the French Quarter. Their shenanigans continued later that night. At 3 A.M., Bennett demanded that Mel Larson, the casino's publicity director, come to his hotel suite to officiate at a touch football game. "He and Pennington had pushed all the furniture to one side so they could play," Larson recalled. "Both of them had had plenty to drink. Bennett had this pillow, which was supposed to be the ball, and he was going for a touchdown and Pennington just stepped out of the way and Bennett ran headfirst right into the wall and almost knocked himself out. I mean, they were just having fun and why shouldn't they? These two guys had all the money in the world that they could possibly want."

Not long after that trip, Angel Naves told Bennett over drinks in the casino's Gilded Cage Lounge that he wanted out. Naves had been working nonstop for three years, and he wanted to spend more time with his family and move back to Lake Tahoe, where his elderly parents lived. It was not an easy decision because he and Bennett had been close friends for nearly a decade. Naves thought so much of Bennett that he had named one of his sons after him. The two men's wives had become inseparable too. But Naves was spent. Bennett understood. There were times when he wished he could retire, he said, but not yet. They reminisced about how tough it had been when they first bought Circus Circus; how they had taken a big risk by giving up their steady jobs. As the conversation wound down, they quickly agreed on a price for Naves's 10 percent share. During the next few days, Naves went through a round of going-away parties, speeches, and farewell toasts. Bennett couldn't say enough about how great he was. Naves was stunned, therefore, to discover when he drove to the attorney's office to formalize his departure that neither Bennett nor Pennington was there. When he read the sales document, he got angry. "The price . . . was nowhere near what we had settled on!" Naves charged years later. "It was much, much lower."

Bennett would later insist that he gave Naves exactly what they had agreed to, and while Naves balked at signing the sales document and called an attorney of his own for advice, he nevertheless signed it before leaving that afternoon. He was paid $1.5 million for his 10 percent share: $100,000 per year to be paid out over a fifteen-year period. Bennett and Pennington already had negotiated a similar buyout with Mickey Briggs for his 10 percent. They now owned Circus Circus fifty-fifty.

Naves left Las Vegas bitter, and as of this writing, he has never spoken to Bennett in person again. What surprised him the most, he said later, was that he hadn't had a clue until he walked into that lawyer's office that he and Bennett were about to be at odds. There had never been a hint of trouble brewing between them. Over the coming years, Naves would often think about his relationship with Bennett, and he would decide that there was only one incident during their entire friendship when he had thought Bennett had acted strangely. One afternoon, Naves had accidentally overheard Bennett taking credit for lowering the Circus Circus hotel rates even though it had been his idea. Naves had thought it harmless boasting. In retrospect, he wondered if it had been an omen.

On June 14, 1977, *The Reno Evening Gazette* announced in a banner headline that Circus Circus was going to expand into Reno. A photograph on the front page showed Pennington sitting on the ledge of a roof at the abandoned Gray Reid Department Store. Circus Circus was planning to convert the downtown building into a hotel-casino. The first public tip-off of how well the privately held Circus Circus was doing financially came when Pennington announced that half of the $30 million cost of turning the store into a casino would be paid in cash by Bennett and Pennington. The other half would be borrowed.

"I was wrong, you know," Bennett confided to Pennington after the announcement.

"What the hell are you talking about?" Pennington replied.

"It only took three years for each of us to get our casino," Bennett answered. "Not five years like I predicted."

Inside the Casino:
Becoming a Dealer

I was thirty-five, living in Washington State and going through a nasty divorce. You do crazy things when you get a divorce and I decided I wanted to be a dealer, so I drove to Las Vegas with my son and sold my car to get money to rent a place and buy furniture and enroll in a dealers school. Now Vegas can be an awfully tough town. I always say that it either makes you or breaks you. And it nearly broke me. I remember I was going to dealers school all day and practicing all night. In those days it was tough to break in if you didn't know someone with juice and I didn't know anyone. Finally, the teacher at the dealers school told me I was ready for an audition. This is where you put on a pair of black pants and a white blouse and walk into a casino and ask to try out for a job. They usually let you deal a few hands. They don't pay you. They just watch. Some guys will have you deal an entire shift and then send you home and tell you they don't want to hire you. It was brutal.

This shift boss in this casino told me to go over and tap this dealer at a blackjack table out. You are supposed to tap her on the shoulder and she is supposed to finish her hand, gather up everything, set the cards down in a certain way and clap out—which means she claps her hands over the table so that the eye in the sky can see that she doesn't have any chips hidden in her hands. Then she's supposed to step back to the right and then you step in at the left. There's a protocol for everything and if you make a mistake, some floorman will be yelling at you within seconds. So I go over and tap this girl out and then go completely blank. Nothing. I had dealt about four hands and the shift boss comes over and says, "That's enough." Then he says, "I think you should try another line of business." I told him that I was smart enough to deal and he says, "It's not a question of being smart. It's: can you relax enough to do it?"

Next I went to Bob Stupak's Vegas World casino, one of the crappiest joints on the Strip. I walked in and asked if I could audition and the shift boss says, "You a dealer or a break-in?" which is what they call people who are new dealers, and I said, "I'm a dealer. I have been to dealers school." And he says, in front of the customers and everyone, "That don't mean a fucking thing! You're a break-in and I'm not hiring any break-ins." I said, "I'd like a chance," but he just told me to get out.

I got so desperate I went downtown to a place called the Friendly Club. It is closed now but it was a real downtown dive. They put me to work on a blackjack table that was actually out front on the sidewalk. It was a 25¢ minimum bet and every bum was trying to turn a quarter into 50¢ so he could buy a bottle of muscatel. They were miserable to me. I had to buy my own dealer's apron, which cost six bucks, and they refused to pay me a salary at first—only a portion of the tips. These bums would walk up to the table and play a hand and lose and curse at you. Finally, I just walked out. I couldn't take it. I was dead broke. I ended up driving home and doing one of those Loretta Young things where you just fall apart weeping and throw yourself to the floor, and my son says, "Mom, some guy called and wants you to start work at the Silver City."

I went right in and really did well there. I learned how to relax and enjoy myself. But it was still a very tough job. In those days, if you lost, the shift bosses would be really mean to you. They would call you Sally the Dumpster. They'd lean down and whisper in your ear, "You stupid bitch! Can't you win a hand?" But luck is a strange thing. I would get on hot streaks and then they would come up to me if they had some guy at the end of the pit winning and they would say, "Sally, get down there. He's beating us bad."

I dealt for several years and then one day they put me on a table with a young, attractive guy who had won a lot of money. He had greens [$25 chips] stacked up real high—I mean twenty-five chips high—and we played a lot of hands and I kept winning and I started trying to warn him that I was hot. I'd say, "Oh, God, I'm hot today. Maybe you should know it." I was trying to be nice and I had to make sure that they didn't see me talking to him because I was giving him a warning and then he says to me, "You're hot, so what?" so I decided not to talk. I just dealt and I won all of his money. I was getting a lot of black-jacks and I took all of his greens until all he had left was this stack of silver. Now these were really heavy $1 silver tokens. After I took his last green chip, he suddenly picked up that stack of silver and he threw it right at me. It smacked me in the shoulder so hard that it knocked me over. The pit boss flew over the table at this guy and chased him out the back door. They took me into the coffee shop and I had bruises all over my shoulder and I drank a couple cups of coffee and I said, "I don't want to deal anymore, okay?" I moved over to a secretary's job. It's like I said: Vegas can be a tough town.

—*Sally Krakora Smith*

CHAPTER FOUR

....

Riches Beyond Belief

Bill Bennett didn't say much when he met someone, and people who didn't know him sometimes mistakenly thought he was shy. He preferred to listen before offering his opinion. It wasn't just other people's words that he mused over. He watched how they stood, noticed if they crossed their arms or averted their eyes when speaking. His friends would later claim that Bennett had mastered many of the same skills as a psychiatrist when it came to identifying strengths and shortcomings in others, and this proved extremely useful to him in business.

It is simplistic, of course, to believe that a man is the way that he is entirely because of his childhood, but Bennett himself would say that his father had taught him how important it was to judge a person and assess his mood quickly. This wasn't meant as a compliment. Bennett's father, Allan Milton Bennett, was a heavy drinker, brazen womanizer, and hot-tempered tyrant at home. Bennett learned how to read his father's mood as soon as the old man burst through the door. "I used to watch my father beat the hell out of my older brother all the time," said Bennett. "I kept saying to myself, I am not going to let that happen to me." One of the first stories that Bennett recalled about his childhood in Glendale, Arizona, was how his father had beaten four men at an air show after they took his three children's grandstand seats while he was buying hot dogs at the snack bar. "Those guys got their butts whipped," Bennett recalled. "I mean he cleaned their clocks with his fists." Allan Bennett wasn't afraid of anyone, and he expected his wife and their two sons and daughter to carry out his orders without question. Bennett fled home in 1942 by enlisting in the navy just before his eighteenth birthday. He scored so high on the entrance tests that the navy thought he had cheated, so it ordered him to take a second test prepared just for him. He aced this one too, so the navy put him at the front of its line for fighter pilot training and sent him to fly combat missions off an aircraft carrier in the South Pacific. He had signed up, as he put it, "to kill Japs," but after seeing several of his buddies die and kamikaze pilots crash into his aircraft carrier, he lost his blood lust and simply wanted the war to end.

When it did, he enrolled in college but discovered that he had little patience for homework and fraternity pranks. "I'd seen too much during the war." Instead, he took a job selling furniture on commission in a local store called Traders. In the postwar boom, the store was swamped with orders from customers who had suffered through years of shortages. Bennett felt uneasy because he wasn't good at small talk, but he soon found a way to turn his awkwardness to his advantage. One afternoon he asked a farmer and his wife if they wanted help. A slick salesman had approached them first but quickly dismissed them because they seemed poor and shabby. The couple responded to Bennett's low-key approach and asked him to write up their order. It turned out that they had just built a new house and needed to furnish every room. "Their bill was thirteen thousand dollars," he recalled, "and that was a significant amount of money in those days." When he asked how they wanted to finance the purchase, the farmer started pulling tobacco tins from his pockets. Each tin was jammed with wads of bills. The incident stayed with Bennett. "The best way to sell someone something is to just be yourself," he said. "It also taught me that you can't tell how much money someone has based on their looks."

The owner of Traders liked Bennett and taught him the furniture business. Two years later, when his mentor retired, Bennett bought the store and eventually expanded it into a chain of eight stores. At age twenty-seven, he was a millionaire with an idyllic life: happily married, with two healthy children, and a prominent member of the Phoenix Country Club. When it came to business, he seemed to have a gift. Together with a friend, he opened a successful fast-food chicken restaurant and a popular Polynesian-style steak house called The Islands. "If you went to The Islands between five and six o'clock," he recalled, "everyone who was anyone in the Phoenix business community would show up." Bennett proved to be as skilled at running his restaurants as he was his furniture stores. At one point, local liquor distributors were overstocked with rum, so they began requiring their customers to buy a case of it each time they ordered whiskey, which was always in demand. "Other restaurant owners were going nuts trying to get rid of all this rum," Bennett said. But he ordered his bartenders at The Islands to push tropical rum drinks at a cut-rate price. "The drinks fit with our restaurant's Polynesian theme, and people couldn't get enough of them." Each drink cost the bar less than a quarter but sold for $3.50. Bennett would later brag that *Life* magazine put his photograph on its cover in the 1960s to illustrate a story entitled "The Young Millionaires of Phoenix." It described how a handful of tough entrepreneurs, most without formal educations, used grit and sweat to wring fortunes out of the desert.

Bennett's financial ruin came as quickly as his rise. In 1960, he returned from a month-long vacation in Mexico and discovered that his furniture empire was in the red. He blamed a sluggish Phoenix economy. Business at his restaurants also fell, and then he was hit with a personal calamity. His wife, Barbara, was diagnosed with a fatal heart problem. During the next two years, Bennett sold all his businesses so he could focus on his wife: "Time was suddenly the most precious commodity in my life." He and Barbara planned a world cruise, but only days before they were scheduled to leave, she died. For the next three years, Bennett drifted. Nothing held his interest until he met a businessman who talked him into investing everything he owned in an upstart financial company. In a matter of weeks, the stock went from $37 a share down to $2. Bennett was forced to declare bankruptcy.

Badly humiliated, he turned for help to his country club pals. L.C. Jacobson, a senior executive with the Phoenix-based Del Webb Company, offered Bennett a job as a casino host at the Sahara Tahoe, one of several Nevada casinos that the company owned. Bennett and his children moved to Nevada, where he was paid $750 per month to squire around high rollers. It was up to him to see that they got credit in the Sahara Tahoe casino, free tickets to casino shows, and dinner reservations. For the fallen millionaire, it was demeaning work, especially since many of his customers were his former cronies from Phoenix. Bennett fumed, but only in private. He was not the sort of man who shared his inner feelings with others, especially when it came to anxieties that he might have felt about his own self-worth. At work, he befriended Angel Naves and learned as much as he could from the veteran casino manager. Within two years, he was the second-in-command at the Sahara Tahoe, convinced that he knew more about operating a casino because of his business background than nearly anyone else. "The only guy in northern Nevada whom I really respected was Bill Harrah at Harrah's Club," he said later, referring to the dean of Reno's casino operators. "The rest of those owners were real dummies." Bennett also thought the Del Webb Company was poorly run. It paid its managers a bonus regardless of whether or not their departments earned a profit. "The guy who worked hard got the same as a guy who screwed around." This was no way to run a business.

For Bennett, there was much more at stake in his accomplishments at Circus Circus than dollars and cents. He was determined to prove that his earlier success in Phoenix had not been a fluke. Yes, he had made a fortune and had lost it, but he had come back, and he now was earning another fortune even bigger than the first. How many of his old country club pals could make that claim?

Not long after Circus Circus expanded into Reno, Bennett's business skills were again put to the test. On Memorial Day in 1978, the Resorts International Hotel and Casino opened on the Boardwalk in Atlantic City, bringing legalized gambling to the East Coast. The Las Vegas economy fell into a tailspin. The number of gamblers flying from New York City to Las Vegas plunged so dramatically that the nation's airlines stopped offering direct flights between the two cities for the first time since the 1940s. Las Vegas took a second economic hit when the entire country slipped into a recession during the final years of Jimmy Carter's presidency. Several casinos went broke. Then tragedy struck. On November 21, 1980, a kitchen fire raced through the MGM Grand Hotel, injuring seven hundred people and killing eighty-four in the worst disaster ever to strike a Las Vegas resort and the second-worst fire in the nation's history.

This was not today's MGM Grand on Tropicana Avenue; it was the original MGM Grand Hotel, located at the very epicenter of the Strip at the same intersection as the Flamingo, the Dunes, and Caesars Palace. The fact that the fire was at the MGM Grand Hotel and not some lesser casino made the public relations fallout even more damaging. The hotel was the creation of Kirk Kerkorian, who had returned to the Strip after recovering from the financial strains of buying MGM Studios. As was his style, Kerkorian had built a resort even bolder than his last creation, the International. Its three thousand rooms made it the largest hotel in the world. The disaster, and rumors of dubious safety standards on the Strip, sparked a morass of multimillion-dollar lawsuits and eventually led Kerkorian to sell the MGM Grand to Bally Entertainment, which renamed it Bally's. Bally's no longer exists. By the time of that sale, however, thousands of tourists had canceled their trips to Las Vegas. Always a superstitious lot, many gamblers considered the Strip jinxed.

Yet in the midst of this financial carnage, Circus Circus continued to make money. "We didn't depend on high rollers or big East Coast gamblers to earn our profits," Pennington explained. "Our customers were working people, coming to us mainly from Southern California, and the recession didn't hit them like the big guys who suddenly didn't have extra cash to spend. Our customers formed car pools and came to our little casinos every Friday night and stayed until Sunday afternoon, week after week."

Bennett took advantage of the hard times. He snatched up fifty-one acres next door to Circus Circus at a bargain price and turned it into a recreation-vehicle park with room for four hundred RVs and trailers. He bought two puny casinos on the Strip—the Slots-A-Fun casino next door to Circus Circus and the Silver City directly across the street. While other owners hurried to open casinos on the Atlantic City Boardwalk, Bennett bought a failing casino named the Edgewater on the bank of the Colorado River, in one of the most ungodly spots in all of Nevada. It was on the state line, in the southeastern wedge of Nevada that jags down between Arizona and California. Temperatures there often were the hottest in the state, yet for more than twenty years, a gambler named Don Laughlin had been trying to develop a resort along the river. His bait shop, motel, and casino were the first businesses that motorists saw when they crossed the bridge into Nevada from Arizona. Despite his unwavering efforts, Laughlin's town, which was named after him, hadn't flourished, although he did convince a group of speculators to build the Edgewater casino next to his property. But Bennett's timing proved to be brilliant. Southern California Edison had just finished building a coal-fired power plant a few miles up the Colorado River and the construction brought new growth into the searing valley. During the following months, the river at Laughlin became a popular recreational site and the town mushroomed into a multimillion-dollar gambling center.

In 1980, when other Strip casinos were declaring bankruptcy, Circus Circus earned $8 million in profit. By 1982, that figure doubled. The company was expected to earn in excess of $20 million in profit by the end of fiscal 1983. Most of it came from its two large casinos, but the three smaller ones that Bennett had bought were also reporting healthy returns. Typical was Slots-A-Fun, which had been bought for $7.7 million in a shrewd deal that required him to pay only $1 million up front. The rest of the $6.7 million sales price was stretched out over a thirteen-year period. Under Bennett's management, it produced a $4 million profit during its first year.

By 1983, Bennett and Pennington were paying themselves $1.2 million a year each in salary and bonuses, more than any other Strip owners. They co-owned two company jets and a $6 million yacht. Both men enjoyed racing speedboats, so their partnership underwrote the cost of a professional speedboat racing team. They were making so much money that their tax advisers told them that they needed to turn Circus Circus into a public corporation. "If either Bennett or I had died unexpectedly, our families would have not been able to afford the federal inheritance taxes," Pennington explained. "They would have been forced to sell their shares simply to pay taxes, and neither of us wanted that to happen."

Bennett and Pennington didn't know much about Wall Street, so their tax advisers suggested they get help from Michael Milken, who was then a bond trader in Los Angeles at the financial house of Drexel Burnham Lambert. Five years earlier, Milken had made a splash by helping Las Vegas casino owner Steve Wynn raise $160 million to finance the construction of an Atlantic City casino. Milken had been the first bond trader to dip his toe into the gambling business, and he had raised the cash that Wynn needed by creating a new form of financing, which the media quickly dubbed "junk bonds" because they were extremely risky investments. In Wynn's case, his entire company had been valued at only $15.3 million, yet he used it as collateral to borrow ten times its worth. The investors took the risk because he was willing to pay them a much higher yield than what more secure bonds were paying. Milken and his junk bonds had become famous on Wall Street, turning Drexel Burnham Lambert into a financial powerhouse. Bennett and Pennington figured that if Milken had been willing to help Wynn, he would also help them. They were right. As soon as Milken saw their financial records, he arranged a series of meetings between them and prospective investors in anticipation of the public stock offering.

On October 25, 1983, Milken began selling stock in Circus Circus Enterprises to preferred buyers at $15 per share. Four million shares were gobbled up within a few hours, 85 percent of them by institutional investors, including insurance companies and corporations such as American Express. The demand was so great that both Bennett and Pennington sold $12.5 million worth of their own stock, but retained 39.2 percent each of their new corporation. On the first day of open trading, Circus Circus stock jumped from $15 per share to a high of $16.87, which meant that on paper, the stock that Bennett and Pennington owned was worth $119.5 million each. Their former partners, Angel Naves and Mickey Briggs, had been paid $1.5 million apiece for their 10 percent shares. Had they kept them, those same shares would have been worth twenty times more.

Nine years had passed since Bennett and Pennington had bought Circus Circus. In that time, they had turned it from a financial fiasco losing $500,000 a month into a company whose stock was worth $300 million. Now that it was a public corporation, Circus Circus was required to open its financial records to the public, and other Strip casino owners were stunned to see how rich Bennett and Pennington had become operating grind joints—so called because profits were ground out a penny at a time.

Bennett relished being in the spotlight and especially enjoyed being cast as a renegade. He opposed the Las Vegas Chamber of Commerce's efforts to bring conventions into town, complaining that conventioneers came simply to eat the cheap food and take advantage of the inexpensive rooms, not to gamble. He outraged other casino owners in 1983 by breaking ranks during a strike of the local hotel workers' union and giving Circus Circus hotel employees the raise that they were demanding. "How could a man like myself," he asked reporters, "with my employees—who know how well the property is doing largely because of them—how can I go to them and not give them a raise?"

In Reno, meanwhile, Pennington kept a low profile. He avoided reporters, rarely issued press releases, and made few public appearances. He did not object when Bennett named himself chairman of the Circus Circus board, leaving him the lesser post of president. Up to this point, the two men had always appeared to be close friends. They often socialized together and even joined each other on family vacations. But this now changed.

Bennett would later claim that he had grown tired of Pennington almost from the start of their relationship. He simply had hidden his disdain. "When we first opened Circus Circus, Pennington would come up from Reno," Bennett said, "and I would be having meetings with my people and he didn't know anything about the gambling business and he would say, 'Hey, why don't we try this?' and that was fine, except that what he was telling us was stuff that had been thrown out ten years ago." Bennett acknowledged that he had needed Pennington's help in the beginning because he couldn't have bought Circus Circus without him, but after they acquired their casino, he had decided Pennington was a detriment. "The only reason why I said, 'Let's build a casino in Reno for him to fool with,' was so he would stay the hell out of my business," Bennett said later. Now that Circus Circus was publicly held, Bennett saw no reason why he needed to continue the friendly relationship. Instead, he began looking for ways to get Pennington out of the company.

Understandably, Pennington defended his role in Circus Circus. "Bill Bennett didn't make a move in those early days without clearing it with me," Pennington said later. While it was true that he had devoted his time during those early years to running Western Equities in Reno, he said he was just as responsible as Bennett for turning Circus Circus around financially. "We talked on the telephone ten or twelve times a day about every change, every one of them." After the two men opened their Reno casino, Pennington had taken charge of it and had sold Western Equities. Focusing his attention on the Reno casino, he left Bennett to run the rest of the company. Still, he would later insist that Bennett had not made any major decisions without first clearing them with him.

He also said he had no idea that Bennett had not felt warmly toward him during their partnership. "I thought we were good friends up to the time we took the company public and then suddenly Bennett turned on me," Pennington said. "I would come down from Reno in my airplane and the minute I hit his office, Bill would get nervous as hell. He was scared to death of me and I didn't know why. Then I would discover that he had done something without telling me. He was cutting me out of the loop. I felt that I was smart enough to protect myself, but it was very difficult to deal with and I didn't have a clue why he was suddenly turning against me."

Rather than confronting Bennett, Pennington simply dug himself in at Reno. "I thought maybe this was just some crazy phase Bennett was going through."

Now that the company was public, Bill Bennett needed help dealing with Wall Street, but from whom? Mike Ensign, who now was the company's chief operating officer, had become Bennett's right-hand man. Intensely private and unassuming, Ensign had climbed the company ladder by working long hours and learning as much

as he could from casino veterans like Angel Naves. He
had proven to be an innovative and popular manager.
Not only did he treat employees fairly, he often helped
his workers when they had personal difficulties. Over
time Ensign had become one of the most respected
casino operators in the state, but he had no Wall Street
training. Neither did Richard P. Banis, the company's
chief financial officer, who was next in line. Quiet and
studious, Banis was a certified public accountant from
Reno whose expertise was casino auditing. While he
was a whiz with numbers and an affable manager, he
too didn't have a clue how to handle Wall Street. There
was something else that made Bennett anxious about
Wall Street. Circus Circus Enterprises had expanded by
buying run-down casinos and making them profitable.
Each of those deals had been one-shot opportunities.
No one in the company had ever developed a long-
range growth strategy, and stock analysts were besieg-
ing him with questions about how he intended to keep
Circus Circus growing.

Once again, Bennett asked Michael Milken for help,
and Milken suggested that Bennett hire Glenn Schaeffer,
an ambitious twenty-nine-year-old executive at Ramada
Inns, to handle Wall Street. Milken had first met him in
1981, when Ramada was having problems paying for a
casino it was building in Atlantic City. Milken had been
impressed because Schaeffer was a former stockbroker,
which meant that he could talk to investors, and a former public relations executive, which meant he could
talk to the media. Bennett called Schaeffer that same
day and arranged an interview.

Schaeffer found it a strange one. They met in
Bennett's office at Circus Circus on a Saturday morning, but Bennett barely spoke a word. Then, a few days
later, he telephoned Schaeffer and asked how much he
was earning at Ramada. "Seventy-five thousand a year
in salary," Schaeffer replied, plus a year-end bonus of at

least $15,000. He was also provided with a car. "I like BMWs," he volunteered. Bennett offered him a job at the identical salary. He added that he would give him a Cadillac because he wanted his executives to use American cars made by union workers, and a year-end bonus that would be tied to his performance. "I figure your bonus will be at least fifty thousand," said Bennett. "If you don't earn more than that, we will both have made a mistake."

Schaeffer asked about stock options but Bennett said he wasn't sure if he wanted to issue any. Circus Circus had never had stock options to give before. But Schaeffer persisted. "Okay," Bennett finally said, "how about options to buy fifty thousand shares at fifteen dollars a share?" If the stock went up, Schaeffer would make money. If not, the options would expire.

"What's my title?" Schaeffer asked.

Bennett said he didn't pay much attention to titles, but Schaeffer said he had to be called something, so they agreed on his becoming a "senior vice president in charge of corporate development."

Although Schaeffer thought the way he was hired was unorthodox, it didn't disturb him. "I knew Mr. Bennett was exactly the sort of mentor I wanted," he said. "This guy had made one million dollars while he was in his twenties, had lost it all, and then had made not one million but a hundred million dollars!"

Schaeffer soon discovered that he was not the only ambitious young manager whom Bennett had hired. "Bill Bennett liked the energy that young men brought to a company," Schaeffer said later. "He compared himself to being a football coach. He drafted the best athletes that he could get, even if he didn't have a specific job for them, and then he served as their mentor. He had been helped early in his career in the furniture business and I think he was trying to emulate that by giving us younger guys opportunities."

William Paulos, a scrappy New Yorker, had under-
gone a similarly clumsy interview process with Bennett
some years earlier. He had arrived in town carrying
everything he owned in a single suitcase, and after
graduating from the hotel and restaurant school at the
University of Nevada at Las Vegas, he was hired to
manage the hotel at the Marina, a Strip casino. When
the FBI threatened to close the place, Bennett had toyed
with the idea of buying it, but ultimately decided it
would be a poor investment. While reviewing its
records, however, he had noticed that its hotel was ex-
ceptionally well run, so he telephoned Paulos. "I was
only twenty-seven years old and I will never forget what
Mr. Bennett said to me," Paulos recalled years later.
"These are his exact words: 'I have every intention of
making you a wealthy man if you come to work for
me.' Now, I knew how much money this guy had made
so I said, 'I only hope I am worthy.' " Bennett had put
Paulos in charge of the hotel at Circus Circus and paid
him exactly the same salary he had earned at the
Marina. That irked Paulos, but Bennett had promised
him a hefty bonus if "you are worth it." At the end of
the year, Bennett gave him a bonus twice as much as his
salary. He also promoted him. Tossing him a set of
keys, he said, "You are now in charge of the Silver City
casino." It didn't have a hotel attached to it, he explained, so Paulos was now going to have to learn how
to run a grind joint. A few weeks later, Paulos returned
to Bennett's office with a long list of expensive casino
equipment that he wanted to buy. Bennett approved it
without asking a single question.

"Boy, that was easy," Paulos said.

Looking up from his desk over a pair of thick black
eyeglasses, Bennett replied, "Young man, I don't want
you to say that I didn't give you all the tools that you
needed to work with when I fire you."

In fact, Paulos succeeded in making Silver City profitable and was rewarded with another generous bonus and promotion. By the time that Schaeffer came on board, Paulos was running the Edgewater casino in Laughlin.

"Bennett was incredibly tough to work for because he was so demanding," Paulos said later, "but he was always a gentleman. When he brought me into his office and verbally undressed me, before I left his office he fully dressed me again. He was the type of guy who could absolutely make you feel like the dumbest human being on the face of the earth, but when you left you said, 'Oh boy! I am still part of the team and he makes me feel good.' "

In addition to Schaeffer and Paulos, Bennett brought in Michael H. Sloan, one of the city's top attorneys, to handle Circus Circus's legal affairs. Sloan was a former newspaper reporter and ex–state legislator with extensive political connections in the Nevada statehouse. Bennett hired several other promising managers too, including a few who didn't measure up and were quickly fired. Those who succeeded joined his band of Young Turks.

On the Strip, Bennett was becoming a larger-than-life figure. His employees revered him because of his open-door policy. If a dealer, a maid, or even a parking valet had a complaint, all they had to do was walk up to the chairman of the board's office on the second floor of the casino and complain directly to Bennett. When a dealer gave birth to a baby with severe medical problems not covered by insurance, Bennett stepped in and personally picked up the tab. Stories circulated about him wandering through the casino handing out $100 bills to gamblers who had gone bust. His largesse extended outside the casino too. Each time a police officer was killed in the line of duty in the Las Vegas area, Bennett quietly instructed his accountants to send the grieving family a check. He donated several million dollars to help abused animals in Las Vegas, including wild horses and abandoned pets. He wrote out checks for relief efforts in other states whenever natural disasters struck. He infuriated the owners of the nearby Frontier casino when its union employees went on strike by sending the protesting workers box lunches and coffee on the picket line.

Nearly every day, Bennett ate lunch at the Pink Pony Café, and over $1.95 club sandwiches and 69¢ slices of apple pie, he dazzled his Young Turks with stories about how he had made his first fortune in Phoenix. One day, when a manager treated a waitress curtly, Bennett scolded him and made him apologize. "Never forget that it's these people who are the backbone of this company," he lectured, referring to the waitress. "They are the ones who keep the customers coming back."

Pennington watched the goings-on in Las Vegas with skepticism. All of Bennett's Young Turks knew who Pennington was, but few had dealings with him. When a manager mentioned that he was scheduled to fly to Reno one afternoon to brief Pennington about a legal matter, Bennett ordered him to stay put: "Let Pennington hire his own attorney if he wants to know what's happening." Pennington recognized that Bennett was trying to isolate him inside the company. "Bennett wanted to hog all the credit," Pennington said later. "I was a threat to him because he couldn't take credit for things we had worked on together and that really bothered him." During his more cynical moments, Pennington wondered what would happen if one of Bennett's Young Turks began getting more attention than his boss, but for the most part, he didn't spend much time fussing about Bennett. He was sixty-one now and was enjoying his wealth. He began buying vacation homes and taking hunting trips.

On June 23, 1984, Pennington was shooting across Lake Tahoe in his nineteen-foot speedboat when it suddenly went out of control near the shore. Pennington clung to the wheel and tried to keep the craft from flipping over, but he lost control and it capsized, striking him in the head and knocking him unconscious. Onlookers tried to reach him, but the water was too deep for them. Then, by chance, an experienced swimmer happened on the scene, took a deep breath, dove straight down, and grabbed Pennington by the shirt, pulling him to the surface. By then, Pennington had been underwater for nearly eight minutes and his heart had stopped, but the young rescuer applied CPR. Ten minutes later, his heart started beating, but he was still comatose and doctors at Tahoe Forest Hospital gave him little chance of recovering. Even if he lasted the night, they warned, the shock to his system would kill him. Though Pennington survived the night, he remained in a coma and was hurried to an intensive care unit in a Reno hospital. Once again, doctors warned that the prognosis was poor. Five days later, he opened his eyes and asked a nurse for a drink of water. Astonishingly, he had suffered no lasting impairment.

Over the next several weeks at home, Pennington tracked down the young swimmer who had saved him and then left the lake. Gary Schmidt was a nineteen-year-old college student from San Francisco. Pennington gave him a red Porsche convertible as a reward. But he could not shake off the experience. He felt cold all the time, so he flew to Hawaii to convalesce. As he warmed himself in the sunshine, he was haunted by whys. Was there some mysterious reason that his life had been spared?

A month later, an executive from Drexel Burnham Lambert called him because there were rumors on Wall Street that he was incapacitated and fears about Circus Circus Enterprises' stability. The analyst suggested that he and Bennett host a party on the corporate yacht in the New York City harbor so their biggest investors could see for themselves that he was fine. When Pennington came aboard, Bennett greeted him as if they were still the best of friends, but Pennington knew better. He found a rail to lean against and had his doctor and secretary stand on each side of him in case he felt faint. The party went well, but toward the end a worried investor approached Pennington. Nodding toward Bennett, who was on the other side of the deck, the investor whispered: "Your partner still doesn't look very good. He's so pale. Are you sure he's recovered from his boating accident?" Pennington fought back a laugh. The investor had mistaken them because Pennington was well tanned from the Hawaiian sun, while Bennett was pale since he spent all his time in his windowless office at Circus Circus. Pennington decided the incident made the entire trip worthwhile.

But back in Reno, he fell into a funk. His heart wasn't in his work anymore. Then a friend whom he had known from childhood died. The man had been rich but died without ever really enjoying his money. What was the point of being wealthy if you were so busy working that you couldn't savor your life? He had always suspected that his father never had been happy because he spent all those years chasing money. He began thinking about his own life. Then, late one night, his telephone rang with more bad news. There had been an accident on Freeway 280 in California. Gary Schmidt, the college student who had rescued him, had been killed when the red Porsche that Pennington had given him skidded out of control on wet pavement. At the funeral, Schmidt's father told him: "Mr. Pennington, you must never feel guilt. Some things are meant to be." Pennington didn't reply. He didn't know what to say. "I shouldn't have survived, but I had," he thought, "and now this young man, with his whole life before him, was dead, and there was nothing that could be done about it."

Inside the Casino: Fire

I was working as a plainclothes investigator on the security staff at the MGM Grand Hotel on November 21, 1980, when I spotted a woman sitting by herself at the bar. She was wearing a very short dress and when I looked at her, she gave me a come-on look, so I sat down and within a few minutes she was making her pitch and we started discussing her price. That's when I busted her. I took her into the security office, where she was photographed, and then I escorted her out the side door. These gals were pretty well known, and if one of them was already with a guest who wanted her company, then we left them alone, but we didn't want them hanging around the bar looking for customers. I had just stepped back inside the building when I heard some noise to my left. There was a coffee shop about forty yards away from me and I looked over and people were running out its door. I started toward it to investigate and that's when I saw the flames. I froze for a second, and in that second those flames seemed to leap to the ceiling and explode—flying across the ceiling of the casino at lightning speed. I heard later that it took only six seconds for the fire to engulf the entire casino.

Everyone bolted for the door. There was screaming and yelling and flames everywhere and when I got outside, you could see people just piling out the door and you could hear the flames inside and you knew that people were trapped inside and there was nothing that could be done to save them. By the time that the fire trucks arrived, several of us on the security force began climbing

up the fire escapes and going onto the floors
where guests were. The fire was contained on the
first four floors, which was where the casino,
lounges, and executive offices were. The guest
rooms started on the fifth and when I went up the
fire escape onto one of the guest room floors, I
had to drop to my knees because the hallways
were filled with so much toxic smoke that you
couldn't see. I began crawling down the hall, stopping at doors, banging on them. I bumped into
something. I felt it and discovered it was a human
being. I checked for a pulse but it was too late.
The smoke had killed him. I crawled over the
body and kept going down the hallway. Whenever
you found someone, you led them outside and
then went back in, and each time you prayed that
you wouldn't find another body and sometimes
you didn't but several times you did. We did that
for four or five hours, and by that time the fire
was out and the security team was called to go inside the casino to get the cash out of the safe.

We went inside the casino and it was like a war
zone. We were standing in knee-deep water. The
huge twelve-inch steel I-beams in the ceiling had
been warped and twisted by the intensity of the
heat. The rows of slot machines looked like melted
pieces of candles. The coins were melded together.
But it was what I saw as we crossed through the
casino that gave me nightmares later. Sitting in
front of the slot machines were charred bodies. I
mean, these were people who were burned alive sitting in the casino. Later some people said it was because the people playing the machines didn't want
to leave them, but I don't know if that's true because the fire came so fast that it just caught people

totally by surprise. There was no time for many to escape.

We got to the safe and the money was perfectly fine inside, so we began loading it into pillowcases, which is what we had handy, and carrying the full bags to a pickup truck that we had parked outside. We just tossed these pillowcases into the back and then drove to a nearby motel. We made five or six trips with this truck and we put all the money into one motel room and I was chosen to stay in the room with my pistol overnight. We had guards walking up and down the hallways, but there were no extra precautions and I was locked in this room with pillowcases stuffed with millions—and I mean millions—of dollars. It would have been a huge heist if someone would have come for it. We guarded the money for three days and then a Brinks armored truck came and took it to a bank. After that I was assigned to guard the president of the company and the vice presidents, but after the fire, it wasn't the same. I had nightmares about the fire. When we first went inside the casino, we opened the doors to an elevator. There were sixteen bodies inside. Sixteen. You don't see something like that and not have it affect you.

My wife and I decided to move to Florida, where we had relatives, but after three years, we came back. We missed the twenty-four-hour excitement. They have a saying here: "Once you live in Vegas and get sand in your shoes, you may leave, but you always come back." I guess that's true no matter what you have seen.

—*Bud Boor, Luxor casino collections manager*

CHAPTER FIVE

....

Bennett Rules Supreme

Glenn Schaeffer, Bennett's new senior vice president for corporate development, climbed aboard one of Circus Circus Enterprises' corporate jets in early 1984 and set off on what he called a "proselytizing tour." He stopped in New York City first to meet with money managers and bankers, and then went to Chicago, Los Angeles, and San Francisco to meet other financiers. At each stop, he gave the same spiel: "Our hotels at Circus Circus are averaging one thousand 'turnaways' every day, which means we have every one of our rooms filled and there are still another thousand people outside wanting to check in." Obviously, Circus Circus needed to expand, but Schaeffer was convinced there was more to this trend than a shortage of rooms on the Las Vegas Strip. "The public's attitude toward gaming is changing," he explained. Delving into a briefcase filled with statistical studies, Schaeffer talked about how baby boomers were coming of age and how many of them had two incomes and were looking for somewhere to go on vacation besides grandma's house. President

Ronald Reagan was finishing his first term and the economy was rebounding. People had money to spend again. He used charts to show how Circus Circus had earned huge profits during lean times by targeting the working class and providing its customers with "more value for less money." He predicted Las Vegas was on the verge of a tremendous growth spurt.

Most of the money managers meeting with Schaeffer had never met an executive from a casino and several asked him about the mob. "Those guys are dinosaurs," Schaeffer replied. "They're gone because they can't compete in today's corporate environment. This is a new era. Casinos are legitimate businesses now." Most of the money managers politely rebuffed him, but a few did not, and Schaeffer returned with a $30 million line of credit for Circus Circus. It was a financial first. The few money lenders who had done business with casinos in the past, such as E. Parry Thomas at Valley Bank, had always charged high interest rates and demanded collateral. Other casino owners, such as Steve Wynn, had been forced to use junk bonds to finance their expansion projects in Atlantic City. Schaeffer was the first on the Strip to obtain a revolving line of investment credit for a casino company. His feat gave Circus Circus Enterprises a clear edge. It now had access to $30 million at a 9 percent interest rate while other casinos were paying 14 percent interest or higher—if they could get a loan at all.

Armed with Schaeffer's cash, Circus Circus went on a building spree. It added extra hotel towers to its Las Vegas and Reno casinos, and expanded the hotel at the Edgewater in Laughlin. Altogether, those projects added 3,263 new rooms, and every one of them was rented as soon as it was ready. The company was averaging an unheard-of 99.9 percent occupancy rate. There seemed to be no end to the hordes of visitors now pouring into Nevada. Buoyed by his first trip, Schaeffer went on another financial proselytizing tour, followed by another and another. Each time, he returned with a bigger line of credit. In the corporate boardroom, "unit growth" became a Schaeffer catchword. Here's how it worked: Whenever Circus Circus added more hotel rooms, more guests checked in, which meant there were more gamblers in the casino. Profits increased, and bigger profits pleased investors, who bought more stock. Rising stock prices delighted money lenders, who quickly agreed to lend Circus Circus more cash to expand. It was Economics 101 in its purest form, and it was making the company's two biggest shareholders and many of Bennett's Young Turks rich.

In 1986, *Forbes* magazine placed Bennett and Pennington on its annual list of the four hundred wealthiest Americans. Each man's estimated worth was $250 million. Only three other Nevada residents were on the list, and Bennett and Pennington were the only ones whose fortunes came from gambling. And Glenn Schaeffer had become a millionaire within sixteen months after going to work for Bennett, thanks to stock options and bonus pay.

Now that Circus Circus had added hotel rooms to each of its major casinos, it had nothing else to enlarge. If it wanted to keep its speeding unit-growth train on track, it had to begin building new casinos. Bennett chose Laughlin as the site for the company's first new project because the river resort was overflowing with customers. In 1986, he unveiled plans for the construction of a 1,238-room hotel and casino next door to the Edgewater. The new casino was designed to look like a giant Mississippi riverboat and was named the Colorado Belle.

Within the company, Bennett's griping about Pennington was getting worse. By now, Bennett's next-in-command,

Mike Ensign, had resigned to start his own casino company and there were no other corporate officers strong enough to serve as a buffer between the two men. In one widely gossiped-about incident, Bennett became furious after he and Pennington appeared together before a state gaming panel to answer questions about the Colorado Belle. The two men had been cordial during the public hearing but Bennett left the meeting steaming. The reason: a state official had complimented both of them for making Circus Circus profitable. "Pennington doesn't do a damn thing around here," Bennett snapped.

Not long after that incident, Bennett got angry when a manager mentioned that Pennington had been the wealthier of the two when they first bought Circus Circus. Glenn Schaeffer was sent to dig through the company's financial records and determine who had had the most money. Those documents showed that Pennington had indeed been better off and that irked Bennett even more.

"Mr. Bennett felt very strongly that he was carrying Mr. Pennington," a former Circus Circus executive explained later, "to the point that he really became obsessed with it. His complaining was really pitiful because he was a very brilliant man and everyone knew he was the driving force behind Circus Circus. He didn't need to prove anything but he felt that he did."

Bennett's constant sniping grated on Pennington. "It was disgusting," he said later. "When I first met Bill Bennett, he didn't seem this way, but once Circus Circus became successful, it was all 'I, me, and my' with him. It was sad to see a man like Bennett . . . make up stories and try to convince everyone that he was the big-ass rabbit."

Bennett soon found a way to rid himself of Pennington. He put in a call to one of the company's financial advisers at Drexel Burnham Lambert and outlined his scheme. "We came up with a way for Pennington to sell some of his stock through a public offering and get one hundred million dollars," Bennett said. "I got the attorneys to draw up the papers because I wanted Bill out of the Reno property. I wanted to put my own people up there. Anyway, that one hundred million dollars hit Pennington between the eyes. He said, 'Where do I sign?' The only mistake I made was that I should have gotten him to give up his seat on the board of directors as well as retire, but I didn't, and that later came back to cause me trouble."

Drexel Burnham Lambert sold Pennington's shares in a single block when the stock hit $32⅞ a share, making the sale the largest by an individual in the history of the New York Stock Exchange. Even after selling three million shares, Pennington still owned 16.1 percent of the company, but Bennett held even more with his 25.8 percent share. As part of the deal, Pennington announced he was retiring. He was sixty-five and he had problems more important than Bennett on his mind. His second wife was in the advanced stages of Parkinson's disease and doctors gave her little hope of surviving.

Bennett was at last finally undisputedly in charge.

Glenn Schaeffer was delighted that Circus Circus had constructed a new casino in Laughlin, but he had much bigger plans in mind than building replicas of Mississippi riverboats. By 1987, he was the company's chief financial officer, a promotion that made him, at age thirty, the youngest CFO on record at any New York Stock Exchange company. Just as important, he was working for the most powerful casino owner on the Strip. Only two other Strip owners were as wealthy as Bennett. Hilton Hotels magnate William Barron Hilton owned the International and the Flamingo, and Kirk Kerkorian owned the Sands and the Desert Inn. Both men, however, were busy focusing on other nongaming business deals and were rarely in town. None of the other casino owners on the Strip had as much money or clout as Bennett. (After Howard Hughes died in 1976, his Summa Corporation divested itself of his casinos.) His corporate counsel, Michael H. Sloan, had helped cement Bennett's power by doling out hundreds of thousands of dollars in political contributions to state legislators, but ironically Bennett rarely used this clout. Simply having it seemed enough.

In a lengthy internal memo written in late 1987, Schaeffer urged his boss to seize the moment by building a new hotel on the Las Vegas Strip. He recalled that Jay Sarno's Caesars Palace had been the first-ever themed resort, and that Circus Circus had boomed under Bennett by becoming a family-oriented casino. He talked about the emerging financial clout of baby boomers, and he urged Bennett to construct the first family-themed resort on the Strip. His model was Disneyland.

Not everyone in the company liked Schaeffer's idea. No one had built a new casino on the Strip in sixteen years. Some managers argued that Circus Circus needed to expand into Atlantic City. A few favored simply doing nothing. After all, there were no guarantees that Las Vegas would continue drawing large crowds.

While Bennett's underlings argued about the memo, rival Las Vegas casino owner Steve Wynn announced plans to build a Strip resort that would be larger and grander than anything anyone had ever seen. He was calling it the Mirage and promising it would be open by 1989.

Circus Circus had lost the lead.

Bennett called Schaeffer into his office.

"How many rooms do you think we should build?" he asked.

"Three thousand," Schaeffer replied. That was the same number as the Mirage.

"I want to build more rooms than Steve Wynn," said Bennett. "Let's build four thousand." No one had ever built a hotel that large.

A few days later, Bennett announced that Circus Circus Enterprises was beginning construction of a $300 million resort on Tropicana Avenue. The casino would be built in the shape of a medieval castle. The similarity between the architectural drawings that Bennett released to reporters and the magic castle at Disneyland was not a coincidence. Just as Schaeffer had suggested, Circus Circus was going after the identical market as Mickey Mouse.

Bennett told reporters that Richard Banis, age thirty-nine, who had replaced Michael Ensign as the company's executive vice president, would be in charge of building the castle. Schaeffer would raise the $300 million it would cost and William Paulos, age thirty-six, would be its general manager once it opened. Bennett was sending his Young Turks into battle with his upstart rival, Steve Wynn.

CHAPTER SIX

....

Steve Wynn, Visionary

Bill Bennett's net worth was more than the value of
Steve Wynn's entire company, but Wynn had bragged
that someday he would build the greatest hotel-casino
in Las Vegas and he made good on that promise when
he unveiled his plans for the Mirage. Wynn estimated it
would cost $600 million, making it the most expensive
resort ever built on the Strip. His plans called for three
hotel towers, each with one thousand rooms and exteriors tinted with gold glass. They were to rise above an
atrium that contained a tropical rainforest with cooling
mists, live orchids, exotic trees, waterfalls, and streams.
From this glass-domed hub, guests would be able to enter a galleria of high-end retail shops, dine in gourmet
restaurants, or relax in intimate lounges. All paths
would crisscross the 95,500-square-foot casino, which
would be decorated in a festive tropical motif and have
polished wood gaming tables and piped-in Jimmy Buffet music. There would be tons of marble, miles of
brass, carpets so thick your toes would disappear in
them. Outside, the swimming pools would be edged

with greenery, fountains, and more waterfalls, creating an atmosphere of private lagoons.

Wynn designed much of the Mirage himself and architecture critics were quick to praise his skill. One described his creation as a "spectacular environment that artfully integrates casino, showroom, shopping, restaurants, and lounges." "The Mirage will challenge all of the old rules and succeed in setting new standards for design, ambiance, and entertainment," wrote another. But even those lavish endorsements were not enough for Wynn. He paraphrased George S. Kaufman by saying that the Mirage was "the way that God would do it if He had money." A joke soon made the rounds on the Strip. "What is the only thing bigger than Steve Wynn's brass balls?" His friends and enemies alike quipped, "His ego." Not since the days of Jay Sarno had the city seen such an unabashed self-promoter. With his carefully groomed good looks, perfectly tailored silk suits, and gleaming white teeth, Wynn strutted onto the Strip with the cockiness of a riverboat gambler and quickly challenged Bill Bennett's kingpin role.

The story of Wynn's success was so intriguing that it proved impossible for reporters to ignore. Nearly every major national magazine published a flattering profile of Wynn after he started work on the Mirage. He always proved a willing subject. Usually, he wore snug-fitting polo shirts and tight blue jeans that displayed a physique kept taut by bodybuilding and his many hobbies, which he was proud to mention: downhill skiing, windsurfing, rock-climbing, Jet Skiing, and rodeo steer-roping. His stories were perfectly paced. Whenever Wynn was asked about his background, he always began by recalling his humble roots and talking about how much he loved and missed his father, Michael M. Wynn. In nearly every interview, there would come a moment when Wynn would talk about his dad. With tears welling in his eyes, he would describe how he had been in college when his father died. "I would trade all of this," he would say, sweeping his arms toward everything around him, "for fifteen minutes now with my father." After a pause, he would add, "To have him . . . see how this has all turned out." Not even Wynn's harshest critics doubted that Wynn's adoration of his dad was sincere, but it was hard not to register the timing and delivery of these moving comments, which always began as soon as the tape recorders and television cameras flipped on.

Steve Wynn's father had introduced him to gambling. It was in Mike Wynn's blood. He was a compulsive bettor. He had found his niche at the age of seventeen, when he got a job in a bingo parlor in Revere, Massachusetts. Playing bingo for prize money was illegal, but the game was so popular that the police didn't interfere. Within three years, Mike Wynn owned the hall and was expanding his bingo operations into three other states. Shortly before World War II, he moved to New Haven, Connecticut, with his bride, Zelma Kutner. Their son, Stephen Alan Wynn, was born there on January 27, 1942. Life inside the Wynn household was raucous. Mike was hyperactive, Zelma was dramatic, both were loud. A childhood friend of Steve Wynn's would later recall that no one in the Wynn family ever spoke in a normal voice. They screamed. Nor was any family event ever routine. To be average was unacceptable. It bore the scent of defeat.

As Mike Wynn's bingo operations spread into seven states, he tried to expand into Las Vegas, but his application for a gaming license in 1952 was rejected for reasons no one now knows. At the time, Nevada was issuing gaming licenses even to suspected mobsters, yet the senior Wynn didn't pass muster. Some claimed his request was blocked by rival bingo operators, others

that he didn't have enough "juice," still others that he
had unsavory connections in New York City that worried state gaming officials. Whatever the reason, Wynn
gave up the idea and stayed in the East. But he had
brought his ten-year-old son with him to Las Vegas
when he made his license appeal and Steve Wynn later
said he had been smitten by the place. Las Vegas had a
special feel to it, he would tell reporters. It was a town
where anyone with dreams could make a lot of money.

In June 1961, Mike Wynn shut down all his operations and moved to a crossroads known as Wayson
Corners, just outside Annapolis, Maryland, where he
bought a legal bingo hall. "If you ran a bingo parlor,
some people looked at you as if you were a bookie,"
Zelma Wynn recalled years later in the Nevada *Casino
Journal*. She and her husband had bigger plans for their
oldest son and his brother, Kenneth, who was ten years
younger. Steve was sent to an elite preparatory school
and then to the University of Pennsylvania to prepare
for a career in law or possibly politics. During a break
between semesters, he joined his family on vacation in
Miami at the luxurious Fontainebleau Hotel and while
there, his father arranged a blind date for him with the
daughter of a gambling friend. Elaine Pascal was a political science major at UCLA, a beauty pageant winner,
and a college cheerleader. "I wasn't sure what Steve was
going to do," she later confided, "but on the first date I
knew that we were going to do it together. There was
something about Steve. He had, I don't know, I call him
the flimflam man. And he flimflammed me . . . I thought
that, 'Here's a guy who I'm going to latch onto because
it's going to be an exciting ride.' " She transferred to a
university closer to him and they planned to marry.

In early 1963, however, Mike Wynn was hospital-
ized after experiencing an irregular heartbeat. The doctors recommended open heart surgery, an operation

that was still rare in those days. The night before the surgery, he called his son to his bedside and said that if he didn't survive, he wanted Steve to pay his debts to Charlie Meyerson, his New York bookie. He owed Meyerson $15,000. Mike Wynn died on the operating table at age forty-six. At twenty-one, Steve Wynn was suddenly responsible for his mother, younger brother, and the running of the family bingo parlor. The first thing he did was go to see his dad's bookie. Charlie Meyerson laughed. "Don't you know a gambler's debts die with him?" he asked Wynn. It was the start of an enduring friendship, and even though it would later cause Wynn a considerable headache with gaming regulators who disliked Meyerson's colorful past, Wynn was never to back away from his friend.

Wynn married Elaine and took charge of the Maryland bingo operation. He had been accepted at Yale Law School, but decided not to go. "I was calling the numbers at the bingo hall and Elaine was counting the money," Wynn said. "We worked constantly. We had no life. We had no friends."

In June 1967, Wynn decided to move his family to Las Vegas. Over the years, he has told at least two different stories about what led him to the Strip. One version, which he gave to nearly all the reporters who wrote profiles of him in the 1980s, repeated to the author of this book, and reiterated during sworn testimony in an August 1997 court hearing, has him deciding to move to Las Vegas at the request of a multimillionaire.

"I didn't want to spend my life in the bingo business," Wynn explained, "so I looked around for other ways to make money." The corridor between Washington, D.C., and Baltimore, Maryland, was booming with new homes and businesses, so, Wynn said, he picked a plot of land he thought was ripe for development and contacted

John MacArthur, the owner of Bankers Life & Casualty Company in Chicago. Wynn had heard MacArthur was willing to lend money to young businessmen who needed help getting started, so he asked the insurance magnate for a $1 million loan and offered him part of his family's bingo operation as collateral. According to Wynn, MacArthur wasn't interested in the land deal but was intrigued by the bingo operation, and sought his advice. MacArthur's insurance company had taken control of the Last Frontier in Las Vegas after its owner died. It had been built in 1942, only the second casino on the Strip, and over the years it had fallen into disrepair. The casino was now closed but a group of investors was offering to buy it.

"MacArthur asked if I would be interested in going to Las Vegas and meeting these people and being a representative—his representative—and he said that maybe he could get me stock in the Last Frontier at a preferred rate."

Wynn jumped at the chance. With MacArthur picking up the tab, Wynn and Elaine flew to the Strip and met with two of the Las Vegas investors, T. W. Richardson and Maurice Friedman. After their meeting, Wynn urged MacArthur to go forward with the lease purchase deal.

Over the years, Wynn's critics have questioned why a multimillionaire would suddenly ask a small-time Maryland bingo hall operator whom he hardly knew for advice about a Las Vegas casino, especially since Wynn had never operated one, and then cut him in on the deal. Wynn always replied that he was as surprised as his critics. "I told MacArthur that running a bingo parlor was entirely different from running a casino, but he said, 'Gambling is gambling.' "

Back in September 1981, however, at a licensing hearing before the Casino Control Commission in New Jersey, Wynn told a much different story.

My father was an inveterate gambler. He bet
baseball, he bet football, and anything else
that he could bet, and he bet with two fellows, one by the name of Charles Meyerson
and one named Herb Liebert. They were his
bookmakers. . . . One day Herb Liebert
mentioned that he was going to Palm
Springs and I said, "Boy, it would be nice for
Elaine and me to go away. We've never had
a vacation."

Wynn said Liebert took them along to Palm Springs in
1965, and while they were eating dinner one night at
the popular Ruby Dunes restaurant, Frank Sinatra
came waltzing in and recognized Liebert.

Sinatra came over to the table and said hello
to us. He said, "I'm opening up at the Sands
Hotel in Las Vegas in two days, why don't
you come over for the opening? You will be
my guests." Herb Liebert looked at Elaine
and me and said, "Would you like to go?" I
said, "Sure." We went to Las Vegas and saw
Frank Sinatra perform . . . it was the days
when he used to work with Dean Martin
and Peter Lawford and Sammy Davis Jr. and
it was the very epitome of glamour. When
we went to dinner that night, T. W. Richardson and Maurice Friedman came over to our
table to say hello to Herb Liebert. I had no
idea who these people were. But Richardson
and Friedman said to Herb Liebert, "We're
going to build a hotel" . . . and Liebert introduced me and said, "This is Steve Wynn

> and he is in the bingo business in Maryland
> and is a very successful businessman." ...
> Richardson says, "Well, maybe he can be an
> investor." That's the way things worked in
> the early days of Las Vegas. They were al-
> ways looking for people to put up money
> and they weren't too discriminating.

Wynn testified that T. W. Richardson called him soon afterward to say he and Friedman had decided to lease the Last Frontier casino from John MacArthur and renovate it. He asked if Wynn wanted to become one of their partners.

Why Wynn would tell different stories about how he met Richardson and Friedman is unclear. Perhaps it has something to do with the timing of the stories. In 1981, when he testified before the New Jersey Casino Control Commission, Wynn still fancied himself as a rogue in Las Vegas and apparently didn't mind discussing how his father's bookmaker had squired him around the Strip. But in 1989, with the opening of the Mirage, Wynn began seeking greater respectability; better to have been introduced to Las Vegas by a multi-millionaire businessman than a bookie. What is undisputed is that Wynn bought a 3 percent ownership in the casino for $45,000, which he borrowed from his family's bingo operation and a family friend, and he, Elaine, and their infant daughter, Kevin, moved into a rental house in Las Vegas so that Wynn could begin work as the slot manager at what was now being called the Vegas Frontier.

Scandal struck before the casino even opened. State gaming officials discovered that Maurice Friedman and three of the casino's other big investors were actually front men for a Detroit-based mob family. A horrified

Wynn was called before a grand jury looking into the casino's investors. He was cleared of any wrongdoing but he would recall later that the incident had embarrassed him. Even though it was widely known that most Strip casinos were mob run, Wynn said he had honestly believed Friedman was a legitimate businessman. He didn't know anything about the other investors, although he wished later that he had checked. Friedman cut a deal with prosecutors and agreed to testify against his cohorts in return for immunity. All three were found guilty of conspiring to hide the real ownership of their shares, were forced to divest, and were fined heavily. For his part, Friedman fled to Los Angeles, where he was arrested a few years later for cheating at cards in the Friars Club, a popular Hollywood hangout for movie stars. Friedman had drilled holes in the ceiling of a card room where as much as $50,000 was gambled each night. His accomplices used the peepholes to spy on the gamblers below and relayed messages through radio transmitters to Friedman. This time, he was sent to prison.

After the state kicked out the investors with ties to organized crime, Wynn and the remaining shareholders were free to open their casino. "It was a mess," Wynn recalled. "I knew the place was going to be a financial disaster." Friedman had installed his cronies in most of the top casino jobs and the new owners weren't sure who was honest. Ten days before the Vegas Frontier's scheduled July 1967 grand opening, E. Parry Thomas, the president of Valley Bank, approached Wynn and the other investors with a solution to their problem. Howard Hughes, who had bought the Desert Inn four months earlier, was willing to pay $10 million for the Vegas Frontier, for which Wynn and the others had paid $3.6 million—but only if every investor agreed to the deal. "I was delighted," said Wynn, who would have received $195,000 for his $45,000 worth of shares. Wynn urged the other investors to sell, but one of them refused and Hughes withdrew his bid.

As Wynn had predicted, the Vegas Frontier was a financial flop, and a few months later, when Howard Hughes again sent banker Thomas to negotiate a sale, Wynn and his fellow investors agreed—this time to a much lower offer. Wynn recouped $45,000 but nothing more. As soon as the purchase went through, Hughes fired the Vegas Frontier's managers, including Wynn. He thought about moving back to Maryland, but banker Thomas convinced him to stay. By then, Wynn said, "Parry Thomas had taken a shine to me. I had lost my father . . . and Parry adopted me. Everybody teases me about it. I'm like his sixth child. . . . He said: 'Steve, you ought to stay in Las Vegas. It's a great place for a young guy and you will get into something. This town is changing very quickly.' "

Wynn dreamed of owning his own casino and knew how much power Thomas wielded. He cemented his bond with Thomas for nearly a year, living off checks sent by his mother from the family's Maryland bingo operation. The two men went skiing, joined each other on family picnics, and frequently ate dinner together. His determination paid off when Thomas finally suggested it was time for Wynn to buy a business. He didn't offer him a casino, however. Instead, he lent $65,000 to the twenty-five-year-old Wynn so he could buy a liquor distributorship called Best Brands. Three years later, Wynn sold it and a warehouse he had built for a tidy $130,000 profit.

Wynn's next venture still ranks as the biggest financial coup in the history of the Strip. With Parry Thomas's help, he bought a 1.1-acre tract next door to Caesars Palace for $1 million, borrowed, of course, from Valley Bank. He bought it from Howard Hughes, who had been leasing the narrow strip to Caesars

Palace to use as a parking lot. "It was the first time Hughes had ever sold anything," Wynn boasted. "I got a phone call from Walter Cronkite's office at the CBS Evening News, the *Wall Street Journal* called about the sale . . . I was just dancing. . . ."

Caesars Palace chairman Clifford Perlman wasn't. He claimed Hughes had promised to give Caesars Palace the first shot at buying the tract if he ever decided to sell it and he suspected that banker Thomas had somehow engineered the sale to Wynn. Perlman called Wynn on the day the purchase was made public and offered him $250,000 more than he had paid, but Wynn told him it wasn't enough. When an outraged Perlman threatened legal action, Wynn replied with a threat of his own. Unless Caesars Palace paid him a handsome profit, he would build a "parasite" casino on the land. Parasites were tiny casinos, filled mostly with slot machines, built next to larger casinos so they could feed off their business. If Wynn had not had the financial backing of Thomas, Perlman might have laughed. But he did, and the thought of having a parasite next door to the posh Caesars Palace was intolerable. Perlman caved in and paid Wynn $2.2 million for the tract. Wynn's personal take was $800,000. He was close to earning his first million dollars and had yet to own a casino. Details of the sale were published in the *Las Vegas Sun*, which wrote: "Steve Wynn, at age thirty, closed a deal many men his senior would give their eyeteeth to have." Wynn had only been in town for five years, but he was quickly becoming "one of Las Vegas's brightest business luminaries," said the newspaper, and was "on a rapid rise to fame and power." Perlman was not as complimentary.

Parry Thomas and his protégé next turned their sights to an even bigger fish—the Golden Nugget, a downtown casino that had fallen on hard times. They chose it because the Golden Nugget was a rarity in the business—one of the only casinos in Las Vegas owned by stockholders, who traded its shares publicly on a tiny California stock exchange. Thomas had tried to buy the casino in 1969 but had failed, so he sent Wynn after it, armed with his new $800,000 bankroll. When Wynn ran out of cash, he borrowed more from Valley Bank, until he owned a big enough block of stock to demand a seat on the Golden Nugget's board of directors. "The place was in pathetic shape," Wynn said later. "Stealing was rampant." Wynn threatened to sue the board for mismanagement unless he was put in charge. The board's chairman, who was close to retirement and wanted to avoid a nasty fight, agreed to step down after he was told that he could keep his lucrative retirement package. At the age of thirty, Wynn finally had a casino to run. He was the youngest casino owner on record in the history of Nevada.

Although Glitter Gulch sparkled with neon lights, downtown casinos were still considered grind joints. Urban seediness, however, didn't fit with Wynn's ambitions. His first month in charge, he closed half of the casino and began remodeling it with loans from Valley Bank. Other downtown casino owners said he was wasting his money. If their customers wanted marble and mahogany, they could visit the Strip. But Wynn ignored them. He made the Golden Nugget building sparkle and then he turned his attention to its lounge.

In what would prove to be a brilliant move, Wynn hired singer Kenny Rogers as the casino's entertainment director. Rogers had achieved some fame with his band, The First Edition, but he was not yet well-known and he needed a job. Rogers was embarrassed to be working in downtown Las Vegas because of its shoddy reputation, but Wynn assured him that his new job would be "the best thing that has happened to either of us." A few weeks later, Rogers released one of the biggest hits of his career, a song called "Lucille." It was the first of a string of country-western hits, and Rogers took advantage of his rising fame to recruit other top country-western stars—singers such as Dolly Parton and Willie Nelson—to the Golden Nugget. Wynn capitalized on the tiny size of his five-hundred-seat lounge by announcing that he wasn't *booking* big-name entertainers into his casino; he and Kenny Rogers were *inviting* their friends to come and perform there. "Suppose I could sell discriminating people on the idea of being involved in an atmosphere almost like a concert in the East Room of the White House," Wynn told a reporter, explaining his philosophy, "like a private show with Frank Sinatra. Wouldn't that be fetching? And suppose, as part of the weekend, they could meet him, and we had special parties, and we did the whole weekend. And suppose the service in this hotel was so elegant we could build a special event around our entertainer, and I could take Frank Sinatra and Diana Ross and Kenny and Willie and they could be a gift for the weekend. Come for a special weekend—a theme party at the Nugget. That's not the same as the star policy. That's another dimension altogether."

The Golden Nugget lounge became the most fashionable gathering spot in town. "It was the best way to see and get close to these wonderful stars," recalled Diane Spataro, who worked there as a "showroom server," the union's title for the waitresses who serve drinks in Las Vegas lounges and theaters. (The price of two drinks is traditionally included in each show's ticket.) "Steve Wynn worked us like dogs," said Spataro. "We were paid union minimum wage for six-hour shifts and only six hours, but you came in an hour early and you didn't leave until two or three in the morning. It broke the union rules, but no one ever complained because we were working for tips and we were making such good money that you would do anything. You see, even though we were working hard, Steve

Wynn was very good to you. He made you want to do your best and he rewarded you—it's just that you just never wanted to get on his bad side."

When Wynn had first taken control of his father's Maryland bingo operation, he had told his younger brother that if an owner really wanted to learn what was happening in his business, he had "to walk around and have the sniff of the place." Wynn left no area of the Golden Nugget unsniffed. He ordered his custodians to paint the white line on the curb in front of the casino daily because it got scuffed so often. He designed the uniforms for the security guards and ordered specially made pistols for each guard that resembled old Wild West .45 revolvers. If he spotted a burned-out lightbulb, he threw a fit. Spataro described the time when Paul Anka complained that the showroom servers were distracting the audience by delivering drinks during his performance. Spataro and her coworkers were ordered to have all five hundred ticketholders served before the lights were dimmed. "This was impossible, so we literally would get down on our knees so that Anka couldn't see us and we would crawl along the floor with a tray filled with drinks, serving people."

During Wynn's first year in charge, the Golden Nugget showed a 400 percent increase in revenues, earning $4.2 million before taxes and delighting Wynn. But in its second year, the amount didn't change. The casino wasn't growing. Wynn decided to add a hotel on the theory that "the more rooms you have, the more money you make." It was the same premise Circus Circus was following, but no downtown casino had ever added rooms because no one thought tourists would want to stay there. When the Golden Nugget's general manager, Bob Maxey, argued against borrowing the money, Wynn replied: "The Golden Nugget is going to be a growth company. . . . We are not going to sit back and clip coupons." He got a $12 million loan from Valley Bank and built a parking garage and a six-hundred-room hotel. Before-tax profits shot to $12 million the next year. But Wynn still wasn't satisfied. This was chump change compared to the profits being pocketed by Strip hotels, and in early 1978 he hired an architectural firm to design the first skyscraper hotel to be built in downtown Las Vegas. But he dropped the project a few weeks later—with good reason. Legalized gambling had arrived in Atlantic City.

The grand opening of the Resorts International casino on Memorial Day weekend was heavily covered in the media, and on Tuesday morning Wynn called the company's president, Jack Davis, to congratulate him. Wynn knew Davis because their families often vacationed at the same ski resort. He had seen television reports about the huge lines that had formed outside the Atlantic City casino and he asked Davis if he wanted to "trade numbers." The Golden Nugget's weekend casino earnings had set new records and Wynn was eager to boast about them. Davis said he had been so busy that he hadn't gotten an accurate count yet.

"Okay, Jack," Wynn replied. "Let's just exchange our slot figures." Slot machines were tracked by computers, making their winnings easy to tabulate. The eight hundred slot machines at the Golden Nugget, Wynn bragged, had collected $210,000 in winnings. "Davis was real quiet on the phone and then he said the slots at Resorts had earned *five times* that amount," Wynn recalled. Wynn didn't think that he had heard Davis correctly, so he asked him to repeat himself.

"I said, we earned about five times what you did," Davis replied.

"How many machines were you operating?"

"We have eight hundred, but only six hundred and twenty were working."

"Are you telling me, Jack, that you won a million dollars just in your slot machines?"

"Well, actually, it was a little more."

"How about the games?"

"About the same—a million in winnings."

Wynn was flabbergasted. "For a gambling person, those numbers were insane. No one had ever approached those sort of numbers—ever," he said. Ten days later, he flew with Bob Maxey to Atlantic City to see what was going on. Wynn had convinced himself that the Resorts' casino's weekend take was a fluke, caused by its holiday opening. But when he stepped inside, he knew better. It was jumping. "Everywhere there were human beings. This was a Thursday, in the middle of the afternoon—a slow time for us normally—and the place was packed." Wynn strolled over to a blackjack table. He was looking for the sign on the table that specified the minimum bet for each hand that a player had to wager. It was $25. The table had people waiting in line to play at midday at $25 per hand—that was unheard-of in Las Vegas! "We've got to get ourselves a piece of land here," Wynn told Maxey. "We've got to do it now."

Within hours, Wynn had bought the aged Strand Hotel on the Boardwalk for $8 million. On the flight home, he calculated that he would need between $80 and $100 million to raze the hotel and construct a new one. That was more than Las Vegas banker Parry Thomas could swing, so Wynn began looking elsewhere. His search soon led to Michael Milken at Drexel Burnham Lambert in Los Angeles. Although Milken's bosses had always been against getting involved in gambling operations, Milken convinced them that gaming was a legitimate, lucrative, and untapped industry ripe for growth, so they accepted Wynn as a client. Not long after that, Wynn and Milken left on a twenty-six–city tour to raise cash from lending institutions, but they couldn't find a single backer.

By December 1978, Wynn was sweating financially. His interest payment on the $8 million that he had borrowed to buy the Strand Hotel was coming due, and he was hard-pressed for cash. He turned to a Las Vegas CPA named Clyde Turner for help. Turner had drafted many of the state's modern gaming laws when he worked for the Nevada Gaming Commission, including those that dealt with corporate takeovers of casinos and high-level casino financing. Turner became the Golden Nugget's new CFO at a salary of $100,000 a year, plus lucrative stock options—more than Wynn had ever paid anyone. He proved to be worth it. Working with Milken, Turner devised a new financial plan for the Boardwalk casino. Banker Parry Thomas then arranged to have Milken, Turner, and Wynn present this plan to a group of Mormon bankers in Salt Lake City. Although their religion prohibited its followers from gambling, the Mormons agreed to invest $160 million in Wynn's Boardwalk casino after hearing him speak. In return, the Mormons were given the first high-interest junk bonds ever issued by Drexel Burnham Lambert. "The riskiest move that Steve Wynn made in his entire career was not when we opened the Mirage, as everyone likes to think," Clyde Turner said later. "It was when we made our move into Atlantic City. That is when he could have lost it all."

The construction of Wynn's 506-room Atlantic City Golden Nugget hotel and casino began in July 1979 and Wynn designed his new property to be the most elegant on the Boardwalk. Its front doors opened onto a five-story-tall atrium with a giant golden birdcage holding five mechanical parrots that spoke in the voices of Louis Armstrong, Bette Midler, Maurice Chevalier, Mae West, and Don Adams. The lobby glittered with glass, brass, and marble. The casino had more bells and whistles than any other. Wynn bought jet helicopters to ferry high rollers back and forth from New York City. He designed suites that were as opulent as any Park Avenue residence.

New Jersey officials were being deluged with so many requests for gaming licenses that they let known casino operators, such as Wynn, begin constructing their casinos before they were officially issued state gaming licenses. This wasn't normally a problem because the casino owners already had passed muster in Nevada. But a few weeks before Wynn's Boardwalk casino was about to open, the New Jersey Casino Control Commission announced it had received "allegations from a number of sources which suggest that Stephen Wynn may have been involved in the use of cocaine in Las Vegas." During the next nine months, a team of New Jersey investigators pored over Wynn's past. Finally, he was called before the full commission where he was grilled for three days. The most dramatic testimony came when Wynn was asked if he had ever used cocaine. "I have not," he answered. The commission then questioned him about sworn statements signed several months earlier by three women who claimed they had seen Wynn snort cocaine at parties. Wynn's attorneys promptly submitted signed recantations from two of the women. One of them admitted that she had made up the charge against Wynn to embarrass him because she was a disgruntled former Golden Nugget employee. This left a single witness still sticking by her story and Wynn's attorneys produced evidence that showed she was an admitted prostitute. They gave the commission statements signed by prominent Las Vegas residents who swore that Wynn had been with them on the night when the prostitute claimed she had watched Wynn using cocaine. The commission ruled that Wynn's lone accuser was not a credible witness, and in a unanimous vote, issued him a New Jersey gaming license.

The Atlantic City Golden Nugget earned nearly $18 million in profits during its first six months, a record that stunned its five Boardwalk rivals. Wynn later credited a quick change in his marketing campaign with much of the casino's success. Initially, he had planned to attract customers by doing exactly what he had done in Las Vegas: booking big-name entertainers into his lounge. But he soon decided that was a waste of money. "The people coming to Atlantic City were only interested in coming to gamble," he said. "The shows were a time-consuming diversion that they didn't have time for." Wynn slashed his entertainment costs and instead bought his own fleet of buses to bring day-trippers into Atlantic City from nearby cities like Philadelphia and New York. There was a shortage of buses at the time, so gamblers scrambled for seats on Wynn's new coaches. Naturally, his drivers delivered them to the Golden Nugget.

There were other reasons for the high profits. Steve Wynn's Golden Nugget had style. He flooded the local airways with television commercials that showed him greeting Frank Sinatra as the veteran crooner strolled into the hotel.

"Hi, Mr. Sinatra, I'm Steve Wynn. I run this place."

"You see I get enough towels," Sinatra replied.

Wynn's Boardwalk casino attracted not only hordes of day-trippers, but several mobsters. Wynn had hired his father's former bookie, Charlie Meyerson, as the New York marketing director for the casino, and state investigators would later allege that Meyerson had arranged for free hotel rooms, food, and beverages for fifty-nine convicted criminals. Meyerson would insist that he had never knowingly invited anyone with a criminal record to gamble at a Wynn-owned casino. If a mobster had visited the casino, Meyerson said, he had learned about the player's shady past only after the gambler was gone. Gaming officials in New Jersey and

Nevada later agreed that Meyerson had done nothing improper as a casino host. There were no rules in place that required casino employees to know whether or not their customers were mobsters.

Still, Wynn began being criticized in the media because of several sensational incidents at his casino. One such affair began late one night in November 1982 when a Harvard-trained Manhattan lawyer named Anthony C. Castelbuono arrived at the Golden Nugget with his bodyguard, a personal valet, and several suitcases stuffed with small bills. Castelbuono handed over his suitcases to accountants in the casino's cage and announced that he wanted to play baccarat. Charlie Meyerson arranged for him to begin playing while his money was still being counted. It took nearly six hours to add up the bills. The total: $1,187,450. Because it was decidedly unusual for a gambler to bring in such a large amount of cash, the casino made a list of the bills by denomination. Castelbuono gambled for three days and when he got ready to leave, demanded he be paid in cash. He was given $800,000, the amount he had left. FBI agents arrested him a short time later and accused him of laundering money at the Golden Nugget for a Sicily-based heroin smuggling operation. An IRS investigator claimed at Castelbuono's trial that he had entered the Golden Nugget with the equivalent of 280 pounds of bills. When stacked together, they measured six feet high, six feet wide, and six feet deep. But he had left the casino with only 16 pounds of bills. His $800,000 was in $10,000 bundles of $100 bills and was small enough to fit into a briefcase. Castelbuono was convicted, sentenced to fifteen years in prison, and fined $50,000. Although the Golden Nugget cooperated fully with the FBI, the money-laundering incident was so widely publicized that Wynn felt compelled to issue a written statement. He reminded the public that the Golden Nugget was "not a church or tower of theological construction."

The Golden Nugget's huge profits in Atlantic City didn't last, in part because a new player moved onto the Boardwalk and opened two even grander casinos. New York real estate developer Donald Trump and Wynn publicly clashed from the moment they became rivals. Ironically, Trump ended up helping Wynn line his pockets. By 1986, the Boardwalk Golden Nugget was losing money. That same year, Trump began buying shares of Bally Entertainment because he had set his eye on taking control of Bally's Park Place casino, a jewel on the Boardwalk. Alarmed that their company was a takeover target, Bally's management hired a team of advisers to help them stop Trump. The advisers came up with a foolproof plan. According to New Jersey law, no one could own more than three casinos in Atlantic City, and Trump already owned two. He could only buy one more. The way to stop him from taking over Bally Entertainment, the advisers said, was for it to buy a second Boardwalk property. That would give the company two casinos, or one too many for Trump to be allowed to swallow the company. Bally decided to go after Wynn's money-losing casino because it was the only one available. Wynn figured out what was happening and took advantage of it. He demanded $440 million for his Golden Nugget, which analysts estimated was worth $160 million at best. Bally paid his price.

Wynn's personal net worth was $2 million before he expanded into Atlantic City. Seven years later, he had a net worth of $75 million and a company with a potful of cash. But while his downtown Golden Nugget casino in Las Vegas was still thriving, his personal life was in turmoil. He and Elaine were divorced, although they remained friends and continued to live in the same house. Neither would discuss why they had separated.

Wynn also revealed that he had been diagnosed with retinitis pigmentosa, an inherited, progressive, and incurable retinal disease that eventually leads to blindness. Undeterred, he had special lights installed in his office to enhance his vision and announced his next project.

"A statistic that sticks with me time and time again is the one that concerns the Disney organization's attendance figures," Wynn announced to his staff one morning. The Vatican in Rome attracts two and a half million visitors a year, he explained. About three million Muslims visit Mecca during Holy Week. By comparison, more than thirteen and a half million people visited Walt Disney World in 1980 and another twelve million went to Disneyland. "I am not going to suggest that Mickey Mouse is innately any more attractive than Mohammed," Wynn cracked, "but I am saying that maybe it is a function of our time . . . that people are in love with the happy fantasy environment that Disneyland created." It wasn't just kids, he continued. Adults liked Disneyland too. "Why? Because of that complete release and relief from the responsibility and the seriousness of everyday life . . . and that's what a casino is about in the first place." Wynn had reached the same conclusion that Glenn Schaeffer was suggesting in the internal memo he was circulating at Circus Circus. It was time, Wynn told his managers, for Disneyland to come to the Las Vegas Strip.

While some thought he was foolhardy when he announced plans to build a three-thousand-room resort, Wynn felt confident about the Mirage, in part because he had studied his competitors' financial statements. Bally's, which was the former MGM Grand Hotel, was attracting customers by offering them high-class entertainment. Hilton's International Hotel was earning a profit catering to conventions. Caesars Palace wooed high rollers with its baccarat pits and generous credit lines. "Every one of the components needed for a megaresort already existed on the Strip," Wynn recalled, "and all of these components had grown from chance. There was none conceived as a single entity. Physically, they were spread out and inefficient. All the hotels had been added onto and added onto, making them ramshackle, wandering things. Now just imagine if you put all of these components under one roof. We knew that if we had entertainment as good as Bally's, as many rooms and conventioneers as Hilton, and a casino that offered high rollers the baccarat pits and magnificent suites that Caesars had, then we would be profitable." Wynn also knew another piece of critical information. His downtown Golden Nugget casino was turning away hundreds of people each night who wanted to book rooms but couldn't because there weren't enough in town to keep up with the demand. "Deciding to build the Mirage was as risky as spitting and trying to hit the floor," he quipped. Investors agreed. Wynn telephoned his pal Michael Milken, and this time they were able to raise the $600 million that Wynn needed through junk bonds without the need to go on a cross-country tour to solicit money lenders. It was all done by telephone.

The grand opening of the Mirage in November 1989 marked the beginning of a new era on the Strip. The super casino was born. Wynn's resort soon replaced the Hoover Dam as the most visited tourist site in all of Nevada. Its casino was so crowded that it was difficult even for high rollers to find seats. In glowing press reports, Steve Wynn was declared a visionary. One journalist wrote: "His face is now the face of Las Vegas."

Bill Bennett watched Wynn's soaring popularity without comment. His Young Turks were entering late into the race to build a new Strip resort, but Bennett felt confident that they would outdo his newest rival.

Inside the Casino:
Cocaine and Sex

This town really rocked during the 1980s before
everyone started worrying about getting AIDS
and the corporate bigwigs started requiring employees to take drug tests. There was cocaine
everywhere. We called it enjoying the three "C's"
of Las Vegas—cocaine, cocktail waitresses, and
cognac! I was working in a downtown joint where
dealers were doing lines in the employee lounge
and everyone looked the other way. It wasn't just
dealers back in those days either. I was younger
then, of course, and single, and I remember that it
wasn't uncommon for me to have women slip me
the keys to their rooms after they had played
blackjack at one of the tables where I was dealing.
Hell, I had them get up and follow me around the
casino when the floor manager would rotate me
to a different table to give another dealer his
break.

One night I had this gorgeous blonde, about
twenty-nine years old, sitting at my table. Looked
sorta like Marilyn Monroe. She was married to
this slug. He was overweight and ugly and he was
losing big, so he went to play dice [craps] and she
and I started talking. I knew right off she didn't
like her husband because every time she saw him
coming, she rolled her eyes. One time, she just
flat-out says, "Oh hell, here he comes again. Why
can't he just leave me alone?"

Now this broad doesn't know much about
cards and she is making plenty of dumb mistakes
so I start helping her. When she needs to take a
hit, I don't even ask her, I just pull a card out of

the shoe and give it to her. If she shouldn't take a hit, I just skip her without waiting for her to ask for a card. She catches on and just sits there and we start winning. I mean, she's kicking my butt— or should I say, I'm kicking my own butt. She starts giggling and getting excited and pretty soon the shift is about over, so I bring up how I'm going to leave. Now, I'm pressing her for a tip but instead she says to me, "How'd you like to have a drink in my room?" Luckily, there wasn't anyone else at the table because I could lose my job over this. But I figure no one will know, right, so I say, "Sure." And she starts to take out her room key and hand it to me and I'm thinking: Jesus! The guys watching this from the eye in the sky are going to be busting my butt because this broad has just won a couple hundred from me and they are going to figure that I was cheating for her and now she's paying me off. So I tell her just to tell me the room number. About this time, her husband comes up and this gal is slick. She gives him all the cash that she has won so he can keep playing craps and then says that she has a headache and needs the key to their room. He asks her where her key is and she says she lost it. I told you that she was smart. Now she has his key and her own 'cause she never really lost it.

Fifteen minutes later, I am in this broad's room having sex and she is acting like she has spent the last ten years on a desert island. I get out some coke and we do some lines and all of a sudden there is this knocking on the door and I hear her husband's voice. I figure I'm dead. Now I know I'm going to lose my job and probably some teeth too. But this broad is totally cool. She tells him that she doesn't want to see him because she has been throwing up. She drank too much, she says. She tells him that she'll meet him in the bar in twenty minutes. Now he complains, but she gets him to leave without ever opening the door. Meanwhile, I'm pulling on my pants and getting ready to climb out a window.

Now here is the wacky part. This broad says to me, "Do you know anyone who I could hire to kill my husband?" I said, "What?" She says, "C'mon. All you Vegas dealers have connections with the mob, don't you?" It was the damndest thing. I got the hell out of there and told myself that I would never take another chance like that again. You know what happened? The next night, this broad and her husband sit down at my table and they spend the entire night playing there. Her husband wins a couple hundred dollars and hands me a fifty as a tip. He was a real George [good tipper] and the dumb son of a bitch didn't have a clue that I had nailed his wife the night before and that she was looking for someone to kill him.

                              —*Veteran Las Vegas dealer*

CHAPTER SEVEN

....

Family Feud

Seven months after the Mirage opened, the Excalibur, Bennett's castle casino, lowered its drawbridge and seventy thousand customers walked through its doors the first day. It had the look and feel of a family theme park. Guests were called "lords" and "ladies," employees dressed in medieval costumes, the hotel's hallways were lit with fixtures shaped like torches, even the telephone operators dropped "ye olde English" into their speech. Its 4,025 rooms made the Excalibur the largest hotel in the world, and its size created a slew of problems for general manager William Paulos. There was no computer software capable of handling the 2,500 daily check-ins and check-outs. "We had more people checking in and out every day than the third-largest hotel in the world had in total rooms," Paulos said.

From the air, the Excalibur resembled a giant square. Each of its sides was a twenty-eight-story hotel tower. Visitors crossed a moat to enter the castle facade. The courtyard within the four towers contained four levels. The drawbridge entrance led to the casino, a sprawl of gaming tables and slot machines that was 20,000 square feet larger than the Mirage's 95,500-square-foot casino. Just as he had done at the original Circus Circus casino, Bennett insisted that the Excalibur stick with a meat-and-potatoes approach to gaming. There were no baccarat tables or exotic table games. Guests were offered blackjack, craps, and roulette. The Mirage had 119 gambling tables in its casino: the Excalibur had only 62. Bennett used the remaining floor space for slot machines—2,706 of them, or 500 more than were in the Mirage. There were more slots in the Excalibur than in any other single casino in all of Las Vegas. On the second level of the courtyard were the resort's restaurants and shops. Once again, Bennett stuck with what he already knew was successful. There was a fancy restaurant where mom and dad could eat without the kids at least one night during their vacation, a cheap all-you-can-eat buffet, an Italian restaurant with pizza, and a steak house that also served hamburgers. The Excalibur's retail shops were tailored for tourists too. The Dragon's Lair sold miniature crystal castles for moms, armor paperweights for dads; Merlin's Mystic Shoppe sold magic wands for kids. The Canterbury Wedding Chapel and banquet rooms were on the third floor. Couples could say their marital vows wearing crowns and medieval attire. In the basement under the casino were a video arcade for kids, amusement park rides, and a vast arena where the Lipizzaner stallions performed in the afternoons. At night, knights on horseback jousted in the arena during *King Arthur's Tournament*. The resort had as much of the feel and look of a Walt Disney resort as Circus Circus could emulate.

During its first year, the Excalibur became the most profitable Circus Circus casino. It had cost $300 million to build and it earned $80 million before taxes, netting a 26.6 percent return. "The Excalibur produced the highest return on an investment of any casino that I know of in Las Vegas," Paulos later bragged. It clearly wasn't as luxurious as Steve Wynn's elegant Mirage, but it had never set out to be. Instead, it had targeted moms and pops, in keeping with Bennett's philosophy that there were a lot more working customers to draw from than rich ones.

Bennett's hiring and grooming of his Young Turks had paid off. The Excalibur was the best of everything they had learned from him. In February 1991, he announced that he would retire as chairman within a year. He was sixty-six. As part of his announcement, Bennett sold nine hundred thousand shares of his stock at $60.25 per share, pocketing $54.2 million. He picked Richard Banis, the CPA who was the second-in-command, as his successor. Glenn Schaeffer was chosen to become the company's president. Wall Street signaled its approval by recording steady gains in Circus Circus stock. By June 1991, it had reached an all-time high of $76 per share and the company declared another two-for-one stock split. Despite an industry slowdown in gambling caused by a lackluster economy and the Persian Gulf War, Circus Circus was posting its highest-ever earnings. The company was a rocketship, the best-rated and most often recommended gaming stock on Wall Street. *Forbes* magazine estimated Bennett's personal wealth to be between $500 and $650 million. He was retiring at the top of his game as one of the most respected casino owners in Nevada.

And then he upset the cart.

Three weeks after the stock split, Bennett changed his mind. In a move that completely dumbfounded his protégés, he announced that he had discovered he and Banis had "pretty deep philosophical differences" about how the company should be run. Without further explanation, Bennett demanded that Banis resign. Wall Street recoiled. Circus Circus shares dropped $2 in one day. Bennett moved quickly to quiet investors' fears by naming the company's new president Schaeffer as his heir apparent. He went on to explain that he was postponing his retirement indefinitely in order to keep the company stable. At the time, neither Bennett nor Banis would discuss what prompted their falling-out, but this is how Bennett explained it later during an interview for this book: "I had tried to help Rick out because he had seemed unsure of himself. That is why I announced at a stockholders meeting that Rick would be the next head of the company. I thought that would settle him down, but it made him goofier than he was. He would say, 'Boy, you sure are lucky to have me.' Now, the first time he said that, I thought he was kidding, and then the next time he says, 'Boy, you sure are lucky to have me,' I gave him a dirty look. . . . Then the third time that he said that . . . I said: 'Just keep your yap shut.' . . . Well, he stopped for about two weeks and then he came in and said, 'Boy, you are lucky to have me.' I wanted to kill him. . . . I called every board member and said, 'We got a problem.' Every one of them said get rid of him."

Banis was prohibited from discussing his departure by a lifelong confidentiality clause in his severance contract, but several other managers who were at Circus Circus would later challenge Bennett's version. "Rick never did anything wrong," Paulos said. "The truth is that Bennett just wasn't ready to turn over the reins to his company, so he chopped off Rick's head."

The firing of Banis made Bennett's other Young Turks nervous. Each of them could cite times when Bennett had chastised them for no apparent reason. Such a moment had come for Paulos when he was making a name for himself running the company's Laughlin operations. When he was first sent there in 1983, being transferred "to the river," which is how Laughlin was referred to inside Circus Circus, was akin to being banished to Siberia. The boom there had not yet hit and there was little for employees to do but sweat in the scorching valley. Paulos had worked hard to improve working conditions by hosting employee picnics and demanding that his workers learn each other's first name and say "hello" to at least one hundred people—guests and fellow employees—during their shifts. "We became like a family in Laughlin," recalled Sally Smith, one of the first Circus Circus employees sent there. "We were a bunch of nobodies out of nowhere who went to this really horrible place, worked really, really hard, and turned it into a major resort. Everyone in the town loved Bill Paulos." Even the competition admired him. He was so well liked, in fact, that the town council voted to name a street after him when the resort began to boom. A short time later, Bennett summoned Paulos to Las Vegas.

"I have received an anonymous letter from someone who says you are in charge of all drug trafficking in Laughlin," Bennett declared.

Paulos noticed that Emmett Michaels, the director of corporate security for Circus Circus, was in the room with them.

"Are you using drugs?" Bennett asked.

"Of course not!" replied Paulos, outraged that his integrity was being questioned on the basis of an anonymous accusation.

"Then you wouldn't mind peeing in this jar?" Bennett said, nodding toward a plastic container on his desk.

"I have no fucking problem at all," Paulos retorted. He motioned toward Michaels. "What's he going to do?" Paulos asked. "Hold my dick?"

"No," said Bennett. "Just step into the bathroom and get this taken care of."

Paulos returned minutes later with the urine sample. "I will send you a fucking cup every day if you want it."

Bennett's face betrayed no emotion, neither embarrassment nor regret. "That will not be necessary," he replied.

Back in Laughlin, Paulos had set out to discover who had sent the anonymous letter but he never found the source, and as time passed, he began to wonder if Bennett had simply wanted to prove that he was still in charge, powerful enough to make Paulos pee in a bottle if he wished.

After Banis was fired, the Young Turks began taking bets about who would be next to fall. Although Glenn Schaeffer was in the risky role of being Bennett's declared successor, he seemed the least worried. He had worked for Bennett nine years and had come to think of him as a surrogate father. No one had worked harder to please his boss. Schaeffer had never called in sick, even when he had been running high temperatures. He had accepted every assignment given him, and had always been the first to volunteer. "I was closer to Bennett than I was with my own father," he said. "That is how much he had come to mean to me." There was another reason why Schaeffer didn't think his job would ever be in jeopardy. Circus Circus had increased sixteen times in value since it had become a public company, and Schaeffer deserved much of the credit for its phenomenal growth on Wall Street. It was his opinion that stock analysts trusted, he bragged, not Bennett's.

Now that the Excalibur was open, Schaeffer pushed Bennett to keep expanding. Chicago mayor Richard Daley had expressed interest in bringing legalized casino gambling into his city and Schaeffer wanted Circus Circus to get involved in the pro-gambling political campaign being organized there. He also urged Bennett to build another super casino next door to the Excalibur. Steve Wynn already had announced that he was going to construct a $450 million pirate-themed resort called Treasure Island next door to the Mirage, and financier

Kirk Kerkorian had unveiled plans for a new MGM Grand resort, directly across the street from the Excalibur. Circus Circus needed constant "unit growth" if it wanted to keep earning hefty profits.

Bennett was just as eager as Schaeffer to build another super casino, but no one at Circus Circus had a clue what it should be, so Las Vegas architect Veldon Simpson was hired to come up with an idea. His initial sketches were of a five-story hotel with what he called "stepped-back" layers. It was in the shape of a "U" and each floor was stepped back by two rooms, giving it the profile of a Mayan temple. The interior of the "U" was covered with glass, and this atrium was where the casino would be. As Simpson played with the design, he suddenly realized that he was wasting space and money by keeping the U-shaped hotel and the atrium separate. "I thought, 'Why don't we use the rooms to actually make the shape of the atrium?' So we put the hotel rooms into the actual skin of the building." When he did that, Simpson found himself staring at a pyramid.

In November 1991, Bennett announced that Circus Circus would construct a super casino in the shape of a pyramid. He called it Project X because its name hadn't been chosen. It would be thirty-six stories high and its four sides would be covered with gold-tinted glass just like the Mirage's. There would be 2,500 hotel rooms built into its walls and its hollow interior would contain the largest atrium in the world. It would have three public levels. On the basement level there would be a giant arena patterned after the one in the Excalibur; on the next one the casino; and on the floor above, restaurants and amusement rides. The total price tag: $300 million.

Schaeffer saw Project X as his chance to prove all of his theories about how Las Vegas was becoming an "entertainment destination city" and not just a place to gamble. He began appearing on network television

morning shows talking about "entertainment architecture" and how Las Vegas was now a "family resort."
When a consulting firm proposed naming the project
Pyramid Pyramid, a take off on Circus Circus, Schaeffer
intervened. He suggested "Luxor," from the city in central Egypt where the famous temple and tombs of
Amenhotep III and Ramses II were located. The word
had an echo of luxury and good luck, and Schaeffer
liked the Egyptian theme. Circus Circus could brag
that it was building the first pyramid in a desert in
more than six thousand years. Bennett enthusiastically
agreed.

Having everyone dress in Egyptian costumes wasn't
going to be enough to make the Luxor into a themed resort, Schaeffer decided. Every aspect of the pyramid
needed to be linked philosophically, so that the resort
would become a "total entertainment package." Circus
Circus hired a special-effects studio headed by Douglas
Trumbull to work with architect Simpson and turn
the pyramid into "a doorway into another world."
Trumbull had created many of the groundbreaking effects seen in such futuristic films as *2001: A Space
Odyssey, Close Encounters of the Third Kind,* and
Blade Runner, and he had recently designed a ride for
Walt Disney World based on the movie *Back to the
Future.* Trumbull recommended that Circus Circus use
the amusement rides in the Luxor to tell a story. Costs
soared, but Circus Circus had plenty to spend. Bennett
told reporters that his company was so profitable, it
could finance the $300 million complex with its own
cash. If the company needed more, it could tap into the
$600 million in credit lines that Schaeffer had obtained.

It was a heady time for the thirty-seven-year-old
Schaeffer. In a flattering profile published in the *Wall
Street Journal,* he was credited by several New York
stock analysts as the financial whiz behind Circus
Circus's tremendous growth. The newspaper noted that

he had gotten the company nearly all of its loans from traditional banking sources rather than junk bonds. This now seemed farsighted, because the king of junk bonds, Michael Milken, had pleaded guilty in April 1990 to six felony counts of security law violations in various junk bond schemes, and had been sentenced to ten years in a federal prison and fined more than $1 billion. His former company, Drexel Burnham Lambert, had been forced out of business.

As 1992 began, Schaeffer started getting still more media recognition. Reporters who had scrambled to write flattering profiles of Wynn in the 1980s returned to Las Vegas to interview Schaeffer. With his button-down collars and finance-laced jargon, he was portrayed as the new "corporate" executive now taking charge of the Strip. He didn't gamble and his background was much closer to that of a Fortune 500 chief executive than to Steve Wynn's.

From childhood, the California-born Schaeffer had been self-directed, focused, and highly motivated. A bullied ninety-five-pound kid at the age of fifteen, in a single year he had turned himself into the strongest boy in school, pound for pound, by dedicating himself to a rigorous bodybuilding regimen that he still followed. He became a starting defensive back on the football team and dated a cheerleader. On their first date, he drove her into Beverly Hills to gawk at the mansions. "I'm going to have enough money someday to live here if I want," he told her.

He held to his own way throughout college. When his hard-driving father pressed him to study chemistry at the University of California at Irvine, Schaeffer rebelled by getting high marks in every subject but chemistry. He discovered he had a gift for writing, won a first-place award for an essay on *The Catcher in the Rye,* and graduated summa cum laude as an English major. His eventual goal was to become a novelist.

Now married to his high school cheerleading sweet-heart, he gained a coveted slot at the prestigious Iowa Writers Workshop. But he felt out of place—"It was my first exposure to rich kids," he remembered. "I'd never met anyone from an eastern prep school who was living off his daddy's trust fund"—and he soon realized that most literary novelists didn't earn much from their writing. "I was afraid that I was going to become a writer whom other writers might have heard of, but who would be starving nonetheless."

That wasn't good enough for a young man determined to become rich.

Schaeffer sent resumes to one hundred public relations firms in Los Angeles but got no response, so he decided to become a stockbroker because he knew that successful ones were highly paid. "I went into the same area of Beverly Hills where I had gone on my first date with my wife and stopped at every brokerage house on Wilshire Boulevard and asked for a job." The Dean Witter company hired and trained him. "I liked the idea of selling something that you can't see," Schaeffer recalled. "You are really buying the person who is selling you the idea." On weekends, he would pick a high-rise office building, walk from door to door looking for lawyers and CPAs working overtime, waltz inside their offices, and pitch a stock. One afternoon, he got a call from a public relations agent who needed financial information for a client and knew nothing about Wall Street. It dawned on Schaeffer that he had two marketable skills: he understood finance and he knew how to write well. He switched over to a job with the giant public relations firm Hill and Knowlton, and aligned himself with the company's expert on public financing. "The way for me to rise, I decided, was by attaching myself to one of the generals in the company—someone who was clearly a rainmaker. I became the guy who raised his hand and volunteered." His timing was good.

Wall Street was buzzing with proxy fights, buyouts, tender offers. He was assigned the Caesars Palace account and was soon writing speeches for Caesars Palace executives in defense of gaming. In a speech later reprinted in the magazine *Vital Speeches,* Schaeffer predicted that the public would eventually accept gambling as simply another form of entertainment. One day in 1980, he was eating lunch at his desk when an executive from Ramada Inns called and asked to talk to "whoever is handling the Caesars Palace account."

Hoping to cash in on the Atlantic City boom, Ramada Inns was building a casino on the Boardwalk. Its president had admired the Caesars Palace advertising campaign and wanted Schaeffer on board. Schaeffer, who was now in the midst of a divorce, moved from Los Angeles to the Ramada Inns headquarters in Phoenix. A few months later, the company fell on hard times, primarily because costs were out of control at the casino it was building in Atlantic City. A new chairman was brought in to run the company, and he became Schaeffer's mentor. When Bill Bennett called him in December 1983 at Michael Milken's suggestion, Schaeffer saw Circus Circus as a perfect match for his financial and public relations talents. "I recognized that gaming was where a tremendous amount of money was going to be made."

Schaeffer's rising status on the Strip during 1992 didn't go unnoticed by Bennett. "Glenn is outselling himself," he grumbled one fall afternoon. "He is letting his ego get ahead of him." It was a comment chillingly similar to what Bennett had said about Rick Banis before firing him.

Over lunch just before Christmas, Michael Sloan, the company's politically savvy attorney, warned Schaeffer to be careful. He had seen a magazine lying on Bennett's desk a few days earlier that had a photograph of Schaeffer and Steve Wynn on its cover. The story described how both men were responsible for "Disneylanding" the Strip. Bennett always kept his desk absolutely clean, yet when Sloan went into Bennett's office later, he noticed the magazine was still there. "Mr. Bennett is noodling over that picture," Sloan said. "I suspect that he isn't happy about all the publicity you are getting."

Not long after that, the directors of a national hotel chain met secretly with Schaeffer, Sloan, and Bennett to discuss merging with Circus Circus. The talks were going well until hotel officials said they wanted Schaeffer to head up the company after the merger. Bennett was visibly shaken. He pointed to a chair and spent the next several minutes insisting that Schaeffer would make a lousy chairman because he wouldn't be able to tell the difference between that chair's fabric and a lesser-quality fabric if he needed to order chairs for a hotel. He was a financial officer, not a hotel or casino operator. The next day, Bennett told Schaeffer that the merger was off. Moreover, he no longer wanted Schaeffer issuing orders to managers involved in Circus Circus's daily hotel and casino operations. He was to restrict himself to dealing with Wall Street.

"This is bullshit," Schaeffer protested. "You are setting me up to fail."

"Listen, Glenn," Bennett lectured, "I don't talk to you like that and I don't expect you to talk to me like that either."

Soon after their exchange, Bennett summoned Schaeffer into his office and announced that he had written out a list of rules he wanted Schaeffer to follow.

"I've never had a set of rules," Schaeffer replied, "and if I told you that I was drawing up a set of rules for you, you wouldn't accept it. So why are you asking me to accept treatment that you would not accept?"

Bennett accused Schaeffer of being insubordinate.

"I can quit," Schaeffer replied, "and if you want me to quit, it won't take long—just say so."

Bennett changed his mind about issuing the new rules and an angry Schaeffer left the room. "I was probably closer to Bill Bennett than any employee had ever been," Schaeffer said later, "but there was always an understanding that I worked *for* him, not *with* him. I began to sense that he felt I had violated my role."

During the coming weeks, relations between them became so strained that neither spoke to the other. In late January 1993, a frustrated Schaeffer invited four top managers to his house over the weekend to talk about what he should do. One of them suggested that Schaeffer take his case directly to the Circus Circus board of directors and ask it to force Bennett to retire. After all, Bill Pennington was still on the board and was the company's second-largest stockholder. Surely he would understand Schaeffer's quandary. Schaeffer considered it briefly, then said he wouldn't feel comfortable taking so drastic a step.

Two days after the secret weekend meeting, Bennett called Schaeffer in. "I don't think you will ever be chief executive of this company," Bennett said. "I have talked to several members of the board and they don't think you have what it takes."

"Fine," Schaeffer replied. "I have no interest in working with someone who doesn't want me to succeed. . . . If you don't want me here, it is your board and your call, but I think you are making a big mistake. You are undoing the management of this company, piece by piece."

"I'm going to do just fine without you," said Bennett. "I made a lot of money before I met you and I'll make a lot without you."

Schaeffer resigned, and a few days later, one of the other managers who had attended the weekend meeting abruptly resigned too. Bennett was cleaning house. Circus Circus's stock plunged six points before settling at $42.25 per share. At first, Bennett refused to comment on Schaeffer's departure, but on April 1 he lambasted his former heir apparent in an interview with a local reporter. He did the same when the *Wall Street Journal* called. Bennett accused Schaeffer of plotting a palace coup and claimed Schaeffer had urged managers to sign a legal document calling for Bennett's ouster as chairman.

It was almost unheard-of on Wall Street for inside politics like this to be aired in public, and Bennett's juicy comments caused Circus Circus's stock to tumble another seven points. Bennett reacted by recanting his charges, only to repeat them a day later. Schaeffer had signed a nondisclosure clause in his severance agreement, so he couldn't comment when reporters called, and during the following days, Bennett kept punching away. He accused Schaeffer of bungling the company's attempts to open a casino in Chicago. With each new interview Bennett offered the media another "Schaeffer screwup." At one point, he claimed Schaeffer had resigned because he was greedy and wanted even more stock options than the seven hundred thousand shares Bennett had already generously given him. Circus Circus's stock continued to fall, so Bennett hurriedly hired Clyde Turner, who had left his CFO job at Mirage Resorts. He was highly regarded and the stock began to stabilize, but Bennett still could not stop his attack. "Glenn hasn't done anything to contribute to the earnings of this company," he said, throwing one last punch. "Glenn Schaeffer has been taking credit for years for things he had nothing to do with."

Circus Circus was his company, Bennett declared. He was responsible for its success and he didn't need anyone's help running it.

Inside the Casino:
Special Rooms

I'm twenty-three years old and fresh out of college and I get a job at the Tropicana and end up working there as the assistant hotel manager. My main job was to make sure the hotel had 100 percent occupancy every night, and there was so much demand in the early 1990s that we often oversold the rooms. If you had fifty people who had reservations and you had no place to put them, that was tough, but when you had four hundred and you had promised them all a room and there were none, now that was a real challenge. Ten months into the job, two guys come in wearing sunglasses and trying hard not to be recognized, but I recognized them instantly. It was Johnny Depp and Charlie Sheen, the movie stars, and they say, "We need a room." And I say, "Sorry, we are sold out." And they say, "Money is no object." Suddenly, I remember that we have luxury theme suites available. Now these are two-story high-roller suites and each has a different theme and decor. There is the London Suite, the Bombay Suite, the Parisian Suite, and they are beautiful, so I tell these guys that they can rent the London Suite but it will cost them five thousand for one night. Charlie just whips out his credit card and I'm thinking, cool, I just sold a room for $5 thousand! The next morning, I get this call from my boss telling me to get right in. He meets me at the door and takes me to the lounge where the casino vice president and the vice president of Asian casino operations are waiting. "Did you rent out the London Suite last night?" one of them asks me. "Yes, I got five thousand dollars for it," I reply proudly. I figured they were going to congratulate me but instead both of them are furious at me. One of them says, "No one is supposed to rent those suites out except for the casino hosts—no one, not even the hotel manager, and certainly not you. You got that? We had an Asian player stop over last night on a return flight from New York City to Hong Kong and he only likes to stay in the London Suite and he keeps two hundred and fifty thousand dollars on deposit in our cage. You got five thousand for that room—this guy bets five thousand a hand! Now what are we supposed to tell him when he expects to check into his lucky London Suite?" They were really busting my chops. I was so nervous, I knocked over the casino vice president's coffee on the table into his lap. By this time, I figure I am doomed. But he says, "Kid, we aren't going to fire you. You can't be blamed for something that no one told you. But if you are gonna stay in this business, you got to understand a basic fundamental. This is not a hotel-casino. It is a casino-hotel. Without the casino, there is no reason for people to come here, no reason for there to be a Las Vegas. Everything revolves around the gambling and don't you ever forget it."

—Leon Symanski, Luxor safety coordinator

CHAPTER EIGHT

....

The King Falls

Clyde Turner had been retired for five months when Bennett offered to make him president of Circus Circus. The fifty-five-year-old Turner had not been looking for a job. During his thirteen years working as Steve Wynn's CFO, Turner had become a multimillionaire. But he had never been the boss of a giant casino company, and the offer proved to be too tempting to pass up. The fact that he would now be competing against his former boss made it even juicier.

After moving into Glenn Schaeffer's old office, Turner decided to see what he had been hired to run. He flew to Reno and Laughlin to inspect the company's casinos there. "Bill Bennett and Bill Pennington had bled those places dry," he recalled. "They were in deplorable shape." Turner was used to Wynn's impeccable standards and he decided that his first act as president would be to launch an immediate remodeling campaign. Bennett cut him short. He was trying to get the Luxor completed before Wynn's new Treasure Island casino opened, and costs at the pyramid were soaring.

Turner backed off for a few weeks and then brought up
the remodeling subject once again. This time, Bennett
said he would go with Turner on an inspection tour of
the hotel at the Las Vegas Circus Circus resort. If it
needed refurbishing, then Bennett would give Turner
permission to remodel all of the company's older hotels.
Unbeknownst to Bennett, Turner already had checked
the hotel and felt it was ragged. The two men met the
next afternoon and Bennett chose a room at random.
Opening the door, he peered inside and announced that
it looked acceptable to him. Turner glanced in. In his
view, the place was a mess. The carpet was worn and
stained, the wallpaper was dated, the room reeked of
cigarette smoke. Without further comment, Bennett declared their impromptu tour over. Turner said nothing.
He would later explain that he and Bennett had struck a
deal during their hiring negotiations. "Bennett had told
me that he would retire within six months—that was
one of my conditions when I took the job—so I decided
I'd simply wait for him to leave."

Even though Schaeffer had been gone two months
by then, Circus Circus was still reeling from his forced
departure. In May 1993, *Business Week* magazine declared that Circus Circus's stock was stuck in the dol-
drums because Bennett had "purged what was long
considered the gaming industry's strongest management team." The article quoted a Wall Street analyst
saying "Bennett doesn't know when it's time to quit."
Another complained that he was well past his prime.
When asked by the magazine when he planned to retire,
Bennett said he didn't expect to be running Circus
Circus "in seven or eight years," but added that he
wasn't planning on retiring "anytime soon." The quote
surprised Turner, who said later that he had immediately reminded Bennett of their six-month agreement.
Bennett assured him in private that he would step
down, but not until after the Luxor opened. It was still

five months away from completion. Turner didn't protest, but he was no longer sure he believed Bennett. He was beginning to have misgivings about working for him.

After spending five years apart, Steve and Elaine Wynn remarried. "Steve just never got around to moving out," Elaine joked. Wynn deadpanned, "We regret to say that the divorce just didn't work out." Wynn's friends speculated that the couple had reconciled, in part, because Wynn had matured. During the late 1970s and early 1980s, he had enjoyed hobnobbing with Hollywood celebrities and entertainers. Now he seemed much more intent on expanding his empire and influencing state and national politics. Simply put, he wanted to be taken seriously. He began making hefty campaign contributions and speaking out on national issues. He set up a sophisticated polling operation so that he could learn what the public was thinking about any issue that struck his fancy. He also began flexing his political muscles. Some reporters began referring to him in stories as "Nevada's most powerful citizen." Along with their daughters, Kevin and Gillian, the Wynns were described in society pages as the state's "unofficial first family."

Shortly after 9 P.M. on July 26, 1993, the Wynns finished dinner at the Mirage and Kevin, who was twenty-six years old, left for home. She lived by herself in a gated condominium complex west of the Strip. Nothing seemed out of the ordinary when she stepped into her kitchen that night, but as she flipped on the lights, she saw someone jump toward her. Before she could react, two men knocked her down and pinned her to the floor. One covered her eyes with duct tape. Dragging her into the bedroom, they ordered her to strip. Kevin thought she was going to be raped, but when she had removed all her clothing except her bra and panties, they told her to stop. One of them called the Mirage on her bedroom phone and demanded to talk to Wynn. "We have your daughter," he announced. Wynn thought it was a prank until a terrified Kevin took the phone. As soon as she had identified herself, one of the kidnappers snatched back the receiver. If Wynn wanted to see his daughter alive again, he would have to pay $2 million in ransom. Wynn told the kidnapper that he couldn't take that much cash out of the casino without calling attention to himself.

"How much can you get?" the kidnapper asked.

"How the hell do I know?" Wynn replied. "The chairman of the board doesn't come down to the vault every day."

Confused, the kidnapper said he would have to call Wynn right back. Two minutes later, he called and demanded that Wynn bring $1.45 million in ransom to the parking lot of a bar just off the Strip.

"I can't do that," Wynn said.

"Why not?"

"I can't drive at night," replied Wynn, explaining that he was going blind. He offered to send someone else.

"Okay, but remember we are watching you right now," the kidnapper said. "Don't forget that."

As Wynn hurried toward the casino cage, he signaled Charles Price, one of his hotel security officers, and whispered what was happening. Price agreed to deliver the ransom and promised not to do anything that would jeopardize Kevin.

Back at the condominium, the kidnappers snapped photographs of Kevin in her underwear and warned her the pictures would be mailed to the *National Enquirer* to embarrass her father if he told anyone about the kidnapping. With her hands tied behind her, Kevin was shoved into the backseat of her car, covered with a blanket, and driven to McCarran International Airport, where she was left in a remote parking lot. The kidnappers told her that she was being watched and would be shot if she screamed or tried to leave the car.

An accomplice was waiting when the ransom was brought to the parking lot at the bar. The three kidnappers rendezvoused moments later at a 7-Eleven convenience store one block away and called Wynn from a pay phone there. "Your daughter is at the airport," the ringleader told him.

A friend drove Wynn to McCarran, and they soon spotted Kevin's vanity license plate, BIONDA, which is Italian for blond. Wrenching open the car door, Wynn called out her name.

"Daddy?" she cried.

The crime had taken about two hours, and it was solved almost as fast. The kidnappers had telephoned Wynn so quickly after the ransom pickup that the FBI correctly deduced they had used a pay telephone close to the bar parking lot. Agents checked the records of nearby pay phones and found the one that had been used to call Wynn at the Mirage. Incredibly, the three kidnappers had all placed long-distance calls to their girlfriends in Sacramento, California, on the very same pay phone so they could brag about the crime. As if that wasn't stupid enough, less than twenty-four hours later, the trio's ringleader, Ray Marion Cuddy, strolled into an exotic-car dealership in California and tried to pay cash for a $196,000 Ferrari Testarossa. When the salesman told him that all cash transactions over $10,000 are automatically reported to the federal government, he left a small down payment along with his name and promised to come back later. The FBI was waiting when he did. His buddies, Jacob Sherwood and Anthony Watkins, were arrested soon afterward. Cuddy had chosen Kevin as his kidnapping victim because he had once worked for a Las Vegas health club where she exercised. All three men were sentenced to prison after a highly publicized trial. Afterward, Wynn hired a bodyguard for Kevin and bought a trained attack dog for himself. It was time, he told Elaine, for the family to rethink its high profile.

The Luxor opened on October 14, 1993, twelve days before Steve Wynn's Treasure Island resort. Bennett had won his race with Wynn but it was a small victory. Dozens of water pipes burst because they had been incorrectly installed and never tested. Water gushed from guest rooms and cascaded over the balconies, creating twenty-story waterfalls inside the atrium. Many of the 2,501 guest rooms were not ready. One guest was sent to a room with five television sets but no bed. "The problem with the Luxor's opening was that when Glenn Schaeffer left, a real driving force in the company left," recalled the pyramid's general manager at the time, William Paulos. "Glenn was held in high esteem within the company and Turner was trying to fill his shoes—so all he could say was how fucked-up everything was because Glenn had done it. And then Bill Bennett decided to put his stamp on the Luxor and he ripped the heart out of it. It was twenty-five million dollars away from being perfection and Bennett stopped short. All those things that could have made for a great grand opening were cut. Then Bennett heard that Steve Wynn was going to open Treasure Island on the same day as we were opening the Luxor, and he got completely crazed. All of us in management kept saying, 'It doesn't fucking matter who opens first,' but he refused to listen and Wynn absolutely won the psych-out battle. We opened thirty days before we should have and we opened to tremendous criticism."

To save costs, Bennett had insisted the Luxor be built without service elevators to the guest floors, so bellhops pushing carts stacked with suitcases had to ride on the same elevators as the guests. So did the maids. Worse, the hotel's main elevators did not go down into the basement. They stopped in the lobby, which meant the maids had to push their carts of soiled linen through the lobby area to a different set of elevators. Room service also had to use two different elevators, making deliveries slow.

The Luxor seemed cursed. A monorail that was supposed to transport guests between it and the adjacent Excalibur broke. "Instead of saying, 'Let's spend two million to fix it' and then worry about whose fault it was, Bennett decided to litigate," Paulos said. "The money that was lost by not having that monorail working was incredible, but all the bosses wanted to do was blame someone—usually Schaeffer." There were so many problems that whenever a new one surfaced, employees would joke: "What do you expect? Pyramids are supposed to be tombs, not resorts." The Luxor's evening show, called *Winds of the Gods,* became symbolic. Because of Bennett's rush to open, the Luxor skipped an important Las Vegas tradition—inviting taxi drivers and travel agents to a special free preview before the show opened to the public. Snubbed agents and cab drivers steered passengers away from the Luxor when asked what shows in town were worth seeing. Bennett slashed the show's advertising budget too, crippling it further.

In comparison, the grand opening of Treasure Island went flawlessly. Crowds flocked to the casino to see the mock sea pirate battle that Wynn choreographed in front of his resort. Inside, Wynn's new show, called *Mystère,* opened to rave reviews. *Time* magazine called it a "must-see" and ranked it in its "Best Theater" listings.

Once the Luxor opened, William Paulos assumed his career at Circus Circus was through, not because of the numerous problems that plagued the new casino,

but because he had been one of the managers who had
participated in Glenn Schaeffer's secret weekend meeting, now being referred to as the "mutiny" session. The
only reason he had not been asked to resign earlier,
Paulos decided, was because Bennett had needed him to
get the Luxor built. Not wishing to wait for the in-
evitable, Paulos resigned three months after the pyramid opened and accepted a job with a company that
was building a super casino in Australia.

"Telling Bennett was one of the strangest moments
in my life because he had kept his promise to me about
making me wealthy and teaching me the casino business," Paulos said. "I respected him. When he was on
his game, there was no one better. He was a genius. But
near the end, he just couldn't let go and retire." Bennett
threw Paulos a going-away party and never mentioned
his attendance at the mutiny weekend. After cashing
in his stock options, Paulos left Circus Circus with
$10 million.

Paulos was among the last of Bennett's Young
Turks, and in interviews with the author, Bennett would
later bitterly complain about them all. Every one of
them had disappointed him, he said. At the Luxor gift
shop, a videotape went on sale called *The Making of
Luxor.* It identified Bennett as the sole founder of
Circus Circus Enterprises and the mastermind behind
the pyramid. There was no mention of Jay Sarno, Bill
Pennington, or Glenn Schaeffer.

Glenn Schaeffer began getting job offers on the night he
resigned. Michael Ensign was the first to call. Ensign
was the popular former Circus Circus executive who
had served as a buffer between Bennett and Pennington
before leaving to start his own casino company. In the
nine years that had passed since then, Ensign had
amassed four casinos together with his business partner

and best friend, William A. Richardson. The two of them wanted Schaeffer to help them with Wall Street, just as he had done early on at Circus Circus.

Although Schaeffer didn't know Richardson well, he was familiar with the story behind the two men's success. Ensign and Richardson had started out as neighbors. One night, Richardson had knocked on Ensign's door seeking help. His family owned a one-third interest in a tiny gift shop near the Hoover Dam and the other owners wanted to sell him their shares. But Richardson didn't know if the shop was worth buying. He asked Ensign to take a look because he was thinking about livening up the place with a few slot machines and he knew that Ensign was an expert on gambling. There wasn't much to the gift shop—just a snack bar and souvenirs—but Ensign realized its potential as soon as he saw where it was located. The building was on an old mining claim that had been overlooked when the federal government seized title to all the other land around Hoover Dam. It was the only tourist trap within miles. Ensign urged Richardson to buy out his partners and Richardson cut him in on the deal. They demolished the shop, built a casino there, and were soon making enough money to build two more casinos in towns along the Nevada-California state line. Using their profits from those ventures, the two men entered into a partnership with Hyatt Hotels that led to the construction of the *Grand Victoria,* a riverboat based in Elgin, Illinois, that was the largest and most profitable floating casino in the country.

Schaeffer liked the aggressive way that Ensign and Richardson were building their company—they weren't afraid of taking risks—so he agreed to join them. Together, the three men formed a corporation called Gold Strike Resorts, and Schaeffer immediately came up with a clever way for them to build a super casino on the Strip.

As soon as Treasure Island opened, Steve Wynn announced that he would build yet another super casino. He was calling this one the Bellagio, and he was building it at the site of the old Dunes hotel at a cost of $1.6 billion. That was much too rich a project for the upstart Gold Strike Resorts, but Schaeffer had noticed that Wynn was only going to use half of the Dunes land. He went to see Wynn and with much pluck suggested that Wynn give Gold Strike Resorts the vacant half of the tract to develop.

Wynn nearly broke out laughing. Why should he let a rival company build a casino on his land? he asked. Because, Schaeffer replied, Wynn couldn't focus on building two projects at the same time. But if he formed a onetime partnership with Gold Strike Resorts, it could build and operate a super casino for him on the Dunes land in return for a share of its profits. Continuing his pitch, Schaeffer pointed out that Bill Richardson's family owned a Las Vegas construction company, so he could build a casino faster and cheaper than anyone in town. Ensign was one of the best casino operators in the state. And Schaeffer could use his Wall Street connections to finance the project. All Wynn had to do was give them his land and wait for the profits.

Wynn took the bait. They decided to call the new resort the Monte Carlo. Work began as soon as Schaeffer got a $200 million line of credit from the Bank of America. (The fact that E. Parry Thomas was one of the Bank of America's largest stockholders helped. Thomas had sold his Valley Bank to the giant banking monolith in 1992 in a deal that had netted him $460 million worth of stock. He had then retired.)

Thus, less than one year after he was forced to resign at Circus Circus, Schaeffer was back on the Strip overseeing construction of a new super casino that would be targeting the same customers as the Luxor, which was only two blocks away. It was a strange moment. His onetime adversary, Steve Wynn, was now his business partner, and his onetime mentor, Bill Bennett, was now his rival.

By January 1994, Clyde Turner no longer believed that Bennett was going to retire voluntarily, so he began skirting around him. In a meeting with the company's board of directors, Turner unveiled plans for what he called "the masterplan mile," an ambitious expansion project. He suggested that the company begin work immediately on a new super casino next door to the Luxor. This would give Circus Circus three super casinos in a row—the Excalibur, the Luxor, and Turner's new project. The three casinos would occupy one contiguous mile of Strip frontage, forming a Circus Circus "mall" of super casinos, all linked by monorails and moving sidewalks. This masterplan mile would be larger than Walt Disney World. The board gave him permission to begin buying land south of the Luxor.

Bennett didn't raise any objections to Turner's project. He was too busy fighting his own battles. Bad news seemed to hang over him. Pauline Yoshihashi, a reporter at the *Wall Street Journal,* had started digging into his past after his public feud with Glenn Schaeffer and on April 1, 1994, she detailed her findings in a front-page story.

....

Despite his success, Mr. Bennett has evidently felt compelled to embellish his accomplishments. Over the years, he has spoken with pride of a *Life* magazine profile in the early 1960s that lionized him and a handful of other scrappy capitalists as "The Young Millionaires of Phoenix.". . . That tale has woven itself into Circus Circus lore.

But an inquiry to the Time-Life archives fails
to produce such a story. A similar piece ran
under that headline in the September 30,
1961 *Saturday Evening Post,* and it fits Mr.
Bennett's recall in most details save one:
He's not in it.

....

Yoshihashi noted that Bennett had been unable to produce a copy of the magazine for her. (Bennett insisted to
the author of this book that he had a copy of the magazine locked in a safe at his house, but he declined to
produce it.) Yoshihashi's story set off a flurry of gossip
inside Circus Circus corporate headquarters. Bennett's
pride was hurt. He complained to a friend that his reputation was being destroyed—all because of his fight
with Schaeffer.

   For the first time in his twenty-year reign at Circus
Circus, Bennett faced a contentious crowd in June 1994
at the annual stockholders meeting. Revenues were flat,
and the stock had dropped so low despite Turner's expansion plans that the *Wall Street Journal* had identified
Circus Circus—on the day before the stockholders
meeting—as a ripe candidate for a hostile takeover. The
session proved to be a disaster for Bennett. He had
trouble hearing questions from the audience, often gave
rambling answers, and seemed confused. Several times,
Turner either had to whisper in his ear or answer questions for him—moves that drew murmurs and some
suppressed laughter from the room. At one point,
Bennett began to blame Schaeffer and Rick Banis for
the company's financial woes. Fearing a lawsuit for
slander, corporate attorney Michael Sloan cut him off.
"It was one of the most pathetic stockholders meetings
I've ever attended," David Ehlers, publisher of the *Las
Vegas Investment Report,* said later. "The attitude of
everybody in there was disbelief. Bennett's performance

illustrated the need for change." After the meeting, Bennett told reporters that he was sluggish because of a pain medication that he had taken that morning for chronic leg problems.

The Circus Circus board always met privately after the general stockholders meeting, and as board members were filing into a dining room at the Excalibur, Bennett asked Turner and Sloan to wait in the hallway. Ten minutes later, they were motioned inside and discovered that he had pinned the blame for the company's troubles on them. He had asked the board to fire them both but it had turned down his request. It was the first time in the company's history that it had overruled him, but there was nothing he could do about it. Although he was still the company's largest single stockholder, his decision in 1991 to sell a block of his shares had reduced his holdings to 15 percent of the company, and that was no longer enough to let him ride roughshod over the board. The board urged Bennett and Turner to begin working together before some Wall Street raider launched a hostile takeover of the company.

As if on cue, Arthur Goldberg, the chairman of Bally Entertainment, disclosed a few days later that he had bought 680,000 shares of Circus Circus stock and had received permission from the Federal Trade Commission to buy another 25 percent of the company. The board called an immediate emergency meeting and during it, decided to replace Bennett as chairman and put Turner in charge. It also adopted several poison pills to make Circus Circus harder for Goldberg to swallow. A few days later, Goldberg sold his shares without explanation, netting a $4 million profit after speculators drove up the stock price.

Now that Bennett had been stripped of his day-to-day powers, Turner focused on buying the land that he needed for his masterplan mile project. The first tract, containing forty-seven acres, was next door to the

Luxor. The Hacienda hotel and casino, a low-budget resort built in 1956, was on this tract. The casino itself was worth an estimated $35 million, but the land around it made it more valuable than that. Through a realtor, Turner offered $65 million to the Hacienda's owner but the offer was rejected. The next morning, Turner discovered why. The front page of the *Las Vegas Review-Journal* reported that Bennett had offered the owner $80 million. In a story printed under a banner headline, Bennett explained that he was going to resign from the Circus Circus board and sell all his stock in the company. He was buying the Hacienda so that he could start over. He told the newspaper that he planned to remodel it and turn it into a super casino. Turner and the Circus Circus board filed a lawsuit to prevent Bennett from getting the casino and land. They claimed he had violated his fiduciary obligations as a Circus Circus board member by offering to buy the casino, a charge Bennett adamantly denied.

After weeks of bitter legal wrangling, Bennett relinquished his claim on the Hacienda and resigned from the Circus Circus board. As soon as it received his resignation, the board dropped its lawsuit against him. Turner bought the Hacienda tract for $80 million, then moved quickly to buy the second parcel that he wanted, next door to the Hacienda, for another $75 million.

Circus Circus did not give Bennett a going-away party. The man who had spent two decades building it into an empire was not even given a gold watch. There were no glowing speeches in his honor. Bennett simply cleaned out his desk and drove himself home. He was seventy years old and bitter. A short time later, he bought the failing Sahara casino at the northern tip of the Strip for $193 million out of his own pocket. He told reporters that he couldn't stand the thought of retiring and not having anything to do. To the surprise of no one, Bennett announced that he was going to turn the Sahara into a grind joint.

Glenn Schaeffer read about Bennett's ouster in the newspaper. "I've got a crazy idea," he told Ensign. "What does Clyde Turner know about building a super casino? Nothing. He has never built one, but we have." He urged Ensign to call Turner and offer him a deal similar to the one they had cut with Steve Wynn— Gold Strike Resorts would build a super casino on the Hacienda site for Circus Circus for a share of the profits.

Ensign's pitch couldn't have come at a better time for Turner. Though Schaeffer and Ensign didn't know it, the new Circus Circus board chairman was in a difficult spot. Bill Pennington didn't like him and now that Bennett was gone, Pennington was the single largest stockholder and most influential member of the board. The two men had clashed from the moment Turner was hired, but Pennington was particularly irked when Turner suggested shortly after he arrived that the company sell its original Circus Circus casino. Turner thought the pink-and-white circus tent casino was an embarrassment, even though it was a steady profit earner. It simply did not fit with the upscale image that he wanted to bring to Circus Circus. Pennington had bristled at the thought of Circus Circus selling the casino that had first made the company great. He considered Turner a snob. He thought that his ideas about upscaling the company were poppycock. The board had agreed with him and the idea of selling the company's first casino had been forgotten—by everyone except Pennington. "Turner is nothing but a Steve Wynn wanna-be," he told another board member. "He's going to ruin this company." Turner suspected that Pennington would eventually seek his ouster. He knew he was living on borrowed time. It was at this point that Michael Ensign showed up to make his pitch. Turner listened politely and then countered with one of his own.

"Why don't we team up permanently?" he suggested.

Ensign was so surprised that Turner had to repeat himself.

"Why don't we join forces?" he said again.

On March 19, 1995, Turner revealed to reporters that Circus Circus was buying Gold Strike Resorts for $600 million. The company paid Ensign, Richardson, and Schaeffer a total of $12 million in cash and issued them seventeen million shares of stock. In one quick move, Turner had cleverly accomplished all of his goals. He had acquired the expertise that he needed to build a super casino on his masterplan mile, and had brought back two executives whom Pennington liked. There was another less obvious aspect to the deal. The merger had made Ensign and Richardson the company's two biggest shareholders. Each now controlled 6.5 million shares. That was more than Pennington owned, and as part of the buyout, Turner had cut a verbal deal with the Gold Strike Resorts team that guaranteed him his job as Circus Circus chairman for at least four more years.

The merger made Circus Circus the largest gaming company in the world. It now operated a total of thirteen casinos. In Nevada alone, it owned sixteen thousand hotel rooms and four hundred thousand square feet of casino space. Its properties were worth an estimated $2.3 billion and during fiscal 1995, it reported $1.2 billion in revenue. Of that, $136 million was profit.

Although Turner remained as chairman, the Gold Strike Resorts team took control. Ensign became the company's chief operating officer, Richardson became an executive vice president, and Schaeffer was named president. It was another ironic moment for Schaeffer. After being forced to resign by Bill Bennett, he had returned victorious.

One of the first decisions the new management announced was that it would completely renovate the Luxor. It was going to turn the pyramid into a luxury super casino that would be elegant enough to compete head-on with Steve Wynn's Mirage. "This company is no longer your father's Circus Circus," Schaeffer told reporters, paraphrasing a popular car commercial. Based on his previous relationship with Bennett, Schaeffer thought the phrase was especially apt.

Circus Circus was about to enter a new era, he said, and the Luxor would lead the way.

Inside the Casino:
We're All Pimps!

People around here all want to be high rollers. But you know what? A high roller is the biggest loser of all. That's right. Just stop and think about it. Why is a casino giving him a free room, free meals, and paying for him to fly out here first-class? Because he is losing thousands and thousands of dollars. High rollers are losers, man, pure and simple, but their egos blind them.

I used to love this city, but I hate it now because I see beyond all the glitter. I see this town for what it is. Las Vegas is about only one thing: greed. Everyone here is trying to make a buck off someone else's misery. That's cold, man, but it's true. These casinos don't manufacture a product. They don't produce anything. They just take your money. And thousands of people come out here every day and gladly hand it over. Why? They think they are going to win something for nothing.

I thought I was smart because I was betting on sports—football, basketball, baseball. I figured I knew enough to win. But the odds are against you and if you do win, then greed kicks in. Every penny I won—I just ended up betting and losing it. No one ever leaves this town a winner. If you do win big, the casinos invite you back and sooner or later you figure, "Hey, I scored big once, I can do it again." Greed kicks in. Talk to the old-timers and they will tell you that if you come to Las Vegas twenty or thirty times a year and you break even at the end of the year, then you are a lucky gambler.

What bothers me is how these casino owners
are trying to say this is a family vacation spot.
Everything now is patterned after Disneyland, but
Las Vegas isn't Disneyland. Hello? Is anyone lis-
tening? Disneyland is based on Snow White,
Mickey Mouse, and good triumphing over evil.
These are good things for children to learn. Las
Vegas is based on getting something for nothing,
which is impossible, because there wouldn't be
any jackpots for someone to win if someone else
hadn't lost the money in the first place. Hasn't
anyone figured out that inviting kids into a casino
to watch a circus act or pirates is stupid? What's
wrong with parents? Would you give your kids a
shot of heroin or a bottle of whiskey or fix them
up with a whore for their first date? Then why are
you bringing them here?

That's why I say this town is like a giant
whore with her legs open and the worst thing is
that all of us—every one of us here—is her pimp. I
drive a cab and you know what? I get a kickback
every time I take a fare to a restaurant or nightclub I recommend. Prostitution is illegal, but if I
drive a fare out to one of the legal whorehouses, I
get a cut. And I always ask for one. That's what
draws you in. The money. There is so much of it
in this town that you learn to close your eyes. I
hate it but I can't walk away. Who can?

—*J. T., a cab driver outside the Luxor*

Part Two

THE LUXOR

....

"I don't care if it's Baroque or Brooklyn, but give me something that will knock them flat on their backsides when they walk in."

—*Morris A. Lapidus, architect*

Winter: Reincarnation

"I too was a gambler, and I became aware of it that very moment: my hands shook, my legs trembled. I felt as if something had struck me on the head."
                    —*Fyodor Dostoyevsky, The Gambler*

CHAPTER NINE

....

Tony Alamo, the Boss

The Luxor was exactly what its creators designed it to be: an eye-popping example of entertainment architecture. Eight million people came to see it the first year it was open. It was on the cover of *Time* and pictured in *National Geographic*. Initially, the thirty-six-story pyramid was supposed to be covered with thirteen acres of gold-tinted glass, but less expensive black panes had been installed to cut costs. At times, these panes appeared to change color. When the sun struck the four-sided Luxor in the morning, the black panels on its east side became a mirror of gold. The southern and northern sides of the pyramid reflected the bluish tint of the cloudless desert sky. Only the western wall stayed stubbornly dark, but it too took on a golden glint after the noon sun peaked over the pyramid's tip. By dusk, the colors had reversed positions. Now it was the western wall that burned in the reddish glow of sunset and the eastern face that was coal black. Veteran employees swore the pyramid became ashen during overcast days. Blowing dust clung to it during windstorms, coating it brown. When it rained, the Luxor sparkled as if it were finely cut onyx, and at night the entire building simply vanished—its black skin perfectly camouflaged in the darkness. From a distance, the few lights that could be seen peeking through the pyramid's tinted hotel windows looked like muted stars.

Every super casino requires a "traffic stopper" to mark its entrance. At the Luxor, it was an earth-toned sphinx, ten stories high and three times larger than its Egyptian inspiration. Where wind and time had destroyed the face of the Great Sphinx at Giza, the Luxor's was intact; under a brightly colored blue-and-gold headpiece, it gazed ahead through unflinching black eyes. At night, thin green laser beams shot from these eyes across a man-made pool onto the side of an obelisk, on which the name LUXOR was emblazoned. Using specially designed fountains next to the obelisk, engineers were able to create a sixty-foot-high screen made of falling water, and on it they projected a hologram of King Tutankhamen's face. The constant movement of the water made the young pharaoh appear as if he were a ghost about to speak.

The Luxor was surrounded by 550 palm trees, gardens filled with red, yellow, and blue flowers, and replicas of Egyptian statues made of sand-covered fiberglass and Styrofoam. There were three swimming pools on the west side of the building. They were only four feet deep, and each had underwater seats built around the edges so swimmers could bask in the sun partially submerged and drink frozen blends of fruit and liquor delivered by tanned men and women in khaki shorts and polo shirts.

When viewed from the Strip, the Luxor seemed small, especially when compared to its neighbors—the sprawling MGM Grand and the boxy Excalibur. This was an optical illusion created by the pyramid's shape. Many guests did not realize how huge the building was until they stepped inside. Its hollow center was big enough to hold nine Boeing 747 airplanes stacked on top of each other. Because the resort's hotel rooms were built into the skin of the pyramid, each had a slanted exterior wall of black glass, which gave guests a tinted view of the Strip during the day, much like sunglasses, and made it difficult to see outside at night. The doors to the rooms faced the atrium. The corridors outside them doubled as balconies. From the ground floor looking up, these corridors looked like rungs on an overhanging ladder, each level diminishing in width as it rose higher and higher toward the pyramid's triangular peak.

The Luxor was actually two separate buildings in one. The pyramid formed a shell around a one-story rectangular building in the center of the atrium. The ground floor contained the Luxor's one hundred thousand–square-foot casino. The flat roof of this building was where the all-you-can-eat buffet, fine restaurants, and rides were located. It was called the "attractions level," and there was no ceiling over it to block the view. Gawkers could stare at the apex far above by craning their necks back. This rectangular building was separated from the pyramid's walls by the "Nile River"—a fifteen-foot-wide concrete channel filled with water that ringed the atrium on the ground floor. Flat-bottomed "reed boats," modeled after those used by ancient Egyptians, moved slowly along the Nile River on tracks concealed under a foot of water. The boats were built to ferry guests from the hotel's registration desk to the Luxor's elevators, which were located in each of the pyramid's four corners. (The Luxor's designers called the elevators "inclinators," because they traveled at a 39-degree angle, up and down each corner.) The reed boats were essential because some of the elevators didn't stop at every floor, so the boats were used to deliver guests to their correct elevator in an entertaining way. Guides wearing Egyptian garb translated the hieroglyphics etched on the walls of the casino as the boats moved slowly along the river.

Despite all the bad publicity that the Luxor received when it opened in late 1993, it had always been profitable. It had cost $400 million to build, or $100 million more than Bill Bennett had initially estimated, but during its first year, it had earned $90 million in profits before taxes. The next year it earned $86 million. Despite the drop, it continued to be the most profitable casino owned by Circus Circus. Still, the company's new managers thought it could do better, so shortly after they took charge in 1995, they sent Antonio "Tony" Alamo to evaluate it.

Alamo was one of the veteran casino employees whom Angel Naves had recruited in 1974 when Bennett and Pennington had first bought Circus Circus, and he had stayed with the company for sixteen years, eventually becoming the general manager at the Las Vegas Circus Circus casino. But like so many others, Alamo had gotten into a tiff with Bennett and had been forced to resign. Rival casino owner Kirk Kerkorian had taken advantage of Alamo's ouster by hiring him to oversee construction of the MGM Grand. He had been in charge of building the world's biggest hotel and its theme park, which contained more rides than any amusement park in the country except Walt Disney World. Kerkorian had promised that the MGM Grand would have the biggest casino on the Strip, and Alamo had obliged him by building not one, but three separate casinos inside the complex. Together, they covered as much area as four football fields. It had taken thirty-nine armored cars two days just to bring in the $3.5 million in coins needed to fill the MGM Grand's 3,500 slot machines. About one year after the MGM Grand opened, Michael Ensign had asked Alamo to join Gold Strike Resorts, because he needed someone to build the Monte Carlo—the super casino that Gold Strike was constructing in partnership with Steve Wynn. Ensign offered Alamo a partnership in Gold Strike Resorts and when it was later bought by Circus Circus, Alamo had returned to the company where he had started his Las Vegas career. This time, however, he was a senior vice president and owned more than $9 million of Circus Circus stock.

As Alamo began his walking tour of the Luxor, he tried to visualize it as if he were a guest checking in. The main entrance was located under the haunches of the Sphinx outside. The creature's belly served as a covered portal where taxis could pick up and discharge passengers. When guests entered the pyramid, they found themselves standing on a ledge, facing a pair of stairways that led down to the ground level. The Nile River flowed underneath this platform and was the first ride that guests saw. The Luxor's architects wanted them to feel as if they were entering "a vast archeological dig" where "the mysteries of ancient Egypt are about to be revealed." To help create this illusion, they decorated the outer walls of the casino with fake rocks and made its entrance look as if it were the opening of a cave. Although Alamo could hear familiar sounds—the electronic ring of slot machines and the clink of cascading coins falling into chrome trays—he could not see directly into the casino from the building's front doors. All he could see was the Nile River ride and the fake rocks, and he thought this was stupid. "The first thing guests should see when they enter the Luxor is its casino," Alamo explained. "Period. Not hieroglyphics, not boats, not fancy rides."

The hotel's registration desk was to the left of the entrance on the same platform that he was standing on, so Alamo walked over to it and saw what he thought was another conspicuous mistake. He was being drawn away from the casino. Many Strip resorts made their guests walk through the casino to check in. Here, the first thing guests did was get their room keys and walk down a ramp to the Nile River to board one of the reed boats. Once again, they were being taken away from the gambling.

On paper, the Nile River ride was a master stroke. "The reed boats were extremely popular from the day we opened," recalled Cliff Hay, the company's director of rides and attractions. "Originally, we only let guests use them but we had so many people wanting to ride them I suggested we begin selling tickets and on the first day we did, there was a long line all around the casino." Hay was thrilled at first. "In the amusement park business, long lines mean a ride is a big success, but when the casino manager saw the line, he chewed me out, because in the casino business long lines mean you have people standing around instead of gambling." Hay was ordered to cut the length of the line, so he raised the ticket price from $2 to $3. The next day, the line was only ten people shorter. He raised the price another dollar and the line dropped in half. "I felt bad about charging four bucks because the reed boats were such a lame ride," Hay said. "They didn't do anything but float around the perimeter of the casino for fifteen minutes. The boats were never designed to be an exciting ride."

Alamo knew that the ride had generated $5.1 million in profits the first year it was open. The next year, those profits had fallen to $4.1 million and he was convinced the ride would only produce $3.5 million during 1996. He thought he knew why. Not only was it lackluster, there was no reason for riders to go on it more than once, unlike a roller coaster that gets plenty of repeat customers. Alamo decided the Nile River was taking up space that could be better filled with slot machines.

Alamo rode an escalator up to the attractions level

on the roof of the rectangular building that held the casino. The Luxor's three amusement rides, fine restaurants, all-you-can-eat buffet, and several gift shops were located here, forming a ring around the perimeter. Alamo looked up at the apex high above him. While the vastness of the atrium was breathtaking, it also created problems. No matter how many high-watt fixtures were installed on the attractions level, the darkness of the atrium above made everything seem dim. There was a dreary feel to the place.

Alamo thought the Luxor's rides and other amusements were boring. They were supposed to be linked together thematically, in keeping with Glenn Schaeffer's initial concept of tying everything together inside the pyramid. Each played a role in telling "the Luxor Story," a sequential tale written by Hollywood special effects wizard Douglas Trumbull. Some Luxor employees jokingly referred to Trumbull's trilogy as "Indiana Jones meets Star Wars in Egypt."

" 'The Luxor Story' takes place in the past, the present, and the future," explained Cliff Hay. "Our hero is an Indiana Jones adventurer named Mac McPherson and audiences were told that he had bought the land where the Luxor is now standing and had discovered that there was a giant pyramid hidden deep beneath the surface. He and this girl, who is our heroine, tunnel down into this underground pyramid and discover a mystical obelisk there that has amazing powers. They then use it to foretell the future."

The first attraction was a motion simulator ride, the second a live performance, and the third a 3-D movie shown on a six-story screen. Guests had to buy a separate ticket for each one and although they were technologically dazzling, the public never really caught on to the fact that they had to be seen sequentially for the story to be effective. Alamo knew that an average of six million people bought tickets each year, generating

$21.7 million in profits, but he was not impressed. Like the Nile River ride, the amusements were one-shot events and he thought he could find something better.

Alamo rode an escalator downstairs into the casino and spotted several problems there too. It appeared lifeless. Every casino on the Strip had the same slot machines and table games as its competitors. Blackjack at the Luxor was played the same way it was at the Mirage. A casino had to offer its customers more than gambling alone, and there was little inside the Luxor's casino to make it special. He rode another escalator into the basement, where he walked past King Tut's Tomb, a museum filled with replicas of Egyptian treasures, and entered Pharaoh's Theater, the resort's 1,100-seat arena. By this time the show, *Winds of the Gods,* had been canceled. An ice skating production had been booked into the arena, but it too was failing.

"People used to come to Las Vegas strictly to gamble," said Alamo. "The average gambler used to spend four hours per day playing in a casino, but now that same gambler only plays two hours per day because there is so much more to see and do on the Strip. We have to give them something inside our resorts other than gambling to keep their attention. If we don't, they will go somewhere else." Besides gambling, the two most popular activities for tourists were dining and shows, and Alamo considered the Luxor weak in both.

He had seen enough. During the coming weeks, he proposed dozens of changes and eventually submitted a $250 million renovation plan that would take one full year to complete. As soon as the new managers approved it, an army of workers began using jackhammers to tear out the Nile River ride. That task alone was estimated to cost $5 million. Alamo also wanted the fake boulders at the entrance of the casino removed and the entire front lobby redone so the casino would be the first thing guests saw when they stepped inside. He estimated this change would cost $20 million.

The spending of millions did not faze Alamo. A distinguished-looking man of fifty-five, he had a confident air about him that some who did not know him well often mistook for arrogance. He rarely doubted the decisions he made, whether at work or in his personal life. He was a staunch Republican, a die-hard fiscal conservative, a devout Roman Catholic, a long-married husband, and the father of two. He was proud of his Cuban heritage and a passionate believer in the immigrant work ethic. Oddly, his life was a testament to nearly everything that gambling was not. Alamo had never counted on luck, nor had he believed that he could get anything worthwhile for free or by chance.

The younger of two sons born to working-class parents in a fishing village, Alamo had escaped from Cuba in 1961 by hiding in a tiny fishing boat. He had been studying agriculture at the University of Havana, but had gotten into trouble for criticizing Fidel Castro in public and had been forced to flee. After nearly being captured at sea, Alamo arrived in Miami with $7 in his pocket and the clothes he was wearing. Although he spoke only broken English, he found work, and when his longtime sweetheart, Maria, emigrated legally from Cuba to the United States one year later, he joined her in Reno, where her aunt lived. They wanted to marry but neither had any money, so Alamo asked a pawnshop owner if he would sell him two gold bands worth $25 each on credit.

"Why should I trust you?" the pawnbroker asked.

"Because I always keep my word," Alamo replied. "I will come by your shop every week and pay you one dollar."

Alamo was so earnest that the pawnbroker sold him the rings. He got a job cleaning toilets at Harrah's

Club, and after he paid off his debt, he used the pawn-broker as a reference so he and Maria could rent a tiny apartment and buy a washing machine. Harrah's was considered the most progressive casino in Nevada and one reason was because it promoted employees based on performance rather than "juice." Alamo took advantage of this. He was never late, never missed a day of work, and did every job assigned him without complaint. The casino rewarded his diligence by promoting him to the casino's coin room, where change from slot machines was counted, but he and Maria were still hard-pressed, especially after their son was born. Alamo worked as many overtime hours as he could and competed against sixty other employees in applying for a job as a craps dealer in the casino. Harrah's ran its own internal school and promised the job to the student who scored the highest. Alamo practiced counting out chips at home until his hands were numb. He won the job and was sent to work at a table with another newly trained dealer, Michael Ensign. The two men became lifelong friends.

During the next eleven years, Alamo followed the traditional route that ambitious employees take to get ahead in casinos. He learned how to deal blackjack and roulette, and then became a "boxman," responsible for watching the action at a craps table. The next step was floor manager and then pit boss, although Harrah's called them pit administrators. After that, he was promoted to a relief pit shift supervisor job. When the economy in Mexico underwent a short-lived boom in the early 1970s, Harrah's Club moved the Spanish-speaking Alamo into its marketing department to recruit Mexican high rollers. It was there that he caught the eye of rival casino manager Angel Naves, who recruited him for Circus Circus.

On his wrist, Alamo now wore a watch worth $11,000, but he also kept his $25 wedding band on his finger as a reminder not only of his love for his wife but of his roots. He was absolutely convinced that anyone who was willing to work hard could get ahead in America. "If I went to work as a dishwasher in a restaurant, I would eventually end up managing that restaurant," he often preached, "because I will do my job well. I will volunteer for extra work, for the toughest assignments. I will work overtime. I will work seven days a week. I will go to work before anyone else and I will go home after everyone else and I will do that year after year after year. This is the secret to success in life—working hard, always putting forth your best efforts."

Birthdays, Christmas, and other holidays were rarely celebrated in the Alamo household on the dates when they happened. They were squeezed in whenever Alamo had a day off. Work always came first, always. He wanted his son and daughter to share his work ethic, so he paid them $5 for every A on their report card to teach them the link between hard work and financial rewards. When his son, Tony Jr., came home one day from high school with two C's and a B, Alamo demanded to know why even though the rest of his grades were A's.

"The other kids are geniuses," the teenager shrugged.

"I don't care how smart or how much of a genius someone else is," Alamo lectured. "If you work harder, you can do just as well or even better."

He required his son to study each night for three hours. The boy protested at first, but finally gave in and from that point on earned all A's. Alamo's son is now a successful physician in Las Vegas. His daughter is a psychologist for the county school district.

Alamo told his staff at the Luxor that remodeling a super casino was a much tougher task than building one. "There is a buzz about a new place," he explained.

"Everyone wants to see the new volcano or the new theme park or see what is inside the new pyramid. But how do you get people excited about a remodeling? Most of our customers have already formed an image in their minds about what the Luxor is. Our job is to change that mental picture by getting them to come back into this property and see what we have done. We only have one chance to do that—so we can't blow it now."

Throughout 1996, Alamo and his band of architects worked feverishly to make the Luxor more exciting. They designed new restaurants, added more retail shops, moved other amenities. Two of their biggest changes were the addition of a 1,200-seat theater and new hotel towers. Both were built outside the pyramid. The theater was added near the southwest corner and the two hotel towers, each twenty-two stories tall, on the north side. To make sure the towers complemented the pyramid, they were covered with the same black glass and their lower floors were stepped back. Their 1,906 guest rooms brought the total number of rooms at the resort to 4,407. Once they were ready, the Luxor would be the second-largest hotel in the country.

The remodeling was far more than a face-lift. It represented a change in how Circus Circus was going to do business. The new management had decided that many of Bill Bennett's ironclad policies were outdated, especially his disdain for conventioneers and high rollers. The new management was adding a grand ballroom to the Luxor for convention use and turning two hundred guest rooms in the new hotel towers into luxury high-roller suites, some as big as 4,800 square feet. VIP passes were also being reintroduced so high rollers could jump ahead of the lines at restaurants.

Perhaps nothing better symbolized the break with the Bennett philosophy than the arrival of baccarat tables. Alamo was adding them to a roped-off, high-limit gaming area being built in the center of the casino. Part of the lore of Circus Circus described Bennett removing the baccarat tables from the original Circus Circus casino and taking an ax to one of them to show how much contempt he had for the game.

Because renovations are not "static undertakings," as Alamo liked to put it, he was constantly revising his designs and adding projects. Microbreweries had become a fad in a rival resort, so Alamo worked one in to his drawings. The biggest high rollers were from Asia, so he added a sushi bar. Nightclubs were becoming popular, so Alamo ordered one. Costs skyrocketed, but no one challenged him. "We are going to do everything we can to make the Luxor the hottest casino on the Strip," he said. No idea seemed too extravagant or bizarre.

One morning, Alamo announced to his staff that he had come up with a way to liven the casino. "I want to put a real Egyptian mummy on display," he declared. He ordered Leon Symanski, the Luxor's safety coordinator, to find one. Symanski began calling museums. "We can deal directly with the government of Egypt, which museum curators have told me is nearly impossible," Symanski reported back to Alamo, "or we can get a museum to loan us one on a rotating exhibit basis, or we can buy one in Germany from a Turkish businessman who has a warehouse stuffed with Egyptian artifacts that he stole in the 1950s. He is willing to sell us a mummy."

"Go through the proper diplomatic channels," Alamo said. Symanski arranged a meeting between an Egyptian diplomat and Alamo. They negotiated a price: $2 million a year in rent. Alamo was about to sign the deal when the diplomat asked where the mummy would be displayed. Inside the casino, Alamo replied. A horrified look spread across the diplomat's face. "We can't allow you to put one of our ancestors on display inside

a casino," he said. "You must build a special museum
for it *outside* of the casino." Symanski later recalled
what happened. "Tony had been ready to shake on the
deal and he suddenly whips back his hand and says,
'Everything we do in this business is related to gaming.
If your mummy can't go in our casino, then we don't
want it.' " That was the last anyone heard about the
mummy.

CHAPTER TEN

....

Luxor Security

Luxor security shift manager Malcolm Fry had just finished roll call and was pouring himself a second cup of coffee when the first telephone call of the night shift came in. A couple had just complained to the hotel's front desk that their room had been burglarized while they were gambling. Fry sent a security officer to investigate.

"You ain't gonna believe this, boss," the officer said minutes later over his portable radio. "They claim someone broke in to take a crap in their toilet." Nothing had been stolen from the room. In fact, there were no signs of a break-in. Yet the couple insisted that someone had used their toilet. "They flushed the evidence before I got here," the officer added. The couple claimed that the incident had ruined their vacation and was causing them so much "emotional trauma" that they wanted cash from the hotel as compensation.

"Did you do a lock interrogation?" Fry asked. Every time someone inserted a plastic room key into the electronic lock on a Luxor hotel door, it kept a record that showed the time, the date, and whether the key had been issued to a guest or a hotel employee. Each lock kept track of the last 150 times that keys had been used to open the door. Because the windows in the room were sealed, the door was the only entrance.

"According to the lock, the only keys that have been used to get inside here are the ones that the couple has," the officer reported.

"Be sure to put that in your report," said Fry, "but don't make a big deal out of it with the guests."

The Luxor's assistant hotel manager offered to move the couple into a different room and deduct two nights' worth of room charges from their three-night bill, but they rejected his offer. "They're demanding a cash settlement," the officer reported via radio to Fry. "If they don't get one, they claim they are going to file a lawsuit against the hotel."

"Stay out of it," Fry ordered. "Just get all the facts for your report."

Because the couple refused the offer, they were told that their complaint would be forwarded in the morning to Scott Kent, the director of risk management for Circus Circus. It would be up to Kent, a former insurance claims adjuster, to decide whether or not they deserved a cash settlement. If not, he would submit their claim to the corporation's in-house lawyers to await a lawsuit. Before making his decision, Kent would investigate to see if the couple had a history of filing frivolous claims or if they had ever been arrested for fraud. He might even dispatch one of his own investigators to interview them. Whatever Kent did was none of the security officer's business, Fry explained. "Our job is to be polite to the guests and get all the information that we possibly can. We are the first eyes and ears on the scene, but we are not there to resolve a dispute. We are not cops. We are not here to make arrests or prove someone is lying."

Understanding that distinction was the hardest thing to teach new officers, Fry said. "We are dealing with our guests, and if they tell us that someone left a turd in their toilet, then we write that down and pass it up the chain of command without comment because we don't know who they are. It might be worth it for the hotel to give them whatever they are demanding, no matter how stupid the claim, if they are a high roller. One lesson you've got to learn quickly in Las Vegas is: what you know is not nearly as important as who you know. It's all about having juice."

Fry suspected that the complaining couple didn't have juice. If they did, one of the casino hosts responsible for watching over high rollers would have resolved the complaint without security ever being called. Still, he couldn't be sure. "You would think millionaires wouldn't bother filing really ridiculous complaints, but some of them are the worst, because they know they can get away with it."

Eighty percent of the security force's time was spent doing what Fry referred to as loss prevention. "We do our best to keep the Luxor from being sued. In the old days, our job was to protect the cash from armed robbers and card cheats. Now we have to watch out for scheming lawyers with greedy clients." Circus Circus was hit with an average of twenty-one thousand claims a year in the late 1990s, filed by angry guests demanding compensation for real or imagined wrongs. The bulk of these claims was resolved quickly within each resort, most often by compensating a guest with free meals or free hotel rooms. However, an average of fifty claims ended up in court. According to Kent, about one out of every five claims is found to be fraudulent.

"A guest bites down and finds some object in his food," Fry explained. "Back home, he would be happy if the restaurant gave him a free meal and the waitress apologized, but guests here see all the slot machines and table games and they think, 'Hey, this place has millions. Someone got rich by suing McDonald's because their coffee was too hot. Maybe I can get rich too.' The next thing you know, they're exaggerating their injuries."

The most frequently filed claim was for a "slip or fall," and on this particular night, Fry got a call about this type of incident two hours into the shift. An elderly woman had stumbled and fallen while stepping off an escalator in the casino. She had gashed her hand, but otherwise seemed okay. She was interviewed, photographs were taken of her injury, and an ambulance was called. "This lady is not trying to cheat us," Fry declared. "I can tell by how she handled herself. She didn't demand an immediate cash payment. She didn't even want to go to the hospital. She was embarrassed about falling." Guests hoping to make a quick buck usually complain about injuries that are difficult to prove, such as neck and back pain, and they often want to settle a claim for cash on the spot. The casino took care of the woman's ambulance and hospital charges and told her that she didn't have to pay her hotel bill.

A thirty-year-old man had fallen in the same spot two days earlier, but that outcome had been very different. The "victim" slipped on banana and orange peels scattered on the floor and cut his shoulders when he fell backward onto the escalator steps. On the way to the hospital, he complained of intense back pain. A video camera mounted in a nearby corner showed him riding down the escalator with another man moments before the fall, both unaware that they were being filmed. As they neared the bottom, the other man pulled the banana and orange peels from his pockets and tossed them on the floor. The video revealed that the "victim" actually had delayed his fall by walking backward up the escalator steps until a group of tourists reached the escalator so that he would have an audience see him fall. Further investigation showed the men were cousins who had filed similar "slip and fall" claims against other Nevada resorts.

Fry's favorite scam involved a grandmother who had staggered into the lobby of the Circus Circus hotel in Reno with blood dripping from several scratches on her face. Her right eye was red and swelling shut and her blouse was ripped. "I've been robbed!" she gasped. She claimed that she had been attacked while waiting for one of the hotel elevators and announced that she was going to hire an attorney to file a lawsuit unless she was paid $500 in cash. What the woman didn't realize was that her "attack" had been filmed by a video camera. The tape showed her standing alone in front of the elevators. Suddenly, she punched herself twice in the face, scratched her cheek with her fingernails, and ripped her blouse. When confronted with the evidence, the woman said she had lost $500 gambling and didn't want to tell her daughter.

Not every claim was so easily resolved. A couple sued Circus Circus after they claimed their toddler found a discarded condom under a bed in their hotel room and began chewing on it. The parents said they were afraid that their son had contracted the AIDS virus. Was the hotel liable or did the couple concoct the story? A guest eating at the Luxor's all-you-can-eat buffet complained that he had chipped his tooth when he bit down on a piece of chicken bone in his salad. A dentist confirmed that the man's tooth was chipped, but couldn't tell when it had happened. Had the man chipped it earlier and gone to the resort because he wanted it to pay his dental bills?

"You get cynical because you see people at their

worst a lot of the time," Fry said. "When I first started out in this business, I had this woman tell me that her purse had been stolen." Fry believed her because she described a common ploy of Las Vegas thieves: a man had walked up to her while she was playing a quarter slot machine and had pointed to several quarters on the floor. "You must have dropped your change," he volunteered. She bent down to collect the coins and he helped her. Only after he was gone did she notice that her purse was missing. She had put it next to her chair on the side opposite to where the change was lying on the floor. The man playing the slot machine next to her had stolen her purse while she was being distracted by his accomplice. Fry felt so sorry for the woman and her four-year-old son, who was waiting nearby, that he gave them $10 out of his own pocket for cab fare and arranged for them to eat at the casino's café without charge. But when he left work late that night, he spotted the little boy playing on the sidewalk outside another casino. It was after three in the morning so he stepped inside to ask why the woman had not taken a cab back to her hotel. She was playing a slot machine and Fry noticed that she had a purse with her. "Oh, just go away," she snapped. "My kid was hungry, okay, and I didn't want to spend my money on dinner so I conned you into doing it. It's no big deal. Just go away."

"She knew I was new on the job and didn't know any better," Fry said. "I heard later that she and her boyfriend had gotten caught stealing purses in a casino. Just guess how they were doing it?"

The Luxor security department was operated much like a small-town police force. Its chief was Andrew Vanyo, a twenty-two-year veteran of the Cleveland Police Department and a former director of the enforcement division at the Nevada Gaming Control Board, which regulates casinos. Vanyo had three shift managers: Fry and two other men, who were in charge of the day, night, and graveyard shifts. Each shift manager had about fifteen officers under his command. Vanyo answered to the Circus Circus corporate security department run by Emmett Michaels, a gregarious former U.S. Marine and a Vietnam War hero. Michaels had been one of twenty-two special agents sent by the FBI to Las Vegas in 1977 to help break the mafia's stranglehold on Strip casinos. He was in charge of the FBI's electronic surveillance of mob enforcer Anthony Spilotro and his best friend, Frank "Lefty" Rosenthal. The bureau rewarded Michaels by reassigning him to its Washington, D.C., headquarters, but he didn't want to leave Las Vegas, so he resigned and joined Circus Circus in 1985. "My FBI colleagues thought I had sold out to the mob," Michaels recalled. "Despite everything the bureau had done, even within our own ranks there was still a lot of suspicion of people who worked at casinos." At the time, each Circus Circus casino had its own independent security force. Security officers carried whatever caliber of handguns they wanted and followed different rules. Michaels standardized procedures, established vigorous training programs, and drafted manuals. Circus Circus now had what was generally considered to be one of the best security forces on the Strip.

Shift manager Malcolm Fry had become a security guard by chance. He had assumed that he would work in an auto plant in his hometown of Detroit after he returned from the Vietnam War in 1971, but there were no jobs, so he went to work as a guard in a department store and discovered that he had a knack for catching shoplifters. "They rarely look at price tags. Instead, they look around to see if anyone is watching them." A buddy from Vietnam invited him to Las Vegas in

1986 and Fry found work in a tiny Strip casino called Westward Ho. Not long after he started, Fry disarmed a drunk gambler who had slashed a dealer with a knife and stabbed a security guard. When the Las Vegas Metropolitan Police arrived to take the drunk to jail, one of the cops pulled Fry aside. "This cop asked me why I hadn't killed the bastard!" Fry recalled. "This cop says, 'Around here we never let anyone attack one of our officers and walk away to brag about it.' " Fry said he later received a snapshot in the mail from the cop. "It was a picture of the drunk. His face was smashed up and on the back of the picture, this cop had written: 'This is how we rehabilitate pricks who get out of line in Las Vegas.' "

At least two times during the night shift, Fry would leave his basement office in the pyramid and walk through the casino to check on his officers. About one-third of them were retired cops, several from Los Angeles. Another third were younger wanna-bes who were hoping that a stint at the Luxor would improve their chances of joining the city police department. The rest simply needed a job. Beginning pay was $9.50 per hour; the most that they could earn was $15.75 per hour. Fry had thirteen men and two women working on his shift. One officer patrolled the grounds and four officers were stationed outside each of the Luxor's "inclinators." (Guests had to show a room key before the officers would let them go upstairs.) Another manned the information booth in the casino, and the rest delivered casino chips to gaming tables, collected the boxes of cash at each table, and investigated accidents. The Luxor also had two plainclothes officers who mingled with the guests, looking for prostitutes, pickpockets, purse snatchers, and other thieves.

On this particular night, Fry received a flurry of calls:

• A woman slapped her husband at a blackjack table and then ran crying from the casino. One of Fry's men stopped the man from chasing her. "See if he wants us to call the police so he can file a complaint against her for hitting him," Fry said. The man didn't want to file a complaint. "Then let him go, but make it clear that we don't want either of them back in here tonight."

• A man was found asleep in one of the unfinished guest rooms inside the new hotel towers. He had gambled away all his money and had sneaked into the towers, which were still not open to the public. "Check with the casino manager. If he really lost a lot of money, they might give him a room; otherwise he has to leave."

• An officer found a six-year-old girl wandering through the casino, looking for her mother. "Take her to the information booth. We will keep her there until the mom shows up."

• A hotel guest parking his car accidentally struck one of the thirty limousines being used by the sultan of Brunei's royal family, who were guests in the hotel. The sultan's bodyguards quickly surrounded the man's car even though the royal family members were safely inside the hotel. The guest was terrified because the sultan's guards had brandished automatic weapons. He was afraid that they were mafia hit men and was refusing to leave his car. "Go outside and show him your credentials and then escort him into the hotel and explain that he doesn't have anything to be afraid of."

Fry took pride in how quickly he handled these incidents. They were trivial events, remembered only because he would have to file paperwork about them. Yet if he had not dealt with each one diplomatically, any one of them might have escalated into a much bigger problem. Fry loved the unpredictable nature of his job. One night nothing would happen. The next, he would have to scramble to keep up.

About two hours before his shift was to end, Fry received the most alarming call of the night. A woman called him and said she had been kidnapped and was being held hostage in the hotel. A stunned Fry asked if she was in any immediate danger. "No," she replied, "but I would like you to send some officers to my room to release me." Fry and two of his officers raced upstairs. An attractive young woman opened the door and asked them to come inside. She was the woman who had called. There was an older man in the room smoking a cigarette.

"You said you were being held hostage, right?" Fry asked.

"I am," the woman declared. "This creep ran an ad in my college newspaper that said a Las Vegas advertising executive was looking for beauty pageant winners to be in a television commercial for the grand opening of the New York New York Hotel and Casino in a few weeks." The woman had won a number of beauty pageants so she mailed in her photograph. "This guy calls and says he is president of his own advertising agency in Las Vegas and he says he can help me get into this commercial if I come here." The man had sent her a round-trip airplane ticket and promised to pay all her expenses during her weekend stay at the Luxor. "I got here Friday," the woman continued, "and this creep takes me to dinner. This morning, he picks me up for breakfast, gives me a tour of the Strip, buys me lunch, and then takes me gambling at the Mirage. I kept asking him when we were going to shoot this commercial, but he just kept putting me off. Tonight, he takes me to dinner and then to this topless show at the Stardust casino. Afterwards, he tells me there never was any commercial. He was just looking for someone attractive and younger to hang with over the weekend! He said he really digs beauty queens."

"Did he sexually assault or rape you?" Fry asked.

"No," the woman angrily replied. "He told me that he had done this with lots of girls and that some of them even had sex with him because they had enjoyed themselves. I told him that I was calling the cops and he laughed and said, 'For what?' "

"Did he ever tell you that you couldn't leave?" Fry asked.

"No, he gave me a round-trip ticket, but he, like, kidnapped me in a way to get me here, don't you think?"

Fry questioned the sixty-two-year-old man in the room. Yes, he had met the woman by placing an ad in her college newspaper. Yes, he had sent her a ticket and paid all her expenses. Yes, he had lied to her about the television ad. "But I really do have some contacts, and if she had read the ad closely, she would have noticed that there was a disclaimer that said she was not being promised a job.

"This woman is the first one to complain," he added nonchalantly. "Most of the other women I've brought out here know how to kick back and enjoy a free weekend in Las Vegas. Most of them think what I am doing is funny. You know, I'm not that bad company but this broad is just too uptight."

Fry asked him if he had pressured the woman for sex.

"Absolutely not," he replied. "I've slept with some of the women who I've brought out here, but it's always their choice."

Fry told the woman that he would call the police if she wished but he doubted they would arrest the man.

"I'd suggest you go home and contact a lawyer,"

Fry told her. "We will stay with you while you pack and I'll have a Luxor limousine take you to the airport."

Fry typed his report as soon as the man and woman left the pyramid.

"I file these incidents under 'Las Vegas moments.' Where else but here could things like this ever happen?"

CHAPTER ELEVEN

....

Keith Uptain, Casino Shift Manager

Just after 9 P.M., the surveillance team that operated the cameras in the ceiling of the Luxor casino called Keith Uptain on his pocket telephone.

"It's bad, boss," the caller said. "You'd better come down."

Uptain hurried into the Luxor's basement and tapped on an unmarked door with a peephole in it. The two men inside played a videotape for him without comment. The black-and-white image flickering on the screen had been recorded fifteen minutes earlier from a camera directly over a roulette table. It showed a dealer spinning the wheel in one direction and tossing a pearl-like ball around its rim in the opposite direction as players hurriedly leaned over the table, putting down bets.

In roulette, gamblers try to guess where the ball will land on the wheel. There are thirty-six numbers around the wheel, not in sequence, plus a zero and a double zero. The odd numbers are red, the evens are black, the zeros are green. The players put different-colored checks—often incorrectly called chips—on the roulette table on numbers that correspond with those on the wheel. These thirty-six numbers are arranged on the table in a rectangular grid made up of three vertical columns and twelve horizontal rows. The first row contains the numbers 1, 2, and 3. The next continues with the 4, 5, and 6, and so on. The zero and double zero are at the top of the three vertical columns. The payoff depends on how a bet is positioned on the table. If a gambler is trying to pick a specific number, he puts his check directly on that number. This is called placing a "straight up" bet, and the gambler will win thirty-five checks for every one that he risks. A "split" bet means betting two numbers at the same time by putting a check on the line that connects the two; a "corner" means betting four numbers. The more numbers that are bet with a single check, the lower the payoff. Besides trying to pick a specific number, a gambler can bet colors—red, black, or green—or bet whether the ball will land on an odd or an even number. He can also bet entire columns by placing a check at the very bottom of one of them.

So far, Uptain had not noticed anything unusual about the game he was watching. But when the ball began its last three revolutions around the wheel, the dealer leaned forward with her right arm extended and swept her palm over the numbers on the table as a signal that all betting had to stop. Just as the ball was about to drop on the wheel, a player lunged forward and dropped several checks on the number five. The dealer quickly picked them up, explaining that it was too late to place a bet. But the man could be seen on the tape arguing with her. By this time, the ball had dropped on number twenty-four and as the dealer scanned the table, she noticed that no one had bet specifically on that number, but a large cash bet had been placed at the end of the third column of numbers on the table grid. She didn't remember seeing it there before, but it was a winning bet because the number twenty-four was located in the third column. Picking it paid two-for-one odds.

"Dammit," Uptain snapped. "You teach these people and tell them exactly what they should look for and then they fall for something as obvious and stupid as this." He rewound the tape and explained what was happening. The man who had caused the commotion by putting down a late bet was a decoy whose job was to distract the dealer. "Keep your eye on the bottom of the monitor," Uptain said. As soon as the dealer reached across the table to pick up the decoy's bet, the videotape showed another man, standing at the end of the table, step forward and drop the cash on the table at the bottom of the third column. The dealer couldn't see him because her back was turned as she argued with the decoy. "Now look at the wheel," Uptain said. The videotape showed the man putting down the cash *after* the roulette ball had fallen onto number twenty-four. "This is called 'past-posting'—making a bet after the winner already has been chosen—and it is the oldest cheat in the book." During the next several minutes, Uptain and the surveillance crew printed out photographs of the two cheaters taken from other ceiling cameras. Although the value of the pictures was questionable since both men were wearing hats and sunglasses, the surveillance crew sent copies and a brief report over a fax machine to surveillance rooms in other casinos on the Strip.

"All it takes is a few seconds for someone to cheat you," Uptain said as he returned to the casino. "We've caught teams who have spent months working on sophisticated scams. They will hit one casino on the Strip and then move on to the next one. But this? This was an old scam that should have been caught. There were all sorts of clues."

To begin with, the bet was in cash. Roulette dealers

are taught to look closely at the table as soon as the betting ends so they can be familiar with what bets have been made. Because most gamblers bet with checks, a cash bet should have stuck out. The way the paper money was stacked together should also have made the dealer suspicious. Several $1 bills had been placed on top of several $100 bills. Cheaters will often have two packets of money in their pockets. One will contain all singles and the other a stack of a few $100 bills tucked behind some singles. The cheater will put the pile of hundreds on a table, and then, if something goes wrong, will try to switch the stacks to keep from losing his stash. The dealer also should have anticipated that she was being set up as soon as the decoy made a late bet. He had been playing at the table for ten minutes and clearly knew the rules. Why was he suddenly causing an uproar?

Nor was the dealer the only employee who had blown it. A "mucker" helping the dealer clear the table of losing bets was supposed to be watching the table whenever the dealer was occupied. Instead, the cameras showed him staring at a well-endowed woman walking through the casino. The floor supervisor responsible for monitoring several table games had also erred. As soon as the dealer realized that someone had bet $4,904 in cash and won, she had stopped the game and conferred with the floor supervisor. She admitted that she had not noticed when the cash had been put on the table. The floor supervisor had called in the pit boss who was *his* supervisor. "All the floor supervisor or pit boss had to do was announce that surveillance was being notified so a videotape of the game could be reviewed," Uptain said. "Trust me, the two cheaters would have bolted out of the casino as soon as one of them lifted up the telephone." Instead, the pit boss had ordered the dealer to pay the two-to-one bet and *then* called surveillance. "What good was that going to do after they had

The famous sign welcoming visitors coming into the Las Vegas Strip from the south. The landscape is subdued compared to what was to follow.

[Courtesy Single Item Accessions Collection, University of Nevada, Las Vegas Library]

"Vegas Vic" atop the Pioneer Club on Glitter Gulch in the 1930s.
[Courtesy Manis Collection, University of Nevada, Las Vegas Library]

Glitter Gulch at night, c. 1948.
[Courtesy Manis Collection, University of Nevada, Las Vegas Library]

THE FIRST MEN WITH
LARGE-SCALE PLANS

Kirk Kerkorian in front of the
site of his International Hotel.
[Courtesy Las Vegas News Bureau
Collection, University of Nevada, Las
Vegas Library]

Howard Hughes in the 1950s.
[Courtesy Las Vegas News Bureau
Collection, University of Nevada,
Las Vegas Library]

Jay Sarno—visionary, clown,
man of excess.
[Courtesy Mel Larson]

THE CREATORS OF CIRCUS CIRCUS

Bill Pennington, *left,* and Bill Bennett, *right,* were all smiles at this 1986 ribbon cutting with then governor Richard Bryan for the opening of their new riverboat casino, the *Colorado Belle,* even though they were actually in the midst of a bitter feud. [Courtesy of Mel Larson]

Circus Circus, where it all started. [Courtesy Mandalay Resort Group]

CIRCUS CIRCUS SUPER CASINOS

The Excalibur. [Author photo]

Mandalay Bay.
[Courtesy Mandalay Resort Group]

The Luxor.
[Author photo]

Steve Wynn and his 1999 super casino, the Bellagio.
[Courtesy Mirage Resorts]

CIRCUS CIRCUS CORPORATE HEADQUARTERS

CEO Clyde Turner wanted to attract a higher class of gamblers than the grind-joint customers targeted by Bill Bennett. [Courtesy Jim Barrows]

President Glenn Schaeffer at a March 1999 press conference to discuss the grand opening of the company's newest super casino. [Courtesy Jim Barrows]

From the left, Luxor casino manager Tom Robinson, Circus Circus chairman Michael Ensign, and Luxor general manager Tony Alamo. [Courtesy Jim Barrows]

A LUXOR GALLERY

Casino expert Keith Uptain.
[Courtesy Keith Uptain]

Maria Tamayo-Soto, security
shift supervisor.
[Courtesy the Luxor]

Kelly Jo Steinfort and
Phillip Millaudon.
[Courtesy Kelly Jo Steinfort]

Poker room head
Don Archer,
right, and daily
player Phil
Friedman.
[Author photo]

been paid and left the casino?" Uptain grumbled. The cheaters had made off with $9,808 in winnings.

One by one Uptain chastised the employees in his office. The Luxor had specific disciplinary procedures that had to be followed whether or not the employees in question were union members. First, Uptain spelled out what they had done wrong and how they should have acted. Then he suspended each of them for five days without pay. Uptain had wanted to fire the pit boss, who was an eighteen-year veteran, for so stupid a mistake, but casino manager Tom Robinson had nixed it. "In my view, all of them got off easy," Uptain said later. He fumed about the past-posting swindle much of the night. Word would go out: the Luxor is sloppy, an easy target. "In this business, you are going to be beaten," he explained. "It *is* going to happen, but when it's something as fundamental as what happened tonight, that's just unforgivable."

Actually, cheating hadn't been much of a problem at the Luxor. Circus Circus's reputation for running grind joints had kept most professional cheaters away because they didn't want to risk getting caught for such small stakes. But now that the resort was becoming more upscale, Uptain suspected that it would draw more cheaters. Every few months, it seemed that the Strip got hit with a new sting. A few years earlier it had been the "Dingo boot" scam, so called because most of the cheaters who tried it wore Dingo brand cowboy boots. There was a reason why they liked the square-toed footwear. The cheaters had attached electronic sensors onto their toes to help them count cards while playing blackjack, and the extra room in the boot made it easier for them to wiggle their toes. If a low-value card was dealt, the Dingo cheaters curled the toes on their left feet. If it was a high-value card, they curled the toes on their right feet. The sensors sent a signal to a van parked outside the casino, where a computer kept track of the count. The players had tiny receivers in their ears through which they received betting instructions. While card counting is legal, in Nevada it is against the law to use electronic devices to do it. Uptain knew a store in Las Vegas that sold Dingo boot devices for $20,000, even though most casinos had found ways to thwart them.

Another sophisticated con involved the use of a remote-controlled camera with a powerful zoom lens. In blackjack, whenever a dealer draws an ace as his faceup card, he is required to peek at his hole card to see if he has a blackjack. If he does, the hand is over. If he doesn't, play continues. One team of thieves positioned a camera hidden in a woman's purse directly behind a dealer so that the zoom lens could see the dealer's facedown card when he peeked at it. The Luxor prevented cheaters from sneaking looks at a dealer's facedown card by installing a small prism in the top of its blackjack tables and by using specially designed playing cards. The tens, face cards, and aces in these decks had their suit and the number 10 or a letter, such as "Q" for Queen, printed in the upper left corner. Whenever a dealer needed to check his facedown card, he slid the card's left corner across the prism. If it were a ten, face card, or an ace, the number or letter printed on the card's edge would appear. If not, the prism would show a blank. There was no reason for a dealer to lift his card off the table to peek at it.

Most of the thieves Uptain had encountered over the years had relied on less expensive gimmicks. The most common was a mirror hidden inside a cigarette package that could be positioned on a blackjack table so that a cheater could see underneath the cards as they were being dealt by hand. This was one reason why the Luxor used a six-deck plastic shoe when its dealers dealt; it meant no one could see underneath the deck. The Luxor also did not allow players to touch their cards. Uptain had seen players in other casinos use their fingernails to nick cards. One nick meant a low card, two a high card. Other players used a minuscule piece of sandpaper glued to the tip of a finger to scratch marks on cards or sand down one of the corners. A few even tried to use a luminous daub to secretly mark cards. The clear daub would be kept close by, perhaps on a dollar bill put alongside several chips, so that a cheater could transfer some of the substance with his fingertips onto the back of a card. The daub could be seen only through red-tinted sunglasses or red-tinted contact lenses. At the Luxor, dealers collected all cards that had been dealt at blackjack and stacked them in a red plastic discard tray. The red plastic walls of this tray acted like a filter and revealed any daubs or special inks. The casino also replaced all of the cards at its blackjack tables every two hours to make sure that none of them had been tampered with. The used cards were sold in Luxor gift shops as souvenirs, but only after their sides had been marked with a permanent black ink.

At the Luxor, gamblers were not permitted to touch their bets once they had been put down on a blackjack table. This was done to prevent the "capping" and "pinching" of chips. Capping took place after a gambler won a hand and quickly covered his stack of chips with his hand, dropping several additional ones that he had hidden in his palm onto his wager. Pinching was the opposite. A gambler might look as if he were simply being a good sport when he reached forward and slid his losing bet toward a dealer, but he also might be trying to palm some of the chips off the top when he covered them with his hand.

Over the years, professional cheaters had found ways to beat every game. Uptain had seen craps players so skilled that they could switch dice without anyone noticing that a loaded pair had been tossed into the game. He had heard of cheaters replacing the white ball in roulette wheels with a loaded one and using powerful electromagnets hidden in wheelchairs to stop roulette wheels on command. One legendary con man once walked up to a roulette table and watched as the ball fell into a number. "Dammit, I lost," he exclaimed and handed the dealer a $20 bill. When the dealer pointed out that the man had not placed a bet on the table, the con man explained that he had placed a "mental bet" by thinking of a number. The dealer laughed and accepted the cash. The con man waited for the next spin and then exclaimed: "I won!" He demanded $3,500 as a payoff for his $100 mental bet. When the casino refused to pay, he sued and argued in court that the casino had agreed to accept mental bets when the dealer had kept his first $20 wager. A judge threw out the case, quipping that a casino was entitled to pay off all "mental bets" with "mental checks."

The hardest cheaters to catch were dealers. During his career, Uptain had caught them using marked cards to help accomplices at blackjack. Others had sent their buddies signals with code words or body movements. Some were skilled at "dealing seconds," which meant they could give a specific card to a player whenever they wanted. Casinos themselves had been known to cheat by employing "mechanics"—cardsharps so adept at dealing that they could ensure a player never won a hand. The Luxor used automatic shuffling machines at many of its blackjack tables, as well as the six-deck shoes, to prevent cheating. But no device was foolproof. Uptain had seen some dealers lift the corner of a card as they pulled it from a shoe so that the player sitting in the last seat on a blackjack table, commonly called "third base," could get a glimpse of it. Sometimes dealers gave players hints without realizing it. Experienced blackjack gamblers in some casinos would watch to see how many times a dealer looked at his hole card when he peeked to see if he had a blackjack. If he looked twice at the same card, there was a good chance that he had a four, because at first glance the top of a "4" looks like the top of the "A" on an ace.

Over the years, Circus Circus had caught more dealers stealing than trying to help someone cheat. The company tried to make this difficult by requiring its dealers to wear uniforms without pockets and to always clap their hands above the gaming tables whenever they took a break. This was done to show the eye in the sky that they were not holding any chips in their hands. Still, there were plenty of ways for an employee to steal. One dealer who had a habit of running his hand through his hair was caught dropping $100 chips down the back of his shirt. Another hid a chip in his hand and coughed, covering his mouth, just before going on his coffee break. A female dealer acted as if she was adjusting her bra strap when she was actually slipping chips into the cup. A dealer at the Circus Circus–owned Slots-A-Fun was caught palming a $100 chip in his hand and then dropping it into a half-filled coffee cup. His girlfriend was the cocktail waitress assigned to his table, and she would leave the cup there as if it was for a player and later pick it up and remove the chip. Another dealer was caught using a "chip cup," a metal cup that had a $5 chip glued across its top and was hollow underneath. The dealer slipped the cup over several $100 chips and then slid it across the table to a cohort when paying off a winning $5 bet. From the eye in the sky, it looked as if the dealer was simply passing a stack of $5 chips to a player when he was actually slipping several $100 chips to his buddy. After that incident, the Luxor required its dealers to separate chips individually on top of the table when they paid off a bet. That way the ceiling camera could see each chip.

"There is usually a specific reason behind everything we do inside a casino," Uptain explained. Most of the procedures were in place because of something that had happened in the past. "I don't care how good a dealer is at stealing," he said, "we always catch them—and the reason is greed. If a guy would just take one chip, he'd be difficult to catch, but after he gets away with it for a long time, he begins stealing a couple of chips at a time, and pretty soon he's taking so much that we know there is a problem because of all of the money that's missing." When the dealer sticking $100 chips in her bra was caught and ordered to undress, more than $2,000 worth tumbled out. She had grown a full bra size from when she had first arrived at work.

Even the language used in casinos has stories behind it. Everywhere else, tips are called tips, but in a casino they are called tokes. The reason: Several years ago dealers had tried to convince the IRS that the cash they received from players was not a tip and therefore did not have to be reported as taxable income. The logic behind this dodge was that a tip was defined by the IRS as a payment in return for special treatment. Since it is illegal for a dealer to provide any sort of favor to a player, the dealers argued that the money they were given was a "token of appreciation" for dealing an honest game, and therefore not a reward for special services. The IRS didn't buy it, but the term "toke" stuck.

Not long after the Luxor opened, a dealer caused an uproar by stealing tokes. Like most other Strip resorts, the Luxor requires its dealers to pool their tokes. The casinos prefer this because it supposedly keeps a dealer from hustling customers for tokes or helping a player in return for a toke. The trouble began when a surveillance crew spotted a Luxor blackjack dealer taking her tokes with her rather than depositing them in a toke box. Casino security was called, but since the woman was not stealing the casino's money, there was nothing the Luxor itself could do. It was up to other dealers to ask the police to arrest her for theft, since she was taking money that was supposed to be split with them. In court, the dealer argued that she had not done anything illegal. How could she be stealing, she asked, if a customer had given a toke specifically to her? A judge found her guilty after ruling that she had agreed to share her tokes with other dealers as a condition of her employment.

The most effective way a casino prevents cheating is by having every employee watch every other employee. The best illustration for this is craps, the fastest game in a casino. Up to twenty players can bet on each roll of the dice in craps, so thousands of dollars can change hands. The action happens so fast that craps often looks more complicated than it is. Simply put, craps players try to guess whether or not a certain number will be rolled before the number seven comes up. That's it.

Most craps games are run by four employees. The boxman sits in the center on one side of the oblong craps table and watches the dice, rules on all disputes, counts out the chips, and collects all the money, which he stuffs into a box; hence the term: boxman. On each side of him is a dice dealer, sometimes called a craps dealer. The two dealers arrange the bets on the table and pay off all winners. They have the toughest job because there are 180 different bets that can be made each time the dice are rolled. The "stickman" stands on the opposite side of the table and uses a limber pole with a hook on the end to collect the dice after they are thrown and push them to the "shooter"—the gambler throwing the dice. He throws the dice until he loses, then they are passed to the gambler on his left.

A craps table is waist-high, with the interior scooped out so that shooters can throw the dice from one end to the other. The table is covered with a felt diagram that is marked with squares and numbers that represent different combinations of dice. There are thirty-six possible ways two dice can be rolled. For instance, only one combination will produce the number two, often called "snake eyes." The same is true for the number twelve, called "boxcars." But there are six different ways to roll the number seven, which makes it the most likely number to appear when dice are rolled. According to the law of averages, a seven should appear once in every six rolls. It doesn't always happen that way, but the casino expects it will. That is part of its edge. The more unlikely the dice combination, the higher the payoff.

Here's one way casinos make money. The odds of rolling snake eyes or boxcars are thirty-five to one. But if a gambler correctly guesses when those combinations are going to be rolled, the casino only pays thirty-to-one odds. For instance, if you bet $1 on snake eyes and the shooter rolls the number two, the casino will pay you $30. If it were paying true odds, you would be owed $35. There's more. Your original $1 wager will be left on the table for another roll without your permission simply because that is how the game is played. Chances are you'll lose it. So instead of making a $35 profit, you will leave the table with $29.

Because players stand along the table opposite the boxman, they often don't realize that there is a mirror on the inner wall of the craps table just under their arms. From his seat, the boxman uses this mirror to watch the game at table level. It enables him to see if a stack of chips are all the same denomination or if someone has put a $100 chip on top of several $5 ones to make the bet look larger to the cameras in the ceiling.

There are several procedures that must be followed when dice are thrown. A shooter can blow on the dice. A shooter can arrange them in a specific order before throwing them. But a shooter cannot bang the dice on the table, because cheaters sometimes try to "round the edges" to get them to roll certain ways. Nor may a shooter drop his hand below the table rail or place it in any position where it can't be seen, in case he is trying to switch dice. A shooter may not throw the dice only halfway down the table, nor can the dice hit the side walls. They must tumble off the end wall. As soon as the dice are thrown, the stickman is responsible for watching one of the dice dealers pay off the bets at his end of the table; the boxman watches the other dealer at his end. The dealers and the boxman are supposed to watch the stickman when he passes dice to a new shooter to make sure they aren't being switched. And the stickman and dice dealers are supposed to watch the boxman when he counts out chips.

So what happens if all four employees at a craps table decide to steal? Each craps table is watched by a floor supervisor. Who makes sure the floor supervisor isn't in on a scam? He is watched by the pit boss, and the pit boss is watched by the assistant shift manager, who is watched by the casino shift manager, who answers to the casino manager. Everyone watches everyone else, and the eye in the sky watches them all.

CHAPTER TWELVE

....

Shawna Gray, Whore

Shawna Gray was sipping a Diet Coke in a booth at a Denny's restaurant on the Strip at 2 A.M. when she noticed a woman sitting behind the wheel of an old Plymouth Duster parked near the sidewalk. Whenever a man walked by, the woman leaned out of her car and spoke to him. Gray figured the woman was a prostitute. As soon as she finished her soda, she sauntered out to the car.

"You an outlaw?" she asked, using the slang term that prostitutes use in California to describe a hooker who works without a pimp.

"What's it to you?" the woman replied.

Gray said she had just gotten into town from Los Angeles and needed money. She was willing to turn some tricks. The woman dialed a number on her cellular telephone and within minutes, a man arrived in what had to be the sorriest Mercedes-Benz in Las Vegas. He waved Gray inside. They spoke briefly and then rode south on Las Vegas Boulevard out of town into the desert. He pulled off the highway near a huge storage lot where rows and rows of late-model cars were parked behind a chain-link fence. Gray would later learn that this was where rental cars were stored until they could be sold at auction. The pimp told her that he wanted a "taste." They had sex and then he introduced himself.

"My name's Jerry," he said.

Back at Denny's, Jerry bought Gray an order of blueberry pancakes and introduced her to his wife, Donna, who had been waiting in the Duster until they returned. He was forty, she was twenty-six. They had arrived in Las Vegas three months earlier from Phoenix, where Jerry had two ex-wives and a gaggle of kids. Jerry had gotten a job installing drywall at a hotel construction site when they first came to town and Donna had gone to work as a waitress, but then Jerry had hurt his back and quit. He was drawing workers' compensation, but it wasn't enough, so Donna had started turning tricks. She asked for $100 for "straight sex," which was missionary-style sexual intercourse, but usually only got half that. Her tricks paid $40 for oral sex, which she preferred because it wasn't as much trouble. The couple lived in a two-bedroom apartment not far from the Strip, but Donna never took any of her customers there. If they didn't want to do it in the Duster, she would go to their hotel room. Most nights, Jerry watched Donna from across the street in his Mercedes. She would drive her tricks to a dark corner in a nearby parking lot. She felt safe because she knew he was close by.

By the time that Gray had finished eating her pancakes, she and Jerry had cut a deal. She would work out of the Duster with Donna, and live with them too until she had enough money to rent her own place. In return, Jerry wanted $15 per night for rent and food, plus half of everything she made turning tricks. Gray and Donna went to sit in the Duster and Jerry drove across the street. About an hour later, a man offered them $100 if they both would have sex with him in his hotel room. Jerry followed them into the lobby and was waiting when they came downstairs.

"Get anything extra?" he asked Donna.

"Naw, nothing I could grab," she replied.

They went back to the Duster, but they couldn't attract any more customers, so Jerry decided around 10 A.M. that it was time to go home. He took $40 of the $50 that Gray had earned—fifteen bucks for the rent that she owed, plus half of her $50. She slept on a couch in the second bedroom and had a nightmare about Marcellus coming after her. He was her former pimp and he had sworn that he would track her down and kill her if she ever ran away. She had just turned seventeen.

Jerry turned out to be more of a thief than a pimp. He'd break into parked cars whenever he could. Donna was a "trick-roller"—a prostitute who stole from her customers. She told Gray it was easy. "Now, some whores use animal tranquilizers to knock out a trick," she explained, "but I just use Visine. I squirt it into their drinks when we get up in their rooms." Visine would give a man diarrhea and painful stomach cramps within minutes after he drank it, she said. As soon as the john hurried into the bathroom, Donna would grab whatever she could—wallets, cameras, even portable computers—and race out the door. "Once this trick asked me what I was doing with the Visine," she told Gray. "He had caught me with it in my hand and I thought he was on to me, but I just said, 'Oh, sugar, my eyes hurt 'cause you're just so damn pretty to look at.' Then I dropped some in my eyes and he didn't think nothing of it when I handed him his drink."

Jerry helped Gray get a Nevada driver's license that listed her age as twenty-one, the minimum for frequenting bars and casinos. She began trick-rolling too. They targeted Asian men because Jerry figured foreigners carried more cash than other tourists. He also correctly assumed that a tourist from overseas would be reluctant to file charges with the police, especially if it meant he would have to come back to Las Vegas to testify in court. Married men attending conventions were also prime targets. Jerry told Gray that prostitution is legal in most of Nevada, but not in Las Vegas. She soon decided that the double standard worked in her favor. "A lot of johns think prostitution is legal, so they think it is safe to pick up girls," she said. After she robbed them, Gray assumed her victims would complain to hotel security. At that point, they would be told that prostitution was illegal and they could be arrested for hiring a hooker. "A john is not going to call the cops if he thinks he might get arrested too," she explained. Anyway, Jerry told her, most tricks have insurance. They could file claims for whatever Gray stole from them. "I figure most of these guys lie about what I stole," Gray said, "so they end up making a profit off their insurance company and no one really gets hurt." At least that is what she told herself.

Gray soon was averaging three to four tricks per night, but she stole from only a few of them and only when she was absolutely certain she wouldn't be caught. "I didn't like using Visine. I was scared one of these old farts would have a heart attack and die or something." A month after she moved in with Donna and Jerry, he began pressuring her for more cash and for sex. Whenever Donna left in the Duster with a customer, Jerry would pick her up in the Mercedes so she wouldn't be stranded in the Denny's parking lot. He'd demand that she have oral sex with him. "Let's just call this 'quality control,' " he'd joke. Gray thought he was a creep, but she was having trouble saving enough money to leave the couple. "I was really dumb. I mean, I did basically whatever Jerry told me because I didn't know better. I figured I needed a pimp to protect me because that's how things had been in L.A. You couldn't work the streets there without one."

Gray had turned her first trick when she was fifteen, after she fled the rental house in Sacramento where she was living with her mother, her mother's abusive, cocaine-dealer boyfriend, and her ten-year-old brother. She moved in with a woman who worked at the same telemarketing company as her mother and got a miserable night job in a laundry, working for minimum wage. She wondered how Joanie, the woman's twenty-year-old daughter, always managed to have spending money even though she was unemployed. Joanie laughed at her. She was a whore, she said—"and I was so dumb," Gray remembered, "that I didn't know for sure what she was even talking about."

Gray had had sex when she was fourteen, and it didn't seem like such a big deal. She asked Joanie how she went about becoming a hooker. "There was this corner in Sacramento where you went to stand and guys picked you up and had sex with you in their cars. It was that simple." And it was, at least the first night she tried it. She earned $150 by having sex with five different guys in their cars and decided it beat washing other people's dirty underwear. But violent experiences followed. One customer kidnapped her and drove her to San Diego, where he raped her. Another held a knife to her throat. When she and Joanie moved to Los Angeles together, Gray was brutalized by a "gorilla pimp" who picked her up off a street corner, threatened her, and demanded that she work for him. She was eventually arrested and when the police realized how young she was, they contacted her mother. Gray agreed to move back home because her mother had kicked out her boyfriend. "My mom was trying to go straight— keep off cocaine—and she wanted me to go back to high school, so we lived together and my mom got me a job working part-time at the same place where she worked. I did well in school and at work for six months. My goal was to get enough to buy a car and get my own place." But Gray was still friendly with Joanie, and one night Joanie telephoned and announced that she was living with an ex-con. He had a buddy still in prison who was looking for a pen pal. Gray, who was lonely, began writing him. "Once you've been a whore for a while, it is hard to get excited about going to the senior dance or making out in some guy's car after a basketball game. Anyway, this convict wrote me long letters. He said his street name was Marcellus, and he was really, really sweet and I fell in love with him. It was exciting."

As soon as Marcellus was released, he drove to Sacramento to meet Gray. "He told me he loved me and wanted me to move with him to L.A. My mother was super angry and told me that I couldn't go, but he was the first man who really made me feel special. He promised he would always protect me and he treated me like a real lady, like I was someone important. Of course, I believed him. He knew from Joanie that I had tried hooking. He didn't say anything about it until we got to L.A., and then he told me that we were going to move in with his girlfriend there, Linda. And then he announces that she is working for him as a street whore." Gray learned that Marcellus had been writing Linda the entire time he was in prison. "Linda was mad at first, but the funny thing was that we became friends. . . . Linda watched out for me on the street and taught me how to be a street whore—all the tricks you need to survive, like protecting yourself, how to talk to johns, how to avoid the cops."

Not long after they all moved in together, Marcellus "sold" Linda to another pimp. "Marcellus was cold. All he cared about was money. That's all pimps care about, I soon learned." Gray worked on Sunset and

Hollywood Boulevards—the same streets where she had been brutalized earlier by the gorilla pimp—but this time, no one bothered her because they knew she belonged to Marcellus. "I used to see Linda after that, but it wasn't the same. She started using a lot of drugs." Gray figured it was only a matter of time before Marcellus sold her too. "You don't have a choice but to do what your pimp says," she said, "because a pimp will kill you if you don't."

A night in a downtown convention hotel marked the end of her time with Marcellus. He had taken her there to look for tricks, and she had gone to a room with three men for sex. Instead, they had become violent, holding her down, stealing her money, forcing her to have sex, and then shoving her naked into the hallway. After they tossed out her dress—keeping her underclothes as souvenirs—Gray found a pay phone and called Marcellus. He sped to the hotel in a cocaine-induced high, burst into the men's room at gunpoint, and made them perform homosexual acts on each other as revenge. Terrified that Marcellus would kill all three men, Gray protested, earning herself a punch in the stomach from her pimp. The next day, she escaped from Marcellus by having a john who had stopped in his car to hire her drive her to the bus station in exchange for a "freebie." There she bought a ticket to Las Vegas because it was the "prettiest city" she'd ever seen. Marcellus had taken her there once. She arrived with $80 and her clothes, headed for the Strip, and spotted Donna.

After two months of living with Jerry and Donna, Gray had saved enough to rent her own apartment. "Jerry was white, but Donna was a black whore and it is tougher for someone who is black to get many dates, so she and Jerry began stealing stuff and basically expected me to do all the whoring." On weekends, Jerry would drive Donna to an outlet mall to shoplift. "I told

Jerry I was moving out. I could get plenty of tricks in casinos because I'm young and white. I've had guys tell me I look like the girl next door. I have an innocent-looking face. Jerry got real angry because he was going to miss my money. He began threatening me, but I wasn't a dumb kid anymore. I had bought pepper spray, and when he started yelling, I just shot him right in the eyes. He was screaming, saying I had blinded him, and I told him I would call the cops on him and Donna because their apartment was full of stolen crap. I just took my stuff and left. Later, I heard he and Donna had moved back to Phoenix, but I don't really know because I never saw them again. I had learned in Las Vegas a whore don't need a pimp because the cops hate pimps and don't let them hang around, especially now that the place is like a family town. I knew I could make it on my own."

CHAPTER THIRTEEN

....

Glenn Schaeffer,
Corporate Headquarters

Glenn Schaeffer was eager to start building a new super casino on the Hacienda tract that Clyde Turner had bought as part of his masterplan mile project. The new Circus Circus management—Schaeffer, Turner, Michael Ensign, Bill Richardson, and Tony Alamo—agreed it should be bigger and bolder than anything Bill Bennett had ever built. They had plenty of cash to spend. Impressed by the stunning success of the Strip's first wave of super casinos, investment bankers had given Circus Circus a whopping $1.5 billion credit line. Schaeffer and the others initially decided to spend up to $950 million on their new casino. They called it Mandalay Bay after the largest city in what used to be Burma.

In keeping with his unit growth philosophy, Schaeffer quickly found other casino projects for Circus Circus to undertake in 1996. By a slim margin, Detroit voters decided to allow limited casino gambling inside the city limits, and Schaeffer persuaded his partners to enter the competition for one of the three gaming licenses the city said it would issue. It was a gutsy move because in order to compete Circus Circus would have to sell its interest in a casino project in Windsor, Ontario, directly across the river from Detroit and dispose of a venture that was earning the company $10 million a year in profits. Simply put, Schaeffer was giving up that $10 million in return for a chance at winning a Detroit license without any guarantees. Donald Trump and Steve Wynn had already announced that they were going after Detroit licenses too. Everyone wanted a piece of the Motown pie, which experts predicted would top $1.5 billion per year in total revenues for the lucky three license winners. But Schaeffer saw even more at stake than hefty profits. If Circus Circus could prove itself in Detroit by creating new jobs and increasing tax revenues, then other major U.S. cities would notice. Detroit would be the first domino to fall. Denver, Dallas, Atlanta—who could guess what city might be next? Schaeffer eagerly took charge of the company's campaign to win a Detroit license.

He also cast his eye on Atlantic City. Schaeffer had always wanted to open a casino in New Jersey, but Bennett had adamantly opposed it. There was now only one tract of undeveloped land left near the Atlantic City Boardwalk, and it was about to be sold at auction. Schaeffer heard that Steve Wynn was interested in buying it too. He had not operated an Atlantic City casino since 1986, when he sold his Boardwalk Golden Nugget casino to Bally Entertainment. Obviously, if Circus Circus and Wynn bid against each other, the price of the 181-acre tract was going to skyrocket. Over dinner one night, Schaeffer, Ensign, Richardson, and Wynn agreed to combine forces and make a joint bid for the land. If they won, they would divide it into two parcels and each company would spend $700 million to build a super casino on its half. Because Wynn had already operated a casino in New Jersey and was used to dealing with the politicians and media there, he told the Circus Circus managers that he would take the lead in preparing a bid.

Everything seemed fine until Wynn called Ensign four hours before the final deadline for submitting bids and announced that he wanted to buy the land by himself. Exactly what was said between the two men would later be disputed. According to Circus Circus officials and their lawyers, Wynn told Ensign that he was worried about submitting a joint bid because it put his company at risk. If their joint bid won and, for some unforeseen reason, Circus Circus should change its mind about building a super casino on the tract, Atlantic City officials could nullify the entire deal and put the land up for sale again. Wynn would lose his piece of property and the money he'd invested in it. Ensign assured him that Circus Circus was not going to change its mind, but Wynn would not be swayed. He demanded that Circus Circus drop out. In return, he promised he would still honor their "handshake" deal—as soon as he took title to the land, he would sell Circus Circus its piece. Ensign telephoned Turner and Schaeffer, who would later admit that they were suspicious of Wynn's last-minute demand, but felt they had no choice but to go along with it. They really didn't have time in four hours to pull together a bid package of their own. If they wanted to get a piece of the 181-acre tract—and they did—they were going to have to trust Wynn. It seemed a safe enough bet. Turner considered him a personal friend, and Ensign and Schaeffer had worked well with him while building their jointly owned Monte Carlo casino on the Strip. Minutes before the bidding deadline, Circus Circus announced it was dropping out. A short time later, Atlantic City officials declared Wynn's bid the winner.

Schaeffer was pleased, until he spoke with one of Wynn's top aides. Wynn had decided that he was going to divide the tract into three pieces, not two, Schaeffer was told. Wynn was selling part of the tract at a profit to Boyd Gaming, a Las Vegas casino company. Even more worrisome, the aide said Wynn wasn't certain how much he was going to charge Circus Circus for its parcel of land. The cost of building a highway onto the tract was going to be higher than he had expected. The aide told Schaeffer that Wynn wanted Circus Circus to pay $40 million of the expenses that he had incurred putting together his bid. He would come up with a sales price for the land later. It was a take-it-or-leave-it deal, the aide explained. If Circus Circus didn't want the land, Wynn was certain some other company would.

A furious Schaeffer accused Wynn of breaking his promise, but by the time that he had returned to Circus Circus headquarters, he had cooled down. Even if Wynn only sold them one-third of the parcel, Schaeffer was certain Circus Circus would be able to build a profitable super casino there and earn hefty profits. Schaeffer also knew that Wynn had incurred higher costs preparing his bid than anyone had expected. This was due, in part, to a costly legal campaign that Boardwalk casino baron Donald Trump was waging in an attempt to stop the sale of the tract. After conferring with Turner, Ensign, and Richardson, Schaeffer sent word that Circus Circus was indeed willing to pay $40 million toward Wynn's expenses. But from this point on, Schaeffer announced, the company wanted all of the details of its dealings with Wynn drawn up in a formal contract. There would be no more handshake deals.

Schaeffer and Wynn soon found themselves butting heads again, this time when they both went after the same seat on a hotly charged national gaming panel. The controversial panel was mandated by Congress in the summer of 1996, but its roots went back several years, when antigambling forces first became alarmed at the boom in gambling across the country. By the early 1990s every state except for Hawaii and Utah had some form of legalized betting, and twenty-three of them had casinos, mostly on Indian reservations. Antigambling groups got U.S. Representative Frank R. Wolf, a conservative Republican from Virginia, to introduce a bill that called for an investigation into gambling's impact in America. Casino operators reacted with horror. Afraid that Congress would use its study to justify placing new taxes and regulations on casinos, they put aside their petty disputes and formed the American Gaming Association, a Washington, D.C.–based lobbying group. Frank Fahrenkopf, the former Republican National Committee chairman under President Ronald Reagan, was hired as the AGA's executive director and ordered to kill Wolf's bill. Casino owners in Las Vegas, meanwhile, began doling out cash to politicians. Senate minority leader Thomas A. Daschle, a Democrat from South Dakota, was invited to the Strip and given $220,000 for the Democratic Senatorial Campaign Committee. In April 1996, Steve Wynn hosted a breakfast fund-raiser at the Mirage for Nevada's newly elected Republican congressman, John Ensign, who happened to be Michael Ensign's son. Wynn's guests donated a total of $70,000 to Ensign at the breakfast, but the big payoff was not meeting him, it was rubbing shoulders with then–Speaker of the House Newt Gingrich, the Georgia Republican who was attending the breakfast as Wynn's personal guest. Gingrich assured the casino owners that if Congress did decide to investigate gambling, he would do his best to limit the scope of the probe. When Gingrich's promise was reported in the media, antigambling forces fumed, but there was little they could do. Two months later, President Clinton stopped in Las Vegas for a $25,000-

per-couple Democratic Party fund-raiser, and casino owners were quick to tell him their views of Wolf's bill too.

In July 1996, antigambling forces did succeed in getting Wolf's bill through Congress, but it had been significantly weakened by the gaming industry. For instance, the National Gambling Impact Study Commission was given the power to subpoena documents but not individuals. Casino owners had lobbied for this limitation out of fear that the religious right would use the commission to subpoena gambling addicts, old-time racketeers, and criminals who had been caught over the years laundering money at casinos, and make it appear as if they were representative of all gambling. Congress gave the commission $5 million and two years to conduct its study.

As soon as the issues about the commission's powers were resolved, pro- and antigambling forces started bickering about who would be appointed to it. Wynn and Schaeffer were in the thick of it. Although Schaeffer was not nearly as well known, he was president of the Nevada Resort Association, the most powerful casino lobbying group in the state, and as part of that job, he had defended the industry forcefully in debates on various national television shows. Wynn, meanwhile, led the Strip when it came to making political contributions to national campaigns and their candidates. At one point, President Clinton had invited him to Washington, D.C., to play golf with him.

It was up to the president, speaker Gingrich, and Senate majority leader Trent Lott, a Mississippi Republican, to choose the nine panel members. Each could name three. Gingrich turned over two of his picks to Representatives Frank Wolf and John Ensign and gave a third to the House minority leader, Dick Gephardt, a Democrat from Missouri, as a favor because he needed Gephardt's help in passing a bill unrelated to gambling.

Over in the U.S. Senate, Trent Lott traded away two of his picks for future favors. He gave one to Republican Senator Dan Coats from Indiana and the other to Senate minority leader Tom Daschle. Lott used his third pick to name his next-door neighbor, a sixty-nine-year-old radiologist with no gambling experience, to the commission. President Clinton said he would make his three picks last.

Wynn and Schaeffer figured their best shot at being chosen for the panel was John Ensign, since he was from Nevada and knew them both. The freshman congressman found himself in a precarious spot. If he chose Schaeffer, it would look to other casino owners as if Ensign was favoring Circus Circus because his father and Schaeffer both were executives there. But the choice of Wynn was bound to cause hard feelings because his bombastic personality had alienated other casino owners. There was also worry that antigambling forces would dredge up questions about the charges that had plagued Wynn in New Jersey, even though he had been exonerated. After much hand-wringing, Ensign skipped over both and selected J. Terrence Lanni, the fifty-four-year-old chairman of the MGM Grand. Schaeffer gave up his campaign for a spot on the commission, but Wynn began lobbying President Clinton for a seat. He reportedly was furious after Clinton chose Bill Bible, the head of the Nevada Gaming Control Board, as his pro-gambling choice.

When all the behind-the-scenes lobbying ended, the casino owners ended up with three pro-gambling members on the commission, while antigambling forces were able to get only two of their partisans appointed. The remaining four members were considered neutral. The first meeting of the commission quickly erupted into a hot-tempered free-for-all. Testifying before the commission, Representative Wolf called gambling a "dubious enterprise." Another antigambling speaker warned that the gambling industry had "more of a history of involvement in corruption than any other industry" in the nation. The casino owners' Washington, D.C., lobbyist, Frank Fahrenkopf, reacted by accusing Wolf of spouting off "typical hysterical rhetoric."

What few seemed to notice during all this hullabaloo was how big a leap the gambling industry had made. In the past, politicians always had shunned Las Vegas. Most were afraid they would be associated in the public's mind with organized crime if they accepted political contributions from a casino or its owner. But not now. For the first time in recent memory, a U.S. president and powerful members of Congress had unabashedly come to Las Vegas with their hands out. The Methodist Church was the only national organization that seemed to grasp the significance of this transition. In a strongly worded letter to the White House, the church condemned President Clinton for accepting campaign contributions from casinos. It reminded him that gambling was still considered a vice by millions of churchgoing Americans, and it warned him against being swayed by the fat checks that casino owners could write. Predictably, the White House pointed out in a brief statement that the gambling industry was entitled to make contributions to anyone it wished, and that any group who thought a politician wouldn't gladly take them was naive.

CHAPTER FOURTEEN

....

Tony Alamo, the Boss

A half-million partygoers swelled onto Las Vegas Boule-vard outside the doomed Hacienda hotel and casino at the southern tip of the Strip as the final minutes of 1996 ticked away. Circus Circus had agreed to implode the forty-one-year-old Hacienda at precisely 9 P.M.—midnight on the East Coast—so that Fox Television could use the demolition to usher in the New Year. The network was televising its 1997 New Year's Eve show from Las Vegas rather than the traditional Times Square in New York City because, as it told its viewers, "Las Vegas is happening!" Across the street from the Ha-cienda, underneath a large tent pitched on a vacant lot and separated from the crowd by a waist-high fence and beefy security guards, Circus Circus executives and their guests readied their champagne glasses. Ten, nine, eight, seven ... At the stroke of the hour, there was a brilliant flash and a thunderous boom. Flames shot from the Hacienda's windows and the building toppled inward, sending a cloud of dust over the revel-ers. The grit swept under the tent and enveloped the ice sculpture in the center of the Circus Circus buffet, but no one seemed to care. A beaming Glenn Schaeffer told reporters that workers would start construction of the company's newest super casino at daybreak. Mandalay Bay would have a tropical theme. "Guests will be able to snorkel with tropical fish along an artificially made reef, or swim in a pool next to sharks enclosed in their own clear tank," Schaeffer said. "This resort will be like a movie set come to life—a little bit of Bali, a little bit of Java, and a whole lot of Shangri-la." An enclosed walkway would connect Mandalay Bay to the Luxor, which in turn would be linked to the Excalibur, tying all three together. "Without ever stepping outside, a guest will be able to visit a medieval castle, an Egyptian pyramid, and a South Seas paradise."

Moving comfortably among the guests, Tony Alamo seemed to be without a worry. In fact, he had plenty of reason to feel overwhelmed. He was in charge of getting Mandalay Bay under way, yet he was still not done renovating the Luxor. The remodeling was supposed to be wrapped up in 1996 at a cost of $250 million. But Alamo and the other Circus Circus executives had made so many changes and additions to the project that it was still months away from completion. Meanwhile, costs had mushroomed to more than $350 million— only $50 million less than Bill Bennett had spent to build the entire resort. The Luxor's lobby was symbolic of the mess that Alamo faced. It resembled a construction site. The sounds of jackhammers chipping into concrete and power saws buzzing through boards could be heard echoing through the atrium.

Not everyone thought the renovations were necessary, including some of Alamo's own department heads. "Alamo, Schaeffer, and Ensign are like dogs marking their turf," one complained privately. "They are pissing on things—like the Nile River ride—simply because Bennett built them." Said another, "We were doing fine financially before these guys came along. Why are all these changes necessary?"

Such comments outraged Alamo. "Egos have nothing to do with this," he insisted. "People always like to see something new and that's why the first year's profits at the Luxor were so high. But if you don't keep your customers coming back, then your profits will fall, and that's what was happening here." Had the renovations not been started, Alamo claimed, the Luxor's profits would have fallen to a low of $60 million, some $30 million less than when it first opened. He felt confident that as soon as the remodeling was finished the Luxor would produce as much as $150 million in profits. "Cheap buffets and cheap rooms used to be enough when Bennett was running things because Las Vegas was the only place you could gamble," he explained. "But most Americans now live within an hour or two of a casino. We have to give them more than what they can see at home, and that's why we have to make this place spectacular."

Alamo had anticipated a drop in profits during 1996 because of the disruption caused by the renovations— "No one on vacation wants to stay in a hotel with a jackhammer making noise in its lobby"—so he had tried to soften the blow during the year by slashing costs. During his first month in charge, he had cut $400,000 in expenses, mostly by eliminating jobs. At the same time, he had told his department heads that the Luxor would be going after a higher-income customer as soon as it was remodeled. "Your better players are going to expect more for their money than what grind players have expected from us in the past," he warned them. He ordered them to improve the quality of service that they were providing guests. Some thought his commands were contradictory. How could they improve service if he was slashing their budgets and firing workers? Still, few dared to complain, and those who screwed up their courage enough to tell him that their department was understaffed found him largely unsympathetic. "This is a twenty-four-hour-a-day, seven-days-a-week industry," Alamo said. "When a bank closes at 5 P.M., the loan officer goes home because there are no more loans being made that day, but nothing ever stops in a casino. If you want a job where you work only eight hours, then you should choose another profession. If you want to continue working here, then you will put in whatever hours it takes to get your job done."

Alamo routinely worked eighteen hours a day, seven days a week. The new rule was simple: if Tony Alamo's car was in the employee parking lot, the cars driven by his department heads had better be parked there too. The Luxor's popular first general manager, William Paulos, had never demanded such long hours, nor had he slashed budgets or reduced staff. There were whispers: "Paulos would have handled this differently." "Paulos would have handled this better."

What happened next was not Alamo's fault, but it caused further unrest within the ranks. Circus Circus chairman Clyde Turner ended Bennett's generous employee bonus pay program. This was no small matter. One assistant casino manager who was paid $65,000 per year in salary during 1995 had received a $200,000 bonus under Bennett's incentive system. The fact that Turner and others in top management kept their bonuses intact did not go unnoticed.

Don R. Givens had been in charge of closing down the Hacienda, and after it was imploded, he was sent to help Alamo run the Luxor. They made an odd couple. Alamo was excitable, notoriously thin-skinned, and a boisterous manager. Givens, thirteen years younger, prided himself on being calm and soft-spoken. He was also the highest-ranking black in the corporation.

He had been sent to the Hacienda to be its caretaker, but to everyone's surprise, he had rallied the mediocre operation during its final days, earning the company $7.6 million in unexpected profits. Fresh from that accomplishment, Givens eagerly took charge of the Luxor's day-to-day operations.

He was introduced to his department heads during the first week of January at their regular Tuesday staff meeting in the Luxor's spacious conference room. The chair closest to the door was always reserved for Alamo, although he didn't plan on attending now that Givens was on board. Givens sat to the left of Alamo's empty seat. No one else ever sat in these two chairs. The Luxor's casino manager, Tom Robinson, sat next to Givens. While there wasn't an official pecking order among department heads, everyone understood that the casino manager was the de facto next-in-command. After him, the most important department head was Michael Starr, director of hotel operations. In many ways, the Luxor's management was structured like a small city. The department heads included:

- a director of security, the equivalent of a city police chief.
- a director of retail sales, responsible for overseeing the clothing, convenience, and souvenir shops and the manufacturing of Luxor-brand toiletries and Luxor logo apparel.
- a director of food and beverage services, responsible for the Luxor's six restaurants, all-you-can-eat buffet, room service, cocktail waitresses, and catering.
- a director of purchasing, responsible for buying everything used in the Luxor from cocktail napkins to bed sheets to lightbulbs to poker chips.
- a financial comptroller, responsible for recording

income, expenses, payroll, and for dealing with countless government auditors.

- a safety coordinator, responsible for making sure the Luxor complied with all federal, state, and local safety codes and regulations, with procedures ready in case of emergencies such as fires and bomb threats.
- a chief engineer, responsible for maintaining the hotel-casino and its grounds.
- a human resources director, responsible for the hiring and training of the Luxor's employees.
- a director of entertainment, responsible for booking shows.
- a director of attractions, responsible for the second-floor amusements.
- a slot manager, responsible for the slot machines.
- a keno manager, responsible for operating the keno lounge, a separate part of the casino.
- a poker manager, whose operations were also run separately from the casino's.
- a casino marketing director, responsible for bringing in high rollers by hosting special promotional activities such as golf tournaments.
- a hotel marketing director, responsible for keeping as much as 50 percent of the hotel filled with guests on tours arranged by travel agents.
- a foreign marketing director, responsible for recruiting wealthy players from overseas, mostly Asia.
- a credit or cage manager, responsible for operating the casino's bank and collecting debts from players. The "cage" was a reference to the iron bars on the casino tellers' windows.

It was this group that Givens was counting on to help him turn the Luxor into a premier resort. As he surveyed those at his first staff meeting, he was aware, as he often was, that he was the only black. There were four women. Nearly everyone else was a white male in his forties or older. Despite this outward lack of diversity, the group came from a wide range of backgrounds. Givens had grown up poor in Las Vegas, one of seven children raised by a divorced maid who was a welfare recipient. Casino manager Tom Robinson had migrated to Nevada from his parents' picturesque ranch in Washington State. Entertainment director Michael Hartzell had been a circus kid, traveling from circus to circus with his trapeze artist parents. Linda Dennis, the hotel marketing director, was a former Miss Kentucky. Safety coordinator Leon Symanski stood six feet, eight inches tall and had played on the University of Nevada at Las Vegas's 1986–87 national championship basketball team. Rides and attractions director Cliff Hay had begun his theatrical career as a stunt man in the vampire movie *The Return of Count Igor,* where his specialty had been drowning in quicksand. One of the department heads was deeply religious, another had a brother dying of AIDS, another had fled to Las Vegas in the 1960s to avoid being sent to jail for running illegal poker games in the back room of a pool hall. Half the managers had been divorced; about this same number had graduated from college. None had dreamed when they were youngsters of working in a Las Vegas casino.

Givens liked to begin his staff meetings by reviewing the daily managerial report prepared by the casino's comptroller. It was a refined version of the original managerial report that Bill Bennett had instituted after he first took charge of Circus Circus. The Tuesday morning report contained the Luxor's financial figures from Sunday, framed in casino jargon. The two most common terms used were the "drop" and the "hold," sometimes called the "win." If a customer tossed a $50 bill onto a blackjack table, the dealer issued him $50 worth of chips and pushed the $50 bill into a locked metal box attached to the table. That bill was now part of the drop, which literally meant cash dropped into a box in exchange for chips. When the customer finished playing blackjack, he would be sent to the casino cage to exchange his chips for money. At the end of each eight-hour shift, the metal boxes from the gaming tables were emptied and a comparison was done. According to the daily report, the Luxor had collected a drop of $656,957 from the eighty-two table games it had operated Sunday. The casino cage had paid $491,130 to gamblers who had cashed in their chips. The difference was the casino's hold or win. On Sunday, it had been $165,827.

The report then listed the statistics from the Luxor's slot machines. Once again, the report used a casino term: the "handle." This was the total number of coins played in a slot machine. Let's say a customer walks into the Luxor with $5 in his pocket and starts playing a slot machine. On his first pull, he wins $10. After that, he never wins again and he leaves the casino broke. Although the customer only had $5 when he first entered the casino, he actually bet $15—the $5 from his pocket and the $10 that he won. In this example, the handle would be $15. According to the daily report, the handle on Sunday at the Luxor slots was $3.36 million. The drop was $747,160 and the hold was $265,413. To make these numbers easier to understand, let's pretend that only one person came into the Luxor on Sunday and he played only one slot machine. That would mean our fictitious gambler entered the casino with $747,160 in his pocket. During the next twenty-four hours, he bet it all. Sometimes he lost, sometimes he won, but he kept playing. After twenty-four hours, he had put $3.36 million through the slot machine—the handle. Of this,

$747,160 was money he had brought to the casino. He had left the casino with $481,747, or $265,413 less than he had come with. That was the casino's hold, or win.

The report noted that each slot machine in the Luxor had won an average of $118.43 on Sunday. That might not seem like much until you realize there were 2,241 machines in operation. It was easy to see from the daily report why Bill Bennett had favored slots over table games. The table games on Sunday had earned $165,827 in revenues, compared to the $265,413 the slots had taken in. Nowadays, most Strip casinos earn 60 percent of their gambling income from slot machines. The poker room and keno operation had contributed a small amount of revenue to Sunday's bottom line, as had the race and sports book where gamblers bet on football games, horse races, and other sporting events. But these sums were insignificant when compared to the table games and slot machines. There were other departments at the Luxor that earned money on Sunday too. The biggest, other than the casino, was the hotel, which generated $248,680 in revenues. The food and beverage department contributed another $126,000; retail shops $50,000; and the rides and attractions $16,000. After all of these sources were added together, some $45,000 in comps was deducted, giving the Luxor a grand total on Sunday of $826,038 in revenues.

The second half of the daily report listed all the expenses. Payroll and employee benefits were the biggest, adding up to $307,626. There were 681 employees working in the casino and another 1,697 working elsewhere. The bulk of these employees were maids, although Luxor managers always referred to them by their politically correct title, "guest room attendants." Other expenses included the cost of food, drinks, hotel supplies, utilities, marketing, administration, taxes, and a slew of miscellaneous expenses. The grand total on Sunday was $670,457 in costs.

The arithmetic was easy: $826,038 in revenues minus $670,457 in expenses resulted in $155,581 in profits before taxes for Sunday. If those daily numbers did not change substantially, the Luxor would report earnings of $4.6 million in January. This was considerably less than what Alamo expected. Glenn Schaeffer was telling Wall Street analysts that the remodeled Luxor would earn a minimum of $120 million in profits during the 1997 calendar year. Although January was traditionally a poor month for casinos, Alamo was counting on the Luxor to earn $7.5 million, not $4.6 million.

There was only one way for them to get the resort's profits up. There would have to be more budget cuts. After Givens finished reviewing the daily report, he suggested that each department head study the number of workers' compensation cases in their department. "We need to find ways to reduce the number of claims that we pay," he said, "and we need to do a better job at getting our employees back to work as soon as they recover from an accident, even if it means having them doing something as menial as sweeping a floor." Then Givens went clockwise around the room so that the department heads could explain what was being done in their departments to cut costs and improve performance.

• Alan Buchholz, the casino marketing director, announced that six hundred gamblers were being invited to a Super Bowl party later in the month. He had arranged for each guest to receive a special Luxor Super Bowl hat and souvenir T-shirt. The gamblers would watch the game on big-screen televisions in the resort's new grand ballroom—if the workers got it finished on time. He was thinking about hiring several Dallas Cowboy cheerleaders to entertain at halftime. Buchholz estimated the Luxor would earn $150,000 in additional gambling revenues because of the party.

• Although only 70 percent of the Luxor's hotel rooms were occupied on Sunday, hotel operations director Michael Starr said he had already sold every room that was available for Super Bowl weekend at an average rate of more than $100 per room.

• Human resources director Tom Peacock said his department was saving money by keeping the Luxor from being sued. An employee had complained on Monday about a Budweiser beer calendar she had seen hanging in an office that featured a photograph of several bikini-clad blondes. The employee claimed the picture made her feel sexually harassed. "I told the supervisor in that office to take down the calendar and you need to take down any calendars that show women in any sexual way," he warned.

• Security chief Andy Vanyo reported that someone had called in a bomb threat at 5:30 A.M. but that his office had handled it without alerting hotel guests. The caller claimed a pipe bomb had been hidden in "A tower"—a reference to one of the new hotel towers being built next door to the pyramid. "The only people who call the towers 'A' and 'B' are construction workers," Vanyo said, "because that's how they are identified on construction blueprints. Everyone else calls them the east and west towers. So we are fairly confident that the caller is a disgruntled construction worker." Several construction workers were being laid off later in the day because the towers were almost finished, he said. "There could be more pranks like this if this guy wants to extract some revenge for the layoffs."

His story prompted another department head to complain that he had seen construction workers stealing food from the employee cafeteria. "They are loading up their coolers with drinks and ice cream before they go home at night." It cost the Luxor $2.5 million a year to provide free meals for every employee who wanted to eat there while at work. When another department head suggested that the Luxor stop serving free meals to cut back on expenses, the veterans in the room laughed. The free meals were not served out of kindness. Casinos fed their employees because they wanted to keep them inside the resort, not wandering off or taking their coffee and lunch breaks in the casino's public restaurants. Vanyo offered to post a security guard at the employee dining hall to keep construction workers from taking food away, but Givens vetoed it. "Obviously, we want to eliminate waste, but we don't want our employees thinking that we don't trust them and are going to penalize them if they take a banana to eat on the bus ride home." Givens's meeting lasted two and a half hours, and he concluded it by saying that he was pleased but wanted future sessions to last a maximum of ninety minutes.

Food and beverage director John Thacker found a wad of messages waiting for him after the department-head meeting. He still had thirty telephone calls to return from Monday. Like other managers, he no longer had an assistant to field them because of Alamo's budget cuts. His department served a minimum of nine thousand meals every day and he oversaw a staff of 1,100, which included 25 chefs, 290 cooks, and several hundred busboys, cocktail waitresses, bartenders, and food servers. He personally signed $1.8 million worth of purchase orders per month. Because the Luxor was not generating the profits its executives expected, Thacker had been told to reduce his payroll even more by firing the equivalent of 55 full-time employees. He didn't know how he was going to do that without sacrificing service.

"Everyone always complains about food," he said. "It's always too hot, too cold; there's not enough, there's too much; it's too salty, it's too sweet; it's too cheap, it's too expensive. But the truth is that the actual preparation of food is easy. The hard part of my job is dealing with employees and the customers. It's how you deal with people in this business that ultimately makes or breaks you."

Thacker had first learned this lesson in 1969, when he was in high school and one of his pals offered to help him get a "juice job" as a busboy at the Regency Room in the glamorous Sands resort. No one worked there unless they knew someone, and Thacker's buddy was related to the maître d'hôtel. Thacker went in for an interview before the restaurant opened. "Carry that tray of dirty glasses around the room," the maître d'hôtel ordered, pointing to a heavy tray filled with glasses. Thacker did as he was told and when he got back, was told to do it again. Other employees chuckled as Thacker lugged the tray. This time, he noticed that the maître d'hôtel was not even watching him. But he told Thacker to do it again, sparking more laughter. Thacker carried the tray around the room a third time, and then a fourth, and finally a fifth. "I later learned this was a test to see if I would follow directions without questioning him, even if it meant that I would be humiliated. He knew that some customers wouldn't think twice about embarrassing me, and you had to be willing to smile and do what you were told without insulting these people even if they were jerks."

Thacker got the job and soon discovered there was a payoff for treating customers as if they were always right: "If I was nice to people, they gave me money." Thacker memorized the name of every high roller so he could greet them when he cleared their table. He learned the habits of every waiter and figured out ways to help them do their jobs. The tips flowed downhill from the waiters, who were receiving as much as $300 to $400 per night. Thacker gave his paycheck to his mother, who was divorced and working as a waitress at a club, but kept the tips for himself. "I went home at night with my pockets stuffed with bills."

At the Luxor, Thacker oversaw the Isis, the pyramid's gourmet restaurant; a seafood restaurant, the Sacred Sea Room; and a Polynesian dining room called Papyrus. None of them was doing well. Thacker received daily reports and the most recent showed the three restaurants had served only four hundred meals. That was about one-fifth of what it should have been. There were also two cafés in the Luxor, the Pyramid Café and the Millennium, and they had served 4,512 meals, which was good but not great. The busiest dining hall was the all-you-can-eat buffet, where 6,221 customers had eaten.

Tony Alamo was in the process of changing the restaurants. He was adding a pricey steak house next to the casino and converting the Papyrus into a Chinese restaurant. He was also building a fast-food court on the amusement level near an expanded video arcade popular with kids. The court featured McDonald's hamburgers, Little Caesar's Pizza, and Nathan's hot dogs. A new buffet, called Pharaoh's Pheast, was being constructed in the basement level and even though it wasn't open yet, Thacker already had instructed his cooks how he wanted the food arranged. Soups, salads, and fruits would be placed at the start of the serving line. Next would come various pastas and Chinese and Mexican dishes. Farther down, there would be omelettes and exotic breads. Only when a diner reached the end would he find prime rib and chicken dishes. "You always put your least expensive items in the front of a serving line," Thacker explained, "because you want your customers to fill up on those items first before they reach the more expensive meats." Vacationing tourists who made pigs of themselves were called "trough monsters" by the buffet workers, who often wondered aloud how it was possible to eat so much at one sitting.

Thacker relied on his three shift managers to handle the everyday problems. Each left him messages in a bound log kept on his secretary's desk. The notes revealed much about the daily workings of a casino food and beverage operation. On this particular day, there were a number of notations:

- Employee tossed out the top of a wedding cake for couple having reception. They were furious so we arranged for them to have a free room for night.
- Guest complained that the price for a drink on the menu was 95¢ but it rang up at $1 on cash register. Someone had recorded it wrong in the machine.
- No fish on the all-you-can-eat buffet line last Friday night. Roman Catholic guests complained today.
- Couple got into fight in restaurant and left without paying. Caught by security. Have a history of skipping out without paying for meals.
- Elderly man seen taking carrots from buffet and putting them into plastic bag to take home. Poor Las Vegas resident. Warned not to take food from buffet.
- Had to suspend busboy for possible theft of tips from food servers. Found $9 worth in his apron that had been left for someone else.

- Guest complained because room service wouldn't let her nanny sign for meal.
- Guest returned six-pack of beer, said it was warm by the time it reached his room.
- Waitress dropped glass, didn't tell anyone, shards fell into strawberries and guest cut lip. Waitress disciplined, guest given complimentary meal.
- Guest complained about seeing cook blow nose in napkin and then continue serving food on buffet line without washing hands.
- Suggestion: we need to have signs in kitchen printed in Spanish as well as English.
- Waitress showed up without bra, told to go home and get one.

Shortly before seven o'clock, Thacker got a call from Tony Alamo, who said Michael Ensign was joining him in the Isis in a half hour for dinner. As soon as Alamo hung up, Thacker called the head waiter. "Make sure Mr. Alamo and Mr. Ensign are seated in a booth away from other guests," he said. "The last time Mr. Ensign ate in our restaurant, some woman complained for ten minutes about her meal when she found out who he was. Oh yeah, and for god sakes don't let Jimmy serve them." Thacker was planning on firing Jimmy later that night for hustling tips.

He explained that the casino often sent high rollers to the Isis for complimentary meals and these gamblers frequently ordered the most expensive items on the menu because they knew they were not being charged. Because of this, the Luxor did not list its costliest bottles of wine and champagne on its wine list. Jimmy had been telling gamblers about them and one high roller recently had run up a free dinner that had cost $1,200 because he kept ordering $120 bottles of champagne.

The gambler had slipped Jimmy a fat tip. Jimmy had been warned twice to stop hustling tips but was still doing it.

After talking to the maître d'hôtel, Thacker telephoned the Luxor's head chef and told him about Alamo and Ensign. "You have some nice stone crabs, don't you?" he asked. "Those would be good to serve tonight, but make sure they're perfect."

Everything was running smoothly until ten minutes before Alamo and Ensign were scheduled to arrive. A sewage pipe backed up in the basement and wastewater began spilling into the Luxor's main kitchen. As Thacker rushed downstairs, he used his portable phone to call the Luxor's in-house health inspector. The inspector had worked for the Food and Drug Administration before Thacker hired him to ensure that the Luxor's kitchens exceeded every city, county, state, and national health standard. As far as Thacker knew, the Luxor was the only resort in Las Vegas that had its own internal health inspector, but Thacker thought the cost was well worth it. The inspector had instituted a number of commonsense safety rules—such as using different-colored cutting boards to make certain that salmonella was not spread by having meat cut on a board where raw chicken already had been sliced. "A lot of Strip hotels have sent two or three hundred people to the hospital with food poisoning," Thacker said. "I want to make sure that never happens here."

The kitchen was a mess when he reached it. Chefs and cooks were wading through a half inch of dirty water as they prepared meals. Thacker called the engineering department and asked where the water was coming from. Something had been jammed into a main wastewater pipe, he was told. Vacuum cleaners were brought in to suck up the water, but they couldn't keep up. By now the water was nearly an inch deep and threatening to splash over the bottom doors of the main cooler where all of the Luxor's ice for drinks was stored. Thacker grabbed a mop and ordered several busboys to help him. "If we can't stop it," the inspector warned, "we'll have to close the kitchen."

Thacker's phone rang. Alamo and Ensign had just been seated at their table upstairs in the Isis. "Oh, Christ!" he said. The two executives had no idea of the bedlam in the kitchen. "They just ordered the stone crabs," the chef called out as he sloshed through the water. Thacker's black dress shoes were soaked. Suddenly the water stopped rising. The chief engineer's men had managed to clear the pipe; someone had stuffed rags into it. An anonymous caller had just phoned security to take credit for the vandalism. Security chief Andy Vanyo figured it was another disgruntled construction worker who had been laid off. Even though Thacker and the busboys had kept the dirty water from reaching the main ice cooler, the inspector ordered that all the ice inside it be destroyed and the entire kitchen floor dried, mopped, and chemically sanitized. Thacker thought it was overkill, but he kept quiet. Hurrying upstairs on a service elevator, he grabbed a towel and wiped off his shoes. Moments later, he strolled across the dining room in the Isis and asked Alamo and Ensign if their meal was satisfactory.

"It's delicious," said Alamo. "Tell the chef that he did a fabulous job."

Inside the Casino:
Hustling Bets

This town was different in the sixties and seventies before the corporations took charge. I married a girl whose father was well-connected and he had sent me down to see a casino manager on the Strip to learn the business. I was only twenty, but they set me up on a craps table and after about three weeks, the stickman says to me, "Kid, it's time for us to have a parking lot party." Later that night he takes me outside and says: "Kid, we've been carrying you, but that stops now. If you don't do something to generate some income for this crew, you will make exactly what you are asking for: nothing." I said, "I'm more than willing to learn. Just tell me what to do?" He says, "From now on, whenever I give you a signal, you hit everyone on your end of the craps table for a bet. I don't give a shit what they are betting, you ask them to put one down for the crew." Hustling tips was not allowed and still isn't, but in those days everyone hustled and everyone knew it. You just didn't do it in front of the pit boss out of respect. The next night, the pit boss walked to the far end of the pit and the floor supervisor went to talk to a hooker. The stickman gave me a signal. Well, I am so excited, I start hollering, "SIR, WHAT ABOUT PUTTING DOWN A BET FOR THE BOYS?" I mean, I am yelling this at least seven times to seven different players and the stickman is turning bright red and thinking, "What an asshole!" The pit boss runs over to the floor supervisor, who is running right toward me and says, "Tell that schmuck to see me before he goes on his break" and I figure I am dead meat. But the pit boss says to me at break, "Look, kid, you got balls, but no brains. We all have to make money and I don't have a problem with everyone getting their fair share, but if I hear you ask for a bet again, I'm going to rip your balls off."

That's when I learned that everyone was getting a piece of the action. The stickman and the other craps dealer and me each gave $500 to the pencil man, who made up the work schedules. In return, the pencil man made sure that the three of us always worked together on the best shift for the next nine weeks and that we were assigned to the craps table directly in front of the theater. There were two shows each night and during the breaks, there was a lot of high play at that table. We made $300 to $400 per night each in tips and that was tax-free and all ours. We had to make it in tips because we were only paid minimum wage. But you see, before we could hustle tips, we each had to slip the boxman at the table fifty bucks per night. We also each had to give the floor supervisor another seventy-five to look the other way. How much of that he gave to the pit boss, I never knew, because you never dealt directly with the pit boss except at Christmas, when you gave him a present and I don't mean a box of your wife's cookies. I knew pit bosses who got cars from some baccarat dealers because they were making a quarter of a million in tips that never were reported to Uncle Sam.

The first time you hustled a tip, you were polite. I'd say, "Hey, we're really calling some good numbers for you tonight, aren't we, sir. How about laying one down for the boys?" And if that was too subtle, I'd say, "It's time for you to put one down for the stickman and show him a little appreciation. You know, some respect." I knew dealers who would just take a guy's bet and divide it and put it down as two bets. Most of the time, guys didn't even know they were betting for the table crew until we took the chips.

At Christmas, everyone in a casino dies because there isn't much action, and one Christmas I was really busted. I was divorced by now and I blew every paycheck either at the tables or on women. I needed to earn some cash but the casino was dead so everyone on the crew chipped in a hundred bucks—I borrowed mine from a pal—and we hired this really good-looking blond hooker with huge tits and had her come over to the table and begin shooting dice. Every time she bent over, her big boobs about fell out and within a few minutes, we had every craps player in the casino at our table.

That's just how things were back then. Money talked. Every hotel had a stable of girls. The bellman ran them. We had hookers who would give us money if we sent them a high roller. We had guys who would buy jewelry from us too, you know, when a player would lose everything and offer you his watch or ring. And the sharks were everywhere. There used to be this steak house called the Flame that was famous for high-priced hookers, loan sharks, and really excellent steaks. I blew all my tokes and bankroll one week and my buddy took me down to the Flame and introduced me to a guy who gave me three thousand at seven percent, which meant I had to pay 210 bucks per week to him until I could pay off the three grand.

A week later, I took a friend down there and the shark gave me a hundred bucks for bringing him in. I even started putting some money out on the street myself. It was okay as long as you had less than fifty thousand on the street. If you were doing more than that, you had to pay off the mob guys. There was always lots of money to go around back in those days. Now, the corporations suck it all up. The sharks are still in town, of course, but the guys who are really making all the cash are the corporate suits who don't ever have to dirty their hands.

—*Veteran craps dealer, Luxor*

Spring: A Spin
of the Wheel

....

"In a daze, I pushed all that pile onto the red, but then I suddenly came to my senses. And that was the only time that night that cold fear ran down my spine and made my hands and legs tremble. With horror I realized what it would mean to me to lose at that moment—my whole life was at stake."

—*Fyodor Dostoyevsky, The Gambler*

....

CHAPTER FIFTEEN

Luxor Entertainment

Entertainment director Michael Hartzell could feel the pressure. The Luxor had never had a hit show. There had been three attempts and each had failed. Tony Alamo was making entertainment a top priority. The company was spending $25 million to build a new twelve-hundred-seat theater. It was Hartzell's job to make sure it opened with a smash.

Hartzell had worked at Circus Circus longer than anyone else. He had been hired in 1968, along with his parents and three brothers, to install the trapeze riggings in Jay Sarno's casino several weeks before it opened. Afterward, the family had stayed on to run the balloon concession in the midway and Hartzell, who was then twenty-four years old, had been picked by Sarno to be the circus ringmaster. For the next twenty-one years, he had introduced performers during the free shows and booked all of the acts in the casino. He had given up his ringmaster microphone when he was named entertainment director at the Excalibur. Initially, the super casino's architects hadn't included a stage show in their plans. They recommended building two movie theaters and a miniature golf course in the castle's basement. But Hartzell had argued strenuously in favor of adding a show. The problem was that circus acts just didn't fit with the casino's medieval theme. At the suggestion of a friend, Hartzell had visited Medieval Times, a popular dinner theater in Los Angeles where performers dressed as knights and fought with swords and lances during a jousting tournament. Hartzell thought Medieval Times was perfect, but its owners and Circus Circus couldn't agree on a contract, so Hartzell hired two producers, Peter and Patrick Jackson, to create a jousting show exclusively for the Excalibur's basement arena. Their drama, *King Arthur's Tournament,* pitted an evil black knight against a heroic white knight in seeking the hand of a princess in marriage. The Excalibur's audience was encouraged to hoot, holler, and pound on tables. Between jousts, acrobats, tumblers, jesters, and jugglers performed while "serfs" and "wenches" served Cornish game hens and hot apple tarts. It was Circus Circus's first foray into operating a major show, and it was such a huge success that the Jacksons were hired to produce another arena show for the Luxor when it opened.

But this time, the show was supposed to have an Egyptian theme and be a bit more upscale. Instead of game hens, the audience was to be served either steak or salmon, and the price of a ticket was to be $10 more than at the Excalibur. *The Winds of the Gods* featured elephants, giraffes, and zebras, as well as dancers, musicians, and acrobats, but what really made the show different was the Jacksons' idea of covering the entire Luxor arena with four feet of water in less than a minute so that its second act could be performed entirely "at sea." Circus Circus signed a five-year contract with the Jacksons, but before the show opened, Bennett began cutting the entertainment budget. The first item to go was the $1.8 million water device. "Everyone convinced themselves that we could do the second half in dirt, rather than water," Hartzell recalled. The show opened with little publicity and tiny audiences. It closed thirteen painful months later after Circus Circus paid an undisclosed fee to the Jacksons to end their Luxor contract. After that fiasco, Circus Circus hired veteran crooner Wayne Newton for fourteen weeks, but even he couldn't fill the arena. Nor could the ice show that came next.

Hartzell had spent much of 1996 crisscrossing the country looking at potential shows. He wanted something similar to *Mystère,* the hottest ticket on the Strip. Created by Cirque du Soleil exclusively for Steve Wynn's Treasure Island, *Mystère* was performed twice nightly in a theater-in-the-round. A cast of seventy that included acrobats, clowns, comedians, stilt-walkers, dancers, and musicians performed during the shows, which were done without dialogue, making it especially appealing to non-English-speaking tourists. "This surreal postmodern circus, combining high-tech special effects, seemingly superhuman ability, and commedia dell'arte whimsy, is like nothing you've ever seen before," Frommer's travel guide raved. ". . . Cirque du Soleil is flawless." Hartzell admired *Mystère* so much that he asked Cirque du Soleil about doing a different show for the Luxor, but its ironclad contract with Wynn prohibited it from working with any other Las Vegas casinos.

Hartzell had found several innovative shows during his search, but none had a track record and no one at Circus Circus was going to risk opening a new show at the Luxor—after three failures—unless it already had proved itself. Just when Hartzell was about to give up, he saw a production called *Mystique* at Harrah's casino in Lake Tahoe. It was the handiwork of Las Vegas producers Dick and Lynne Foster, and Hartzell loved it.

"After flying all over the world, the show that I wanted the most was right here in Nevada." Lake Tahoe had a reputation for being a tough town for entertainers, yet *Mystique* was drawing large audiences. Still, Hartzell hadn't been in a hurry to offer the Fosters a contract. He was determined to make sure the Luxor's next show was a success and he wanted to see how *Mystique* did when it moved outside of Nevada for a stint at the Harrah's casino in Atlantic City. It proved to be even more successful there, so Hartzell started negotiating with the Fosters in late 1996.

Dick Foster Productions had an impressive track record of hits, starting in the early 1970s when they produced the first television special done by Olympic medalist Peggy Fleming. They followed it with shows featuring other ice skating stars, including Dorothy Hamill, and Tai Babilonia and Randy Gardner, and celebrity specials by Lindsay Wagner, Flip Wilson, Dinah Shore, and Perry Como. Their first big stage show in Las Vegas was *Spellbound,* a magic show that opened in 1984 and was still one of the Strip's more popular shows. *Mystique* had been Lynne's idea. It was a three-act production with lots of dancing, acrobatics, comedy, and magic.

The Fosters were well aware of the dismal history of other shows at the Luxor, so they proved to be tough negotiators. It took the two sides six months to agree on a five-year contract, and during that time *Mystique*'s Boardwalk run ended and the cast disbanded. As part of the deal, the Fosters agreed to change the name of the show to *Imagine* and enlarge its cast from twenty-seven to fifty-two.

The Fosters began seeking out the original cast members in the spring of 1997 and placed ads in the New York City and Los Angeles trade papers for dancers and acrobats. They also advertised in the *Dirt Alert,* the weekly Las Vegas newspaper read by showgirls and other performers. The Fosters had been told that the new Luxor theater would be ready in August, so they scheduled auditions for July.

One of the names Dick and Lynne Foster noticed when they went over their list of original cast members was Kelly Jo Steinfort. "She has just the sort of winning personality and attitude that we want at the Luxor show," Dick said. Lynne agreed. "The last I heard, she was touring Japan in a topless revue," she said. "I sure hope she's available." That same afternoon, Lynne sent a letter to Japan telling Steinfort about the casting call.

CHAPTER SIXTEEN

....

Kelly Jo Steinfort, Showgirl

Kelly Jo Steinfort was happy her three-month tour in Japan was finally over. It had been grueling. She was still recovering from a knee injury that had crippled her there. She had hurt herself during a foolish accident in a stupid show. Just thinking about it irritated her. The only good thing that had happened in Japan was meeting Yoji Kawamoto. He had been there to help her and had made Japan tolerable. But thinking about him now only made her sad, so she tried to put him out of her mind as she drove to a gym near her Las Vegas apartment. She had plenty of other worries. She wanted to lose 8 pounds before she met with Dick and Lynne Foster. Even though she weighed 138 pounds, which was fine for someone five feet, nine inches tall, she felt bloated. She was twenty-eight years old and this worried her too. Most of the other showgirls auditioning for jobs on the Strip were younger. How much longer could she keep up?

Her boyfriend, Paul Morgan, hadn't seemed concerned when she had hurt her knee. The two of them had been going together nearly five years, but because he was a jazz musician in New York City and she was a dancer in Las Vegas, they really hadn't spent much time together lately. It was frustrating. She had thought about giving up dancing after her accident. She could have joined Morgan in New York, but a gut feeling had kept her from quitting. That turned out to be wise, because they had quarreled over the telephone just a few days ago after she got back to the States and now they weren't even talking to each other.

Steinfort parked at the gym and went inside to look for Phillip Millaudon. He was part of a three-member acrobatic act that already had been hired by the Fosters to perform in the Luxor's show. She had telephoned him earlier in the morning to see if he wanted to join her in working out. They had become friends when they were members of the original cast of *Mystique*, and he had stayed in touch, writing several letters to her in Japan. In fact, had it not been for Millaudon, Steinfort might not have heard that the Fosters had signed a contract with the Luxor. Lynne Foster's letter had never reached her in Japan. It was Millaudon who had tipped her off. Of course, she had immediately called the Fosters and they had promised to hold a dancing spot open for her. Just the same, they had asked her to attend the show's auditions in July. That's why she was working out in the gym. It was now mid-May and she was still having some trouble with her knee.

Steinfort arrived before Millaudon, so she began warming up. How many hours had she spent in gyms and dance studios? For as long as she could remember, she had worked out daily. It was part of the price she paid for being a dancer. Nothing made her happier than dancing. Her mother had enrolled her in a dance class at age four and except for a brief foray into gymnastics, Steinfort had attended dance and ballet classes almost daily since then. As a teenager growing up in

Binghamton, New York, her dream had been to dance on Broadway, and as soon as she graduated from college in 1991, she left for Manhattan. She stuck it out for three months but no one hired her and she was miserable. Late one night, she called her parents and they picked her up the next morning. Back in Binghamton, she got a job waiting tables at a local Holiday Inn. She was twenty-one and going nowhere.

And then she got a telephone call that changed her life.

Carnival Cruises needed a dancer and one of Steinfort's college professors had recommended her without her knowing it. "We need someone who can be in San Juan on Saturday to catch the boat," the caller explained. It was Thursday. Steinfort flew to Puerto Rico the next morning. The show was called *Rock 'Round the Clock* and was a Disneyland-like production. Paul Morgan was the bandleader and he asked Steinfort for a date the day she stepped on board. She said no at first but eventually agreed, and before long was in love. Eight months later, she got into a salary dispute and left the boat. Back home, she went to work as a store clerk in a shopping mall. Morgan called her every day and as soon as his contract with the cruise line ended, they moved into a loft in Manhattan. This time Steinfort vowed she would land a dancing job on Broadway. They went to auditions and supported themselves doing temporary jobs. He delivered packages, she waited tables. Six weeks after they arrived, Steinfort was offered a role in a show being produced for a Hilton hotel in Tokyo. The pay was $600 a week for three months. "Oh," the producer added, "you got to dance topless."

Steinfort had never been to Japan and had never danced seminude, but Morgan encouraged her to take the job. She was a professional dancer and sometimes nudity was necessary. Besides, she would be in Japan. No one knew her there.

Two days later Steinfort flew to Seattle for one week of rehearsals. There were three other dancers in the cast, along with a comedian, a singer, and a "specialty act." She thought the dance acts were moronic. In one number, she wore what the producer called a "Catholic schoolgirl outfit." The dancers were to strip off their white blouses and plaid skirts and end up in tiny G-strings. In another number, they danced in sheer nightgowns while carrying teddy bears. But they rehearsed in leotards, so Steinfort did not have to bare her breasts until a dress rehearsal the night before the cast left for Japan. The show's producer and his friends came to watch. In the dressing room, Steinfort looked in a mirror. "It was strange seeing my naked breasts, thinking that in a few moments I was going to be out on a stage wearing only a G-string. I had never had my shirt off in public. But I said to myself, 'I can do this.' I went out there and tried not to think about it."

Because everyone had rehearsed at different times, Steinfort hadn't seen the entire show and when the specialty act began, she was stunned. A busty eighteen-year-old blonde dressed as Little Bo Peep and carrying a stuffed lamb pranced onstage and began to strip. When she was naked except for her G-string, she invited a man from the audience onstage, placed the stuffed lamb between them, and engaged in simulated sex. The show's dance captain noticed the horrified look on Steinfort's face. "Look, Kelly Jo," she volunteered, "this sort of thing is expected in Tokyo. It is really stupid and you wonder what sort of people want to see this, but it really will be cute in Japan. Really. You'll see."

In Tokyo, they did three shows a night. At the start, the dancers ran through the audience to the stage.

Steinfort got into position too early one night and a customer pinched her. Another time, she was in a telephone booth talking to her parents after a show when
she saw a man masturbating in front of her. When the
three-month booking ended, the stripper was sent home
but everyone else was asked to spend an additional
three months touring Japan in a new show that wasn't
topless. Steinfort was promoted to dance captain,
which meant that she was in charge of the other
dancers. They performed in eleven different cities, and
even though it meant that she had to spend more time
away from Morgan, she loved it. On the flight home,
the producer asked her if she wanted to dance in two
shows booked at Harrah's in Reno. She called Morgan
and he agreed that she should take the job. "I'm not going to stand in the way of your career," he promised.

The 7 P.M. show at Harrah's was called *Hit City*
and was a family-oriented production. The eleven
o'clock show, called *High Voltage,* was topless. The pay
was $600 a week. Her parents and brother came to see
her perform. It was the first time that any of them had
seen her dance topless and her parents didn't mind, but
her twenty-year-old brother was clearly uncomfortable.
So was Steinfort. "When I came out onstage and saw
him, I went 'Whoa, this isn't right. I'm not supposed to
be uncovered in front of my brother.' For the first time
since I had been dancing topless, I felt embarrassed and
we avoided eye contact."

Morgan came to see her too and didn't care that her
breasts were showing. Steinfort began feeling sexy. She
had never thought of herself as a sensuous woman
whom men would lust after. That began changing and
the reason was the stage. "When I am performing, I feel
a tremendous amount of control that I don't always feel
in my personal life. I am in charge onstage. It is an escape for me from who I really am. My mom said that
if you look at my face, I look like an entirely different

person onstage. *High Voltage* had wild wigs and tiny G-strings. I did things onstage that I would never do in private. Heck, I would never even go into Frederick's of Hollywood and buy anything like what we were wearing . . . but onstage, I lost all those inhibitions and I liked that freedom—that control—a lot."

She began spending her weekends with other dancers at a nude beach in Lake Tahoe where they sunbathed to avoid tan lines. She was now one of Reno's beautiful show people. Men sent her flowers and candy backstage. Others offered to buy her drinks and take her to dinner. "I never was much of a party person, but I was learning that you needed to be one in order to build bridges with producers or others who could help your career." A singer in the show offered to help her learn the ropes. She agreed to go out with him even though she was in love with Morgan. "I felt that whenever someone showed me a little attention, I had to like them back." She was lonely and irritated because Morgan rarely answered her letters. When they had first met, he had doted on her; now he seemed to take her for granted. She complained, but he said he didn't have time to write. That irked her even more. She found time, why couldn't he? She began going out with the singer but dumped him after she discovered he was seeing other girlfriends. She felt like a fool, and the next time Morgan came to Reno to visit, she confessed. He was crushed. "I had violated the trust that we had developed even though I had not slept with the singer," she said. Morgan told her he wanted to break up because he couldn't trust her. She was acting like a different person.

Some dancers in the show invited her to go with them to Las Vegas on her day off because the Stardust was holding auditions for *Enter the Night,* one of the best-known topless revues on the Strip. She didn't have anything else to do, so she tagged along. In New York

City, dancers audition in nude tights, dance slippers, and leotards. In Las Vegas, they dress in high heels, fishnet stockings, G-strings, and a kind of tight tank top that shows how big their breasts are. The dance captain at *Enter the Night* showed the forty women at the audition how to do a "combination"—several dance steps—from the show. Once they had mastered it, the Stardust's entertainment director came in. He was brisk and blunt. Moving down the line of dancers, he rejected several without giving them a chance to perform because he said they were too fat, too tall, or too short. He ordered the remaining girls to perform the combination, and brusquely whittled down the number to twenty dancers. "We only need one girl," he declared. They performed again and he cut several more. After yet another competition, he announced his choice: Steinfort.

"When can you come to work?" he asked.

Steinfort hadn't really been looking for a job and still had ten months left on her contract in Reno.

"We'll wait," he told her. "You're that good."

Steinfort was now a Las Vegas showgirl, one of the leggy beauties whom thousands of tourists came to ogle. Shortly after she joined the *Enter the Night* cast, the director made her an understudy for one of the show's principal dancers. Steinfort had never thought of herself as special enough to perform a solo onstage, but the director assured her that she had potential. At about this same time, the movie *Showgirls* was released, and since it was about a young dancer who dreamed of becoming a showgirl at the Stardust, reporters flocked to *Enter the Night* to learn if Hollywood's steamy, X-rated film version of a showgirl's life fit with reality. The Stardust chose Steinfort to talk with the media. Along with four other showgirls, she also appeared on the *Tonight Show* with Jay Leno and was photographed for spreads in two national magazines. She told reporters that the movie was sleazy, cheesy, and ridiculous. She had never been pressured to have sex in return for a job. If she had been, she would have filed a sexual harassment suit. "The days of bosses getting away with stuff like that are over. Besides, most of the producers and choreographers I know are gay!"

Steinfort liked representing the Stardust and other showgirls. "Insecurity has a lot to do with why I dance," she said. "I think that I am always trying to prove myself, and dancing plays a role in that. I have to push myself to get on that stage. Sometimes it's hard for me because I am basically shy, but when I get up there, I find that I am truly happy."

The show's director told Steinfort that she was ready to perform a solo number called "Surrender." The act called for her to be lowered on a tiny round pedestal from the ceiling to the front of the stage until she was only a few feet above the audience in the thousand-seat theater. She was supposed to dance slowly to a seductive tune while wearing a transparent, cream-colored costume that left her breasts exposed. Steinfort was so nervous the first night that she felt certain the audience could see her legs shaking as she was lowered. Although the spotlights blinded her, she could feel the packed room watching her every movement. She was alone, nearly naked, and about to panic when the music sounded and her years of training kicked in. "It was the absolute highlight of my career."

Audiences liked her dance so much that the director chose her to become the show's understudy for Aki, the star of *Enter the Night* and arguably the best-known showgirl at the time. Photographs of Aki were posted on billboards, buses, and taxis, and Steinfort was only one step behind her. She was near the top of her profession, but privately she was miserable. She missed Morgan. She had gone on a few dates but had not found anyone whom she liked as well. She called him one night and found that he was just as unhappy as she was. He flew to Nevada to see her in *Enter the Night*. After the show, she introduced him to all her girlfriends. When they were finally alone together, Steinfort asked him if he would move to Las Vegas. There were plenty of jobs for musicians on the Strip and they would be together at last.

"You've done great and I'm proud of you," he replied, "but this is just another show in the middle of a desert."

Steinfort was irked at his response, but she didn't show it. Morgan reminded her that she had once had plans that he thought were more impressive than being a topless dancer. She had always talked about going back to college to study physical therapy. She had always talked about settling down and having children. Besides, Morgan enjoyed living in New York City because he had more chances to play jazz there. She said she understood.

After he went home, Steinfort signed up with a modeling agency to keep busy and earn some extra cash. She decided that she had been focusing too much on her dancing career. Morgan was right. *Enter the Night* was just another show. The modeling agency sent her to hand out pamphlets at booths in the convention center. She was paid to be polite and smile. One afternoon, the agency told her that Dick and Lynne Foster needed dancers for a one-day show in Palm Springs, California, that they were putting on for a corporate client. They were paying $1,000 in return for two weeks of morning rehearsals and the performance. Steinfort auditioned for the Fosters' director, David W. Gravatt, and he was so impressed that he offered her a job dancing in a new show the Fosters were putting together called *Mystique*. She wasn't interested until he mentioned where it was going to be performed—Lake Tahoe and Atlantic City. Steinfort jumped at the chance because it would get her closer to Morgan. "I wanted to prove to Paul that I cared so much for him that I was willing to give up *Enter the Night*. I owed him that much after destroying his trust in me in Reno." The director at *Enter the Night* begged her to reconsider. She was on the brink of becoming a lead dancer and possibly a star. Why give that up to dance in an unproven show? She thanked him, but she was determined to move closer to Morgan.

Steinfort enjoyed *Mystique* and when the cast got to Atlantic City, she spent every spare moment with her boyfriend. They lived in an apartment off the Boardwalk and went out for bagels each morning. After the show, they watched videos or went to listen to jazz bands. She loved him.

The Fosters had told the cast that *Mystique* might be sent overseas, but when those plans fell through, they disbanded. Only a few knew that the Fosters were negotiating with Michael Hartzell at the Luxor and that those talks prevented them from booking the show into rival casinos. Steinfort was unemployed. She thought about going back to Manhattan, moving in with Morgan, and looking for work there. It was the sensible thing to do. Still, his attitude continued to trouble her. She could tell he thought of dancing as a pastime, something to keep her busy until she decided what she really wanted to do with the rest of her life.

A friend told her about a company looking for dancers for a three-month tour in Japan. The job paid $800 a week. Steinfort took it. She wasn't eager to go back to Japan, but she needed the money and time to think. She knew she had made a mistake as soon as she arrived in Nagoya. The show was in a nightclub called Erotique Nouveau and the owner expected the dancers to mingle with customers after each performance. In return, they received tips in the form of paper coupons that the customers bought at the door and the dancers could later redeem for cash. The first number in the show was called "Jailhouse Rock." Steinfort's outfit was a leather G-string, several small chains, and a broom that she pushed around as if she was sweeping a cell. "The show actually was on the same level as the show I had done in Tokyo a few years earlier, but now I knew more than I had back then," Steinfort said. "I had done topless shows in Reno and Vegas that were classy, so I knew just how sleazy this show was. I had gone backwards in my career and it just didn't feel right anymore."

She thought about running home to Morgan, but decided to stick it out. On the first night, she told the club's woman owner, Kyoko Aoki, that she would stay for three months but she was not going to "fraternize" with customers. "There were several high rollers who would come in and the owner would rush backstage and say, 'This man—he wants to buy you dinner.' I always said no." Steinfort knew that other dancers were being paid for sex and that made her feel even worse. She became depressed. Morgan rarely called or wrote. The only person who wrote regularly was Phillip Millaudon, her friend from *Mystique*. He kept her up to date on news about the cast.

One night Steinfort found a middle-aged Japanese man waiting outside her dressing room with a bouquet of roses. Dancers got a $10 kickback if they were given roses that customers bought at inflated prices inside the club. His name was Yoji Kawamoto. She thanked him but didn't stop to talk. He was there the next night with roses, and the next night too. He told her that he wanted to learn "English conversation," but she didn't believe him. "Just English, Miss Kelly Jo," he pleaded. "Nothing else to worry about."

She finally agreed to sit at his table and talk. He brought her presents and eventually persuaded her to join him for an afternoon of sight-seeing and dinner. He told her that he was married and showed her photographs of his two daughters. "He was like a father when he was with me." He began teaching her Japanese phrases in return for her English tutoring. Being with him and reading Millaudon's letters became her life-support system in a job she had come to despise. She found herself thinking less and less of Morgan.

Six weeks into the tour, Steinfort stumbled during a dance step and tore the cartilage in her knee. She had to fly home for surgery. Kawamoto offered to drive her to the airport, but she didn't want to bother him so she took a taxi. She found him waiting there anyway to carry her bags. Just before she was about to board the airplane, he handed her an envelope to open later. There was $1,500 inside. She called him from her parents' house and said she couldn't accept the cash.

"You will be out of work," he insisted. "You need cash."

Morgan never called but Kawamoto and Millaudon did. She underwent surgery and three weeks later returned to Japan to finish her contract. Kawamoto was waiting for her at the airport. It was November 1996, and Steinfort's birthday was only a few days away. Kawamoto told her that he had made dinner reservations for them at her favorite restaurant and had bought her some jewelry. "I may never see you again after your tour ends," he explained when she protested. "I want to give you some special jewelry so when you look at it, you will remember me." He promised to call on Thursday to finalize her birthday plans.

Steinfort expected to hear from him that morning, but he didn't call. She waited all afternoon but he didn't call then either. She was sure that she would see him after the first show, but he wasn't there. Moments before the second show, she got a telephone call from one of his friends.

"He died," the caller said. Kawamoto's wife had

found him dead in his bed of a brain aneurysm. Steinfort went to his funeral but stayed only a few minutes because she was the only foreigner there. When she saw his wife and daughters, she felt out of place. "I wanted to scream: 'We were just friends! We weren't lovers!' " He had never touched her, not even a hug at the airport, but she was certain that he had never told his wife about their friendship.

Steinfort had planned on moving to New York City to be with Morgan after the Japan tour ended, but she no longer wanted to do that. When Millaudon called to tell her that the Fosters were casting a new show, she saw a way out. She went to visit her parents and called Morgan from there. They soon were arguing because he wanted her to move to New York City. She had given up her job at *Enter the Night* for him, she said. If he loved her, why couldn't he move to Las Vegas? Why was she the one who had to make all the sacrifices? By the time they finished talking, they had agreed to break up. "I am comfortable being by myself," Steinfort told her mother. "I don't need anyone else to be happy."

Returning to Las Vegas had made her feel good. She had always done well dancing on the Strip. Her next call had been to Millaudon to see if he wanted to begin working out regularly at the gym. Today was their first session.

Steinfort had just finished warming up when Millaudon stepped through the gym door.

"Welcome home," he said.

She liked how that sounded.

CHAPTER SEVENTEEN

....

Tony Alamo, the Boss

Tony Alamo wanted to look inside the women's rest room in the casino. An employee had told him that the locks on the toilet stalls didn't work. Rather than fix them, the Luxor's engineering department had put pieces of duct tape inside the cubicles for women to use to keep the doors shut. He was irritated. Here he was, in the midst of turning the Luxor into a world-class resort, with Circus Circus spending now close to $400 million—$150 million more than originally expected—to upgrade it, and the engineering department was using duct tape to keep the doors on the toilet stalls closed.

Alamo ordered his chief engineer, two other department heads, and general manager Don Givens to meet him outside the rest room, but he did not tell them why. He wanted to see the duct tape for himself.

After seventeen months of construction, Alamo was at last seeing progress. The twin hotel towers were finally open, so the Luxor could now offer high rollers special suites equipped with fully stocked wet bars, big-screen televisions, king-sized beds, and Jacuzzi tubs. Some 6,200 people were eating daily at Pharaoh's Pheast, the all-you-can-eat buffet in the basement. Alamo had greatly expanded the Luxor's spa and the resort had started booking conventions into its new 18,000-square-foot ballroom. But the renovation that pleased Alamo the most was the pyramid's new lobby. All traces of the Nile River ride and cavelike opening down into the casino were gone. Guests now entered the building on the ground level, the same floor as the casino. The lobby sparkled. Its floor looked like tan, brown, and black marble although it actually was less costly sandstone. A life-sized re-creation of the exterior of the Temple of Ramses II now greeted guests as they stepped into the atrium. The ornate facade was more than forty feet high, with stone columns and an archway, augmented with gold and hieroglyphics, that led directly into the casino. On each side of the archway were gargantuan twin statues of seated pharaohs. Blue-tinted pools flowed forward from the bases of the pharaohs toward the front doors of the Luxor like beckoning fingers. More stone columns, statues of Egyptian princesses, and live palm trees were set alongside the pools, creating a semicircle that subtly funneled guests into the casino. It was exactly what Alamo had wanted.

The Luxor's registration desk now was to the right of the entrance and was twice as large as the old one, with a waist-high counter marked by gold-plated signs identifying the different services: concierge, bell captain, hotel registration, check-out. There was a separate check-in area for VIPs behind gilded glass doors, so that passersby could gawk and wonder why those inside were receiving special treatment. The lobby walls were decorated with hand-painted murals depicting Egyptian life.

Much still needed to be done, and Alamo was painfully aware that the remodeling had been scheduled to take only one year. But he was proud of what he was accomplishing. The Luxor had a different ambiance now. Before the renovations, there had been a cut-off-shorts-and-tank-top feel to the place. It wasn't uncommon for arriving guests to bring a plastic ice cooler with them. Now, the lobby was frequented by men in brightly colored polo shirts wearing pressed khaki slacks and brown-tasseled loafers without socks. The women arrived in Nordstrom sundresses and sported Tiffany tennis bracelets. The gaudy red industrial-grade carpet that once covered the casino floor had been replaced with a thick blue carpet. "The old carpeting didn't convey the message we wanted to send," Don Givens had told a local reporter during a recent tour. "I think the town has grown into something more upscale. That's what we're going for."

All the new carpeting, hand-painted murals, and glitter, however, were going to be wasted if the Luxor's employees didn't provide first-class service. "We can't have guests finding duct tape serving as locks on bathroom stalls," Alamo snapped.

His managers were waiting for him when Alamo arrived at the rest room. With the head of housekeeping leading the way, Alamo went inside. The floor had been freshly polished and new locks had been installed on the seven toilet stalls. "Someone figured out what I was doing," Alamo said. While he was pleased by the repairs, he was irritated that his managers had not made them without having him threaten them with a surprise inspection. When asked, the building engineer said he had used the duct tape as a temporary measure to cut costs in keeping with Alamo's campaign to maximize profits. That upset Alamo even more. When he got back to his office, he called in Givens. "We can renovate buildings," he lectured, "but people's attitudes are much harder to change." The Luxor's employees were still acting as if they were working in a grind joint. Attitudes at the pyramid needed to change, and it was Givens's job to change them.

CHAPTER EIGHTEEN

....

Keith Uptain, Casino Shift Manager

From 6:30 P.M. until 2:30 A.M., the Luxor's casino was in Keith Uptain's hands. At age fifty, he was the oldest of the three shift bosses and was considered by many to be the best, in part because he was a "player," and that made him different. Most of the top managers at the Luxor rarely gambled. Uptain had a passion for it. Shooting craps gave him an adrenaline rush. Asking for a hit, when he had sixteen showing and the dealer had a face card, gave him a buzz. Whenever Uptain wanted to unwind after work, he stopped at a neighborhood pub and played video poker. On his days off, he often could be found playing blackjack at a casino near his house. He knew the odds of every game, read each new theory about betting as soon as it was published, and enjoyed talking with other gamblers about various strategies. He knew what it felt like to win big, and to lose big too.

During his shift, Uptain spent his time on the casino floor even though he had an office. On most nights, he oversaw ten gaming pits. Each had a pit boss responsible for watching as many as twelve games. They were assisted by 125 floor supervisors who watched over the four hundred dealers. Uptain was responsible for all of them.

One of the ironies about the Luxor was that it was a modern-day temple of chance, yet little about the place had actually been left to happenstance. Every slot machine had been placed on the casino floor in a carefully chosen spot. Each table game had been meticulously arranged. The half-inch pad under the Luxor's carpet, the "Navajo white" color of the paint used on its walls, the smooth texture of the green felt on its gaming tables—all of these seemingly minor matters had been reviewed with a single question in mind: How will this affect gambling? There were no windows or clocks in the casino to remind players that there was a world outside where day and night came and went and schedules had to be met. This was standard practice in all casinos. But the Luxor's creators had gone even further. The outer edge of the casino was kept darker than the center, where the majority of its table games were located. The lights over the high-stakes games glowed with a warm brilliance, as if to draw customers deep into the casino's belly and away from the darker netherworld at its rim.

The casino's slot manager, Richard Marino, was in charge of positioning the resort's 2,500-plus slot and video poker machines. The casino manager, Tom Robinson, decided where the Luxor's 110 table games would go. Both used their games to entice, manipulate, and excite players. For instance, the first gambling devices that guests saw when they entered the Luxor were a bank of slot machines to the immediate left of the front doors. These machines cost a quarter to play and were positioned in a circle around a bright red Jaguar XJ8 convertible parked on a platform at eye level under flashing yellow lights. The first player who hit three diamonds in a row on one of these slots would get the car. Marino had chosen a Jaguar because he thought it helped reinforce the Luxor's image as a luxury resort. He had put the twenty-five slot machines near the entrance because he knew that games that offered cars as prizes always attracted players. "You want to create an environment that makes a casino look busy," Marino explained. "You want customers to say, 'Look at how many people are playing these machines. They must be good.' " Using that same logic, Marino had placed two carousels, each with six slot machines, near the Egyptian archway that opened into the casino. These machines cost a nickel to play, making them the cheapest slots in the casino, and people were often lined up waiting to play one. The busy scene made the casino look as if it was bristling with action even when it wasn't.

Marino's decision to place Megabucks, one of the hottest slot machines in Las Vegas, in the southwestern corner of the casino was also a calculated move. Megabucks was a linked "progressive" slot machine, which meant that every Megabucks machine—and there were thousands of them throughout Nevada— was connected electronically to a computer that kept track of how many coins they were gobbling. Each time someone dropped a coin into a Megabucks machine, a percentage of it was added to the ongoing jackpot. Electronic billboards above Megabucks machines showed a running tally of how much cash would be paid to the winner. Since this "progressive jackpot" was increasing second by second, no one knew how high it would go until someone won. At least six or seven times a year Megabucks would pay out $10 million or more, so the machines were always busy. Marino had placed Megabucks in the least populous corner of the casino to draw customers into an otherwise dead corner. The

Luxor operated its own progressive slot machines, known as Luxor Riches, and Marino used them to move customers through the casino too. But they were linked only with other Luxor machines, which in general limited the size of their jackpots to less than $1 million.

The greatest amount of floor space in the casino was taken up by slot and video poker machines. Although the internal mechanisms of all these machines worked the same way, Marino used a variety of different models, shapes, and sizes to create exciting displays of flashing lights and noise. There never seemed to be a moment when the metallic buzzers, ringing bells, and the clatter of coins weren't signaling that someone had just aligned a winning combination of spinning diamonds, cherries, or lucky sevens.

Las Vegas residents preferred video poker machines to slots, so casinos that catered to local players usually kept a ratio of 80 percent video poker machines and 20 percent slots on their floors. But at Strip resorts, vacation gamblers preferred the user-friendly slots, so Marino used a ratio of 73 percent slots and only 27 percent video poker machines. Every slot and video poker machine in the Luxor was connected to a computer in his office that showed him at any moment which machines were being played and whether they were winning or losing. He used his computer to help him decide which machines were the most popular and whether he had enough machines to keep his customers happy. "I like to have two machines available for every player," he explained. "I call this the 'Tony Alamo urinal theory.' Tony says that when a man goes into a public rest room and sees a bunch of urinals, he will always select one that is away from other men. The same is true about slot machines. People don't like to play next to a stranger, so we give them room. There is usually an empty machine next to them."

Although the Luxor's slot operations fell under

Keith Uptain's jurisdiction during the night shift, he let
one of Richard Marino's assistants take care of them.
The only time he was called was when there was a big
jackpot and he had to make certain the player had won
legitimately. This left Uptain free to do what he loved
best: watch over the casino's table games. The new
high-limit gaming area was being constructed in the
center of the casino, much like a bull's-eye. The easiest
way to visualize the layout of the casino was to think of
it as a pie that had been divided into four equal wedges.
Each piece of this imaginary pie contained hundreds of
slot and video machines. The high-limit gaming area
was in the center of the pie, and the four cuts in the pie
represented the four paths that led to the pyramid's
north, east, south, and west entrances. Of these, the
main lobby entrance, which faced east, was the most
popular. This is where guests entered the hotel. The
northern entrance also was widely used by guests moving between the Luxor and the Excalibur. The west
entrance led to the Luxor's swimming pools, and the
south entrance was being readied for when Mandalay
Bay opened next door. The casino's table games were
positioned along the two paths that led from the hotel's
main lobby and from the Excalibur to the high-limit
gaming area. They formed a gambling gauntlet.

    The first table game that gamblers saw when they
passed under the lobby archway into the casino was a
Big Six Wheel, also known as the Wheel of Fortune.
Robinson had placed the five-foot-tall wheel here because it is the most recognizable and the simplest game
to play. Most carnivals and amusement parks have
some sort of game in which people try to guess where a
spinning wheel will stop. Robinson wanted to send
guests a subliminal message: Don't be afraid to come inside; the Luxor's games are fun and simple to play.
There were fifty-four spaces on the wheel, each marked
with actual bills in various denominations, and as soon

as the dealer spun it, the wheel would emit a loud ta-da-ta-da-tat amid the shrieks of the players. This sent out another message: Everyone here is enjoying themselves!

The path leading from the wheel to the casino's center was lined on both sides with gaming pits, or small circles of six to ten tables. The dealers stood inside the circles. The first pit contained blackjack tables. The next two pits offered Caribbean Stud Poker and Let It Ride, two popular poker games. As guests moved closer to the casino's center, they found roulette wheels and craps tables. There was usually a lot of cheering going on at both, especially craps, which made the inner circle of the casino loud, sending another message: Come in farther and see what the excitement is all about!

Uptain could usually be found in the high-limit gaming area. It was already in use even though construction there wasn't yet finished. On one side were $5, $10, $25, $50, and $100 slot machines and video poker machines. The other side was reserved for high-limit table games: blackjack, baccarat, and pia gow poker, a dice-and-card game popular with Asians. These tables had "minimums" that ranged from required bets of $25 per hand at a blackjack table to $1,000 per hand at baccarat. During slow nights, the limits were kept low. Whenever the pit got crowded, the minimum bets were raised. These tables also had maximum amounts that players could bet to protect the casino from high rollers on hot streaks. The highest wager was $10,000 per hand at baccarat unless Uptain or his bosses decided to raise it. The busiest nights were Friday and Saturday, when gamblers from Los Angeles arrived. Uptain recognized many of them because they had established credit lines at the Luxor. On this particular Friday night, the first big player to arrive was a college student whose father was a Japanese hotel tycoon. He pulled a five-inch-high stack of new $100 bills from his backpack and slapped it down on the table. When "the kid," as he was called by employees, had first started coming to the Luxor, Uptain asked if he wanted to deposit his cash in the casino's safe or have a security guard escort him to and from his car, since he often carried as much as $40,000. He had said no. He liked to show off his wad and he insisted on betting $100 bills instead of chips. Another player wandered into the pit a few minutes later and Uptain grimaced when he spotted him. He was a "steamer," Uptain's word for a player who couldn't control his temper. Although the Luxor wanted all the high rollers it could get, Uptain had warned this man that he would be banned from the casino if he couldn't keep his outbursts under control. The weekend before, he had become so furious that he had hurled a $5 chip at a brass trash can fifteen feet away from his chair and had barely missed hitting a cocktail waitress. The chip had been thrown so hard it dented the side of the can.

Twenty minutes after the steamer began playing, he leaped from his seat and headed for Uptain.

"Your pit boss just changed the table minimum on me," he protested. He had been the only gambler playing at a blackjack table with a minimum of $100 when a black woman sat down next to him. She had won $7,000 the night before sitting in that same chair and she wanted to sit there again, but on the previous night the table minimum had been only $50. She had asked the pit boss to lower the minimum bet limit and he agreed. "If I wanted company," the steamer complained, "I'd go to a whorehouse. I don't want this woman playing next to me." Uptain glanced over at her. She was betting two $50 chips at a time, probably just to irritate the steamer. He escorted the man over to an empty blackjack table with a $100 minimum and gave him a comp so he could eat dinner for free at the

Isis. That quieted him down. "The pit boss shouldn't have done that," Uptain said later. "That's why I comped him."

Comps came in handy, although Uptain was careful how he used them. They used to be given away by casinos without much scrutiny. In the 1960s, some resorts flew in hordes of players on complimentary junkets, furnishing them with free rooms and food without checking to see if they actually gambled. After the corporations took control and computers were brought into the gaming pits, casinos developed a sophisticated tracking system that now dictates how many comps each player can receive based on time spent gambling and average bet. Anyone could ask to be rated, which was the first step toward earning a comp at a gaming table. A floor person would watch the player for a few minutes, carefully noting the average amount of the bets and how much was either won or lost. He also noted when the player stopped gambling. This information would be entered into the casino's computer, which would then calculate the person's "theoreticals." Uptain now typed the name of the steamer into the computer keyboard in the high-limit gaming area, and the man's full name, address, credit limit, and other personal tidbits, such as his wife's name and their birthdays and wedding anniversary, flashed on the screen. The casino often used this personal information to send cards or gifts to gamblers. The screen listed all the dates when the gambler had played at the Luxor, how much he had won or lost, and how long he had played during each trip. His average bet was $100 per hand, which meant that in one hour of play at blackjack (sixty hands), the computer projected that he would give the casino $6,000 in action. Based on the casino's mathematical edge of about 2 percent, the Luxor expected to win $120 per hour from the gambler. In return, it would credit his account with about $48 worth of comps, which was 40 percent of his expected losses.

Comps were not usually paid in cash. Instead they were given as meals, rooms, airline tickets, limousine service, show tickets, and sometimes Luxor merchandise. Slot and video poker machine players could also earn comps by enrolling in the free Gold Chamber Club. Members were issued a card about the same size as a credit card, which they inserted into the slot and video poker machines whenever they played. The magnetic strip on the card kept track of how much money was being dropped into the machines. For every dollar that they gambled, players received points that could be redeemed for meals, rooms, and other prizes.

What many gamblers didn't realize was that the data collected by the magnetic cards provided slot manager Richard Marino with a gold mine of demographic information. He could now target his best customers and make sure that they were invited to special events, such as slot tournaments. A slot tournament was usually held on a weekend and began with a free banquet hosted by Marino. The next day, the two hundred or so competitors would play for twenty minutes on slot machines that had been set as loose as possible so that the players would hit some sort of winning combination on nearly every spin. Rather than winning cash, they accumulated points. They would play twice each day on Saturday and on Sunday, and the player with the most points would win a $25,000 cash jackpot. The Luxor made money from this event because most tournament participants played the casino's regular slot machines when they weren't playing their twenty-minute tournament games.

Shortly before midnight, one of Uptain's pit bosses told him that a customer was complaining about how she had been rated for comps. The floor supervisor had noted that she had bet an average of $25 per hand at blackjack, but she was now insisting that she had been betting $50. Uptain knew that a lot of players tried to make up for their gambling losses by getting comps. This was especially true after a book called *Comp City* was published in Las Vegas. Its author claimed that he could teach gamblers how they could earn more in comps than they lost gambling. One of his tips was to make it look as if they were betting more per hand than was actually the case. They did this by wagering large amounts whenever a floor supervisor was watching and cutting back their bets when the supervisor looked elsewhere. Uptain was familiar with *Comp City* and a dozen other books like it, but he didn't give them much credence. While the mathematical theory behind the author's reasoning was sound, the book did not take into account human nature and luck. For instance, the casino expected the steamer to lose $120 per hour based on its mathematical edge. In return, it was giving him $48 per hour in comps. If the steamer followed basic blackjack strategy, however, he could reduce the casino's expected winnings to as little as $12 per hour. This would mean he could pocket $36 more in comps per hour than he was actually losing. That sounded easy, but it really wasn't. BBS was based on the playing of thousands of hands, not just sixty, and Uptain had watched plenty of gamblers lose ten or twenty hands in an hour regardless of how skillfully they played. They had simply been unlucky. Their losses could easily be as much as $1,000 during their first hour of play, and the Luxor computer would still offer them $48 in comps. Over time, the mathematics behind BBS would eventually kick in and a gambler's losses would average out to $12 per hour. But how long would that take? No one could be sure. A player would have to have deep pockets and steel nerves to continue betting $100 per hand until his unlucky streak ended.

The same was true of slot machines. The Luxor typically set its machines so they paid back 98 percent of all the coins that were put in them, but what many slot players didn't understand was that the 98 percent payback was based on *one million* spins. A player could sit down at a machine, play for an hour, and win only a few coins because the machine was in a down cycle. Another player might win ten pulls in a row. It all depended on where that slot machine was in its one-million-pull cycle.

Uptain listened patiently to the complaining player, but the longer she talked, the more suspicious he became. The floor supervisor said that he had seen the woman dropping her bet to $10 per hand when she thought he wasn't looking. Uptain called the surveillance room and asked them to check the video from the camera over the table. It showed that the woman was lying and had bet $50 only a few times. Uptain confronted her.

"Oh well," she shrugged. "You can't blame a girl for trying."

By 1 A.M., the casino was bustling and so was Uptain. A pit boss needed help because a high roller had left $1,500 in chips on a table while he went to a rest room. An hour later, the player still hadn't returned. Uptain sent someone to find him. It turned out he had decided to go to bed and had forgotten about his chips. He asked Uptain to take the chips to the casino cage for safekeeping until he retrieved them. Another pit boss called to report that the casino had lost $14,500 to a single player at a craps table. Uptain was irked. He expected his pit bosses to tell him when the losses hit $5,000, not nearly three times that. He went over to watch the game and make sure that the player hadn't slipped in a pair of loaded dice. He hadn't. He was winning fairly. While Uptain was watching the craps game, his assistant, Richard Woods, whispered that a gambler who had refused to give his name had bought $1,000 worth of chips but played only one hand of blackjack. He'd lost $50 and then gone to the casino cage to cash in the remaining chips. Woods suspected the gambler was laundering money. Ten minutes later, Woods called Uptain on his cell phone to report the man had just bought $3,000 worth of chips at a blackjack table, had again played one hand, and was now on his way to cash in his chips at the casino cage. Uptain stopped the man at the cage and asked him why he wasn't gambling. "I decided I don't feel lucky," he replied. Uptain told him that his photograph had been taken by surveillance cameras and he wouldn't be sold any more chips unless he used them to play. The man left in a hurry.

Minutes later, a pit boss asked Uptain to watch a player suspected of card counting. The gambler had won $7,359, but Uptain decided he was simply lucky. A Los Angeles record producer arrived at the high-limit gaming area and asked for Uptain because they had met the previous weekend. He just wanted to say hello. He had two women with him, whom he laughingly introduced as "party girls." The producer lost $35,000 gambling that night but thanked Uptain before he left. At two in the morning Uptain got a telephone call from a friend who was a supervisor at the Stratosphere casino. A player who had just won $75,000 there was on his way to the Luxor and was suspected of being a card counter. He faxed Uptain the guy's picture, taken by surveillance cameras. Next, two gay men demanded to see Uptain because a blackjack dealer had offended them. Every time they won a hand, they kissed each other on the lips, and they claimed the male dealer had gotten a disgusted look on his face. Uptain gave them a woman dealer. A pit boss called to tell Uptain that a husband and wife were betting against each other at a roulette table. The husband bet $100 each spin on the red numbers at the same time that his wife bet $100 on the black numbers. At first glance it didn't make much sense, because whenever the husband won, his wife lost and vice versa. But Uptain knew instantly what they were doing. "They're trying to rack up comps," he explained. The pit boss checked the computer and discovered that the man was close to earning enough comps to get a free room. "What should we do?" the pit boss asked Uptain. "Absolutely nothing," he replied, "because eventually the ball is going to land on green." When the ball hit zero a few minutes later, the couple both lost their $100 bets. It landed on zero two spins later for a second time, and the couple stopped playing. They'd lost $400 without earning enough comps for a free room.

Just before Uptain's shift was scheduled to end, one of his pit bosses called to tell him that a gambler had won $6,500 by walking from one blackjack table to another, making quick $100 bets in cash. Uptain went to watch. The man was in his early forties, dressed in blue Tommy Hilfiger windbreaker and blue denim pants. He seemed to be walking aimlessly through the games, but every five minutes or so, he would rush over to a blackjack table and place a bet. He usually won and sometimes he played a second or third hand, but he rarely stayed for more. He'd walk away, wander around, and then hone in on a different table. Uptain called the surveillance room and asked them to look at the tapes of each game where the man had just won. He wanted to know what the count had been when the player had joined the game and placed his bet. "I'm guessing this guy is part of a card-counting team," Uptain explained, "only he is not doing the actual counting. He has accomplices at several tables and they're signaling him whenever the count is in the player's favor." It was a clever ruse, because Uptain couldn't accuse the gambler of being a card counter. After all, he hadn't sat at a table long enough to count the cards. Nor could Uptain be sure who the accomplices were, because they weren't changing their bets or making any obvious signals. If Uptain didn't stop him, the gambler would keep on winning.

A half hour passed and the gambler's "lucky" streak continued. His winnings were now close to $13,000. Finally surveillance called and confirmed what Uptain had suspected: the count at the table where the gambler had bet had been +8, which meant the gamblers at that table had a 9.8 percentage edge over the house at the point when the player hurried over to make his bet. "He's clearly part of a team," Uptain said. But who was working with him? Uptain had noticed that the man had bet several times at a table where a woman wearing a red blouse was sitting. He also seemed to be following an older man wearing a cowboy hat. Uptain had watched the older man get up and leave his chair so the gambler could take his spot and bet. The man in the cowboy hat had then moved to another table and the gambler had followed him there a few minutes later. Uptain figured the woman and the cowboy were involved, but he couldn't be sure if there was anyone else.

It was at this moment that casino manager Tom Robinson stopped to chat. Uptain explained what was happening and Robinson quietly suggested a way for Uptain to catch the team.

Uptain walked up to the gambler and congratulated him on his success. "I've noticed how well you play blackjack," Uptain said, feeding the man's ego, "and I'd like to offer you a free high-roller suite tonight. We are always interested in keeping good players, and you seem to know your stuff." The player chuckled and gladly accepted the offer. An hour later, he picked up his key and went upstairs. Uptain had already tipped off hotel security so they could have one of their undercover officers follow him. Not long after he entered the room, the woman in the red blouse and the man in the cowboy hat joined him. A younger man also showed up. Uptain hadn't spotted him earlier.

"Now we know who the team members are," Robinson declared.

By now, the surveillance crew had reviewed all the tapes and at every table the count had been in the players' favor when the gambler had joined the game. He had bet only at tables where the woman or one of the two men had been playing. Hotel security officers knocked on the door of the free suite. The gambler seemed genuinely shocked when he was told that he and his cohorts were being barred from playing black-jack at the Luxor and that their photographs were be-ing distributed to other Strip casinos.

It was well after quitting time for Uptain, but he didn't leave until the four team members were escorted out of the hotel. He wanted to take another look at them in case they ever came back.

CHAPTER NINETEEN

....

Luxor Security

Luxor security chief Andy Vanyo usually began his workday with a cup of coffee and a stack of incident reports that his officers had written during the previous twenty-four hours. On this particular morning a statement filed by Malcolm Fry caught his eye. According to the night security shift manager's report, a homeless man had entered the casino shortly after 4 P.M., plopped down in a comfortable chair, kicked off his tattered tennis shoes, and fallen asleep. The derelict had been warned before by security officers not to nap in the casino, so when he was spotted this time, Fry decided to file a trespassing complaint against him with the local police. Luxor security officers could not make arrests, but under Nevada law they could detain people suspected of committing crimes and hold them until the police arrived. The Luxor had strict guidelines that had to be followed whenever someone was detained. Suspects were taken into a special holding room where they were kept until the police arrived. A large sign on the wall warned them that they were being videotaped and their voices were being recorded. The recording devices came on automatically and were in place because Vanyo did not want anyone claiming later that he or she had been verbally or physically abused. The derelict had gone peacefully into the holding room, but after ten minutes he had been released and the police had been told that they didn't need to pick him up. Fry's report didn't explain why. Vanyo was curious. He thumbed through the videotapes on his desk, looking for the tape of the vagrant in the holding room. It was missing. He telephoned Fry, who was at home.

"What made you change your mind about having the vagrant arrested?" Vanyo asked.

"Ah, it wasn't worth it. He promised he'd stay away from the casino," Fry replied. "In fact, he said he was leaving town, so I just let him walk."

"Where is the videotape?"

"It's not on your desk?" Fry sounded surprised. "I turned it over to the graveyard shift supervisor before I left last night." It was standard procedure for the graveyard shift supervisor to collect all the videotapes and deliver them to Vanyo's secretary each morning. "He must have misplaced it," Fry volunteered, "but it's no big deal, boss, because nothing happened."

For a moment, Vanyo thought about dropping the matter. Fry had always gotten excellent evaluations and there was no reason to doubt him, but Vanyo hated loose ends. So after he hung up, he telephoned the graveyard shift supervisor.

"Boss, Fry never gave me any tape last night and if he told you that he did, he's lying," the supervisor said.

Vanyo called Fry again and this time asked him to report to work.

"I swear I left that tape here last night," Fry insisted when he arrived, "and I can prove it." He hurried into the squad room and returned a few minutes later waving a paper. It was a statement signed by a security officer who had worked on the same shift as Fry. The officer swore in the statement that he had seen Fry leave a videotape on the graveyard shift supervisor's desk.

"Maybe someone took it," Fry offered, "but it doesn't matter, because I'm telling you nothing happened. I don't know why this is turning into such a big deal," he repeated.

Vanyo didn't reply. He didn't believe Fry. He couldn't think of a logical reason why the videotape would be missing unless there was something incriminating on it. He asked David Miller, one of the Luxor's plainclothes security officers, to look into it. Vanyo often used him to conduct internal investigations. Miller questioned the two men who had been working with Fry when the vagrant was detained. The first was a veteran Luxor officer, and he backed up Fry's account. The other was a rookie who had worked at the Luxor for only a few weeks. At first he repeated the same story, but Miller thought he was lying, so he kept questioning him and finally caught him in a different lie. The rookie quickly confessed.

"Fry told us not to say anything," he said, "because he really lost it in that room." According to the rookie, Fry had grabbed the homeless man by the neck and started to choke him shortly after they entered the holding room. When the man fought back, Fry slammed him against a wall and the other two officers pinned the derelict to the floor. Fry kicked him in the face three times and was about to deliver another blow when the veteran officer said the old man had been "punished enough" for coming into the casino. Fry had called an emergency medical technician because the man's face was bleeding, and then told the derelict that if he ever came back into the Luxor, he would be beaten again and left in the desert to die.

"Why did Fry attack him?" Miller asked.

"He wanted to teach him a lesson," the rookie said.

Miller interviewed the EMT who had treated the vagrant, and she confirmed that the homeless man's face had been a "bloody mess" when she got there. "He kept saying, 'That man beat me. I didn't do nothing and he beat me.' But Fry said he was lying," the technician recalled. "Fry said the man had resisted."

Miller had heard enough. He briefed Vanyo, who in turn informed Circus Circus corporate security director Emmett Michaels. Following company procedure, Michaels sent one of his detectives to conduct an independent investigation. That way, Fry couldn't claim that Vanyo and Miller had grudges against him. The second investigator reached the same conclusion as Miller. Vanyo fired Fry the next morning. He also fired the veteran officer who had helped hold down the vagrant while Fry kicked him, and the officer who had claimed in a written statement that he had seen Fry give a videotape to the graveyard shift supervisor. Vanyo assumed Fry had destroyed the videotape. The rookie officer who had told the truth was disciplined, but didn't lose his job.

"I don't care how long someone has worked here or how high up they are in this company," Vanyo announced the next day to his officers at a special meeting. "I will not tolerate my officers abusing anyone. Maybe in the old days guys could take a vagrant out back and beat him up to get rid of him, but those days are over. I repeat, those days are over."

Vanyo knew that Fry's actions had made the Luxor vulnerable to a lawsuit, especially if the vagrant learned that the Luxor had statements that would back up his account of what had happened. All the man had to do was hire a good lawyer. Despite this, Vanyo spent a week trying to locate him. "I wanted to make sure he was being treated by a doctor and I also wanted to apologize," Vanyo said. He couldn't find him. Apparently, the old man had had enough of Las Vegas and had left town.

A few days after Fry was fired, Vanyo was at home on a lazy Sunday afternoon when he got a call from a shift supervisor. A housekeeper had been waiting all day to clean a guest room that had a Do Not Disturb sign hanging outside its door. When she finally knocked, there was no answer, so she had unlocked the door and peered inside. A figure was dangling from a rope attached to the ceiling. At first, she thought it was a mannequin and someone's sick idea of a joke. But she wasn't sure, so she had closed the door and called her boss. A security officer had gone inside and found the guest dead. The hotel register identified him as Travis Westfield, age twenty-two. After finding a handwritten journal that Westfield had left behind and determining that no one else had been inside the room during the hanging, the police and county coroner ruled it a suicide.

This was the fourth since the Luxor opened. The first was a middle-aged man who had jumped from the fifteenth floor into the atrium at 3 A.M. shortly after the resort opened. Luckily, most of the guests were in bed, so the incident didn't draw much attention. Not long after that, a twenty-three-year-old woman climbed over the ledge of the twenty-sixth floor of the atrium at eleven o'clock in the morning. A bellhop delivering luggage to the floor had tried to talk her off the ledge, but she let go and her body burst on the floor only a few steps from a long line of customers waiting at the all-you-can-eat buffet. Leon Symanski, the Luxor's safety coordinator, quickly sealed off the area and brought in a biohazard team to clean up the mess. The carpet was replaced and the entire area sterilized, which proved important because unconfirmed rumors began circulating through the resort that the woman had been a prostitute with the AIDS virus. The Luxor offered free counseling sessions with a therapist to the guests who had seen her leap. The third suicide was a man in his late twenties who had barricaded himself in his room shortly after New Year's Eve and then crawled naked under the bathroom sink to smoke a lethal dose of crack cocaine.

Overall, 110 persons attempted suicide in Clark County during 1996, according to police records. Ten were successful. The city didn't think that was an unusually high number for a population of nearly 1 million. Vanyo and other department heads had discussed ways to prevent people from leaping to their deaths in the atrium. One idea was to install Plexiglas on the corridors, but the county fire department had nixed that idea after safety inspectors warned that the shape of the atrium would cause the corridors to become smoke traps if they were enclosed. Wire screens were deemed too ugly, so the corridors were left open.

Vanyo reviewed the paperwork about the suicide when he reported to work Monday morning and noticed the police had copied several passages from Travis Westfield's journal and attached them to the file. He began reading the dead man's handwritten notes. They made him sad. Westfield had come to Las Vegas to have one final fling before killing himself, and he had chosen the Luxor completely at random. This was not the first time that he had attempted suicide. Several months earlier, he had run a plastic hose into his car from its exhaust pipe, but after three hours of sitting in the vehicle, the fumes had only made him sick.

According to his journal, Westfield was being treated by a psychiatrist for chronic depression. It was his psychiatrist who had suggested that Westfield keep a detailed account of his thoughts and actions as part of his therapy. Those passages painted a picture of a deeply troubled but bright and talented young man who suffered spells of numbing depression and feelings of worthlessness. Ironically, Westfield had run into a string of good luck as soon as he checked in at the Luxor. He had planned on losing all of his cash gambling—a move that he felt would help drive him over the edge. But during a five-hour gambling binge at the blackjack tables, Westfield had won more than $5,000. At one point, he had started giving away his winnings, but that had made him feel better.

The next morning, he had returned to the blackjack tables and had won another $7,500. This time, he had given most of it to a fellow player named Paula, who had been so grateful that she had asked him to join her for lunch and an afternoon shopping spree. They had spent the next three days together, and Westfield had written in his journal that he was falling in love with her. That only seemed to escalate his fears.

After spending a Saturday night together, Westfield had retreated to his hotel room and become severely depressed. He noted in his journal that the longer he spent with Paula, the more difficult it was going to be when she abandoned him—and he was sure that she would—as soon as she discovered what a worthless human being he was. He drew a hot bath, swallowed twenty-five sleeping pills, climbed into the tub, slipped a plastic hotel laundry bag over his head, pulled the drawstring tight, and leaned back ready to die from a drug overdose, asphyxiation, or by falling into a coma and drowning. Instead, he woke up refreshed and wrote in his journal that he felt better than he had in weeks because he had finally gotten a restful sleep.

By late Sunday afternoon Westfield had slipped into another depression, and this one proved to be worse than earlier ones. Using a drill, rope, and screw hook that he had brought with him to the Luxor, he hanged himself. A note in the police file said that a woman named Paula Asburn had asked about Westfield at the front desk later that night. When questioned, she had identified herself as his friend and said that they had planned to play blackjack together. She had left the hotel crying after she was told about his suicide.

"This young man's death was such a waste," Vanyo said. It was odd, he continued: Every day he walked through the casino and saw hundreds of people gambling. He always assumed that they were enjoying themselves. "But you really don't know who these people are and what has brought them to Las Vegas. A lot of guests who come think that if they just hit it big, all of their problems will disappear, that somehow Las Vegas is the answer to all their problems. But it isn't."

Vanyo put the file about Westfield in a cabinet. There was no need for any follow-up, and he was soon preoccupied with another matter. Now that Malcolm Fry had been fired, Vanyo needed to choose a new night security shift manager, and he decided that Suzanne Tamayo-Soto was the best qualified. The Luxor had never had a woman as a security shift supervisor. The promotion made her the highest-ranking woman in the security department in all of Circus Circus. She soon learned that not everyone welcomed the idea of having her in charge.

CHAPTER TWENTY

....

Glenn Schaeffer,
Corporate Headquarters

The angry telephone calls started as soon as Wall Street analysts saw the Luxor's revenue figures in early 1997. Glenn Schaeffer had done a good job of preparing them for 1996's lackluster profits. After all, the Circus Circus's biggest moneymaker was undergoing a disruptive renovation. So harsh was Schaeffer's warning that many analysts had been pleasantly surprised when the 1996 year-end figures finally came out and the Luxor reported earning $65 million in profits for the year. While that was less than the $86 million that it had earned in 1995, because of Schaeffer's dire predictions many analysts had expected the Luxor would earn only $43 million.

If anything, Alamo's budget slashing at the Luxor had buoyed analysts' expectations. Near the end of 1996, well before the year-end figures were tallied, they had started urging their clients to buy Circus Circus stock on the expectation that the "new" Luxor would open in January and soon be posting record earnings—as much as $120 to $150 million for the year.

But the balloon burst in March, when analysts realized Schaeffer's minimum $120 million profit goal was going to be nearly impossible for the Luxor to achieve based on its first two months of earnings. The reason was obvious. The remodeling was still not completed and Alamo was having trouble convincing high rollers to stay in a resort that did not have an evening show, nightclub, or steak house, and that still had jackhammers pounding in its atrium.

Schaeffer had been the golden boy of gaming, the whiz kid who had made more money for Bill Bennett, Bill Pennington, and their stockholders than anyone in the history of gambling. Wall Street always had sung his praises. Not now. Several New York City money managers called to tell him that they felt personally deceived. He had estimated that Circus Circus would earn between $1.80 and $2.00 per share during 1997. Based on the latest figures that Alamo had sent him from the Luxor, Schaeffer was now lowering that figure to $1.08 per share. By other companies' standards, that was still a juicy return. But over the years, Wall Street had come to expect returns of 20 percent or more from Circus Circus, and money managers were now going to have to answer to their clients, who had invested millions in the company's stock.

Schaeffer was irked. He had based his estimates on formal budgets that had been computed and defended by the general managers, including Alamo, at the company's thirteen properties. Nearly all of those forecasts were now veering off course, especially at the Luxor and the Excalibur, the company's two biggest money earners. How could he be expected to keep Wall Street informed if Alamo and the others were giving him overly optimistic numbers? "We are going to be punished for not meeting our expectations," Schaeffer warned fellow company officers. "Our stock is going to get hammered."

Shares in Circus Circus, which had been trading in

the mid-$30s range, dropped overnight into the mid-$20s. On June 24, 1997, the day of the company's annual stockholders meeting, the stock was trading at $26.63 per share—a loss of more than 40 percent from where it had been at the company's annual meeting in 1996.

Before the meeting began, stockholders were treated to a breakfast buffet under a billowing tent beside the Luxor's swimming pools. Nearly a thousand of them nibbled on fruit, cinnamon buns, and omelettes served on tables decorated with exotic flowers and ice sculptures. A string quartet played and three busty showgirls clad in scanty belly-dancing costumes mingled with the crowd. But those diversions did little to soothe the angry stockholders.

Chairman Clyde Turner acknowledged that the earnings were down and renovations at the Luxor were still not finished. But he again insisted that the costly remodeling was necessary and that better times were coming. Next, Schaeffer reviewed the company's plans to expand into Detroit, Atlantic City, and also into Mississippi, where Circus Circus had optioned a large tract of land on the Gulf Coast. The goal, he explained, was for Circus Circus to export the super casino concept to all three locations. The company would have "entertainment hubs" in the West (Las Vegas), Midwest (Detroit), South (Mississippi), and Northeast (Atlantic City). From these hubs, Circus Circus could move quickly into other jurisdictions as soon as they legalized casino gambling.

For the next forty minutes, stockholders protested. At one point, Turner reminded them that the company's executives and board members owned more stock than anyone else in the room. "No one wants it to go up more than us," he said wryly. Turner answered every question, including one posed by a twelve-year-old boy who said the Luxor's video games cost too much to play. Only one stockholder drew blood.

"How come Steve Wynn and the Mirage can make a profit when you guys can't?" he demanded. The Mirage's earnings for the same fiscal year had jumped 25 percent, setting a company record. "The Mirage did not have backhoes and jackhammers in the lobby of its flagship property," Turner replied. "Trust me, if it had, then its earnings would have suffered."

The questioner returned from the microphone to his seat, but he could still be heard as he grumbled, "Steve Wynn wouldn't have needed to send a backhoe or jackhammers into his resort, because he does things right the first time and he does them on time."

While Turner was fending off stockholders' complaints, Steve Wynn was preparing to testify in a multimillion-dollar libel suit that he had filed against New York City publisher Lyle Stuart. Wynn claimed that his reputation had been smeared in an unauthorized biography titled *Running Scared: The Dangerous Life and Treacherous Times of Casino King Steve Wynn.* The book, which was written by Las Vegas newspaper columnist John L. Smith, suggested that Wynn had ties to the Genovese crime family. Wynn had been so outraged that he had filed two separate lawsuits. In Las Vegas, he claimed that he had been defamed by two pages promoting the book in a catalog the publisher had distributed to five thousand bookstores. In Kentucky, Wynn claimed that he had been libeled by the text of the book itself. The dispute about the catalog copy came to trial first, amid posturing by both sides. Publisher Stuart bragged that libel suits by big shots didn't intimidate him. He had been sued before (by King Farouk of Egypt), he declared, and he'd stuck by former pornography star Linda

Lovelace of *Deep Throat* movie fame when she had
been sued because of a book she had written for him.
Stuart, who was seventy-seven years old, told reporters
that he had won every libel suit filed against him.
Wynn, meanwhile, said he had no choice but to go to
court. "This trial is about me trying to clear my name
from someone who's called me a member of organized
crime."

The trial began with Stuart arguing that he couldn't
be found guilty of libel because he had printed the truth
in his catalog copy. It said Smith's book would reveal
"why a confidential Scotland Yard report calls Wynn a
front man for the Genovese crime family." Stuart said
he had based the sentence on a report that his author
had obtained from Scotland Yard, which had investigated Wynn in 1981 when he was thinking about opening a casino in London. According to author Smith, the
report concluded that "Stephen Wynn . . . has been operating under the aegis of the Genovese family since he
first went to Las Vegas in the 1960s." Stuart said his
sales catalog had merely summarized what the police
report said, so it couldn't be libelous.

Wynn's attorneys saw the matter differently. They
forced Stuart to admit during questioning that he had
taken poetic license in quoting from the report.
Scotland Yard had described Wynn as an "aegis" for
the mob, but Stuart had used the term "front man" in
his catalog copy. Stuart insisted the two terms had identical meanings; he had substituted "front man" because
he was afraid bookstore owners wouldn't understand
what "aegis" meant. But Wynn's attorneys claimed that
the editing was done to make the Scotland Yard accusation look as damaging as possible. They attacked Stuart
for giving the report so much attention in his catalog
copy when his own author had warned readers in the
book itself that it was biased and flawed. Wynn's attorneys emphasized this point by calling on a former

Scotland Yard investigator, who testified that the report had been so poorly researched that Scotland Yard had ignored it, not considering it credible.

Wynn's attorneys called two character witnesses to praise their client: Nevada governor Bob Miller and Las Vegas mayor Jan Jones. On the seventh day of the ten-day trial, Wynn took the stand. The accusations against him were "hucksterisms," he said. "No one could write any of those words without knowing that they were a lie, just for money to sell books." He had been investigated fifteen times by various licensing panels and he always had come up clean. "I don't think there was a period of time where I was out of investigation," he testified.

Attorneys for publisher Stuart grilled Wynn for hours about every accusation in Smith's book, but failed to produce any evidence that linked him to organized crime figures. They then argued that Wynn was a public figure and, as such, had to prove that Stuart had maliciously set out to ridicule him or had been reckless in what he had published. The publisher's attorneys insisted that their client had not intentionally maligned Wynn.

The eight jurors decided otherwise. They ordered Stuart to pay Wynn $500,000 for emotional distress, humiliation, and mental anguish, $1.5 million for damage to his professional reputation, and $100,000 for injury to his business and professional standing. The jury then tacked on an additional $1 million in punitive damages.

"You can't expect much American justice in a Nevada courtroom," Stuart protested afterward. Author Smith told reporters: "We live in a town with no standard of obscenity, but criticizing a casino boss is a sin. . . . That the powerful Steve Wynn could be hurt by two pages in a catalog that no one read is absurd." A few months later, Stuart's publishing company was

forced to declare bankruptcy, leaving the Kentucky suit
unresolved.

Wynn was not in court when the jury announced
its verdict. The nation's governors had been meeting at
the Mirage and President Clinton had flown in for the
event. Wynn had been too busy entertaining them to
attend.

Clyde Turner was not surprised when his former boss
forced a book publisher to close. He had seen Wynn
play hardball plenty of times. During his thirteen years
as Wynn's financial adviser, Turner too had proved that
he could be hard-nosed. In one controversial episode,
Turner had engineered a deal that earned the Mirage a
cool $15.6 million profit simply by buying and then
quickly reselling a troubled casino's mortgage papers.
Not everyone in that deal, however, had been happy
with its outcome. A group of plaintiffs had sued the Mirage, and after a testy court battle, a judge had ordered
the company to split its $15.6 million with them. Still,
the Mirage had ended up with a $7.8 million profit and
Turner had gained respect within the company.

Respected was *not* something Turner was now feeling as chairman of Circus Circus. Almost every day, he
read reports by Wall Street analysts who described him
as a figurehead. Michael Ensign and Glenn Schaeffer
were being identified as the brains and muscle behind
the company. Such comments stung. Although he had
never said anything to either man, Turner had been irritated by the way both had acted when they first re-
joined the company. Turner had invited them to meet
him at a resort in Pebble Beach, California, to discuss
what role each of them would play after Circus Circus
bought Gold Strike Resorts. Schaeffer and Ensign had
swept in armed with demands. Ensign, in particular,
had irritated Turner by handing him a list of the man-

agers to fire. Who did they think they were? Turner had complained later to his wife, Vera. The masterplan mile had been his idea. He had finally ousted Bill Bennett. And he was the one who had proposed the buyout that had brought Schaeffer and Ensign back into the company. But there was little that Turner could do, since Ensign and Bill Richardson each owned 6.5 million shares of stock. When you added in Glenn Schaeffer's and Tony Alamo's shares, the former Gold Strike team controlled some 17 million shares—a solid voting block. Turner owned 30,000 shares. Total.

When the two companies merged, Turner had assumed that Ensign, Richardson, Schaeffer, and Alamo would see him as a friend. Although Steve Wynn had been a demanding boss, that was what Turner had thought him. Mirage executives had felt "like they were part of a family," Turner said. The Turners had been frequent dinner guests at the Wynns' mansion, and the Wynns had come to their home too. Like the Wynns, the Turners had been active in the city's social events. None of these things seemed to matter to the Gold Strike crowd. Ensign disliked publicity so much that he refused all interviews. He was close to Richardson and Alamo, but rarely did anything after work with other company executives. Schaeffer went home to his family at night and didn't socialize with any of his Circus Circus peers.

In Turner's mind, the stockholders' meeting was a turning point. In the two years since the merger, he had kept quiet and let the Gold Strike team do whatever it wished. But now he decided it was time for him to begin taking a more active role, especially at the Luxor. What did any of them know about running a high-end resort? They had been trained by Bill Bennett in grind joints. But he had cut his teeth working for Steve Wynn, who operated the classiest resorts on the Strip. Turner was especially critical of Alamo. At one point, the head of a five-star hotel had been Turner's guest at the Luxor, and when he called room service one morning to order a pot of coffee, he had been forced to wait forty-five minutes for it to be delivered. If that was how Alamo and his staff treated a VIP who was a guest of the Circus Circus board chairman, Turner could only imagine what sort of service a vacationing tourist from Iowa received. And this was only one instance where Turner had been critical of Alamo. There were others. One morning Turner had ridden the new moving walkway from the Excalibur to the Luxor, and as he stepped off it he was handed a coupon by a shapely woman dressed in Egyptian garb. It entitled him to a free bag of popcorn if he redeemed it in any of the new retail shops in the Giza Galleria. Turner had been disgusted. The Luxor was supposed to be a luxury resort. Wynn never would have permitted such a cheap gimmick.

Turner blamed the Luxor for the company's falling stock prices and Alamo for the Luxor's lackluster performance. He decided it was time for a change in management at the pyramid.

CHAPTER TWENTY-ONE

....

Shawna Gray, Whore

Shawna Gray had decided she didn't need a pimp. She began working out of hotel bars. The Mirage was her favorite, but she quickly ran into trouble there. The resort didn't want street prostitutes hustling customers. She got busted propositioning a plainclothes Mirage security officer who took her photograph and threatened to call the police if she was caught soliciting there again. Gray went across the street to Caesars Palace but was busted within a day. She moved south on the Strip. A bartender at the MGM Grand gave her several helpful hints. "I don't hustle my customers for tips," he told her, "so why do you think I'm going to let you hustle them? Just be cool, sit down at my bar, buy a drink, and wait. If a man approaches you, then that's no one's business but you two. But if you are working your way up and down my bar propositioning men, then we're going to have problems." She gave him a $20 bill every time she returned to the bar after having sex with a trick and, in return, he warned her whenever a plainclothes MGM officer was in the bar. She soon made similar deals with other bartenders. Most times, she didn't even have to explain what she wanted. She simply gave the bartender a $20 tip when she ordered a drink and he knew what she expected from him. After several Las Vegas vice cops began busting girls at the MGM, Gray decided it was too hot to work there. The bartender didn't always realize who the cops were. She moved across the street into the Luxor. Because of the renovations, it wasn't as busy as the other super casinos and didn't seem to have as many undercover security officers or vice cops prowling through it.

Most nights, she would play the quarter video poker machines that were built into the surface of the Nile River bar so you could gamble while you drank. She always waited for a man to approach her and it usually didn't take long. Gray would ask potential tricks a series of questions before she made her pitch. Where are you from? How long are you in town for? What do you do for a living? She was trying to decide whether or not they were cops. With men in their twenties, she was blunt. "Ever date a working girl?" she'd ask. Many were indignant. "I don't have to pay for sex," they'd tell her. That was exactly what she wanted to hear. "Listen, honey," she would reply, "you've paid plenty of times and never even gotten a kiss. Let's pretend I'm some college kid from Idaho, okay? First you'd have to buy me a few drinks if you wanted to get into my pants. Then maybe we would gamble a bit or even go to dinner or an expensive show. Maybe we would go dancing. By the end of the night, you would have spent a couple hundred bucks and the best you might get out of me is a kiss on the cheek. Why waste all that time and money? With me, you don't have to wonder. We can go up to your room right now and you'll have the best sex that you have ever had. I can promise you that. Then I leave. I don't call you tomorrow. I don't make any demands. I don't give you anything but what you really want, because I'm clean. We have to get checked by doctors around here and the whole experience costs you less than what you spend on a date."

With older men she was less aggressive. "I'd always tell them I was earning money to pay my way through college," Gray said. "The older men liked the idea of having sex with a college girl. I guess that made me less of a whore." Gray claimed that she would have sex with three men on an average night and net about $300. "When I'm doing it, all I'm thinking about is how fast I can get this guy's money," she said. "I don't care if he is fat or ugly, if he is old or young, if he's any good in bed or lousy. As long as the money is green and I can get as much of it as I can any way that I can— that's what I want. This is not lovemaking. It is fucking for dollars. I used to fake orgasms when I first started because I figured a trick wanted to hear me moan and groan and come, but then I learned these pigs really don't care if I have an orgasm. It's about them, not me. So the whole thing is really just mechanical, you know. But there are some guys, wow. I mean, what's funny is sometimes I will be in bed with some guy and I will be thinking about something I have to do later that night and suddenly my body reacts. This trick will be turning me on and I will have an orgasm, okay? I'll actually enjoy what we did. Whenever that happens, I really get bummed out and it pisses me off. Why? I guess because when that happens, I, like, don't have any control. It messes with my mind, you know, because I don't want some stranger doing that to me. My job is get the trick off as fast as I can for as much money as I can. I don't like it when there is any real emotional or physical reaction."

One night, a man in his late twenties agreed to pay her $150 for sex. Out of habit, she looked for luggage as soon as she entered his room. "Cops and weirdos never have luggage in a room," she later explained. She asked for her money up front.

"Before I pay, I'd like to ask you a question," the man replied. "Have you ever thought about how Jesus Christ can change your life?" He immediately began preaching to her. "Mary Magdalene was a harlot but Jesus forgave her. Jesus loves you. Will you pray with me right now?"

"You want to pray or fuck?" Gray asked. "Either way, it will cost you a hundred and fifty bucks."

Gray walked out and he followed her down into the casino. At the bar, he gave her a pamphlet and then left. She was still fuming the next morning over breakfast at a nearby Denny's. "I'm not hurting anybody, okay? I'm giving men what they want and they are giving me what I want—no—what I need to survive. To me, sex is like shaking hands. It's just a physical act. You don't have to make sex more than it is. That guy thought he was so much better than me because he's religious. Well, what has he ever done to help anyone? What would he do if he came home and found his kid brother being whaled on by his mom's crackhead boyfriend? I should have fucked him for free—just to show him what sin is really all about. What gets me is that life isn't fair, you know. Just because I wasn't born into a rich family or to parents who lived in some lily-white suburb, that doesn't mean I'm somehow less of a person."

That spring Gray saw a news story on television that scared her. Two men target-practicing with their rifles had stumbled upon a woman's nude body on a steep embankment about four miles outside of town. An autopsy showed she had been hit in the head and strangled. Las Vegas detective Jimmy Vaccaro speculated that she was a prostitute. The only clue to her identity was a rose tattoo near her groin with a man's name etched in it. A few days after her body was found, a local television station reported a theory during its newscast that the woman's murder was the handiwork of a serial killer targeting prostitutes. At least five of them had been killed in recent months and none of the cases had been solved.

"My mom doesn't have a clue where I am and neither does no one else," Gray said. "I'm alone except for this stray cat I got. I call her Beavis because she is such a butthead. If some trick killed me, no one would know who I was. That's not right, you know?"

One warm spring morning, Gray sauntered into the Nile River bar wearing a black slip dress she had bought at Wal-Mart. She ordered an orange juice and began playing video poker. Three men were sitting across from her at the U-shaped bar and a couple was playing video poker a few seats away. Gray felt certain that she was the only hooker there. It had been a slow night. The Luxor had been so dead earlier that she had gone to the MGM and turned two tricks there, but she had noticed a guy watching her and thought he was an undercover cop, so she had returned to the pyramid. She won her first hand at video poker and glanced up at the three men to make certain they had noticed her. She smiled at them. "If you can get a guy to come over while his buddies are watching, then you can usually hook him," she explained later, "because guys don't want their pals to see them get shut down. They don't want to walk back empty-handed, you know?"

Gray felt someone brush against her. "Excuse me," said a woman in her early thirties as she sat down. It was nearly 4 A.M. and there were plenty of other vacant bar stools, but she had seated herself next to Gray. The woman was wearing a black leather miniskirt and a cream blouse without a bra. Gray couldn't tell whether she was a prostitute. "A lot of women dress like whores when they come on vacation in Vegas," Gray said. "I guess they think they can get away with it here." The woman gave the bartender a $100 bill and asked for a "rack," gambling parlance for a plastic container that held one hundred $1 tokens for use in video poker or slot machines. The fact that she had asked for a rack meant that she knew her way around casino bars. Buying a rack entitled her to drink free at the Luxor. There was an unwritten rule in town that gamblers were never asked to pay for their drinks as long as they bought at least $10 worth of quarters if they were playing 25¢ machines, or $20 worth if they were playing $1 machines. The woman ordered a Tom Collins and Gray made another mental note. To keep their minds clear, most hookers drank bottled water or fruit juices while they were working. After the woman had played a hand, she spoke to Gray.

"My name is Ginger and I'd like to ask you a question."

Before Gray could reply, a man tapped her shoulder. He was one of the men from across the bar and he asked if he could buy her a drink. She invited him to sit down and they agreed on a price. Gray could tell from the way he negotiated that this wasn't his first time, because he asked for "half and half," which meant he wanted both oral and vaginal sex, and he had argued with her over her price. Most first-timers were too timid to do that. Thirty minutes later Gray returned to the bar, where Ginger was still playing video poker. She would later recall that she had thought Ginger was a lesbian looking for action. "I was willing to try it if she wanted to pay me." Gray sat down next to her and ordered an orange juice.

"How's tricks?" Ginger asked, rolling her eyes. Her question came across as a joke made by someone who knew what it was like to turn one.

"Okay," Gray replied.

Ginger got right to the point. She wasn't interested in sex. A friend of hers operated an "entertainment out-call service," and he was looking for more girls, especially young ones like Gray. He paid them well and he always sent a driver to escort them to each job. "If you get busted, he'll get you out of jail," Ginger said. "If a sicko tries anything, you got someone who can help you just waiting outside the door."

"What's in it for you?" Gray asked.

Ginger said her friend paid her a $100 finder's fee for every girl she brought him. She handed Gray a business card that had on one side a photograph of a young blond woman wearing a white lace top and nothing else. On the other side there was a telephone number and these words: "Hotel Room Service 24 hours per day! Every hotel. Major Credit Cards Accepted. Our Girls Are Guaranteed To Please!"

Gray took the card and called the number later that day. She mentioned Ginger's name. The receptionist turned her over to a man who asked a few questions and then invited her in for an interview. Gray was surprised when she got to the address. It was a suite in a small office building. A few doors down was a dentist's office. The owner, who said his name was Danny, explained how the operators worked. Each girl was issued a beeper. Calls came into the switchboard and the receptionist beeped the girls whenever they were needed. A driver would pick them up and take them to their "dates," usually at a Strip hotel. Customers were told over the telephone that there was a $150 flat charge for having an "entertainer" come to a hotel room. A caller could request any type of girl that he wanted: tall, young, slim, fat, black, Asian, blond, brunette. If a caller mentioned sex, the receptionist would politely explain that whatever the entertainer and the caller did together was between them.

Within an hour, Gray's beeper went off. "The first thing you did was collect the money up front, I mean, as soon as you walked in, because a lot of guys would get angry when they discovered you were just going to strip for them." The $150 only covered the cost of having a girl come to the room and dance. "You'd try to get them excited and then you'd explain anything more than a look-see was going to cost them a lot more." Gray got lucky on her first date. "It was this guy from Japan and I told him three hundred, which is what Danny told me to ask for, and this john paid it without even negotiating. I took off my skirt and panties but left my blouse on. He asked me to take it off, but I told him it would cost another fifty so he paid it. He tried to kiss me on the lips and I told him, 'No!' I never kiss tricks. I mean, you always washed a guy's prick before you have sex so you know it is clean but I've never brushed anybody's teeth and you don't know where his mouth had been. This guy offered me another fifty to let him kiss me so I said, 'Okay, but no tongue, just lips.' "

Not long after Gray began working for the out-call service, she and Ginger were sent together to a hotel room. "Having two girls at one time is a really big fantasy for a lot of men, and this guy had won a bunch of money playing craps, so he called for us." Gray would later recall being impressed at how skillful Ginger was. "She worked this guy over mentally and physically. She could have just talked to him and had him coming in his pants." Ginger offered Gray some "survival tips": Don't ever wear a scarf, because a trick could use it to choke you. Never take a bath or shower with a trick, because he might drown you. If a trick requests anal intercourse, quote him a price so high that he'd be crazy to pay it, because there is a good chance he probably has done it before and that means he could be gay or bisexual and might have the AIDS virus. Never let a trick put cocaine on his penis for you to lick off. Cocaine makes it more difficult for a man to ejaculate if it is sprinkled on his penis. Ginger also told Gray how to use sponges to disguise when she was having her period.

"I've had sex with guys who didn't have a clue that I was bleeding inside," Ginger bragged.

In late April, Gray and Ginger rented a two-bedroom apartment just off the Strip. Each now began compiling her own list of clients. "We would give tricks our beeper numbers. We weren't supposed to, but we did. That way they could beep you direct." Ginger also introduced Gray to her first "regular."

"Ginger hung out at the Boulder Station Hotel and Casino, where a lot of local residents play," Gray later recalled. "She had about four men who were older, you know, retired guys, and they were her steadies. She would have sex with them every week, usually on the same day, at our apartment, because she knew them and they all had wives at home. One day this steady of hers asked if she would fix me up with a friend of his whose wife had died about a year ago. This guy was sixty-two and was shy. The first time he came to our apartment, we just talked for an hour. That was it. He even showed me pictures of his grandkids and his dead wife. He paid me a hundred bucks just for talking to him and he sent me flowers the next day. When we finally did it, I was surprised, you know, because I didn't think a guy his age could really do much but he was really good, you know. It was weird, me being seventeen and all. But we began getting together about twice a week at my place. His name was David and I really got to like him." In the underbelly world that Gray lived in, Ginger and David soon became, in her own words, "my family—the folks who'd care if I ended up dead in the desert someplace."

Inside the Casino:
Making It Legal Spoiled Everything

I grew up in New Jersey and married a man
whose uncle was "connected." I knew he was involved in organized crime, but I was in love. His
uncle would buy businesses and then send in his
nephews to run them. You got half the money but
never owned the business. Of course, there was
always something going on there: numbers, gambling, loan-sharking, but never drugs or prostitutes. It was harmless stuff really. The only time
anyone got into trouble was if they deserved it.
That's how you felt. You figured if someone got
beat up it was because they had done something
wrong. No one ever forced anyone to gamble or
take money from a loan shark, right?

Every night we went somewhere because my
husband had to make his rounds. We would go
into clubs and restaurants in New York a couple
times a week and everyone knew us when we
walked through the door. It was nice. My husband was not violent. It was just his family. One
Christmas, my husband was going to give me
$1,000 as a present and on his way home, he lost
the envelope. He put out word and two days later,
this kid shows up at our door and he is terrified
because he found the envelope and he had heard
who it belonged to. He was afraid what might
happen if word got back to my husband so he
brought it right over. My husband gave him three
or four hundred.

We always had a lot of cash and I learned that
it was hard to get rid of. You had to watch how
much you showed. I ran a beauty parlor with my

sister and then I bought a building with a laundry in the bottom of it. We were always looking for ways to make all this cash seem legitimate. I mean, how many new suits and fur coats can you buy? You got to launder the money to enjoy spending it.

We bought an old Victorian house and I was happy and started having children. And then Atlantic City opened and the entire thing collapsed. Overnight, all of the gamblers in New York and New Jersey started going to Atlantic City. All of the backroom casinos closed down and the numbers racket too. The businesses that we owned started going downhill. Atlantic City was killing us. We had lived such a nice life. It was quiet, very normal. All of us who were involved stuck together, you know, everyone who was part of this extended family and you never talked business with anyone else. Once in a while the FBI would come down on everybody and there would be phone taps and I would go, "I can't take this." One day I came home and the door to my house was padlocked. It was the FBI. They had broken in, looking for bookie slips. Another time, we were at a restaurant and I noticed this really good-looking guy and I asked who he was and they told me he was a hit man. But other than that, we really lived a quiet life.

I suggested we move to Vegas because gambling was all that my husband knew. My husband didn't want to leave New Jersey but I convinced him that if he stayed, he would end up in jail because he would have to get into other things. A friend got him a job as a floor supervisor at a casino here. He has had trouble making the adjustment. You know, in New Jersey, everyone knew him. He was somebody and got a lot of respect. Out here, he's just another floor supervisor. We got divorced not long ago and now I am a cocktail waitress. I still have my cosmetology license and I have a realtor's license and I have run businesses, so I have a lot of options and experience. But for now, this is okay. Sometimes I look back and laugh. Everyone thought if they allowed gambling in Atlantic City, it was going to be a boom for organized crime. Maybe it was on the Boardwalk, but making gambling legitimate there put the rest of us out in New Jersey out of business.

—*Cocktail server, Luxor*

Summer: Betting It All

"Tell me, do you do anything besides gambling?"
"Nothing at all."

—*Fyodor Dostoyevsky, The Gambler*

CHAPTER TWENTY-TWO

....

Luxor Security

Luxor security chief Andy Vanyo's choice of Suzanne Tamayo-Soto, whom everyone called Maria, as the new night shift security supervisor sparked grumbling among older officers who thought they were better qualified. Her critics accused Vanyo of bowing to political correctness. Tamayo-Soto was better known for bringing in cakes whenever someone had a birthday than for her investigative skills. The fact that she initially had been hired on the recommendation of Circus Circus corporate security director Emmett Michaels, who happened to attend the same Roman Catholic church as Tamayo-Soto's mother, gave her critics even more fodder. She was not physically strong, or aggressive, or experienced. She was a plump, married mother of five who often joked about how addicted she was to television soap operas.

But despite the complaints, Vanyo felt confident in his decision. He had first noticed Tamayo-Soto after he had complained one day about the poor grammar and spelling in the incident reports that he was receiving from his officers. Tamayo-Soto had started staying after work on her own to rewrite all the reports handed in by her coworkers. She had done it to impress Vanyo, and it had. It also had helped her catch two thieves. While working on the reports, Tamayo-Soto had noticed that several guests who had stayed on the twelfth floor of the Luxor had reported items missing from their rooms. Tamayo-Soto began recording the names of the maids who worked on the floor on index cards. Whenever a guest filed a theft report, she checked to see who had cleaned the room and noted that maid's name on a card. Within a month, Tamayo-Soto had found a link between two maids and more than a dozen rooms where items had been reported missing. She told Vanyo and he set up a sting operation. An officer posing as a guest checked into the hotel and left his billfold with $200 in marked bills on the nightstand in his room. When he returned after the room was cleaned, $50 was missing from his wallet. Security officers found the marked money in the maid's pocket. The officer moved to another room the next day and again his wallet was looted. Security officers tracked the money to the other maid Tamayo-Soto had suspected. Both maids were fired.

Vanyo liked Tamayo-Soto's enterprise and also sensed she was a lot tougher than most of her peers realized. She had not had it easy growing up. She had moved with her mother to Las Vegas at age twelve after her parents divorced, and they had lived in a poor neighborhood riddled with Hispanic gangs. As a white student, she was in the minority in neighborhood schools, but she had avoided trouble and excelled academically. She also had worked from the time that she was fifteen—not for spending money, but because her mother had needed her help paying the rent. By the time Tamayo-Soto finished high school in 1983, she had done stints as a hotel telephone operator, pharmacy clerk, and bookkeeper. She also had sold appliances at Montgomery Ward. Her life had not gotten any easier. She had married too young, given birth to a son, and divorced just as quickly. To make ends meet, she had been the opening manager at a McDonald's restaurant in the mornings—a job that required her to get up at 5 A.M.—and had worked as a cashier at a Kmart store at night. In the afternoons, she attended beauty school. Her job at the Luxor was the first she had ever had that paid more than minimum wage.

Tamayo-Soto was now married to Alfonso Soto, whom she had known from her neighborhood since they both were fifteen. It was his second marriage too. He had three children who lived with them, she had one, and together, they had a fifth. Alfonso's elderly parents, who did not speak English, also lived with them. Vanyo joked that anyone who could manage a blended household with five children and two Spanish-speaking in-laws could surely handle a security shift at the Luxor.

Tamayo-Soto heard the disgruntled whispers behind her back. "I'm not going to take any grief at work from anybody," she told her husband. "I can't, because if I do they are going to walk all over me." During her first week on the job, she announced that the officers on her shift would be required to file written incident reports every time a guest contacted them with a problem. Before, they had only been required to write a report if a guest made a formal complaint. But Tamayo-Soto wanted to know about every guest complaint. "I don't want to be in the dark when a guest returns home and decides to write a nasty letter six months later about how he complained to security and nothing was done," she explained. "I want to be able to walk into Chief Vanyo's office with a report in my hand that will explain exactly what we did and why." The extra paperwork caused even more dissension.

Tamayo-Soto began identifying which officers on her shift simply wanted to do their eight hours and go home and which were gung-ho, wanna-be cops eager to dive into trouble. Malcolm Fry had doled out assignments based on favoritism. She began matching her officers' personalities and skills to the jobs that she needed done. The wanna-be cops were assigned to patrol the Luxor's grounds and investigate complaints; the ones who were just putting in time were posted outside the hotel elevators to make sure guests showed their room keys before going upstairs. A retired cop who liked to tell jokes and meet people was put in charge of the casino's information desk.

Within a few weeks, most of her critics had stopped complaining, with one exception. Ralph Long was a retired military policeman who made it clear to anyone who listened that he didn't believe women should be doing "a man's job." If a drunk started swinging, Long wanted a two-hundred-pound man backing him up, not a woman who had five kids to worry about at home. Tamayo-Soto began standing at the door of the squad room after the shift ended so that she could say goodbye to each officer. What few realized was that she was doing this entirely because of Long. He spoke to her at work only when she asked him a question or he had to tell him something related to his job, and she wanted to force him to be cordial. It didn't work. At first, Long tried to slip out before everyone else and then he tried to outwait her. But she made sure that she always beat him to the door so she could cheerfully say, "Good night, Ralph!" The best she got in return was a nod or unintelligible grunt.

Tamayo-Soto had been in charge for about three

weeks when Long made a mistake and she had to reprimand him. She could tell he was seething inside during the lecture. The next night, Tamayo-Soto got a radio call that a drunk was putting glasses on one of the Luxor's escalators and watching them tumble down the steps. One of her officers already had told the man to stop, but he had refused, and threatened to "kick some ass" if anyone tried to keep him from "having a good time." The officer had called for backup and had notified Tamayo-Soto because she required all her officers to contact her before they got into a scuffle with a guest. As soon as she reached the escalator, Tamayo-Soto took charge. She noticed that Ralph Long had responded to the officer's call for backup and was standing nearby. The drunk had gotten another glass and was about to put it on the escalator.

"Excuse me," Tamayo-Soto said politely, "but you have been asked to leave."

The drunk grinned. "You can't make me leave," he replied. "This is a public building."

"No, sir," she replied. "This is private property and we have every right to ask you to leave."

"Are you going to throw me out?" he asked. "You and how many of your girlfriends?"

She wished she was wearing a uniform rather than the purple jumpsuit that she had on. Sometimes a uniform and badge intimidated people.

"We don't want a scene here. I don't want to use physical force to make you leave," she said calmly, "but I will."

The drunk already had taken one step toward her and she had backed away. Now, he took another step and she backed away again.

"Hey, whatever you want to try, go for it," he declared, stepping toward her again.

Tamayo-Soto stepped back. He moved again until he was so close that she could feel his boozy breath on her face.

"I'm not ready to leave yet!" the drunk said.

Tamayo-Soto shot toward him. She did not grab him; instead she leaned forward so that her face was within inches of his. She had been stepping back because she wanted to draw him away from the escalators and the other guests. They were now near a corner with few bystanders.

"Listen," she snapped. "You are going to leave right now! Either you walk out of here or we will escort you out!" Unleashing a battery of expletives, the drunk lunged toward her. Tamayo-Soto did not flinch. She grabbed his arm, as she had been taught in self-defense classes, at about the same moment that Long and the other officer took hold of him.

"Okay, okay," the drunk cried. "I'll leave. Don't hurt me!" The two officers hurried him out a side door. That night, she took her post at the squad room door as always and waited for Long to leave.

"Good night, Ralph," she said, expecting a grunt.

There was a pause. "Good night," he replied.

Tamayo-Soto beamed.

"When you are a manager, I believe you have to keep one of your toes planted firmly back where you came from," she said later. "You have to let your officers know that you are not going to ask them to do anything that you wouldn't do. You want them to know that you remember where you came from. You can't just jump over that line and start shitting on people. Ralph and I still have a lot to work on, but we are making progress."

In June, Tamayo-Soto saw several prostitutes hanging around the Nile River bar and in Nefertiti's Lounge. It made sense. The Luxor was trying to attract a wealthier clientele, and anyplace there was money to be made, hookers would appear. Chief Vanyo didn't want prostitutes soliciting business in the Luxor. "If a guy comes in with a prostitute on both of his arms, that's his business, but we don't want people on vacation getting solicited in our resort." He sent the Luxor's two plainclothes officers into the bars to ferret out the whores. As soon as they mentioned a price, the officers took them into the security office, where they were photographed and then banned from entering the resort. By the end of the month, it appeared that they had gotten the message. A week later, however, several reappeared at the Nile River bar, and this time, when Vanyo sent in his two plainclothes officers, neither man was able to make a bust. Both officers decided that someone was warning the hookers. Vanyo sent in different officers, but the women seemed to know they were working undercover. Vanyo called the Las Vegas Metropolitan Police Department's vice squad and asked for its help. "I think I have a situation here where a bartender is tipping off these girls," he explained. Vanyo suspected a particular bartender who had worked at the Luxor for only a few months. A few days later, the vice squad sent an undercover cop into the Nile River bar to watch the bartender. Nothing unusual happened. The cop was posing as a tourist, and at one point even asked the bartender if there were any hookers around. The suspect had said he didn't know. Vanyo was getting frustrated. "We want word to spread that the Luxor doesn't want hookers plying their trade here," he told his shift managers.

Tamayo-Soto liked to spend her shift walking through the casino, because she wanted to be close by if her officers needed her. Now she began dogging prostitutes at the Nile River bar. Whenever she spotted one, Tamayo-Soto walked over and stood next to her or sent an officer over. This tactic proved effective, because most johns didn't want to pick up a hooker who was being watched by a security officer. One by one, the women began moving to easier sites on the Strip.

Tamayo-Soto didn't feel uncomfortable harassing hookers. "When I was thirteen, I was standing outside the Westward Ho waiting for my mom when this guy comes up and says, 'How much?' I was big for my age but I didn't know what he meant, so I went and got my mom and she really told the guy off. That was the first I had ever heard about prostitution. Since then, I've seen a lot of hookers on the Strip and have heard a lot of their hard-luck stories and I've never met one who I really felt sorry for. You know, I have busted my butt since I was fifteen. I got my first job at a Jack-in-the-Box restaurant by lying about my age. I've worked sixteen hours a day at most of the jobs I've had. Right now, I get up every morning at six o'clock to get my kids ready for school. Then I clean up the house and watch my soap opera and then leave for work at one P.M. I don't get home until after midnight, so I don't see my kids until the next morning. I got a daughter who calls me up at work, crying about how much she misses me. My husband works on commission at his own auto body shop, so he puts in long hours too. Even my husband's father, who is this little Mexican man in his seventies, rides the bus each day to a job here at the Luxor washing dishes. We are all working hard because we want to buy some land and build a house. Maybe we'll get some chickens and a burro for my father-in-law. The point is, we have dreams. Most of these whores will tell you that they don't have a choice or that they were abused, but the truth is that most of them are either lazy or cocaine addicts. There are maids in this hotel who are cleaning seventeen rooms a day. Some of these women don't speak any English and don't have any education. I talk to them in Spanish and some of them tell me they are working two or three jobs doing hard, hard manual labor to support their families. They aren't selling themselves. Now if a Spanish-speaking woman without any formal education can get a decent job, then these whores could too."

The Nile River bar was packed one night when Tamayo-Soto took up her post shortly after ten o'clock and scanned the bar. A rugby team from Austria was staying at the Luxor and the players were wearing purple-and-black-striped jerseys with their names printed on the back. One of them had attached on his chest over his jersey a flesh-colored plastic shell that had been molded to look like the torso of a naked woman with large breasts. He and his teammates were playing a game. The man would pinch the nipples on his costume, alternating back and forth in rapid order. His opponent would try to repeat the same series of pinches in the correct order. If he made a mistake, he had to drink a shot of whiskey. Tamayo-Soto noticed a woman approaching the bar. She had long, bleached-blond hair, was well tanned, and wore a skimpy black skirt with a loose silk top that left little to the imagination. Tamayo-Soto suspected she was a hooker. She watched the woman slip onto a bar stool, order juice, and begin flirting with the rugby team. Tamayo-Soto raised her portable radio to her lips and told one of her officers that she needed him to "dog" a hooker. As she gave the order, the woman spotted her from across the bar and their eyes met. Seconds later, a uniformed officer reported to Tamayo-Soto and she nodded toward the woman at the bar. As the officer moved in her direction, the woman left her seat and started to walk toward the Luxor's exit. Tamayo-Soto fell in a few steps behind her. Outside, the woman flagged down a taxi. As the cab pulled away, she rolled down the passenger window and leaned out.

"Hey!" she yelled at Tamayo-Soto. She curled her fingers in an obscene gesture and then ducked back inside the cab.

"Whatever," Tamayo-Soto said under her breath. She turned and walked back inside.

....

CHAPTER TWENTY-THREE

Tony Alamo, the Boss

Although January and February's numbers had been terrible, the Luxor had posted great figures in March and April of 1997 after the pyramid's new twin hotel towers had finally opened. The 1,906 additional guest rooms caused revenues to surge. In March, the Luxor made $9.8 million in profits, in April, $9.9 million. Those figures gave Tony Alamo hope. He began to think the Luxor might surprise the doomsayers and actually achieve the $120 million minimum profit mark that Glenn Schaeffer had initially promised Wall Street. On an average night, the hotel was renting out 98 percent of its 4,407 rooms at a rate of $90 per room. That meant the hotel was contributing more than $300,000 every night to the resort's earnings, and 70 percent of this was profit. For the first time since the Luxor opened, its hotel was generating as much income as its casino. This was unheard-of in Las Vegas. And in May it happened again: another $8.4 million in profits—again thanks to the hotel.

And then June hit.

Hotel revenues plunged. During June, the hotel dropped its room rate to $70 per night but it still could fill only 90 percent of its rooms. July was just as bad. Half the calendar year was over and the Luxor had mustered only $50 million in profits. It would be impossible to hit the $120 million mark now.

The arithmetic was embarrassing. Alamo and his fellow executives had spent $400 million, so far, remodeling the Luxor, yet they were going to make only $14 million more in profits than the resort had made under Bill Bennett before the renovations began. They could have earned more depositing the $400 million into a savings account. Alamo could almost hear Bennett laughing at him down the Strip at the Sahara.

The Luxor was not the only super casino whose hotel operations were hard hit in June and July. Financial analysts were quick to explain why—greed. In 1996, casino owners had started adding hotel rooms on the Strip as quickly as they could. Everywhere you looked, huge cranes jutted up from the steel frames of half-finished hotel towers. Everyone seemed to be following Schaeffer's unit growth philosophy: if you build hotel rooms, tourists will come. Most of these rooms hit the market at the same time. Between January and May of 1997, 13,126 new rooms opened, pushing the number of hotel rooms in Las Vegas to 101,757—a 12.9 percent increase in capacity. Yet, in that same five-month period, the number of visitors flowing into the city had increased by only 5.7 percent. For the first time in a decade, supply surpassed demand. Doomsayers, always in ample supply in Las Vegas, immediately predicted that the boom was over.

Amid all of this hand-wringing, few seemed to notice that a significant change had taken place. In the past, Las Vegas casinos had not paid much attention to their hotel operations. Rooms had been added as a convenience because gamblers needed a place to sleep. This had been especially true at Circus Circus, where Bennett had once practically given away rooms for $18 per night. The super casinos, with their thousands of guest rooms, had now changed that. At the Luxor, the difference between charging $79 and $80 per night—$1 more—over a one-year period could mean as much as a $1.5 million difference in the resort's year-end profits. The same was true of the occupancy rates. If the hotel stayed 99 percent occupied instead of 98 percent for the year, the difference could mean an additional $1.5 million. In the best of all worlds, the Luxor would do both—maintain a high room rate and a high occupancy rate. If it did, it minted money. Of course, if both rates fell, profits sank.

In Las Vegas, the price of a hotel room could change hourly. If the Tyson versus Holyfield boxing match or the National Rodeo Finals were in town, room rates would skyrocket. On most Sunday nights, when the weekenders from California returned home, the prices hit bottom. There were different rates for different customers too. Many gamblers qualified for the Luxor's casino rate, which was half what others were charged. Tour groups got discounts. When all these rates were added together, they produced what is known in the hotel business as an "average daily rate," or ADR. In the summer of 1997, the term "ADR" was being spoken with a new respect. Casinos were no longer thought of as the premier cash producers, the prime contributors to the bottom line, for better or worse. Hotels had become their equal.

Michael Starr was the Luxor manager who set the hotel's ADR, and he was usually the first department head whom Alamo met each morning. Both men exercised before 7 A.M. in the Luxor's Oasis Spa, and they often discussed business while they sweated on treadmills or rode stationary bicycles. Alamo had brought Starr to the Luxor from the company's hotels in Laughlin and had given the forty-one-year-old manager a single assignment: to raise the Luxor's ADR. When the Luxor first opened, Bill Bennett had told his hotel manager that he wanted 100 percent occupancy no matter what. Bennett had preached that keeping a hotel full was more important than getting a high ADR, and during the Luxor's first three years of operation, the resort maintained close to full occupancy. Its ADR, however, had hovered around $65. Alamo's philosophy was the opposite. He wanted Starr to push the ADR up to at least $86. After the renovations were finished, Alamo expected it to climb to $100. The reason for this had to do with the kind of clientele Alamo wanted to attract.

"Filling a hotel is easy to do," he pointed out. "All you have to do is lower your room prices and you can have guests in every room. The real trick is filling it with the *right* kind of guests at the *right* rates."

If Alamo had a choice between having every room occupied by guests paying $70 per night or having only 60 percent of the hotel occupied with guests paying $117 per night, he would choose the pricey crowd— even though the revenues would be nearly the same. Why? Because people who could afford a $117-per-night hotel room could afford to gamble more in the casino, or so Alamo claimed.

This did not mean Circus Circus Enterprises was abandoning its legions of grind customers. Its chief executives were now trying to tailor their various casinos to fit different markets. At the original Circus Circus casino, guests could still get a room for as little as $29 a night and dine at the cheapest buffet in town. The ADR at the family-oriented Excalibur was kept at around $62, the lowest rate on the Strip at a super casino. The Luxor was now being aimed at a higher social stratum: guests who were forty and older, with annual incomes of $60,000 to $80,000. The company's next resort, Mandalay Bay, would be targeted at the $80,000-and-higher crowd.

Michael Starr was responsible for keeping the "right clientele" happy. Few departments had as many direct contacts with guests as his 1,200 employees. The reservation clerks who answered the telephone when a vacationer called fell under Starr's jurisdiction. So did the valets who parked a guest's car when he arrived; the registration desk clerk who checked him into the resort; the bellboys who carried his luggage to his room; the stewards who cleaned the front lobby where a guest often formed his first impression. Starr was responsible for the legion of guest room attendants who cleaned each room; the room service waiter who delivered midnight snacks; the trainer at the Oasis Spa who advised guests about the best way to lift weights; the lifeguards at the pool who warned children not to run on wet surfaces. "My people are responsible for keeping guests happy, and that's tougher here than in a nongambling resort because guests are usually losing money here. That can make them irritable, especially if their room isn't up to the highest standard."

On most days, Starr left the hotel's daily operations to his seven managers so that he could focus on the ADR. The first telephone call he made each morning was to the room reservations department. It was buried deep inside the belly of the pyramid, in a windowless catacomb filled with rows of shoulder-high cubicles. Here, eighty-six reservations clerks worked around the clock in three shifts, manning telephones. On a busy day, they would answer seven thousand calls. Starr expected them to "convert" 15 percent of these calls into reservations, and it was this ratio—the number of telephone calls coming in and the percentage of those calls converted into reservations—that he used as his primary tool in deciding the hotel's ADR. It was supply and demand at its purest.

Starr was technically responsible for renting 4,407 rooms per day. As many as 50 percent of these rooms, however, already had been booked long before Starr arrived in his office each morning. They were sold months in advance by the Luxor's marketing department to wholesalers who specialized in putting together package tours for travel agents and airlines. The Luxor's casino claimed another 1,000 rooms each night for various VIPs and gamblers who had earned free or discounted rooms with their comps. This left Starr with about 1,200 rooms that his department needed to "sell." On most days, his room reservation clerks had already sold half of them in advance to callers who had made reservations. This left Starr with about 600 rooms that he had to sell each day, and the rates for these rooms could change hourly.

One random August morning, for instance, Starr was told that he had 486 rooms to sell. This was less than what he ordinarily had, so he knew demand was higher than usual. He wanted to squeeze as much profit as he could from each room. At the time, the Luxor had a profit margin of 70 percent—one of the best on the Strip—on its room prices. At 8 A.M., Starr told his room reservation manager that he wanted to charge $85 per night for the vacant 486 rooms. Two hours later, the manager reported that only 9 percent of the telephone calls that her clerks were receiving about rooms for that day were being converted into reservations. She also noted that Steve Wynn's Treasure Island resort, the benchmark the Luxor was using during its remodeling, was charging only $80.25. Starr lowered his rate to $82.50. During the next hour, the "conversion" rate improved, but not by much. Just before lunch, he dropped the rate to $80.50. At 2 P.M., the reservation manager reported that her operators were being flooded by calls. Treasure Island had raised its rate and so had five other Strip hotels. The conversion rate was almost 18 percent. Starr immediately bounced the Luxor's rate to $86. When demand tapered off during the next hour, he cut the price to $84.50. By four o'clock, the conversion rate was about 15 percent, which was where Starr liked it. Early the next morning, Starr checked the hotel's numbers. The Luxor had achieved an 88 percent occupancy rate the night before, with an ADR of $82.25. It was less than what Alamo wanted, but better than June and July. With his gym bag in hand, Starr hustled into the spa.

Luxor general manager Don Givens prided himself on keeping his temper in check, but he was angry as he stormed into his regular Tuesday staff meeting. He had just read a letter from a disgruntled guest who had complained that Luxor employees didn't "know the meaning of 'First Class Service' or 'Customer Satisfaction.' " The letter writer had cited examples. He had been forced to wait thirty minutes for valet service; a maid had walked into his room without his hearing her knock; he had telephoned housekeeping at 9 P.M. and asked for extra pillows but they were never delivered. When he called the front desk to ask how late the swimming pool was open at night, he had been passed from employee to employee and none of them knew the answer. He and his wife had stood in line for more than an hour at the all-you-can-eat buffet and had ended up receiving "average service" at an "average buffet." The Luxor's amusement rides were "lousy" and there was still no evening show. The letter writer had not only complained to Givens, he had posted his complaint on the Internet under the heading: "LUXOR STINKS!"

"I get a lot of good letters from our customers," Givens lectured his department managers, "but when I get one bad letter or two bad letters, that is cause for alarm. In this case, I have received four angry letters from guests and each of them has said the same thing: that our hotel is beautiful but they will not be returning because they were treated rudely. This is simply not acceptable!"

For the next ten minutes, Givens berated his managers for failing to improve the service at the Luxor. "The sort of guests we're hoping to attract come with great expectations," he said. "They want to be pampered. They want to be in a luxurious surrounding. They want to feel good about themselves and the decision they made in choosing us. When I walk through Steve Wynn's Mirage, I feel good. Our mission is to achieve that same feel here while still staying within our departmental budgets."

Givens acknowledged that many departments were short on staff because of Alamo's continuing budget cuts, but he added that this was no excuse. "I can guarantee you that the employees who were nice and courteous and service-oriented before the budget crunch are the same ones who are nice and courteous and service-oriented now. And the people who are rude and causing the problems are the same ones who were causing the problems before."

Givens ordered his managers to hold meetings with their employees and review the way customers were supposed to be treated. "Each of you will be held accountable by me for making certain that the standard of service on our property is raised to a much higher level," he warned.

The next morning, Givens walked through the resort with several managers and pointed out lapses that he wanted fixed. The glass panes in the front doors were smudged with fingerprints. Employees had scribbled numbers in pencil on a wall next to an in-house telephone. There were heel marks next to the service elevators in the new hotel towers where room service employees had leaned. In a Bill Bennett grind joint, finger smudges, doodling, and heel marks might not matter, but in a luxury resort, they did. Givens repeatedly cited the Mirage as his example of how things needed to be done. "We have to 'Steve Wynn' this place," he explained at one point. "We have to make our employees feel as if they are part of a team—like they do at the Mirage."

Not everyone in the meeting liked the comparison. "Steve Wynn has a first-class resort because he spends whatever is necessary to make it a first-class resort," complained one manager. At the Mirage, employees ate in a cafeteria where food was prepared especially for them. The Luxor's employees got the same food that was being served in the all-you-can-eat buffet or leftovers from its restaurants. "We want the Luxor to be like the Mirage, but we are still trying to cut our expenses as if Bill Bennett was running things. You can't operate this like a grind joint and expect to please first-class customers."

A few days later, Alamo announced that every department was going to have to cut its budget still more. Every cent was to be scrutinized. The engineering department turned down the forty-billion-candlepower spotlight that shot a beam ten miles into the sky from the Luxor's apex. The spotlight was made up of forty-five xenon bulbs that cost $1,200 each and had a life expectancy of five hundred hours when burned at their brightest. It cost $600,000 a year to replace the bulbs. Keeping the spotlight at 80 percent of its power made them burn longer. Other departments began using part-time workers to save on benefits. Managers also began laying off employees. Security chief Andy Vanyo was told to cut his 125-member force by 13.

"What these managers don't realize is that low earnings in the hotel and casino don't change my responsibilities," Vanyo complained. "The risk of having a guest being assaulted is not going to change based on whether or not the casinos post high profits."

When keno manager Melinda Winn told her night

supervisor that he was being fired because he had the least seniority, he exploded in anger. "If I had a gun, I would kill Tony Alamo!" he yelled. "I've seen this company's financial sheets. Do you know how much Clyde Turner, Glenn Schaeffer, and Michael Ensign make?" He knew exactly, because he had read the annual stockholders report. Turner's base salary in 1996 had been $839,760, plus a bonus of $540,410, giving him $1.4 million. Schaeffer and Ensign had earned $1.05 million and $1.07 million respectively in salary and bonuses. "This company is making millions of dollars," the angry worker shouted. "If they want to cut costs, let them take a pay cut. I hope every damn one of them dies from a heart attack."

Winn called the Luxor security office as soon as the fired supervisor stormed out of her office. Vanyo called his boss, Emmett Michaels, who immediately sent security officers to guard Turner, Schaeffer, Ensign, and Alamo. "We consider this a genuine threat," Vanyo said.

Alamo was looking over blueprints for Mandalay Bay when his secretary told him that a security officer had arrived to protect him. He didn't like it. "I am not going to live my life being afraid that some angry employee is going to shoot me," Alamo declared. He decided to talk to the disgruntled former employee face-to-face. Vanyo and Michaels urged him to reconsider, but Alamo had his secretary call the man and invite him to a meeting. He came in the next morning and found Winn and Vanyo waiting with Alamo.

"I have been told that you are angry about being laid off," Alamo began. "So angry, in fact, that you said you want to get a gun and shoot me."

"I am angry because it is unfair," the former supervisor replied, "but I shouldn't have said that about the gun. I don't think I deserve to be laid off, though, when you executives are paying yourself such huge salaries."

"Listen," said Alamo, who earned close to $1 million per year in salary and bonuses, "I am proud of what I get paid and I can tell you to your face that I earn every penny of it." Alamo recalled how he had started out cleaning toilets in Reno and talked about how hard he still worked. "Rather than being angry at me and my salary, you should be working hard to get my job," Alamo said. He asked the ex-supervisor why he hadn't appealed his firing through the proper employee channels. The man said he didn't think it would do any good. Alamo chastised him. "You didn't even try then, did you? If you felt wronged, you should have fought for your job back, not threatened to shoot someone." For several minutes, Alamo questioned the ex-supervisor about what he thought was wrong with the Luxor. Then he explained why the budget cuts were necessary and told the man that he was being rehired. He had ordered Winn to reexamine her budget, and she had found a way to keep him by reducing the number of hours her other supervisors worked.

"I was shocked at how Mr. Alamo ended up turning this guy completely around," said Winn afterward. "He confronted him, lectured him, and then built up his confidence, and really got him excited about trying harder at work to get ahead."

Despite this new round of cuts, the Luxor's profits continued to fall, as did Circus Circus's stock price, which was now down to $21 per share and still sinking. Rumors that Alamo would be replaced swept through the pyramid. Although he was fully aware of the chatter, he went about his job without comment. But he felt trapped. It was now late summer and construction crews were still at work on renovation projects. He was being pressured to bring in high rollers, but he worried that they would be disappointed unless the Luxor was completely ready. He felt he had no choice but to continue cutting expenses until the remodeling was finished, yet this was clearly frustrating his employees and making it more difficult for them to meet his expectations for first-class service. Alamo also knew that Turner was breathing down his neck. The question was: What to do?

....

CHAPTER TWENTY-FOUR

Keith Uptain, Casino Shift Manager

During the summer, casino manager Tom Robinson left for Taipei and Hong Kong to introduce himself to several wealthy Asian whales, or million-dollar bettors, and to hire hosts in both cities to represent the Luxor and Mandalay Bay. Circus Circus had never had an overseas office, and Robinson was especially careful to make sure every detail was well planned. He rented space for his new hosts on the eighth floor of office buildings because eight is a lucky number to many Asians, and he handed out business cards that had been modified specifically for his trip. Luxor business cards had a pyramid printed in gold in the center, but Robinson omitted the logo because some Asians considered the pyramid to be bad luck. He also had his title changed from "Casino Manager" to "President, Overseas Casino Operations," because titles were important in Asia, and many of the executives whom he hoped to meet would not want to waste their time talking to a manager. Before leaving, Robinson had pulled a coup on the Strip by hiring Tom Carilli away from Steve Wynn. Carilli was one of the city's premier casino hosts, personally responsible for bringing several million dollars' worth of action into the Golden Nugget each year because of his relationship with high rollers. A national gambling magazine reported in a gossip column that Wynn had been furious. The article cited Carilli's move as another signal that Circus Circus was serious about shedding its grind-joint image.

While Robinson was overseas, casino shift manager Keith Uptain took charge, and shortly before six o'clock on a Friday night, Carilli brought two wealthy gamblers into the Luxor to see the remodeling. Both men had been flown into town by Steve Wynn, who was hosting a golf tournament at the Mirage's exclusive course. Carilli had promised his guests a complimentary dinner at the Isis for stopping by. Of course, Carilli assumed they would stop at the new high-limit gaming area to make a "courtesy bet" in return for his hospitality. Uptain made sure he had experienced dealers on tap because he didn't want anyone getting the jitters if a gambler began betting several thousand dollars per hand. Carilli arrived just before eight o'clock with two men in their late forties, dressed in gray sports jackets and black slacks. Carilli introduced them to Uptain, who had already drawn up "markers" for them worth $5,000 each. (Markers are IOUs issued by the casino to gamblers.) They began playing blackjack at $500 per hand as Carilli stood close by, kidding them. After a few hands, the taller player had won $4,000 and his friend was $1,500 ahead.

"Goddamn!" the first player exclaimed. "I love this place, Tom. You make it easy to take your money." He gave the cocktail waitress a $100 chip for bringing him a shot of whiskey.

"Did you hear the joke about ebonics?" the shorter one asked Carilli in a booming voice. "Two blacks are on that television game show, *Password*, and the secret word is deer, so this one says 'doe' as his clue, and his partner looks at him and says: 'knob!'" Everyone but Uptain erupted in laughter.

"Let's go eat dinner now," said the taller gambler. They each gave the dealer $300 as a tip and left.

Uptain was pleased they had won. "You always want guys like that to have a good taste in their mouths the first time they play because it means they'll be coming back for more."

High rollers didn't impress Uptain. He had seen hundreds of them come and go. He had spent so much time around casinos that it was difficult for him to remember the last time that he had gone an entire week without seeing someone shoot dice or play cards. His mother had been one of the first women dealers in Lake Tahoe and his stepfather, Jim Neff, was a retired casino manager who was still highly respected and well known in the industry. One of Uptain's first childhood memories was the time when he and his younger brother were eating dinner in the casino where their mother worked and the comedian Red Skelton sat down in the booth next to them and bought both boys milk shakes.

Because so few people lived year-round in the Lake Tahoe area, there were only twenty-eight students in Uptain's high school graduating class in 1965, and nearly all of them had worked at nongambling jobs at casinos while they were in school. Most of their parents worked at those same casinos. They were the only jobs in town. The Sahara Tahoe resort opened the summer after Uptain graduated, so he went to work there, first as a dishwasher and then as a parking valet, a sought-after job by teenagers. The casino let him work as many hours as he wanted since he was paid only in tips. Uptain could make fifty bucks a night when it snowed because gamblers from California would ask the valets to put snow chains on their tires for the drive home. Within a few months, he had enough cash to buy a brand-new Corvette sports car, but the job didn't last. One of his coworkers broke into a car that was owned by a pit boss. "Back in those days, everyone wanted to be a pit boss because they really had juice," Uptain recalled. "They all drove Cadillacs." Out of respect to the pit boss, the casino fired every one of its parking valets.

Uptain's stepfather was the casino manager at Harvey's Wagon Wheel Casino and he got Uptain a job parking cars there. But as soon as he turned twenty-one, Uptain began dealing craps. He already knew how to deal because he had been practicing at home since he was sixteen. At night, he would stack several rows of chips on an ironing board and separate them into piles five chips high. "Five, four, three, two, one," he would say out loud as he separated them. "One, two, three, four, five," he would repeat as he stacked them back together. He did this over and over again every night until he could tell simply by touching the chips how many were in a pile.

Lake Tahoe proved to be too small-time for the cocky twenty-two-year-old. Uptain had always heard that the best dealers worked on the Strip, so he quit his job and drove to Las Vegas. A downtown joint hired him, but Uptain had his eyes on the Dunes, which was one of the hottest casinos on the Strip. Every day he asked the pit boss at the craps tables there for a job. This went on for two months, until the afternoon when he arrived at the moment the pit boss was firing a dealer.

"Kid," the pit boss said, "you've been driving me crazy coming in here. Can you really deal?"

"Yes sir!" Uptain replied. The pit boss tossed him a dealer's apron and put him to work. When the shift ended, he told Uptain, "You can't deal worth a damn, but you got great hands at sorting chips, so I'm giving you a job."

Uptain was soon earning as much as $100 a night in

tips. He was single and he felt rich, since his only costs were food and a monthly rent of $75. "There were two ways, I decided, to look at gambling: I could look around me and say, 'Keith, you better leave this alone because these places were built by taking gamblers' money,' or I could say, 'Keith, you deal craps every night to people who are dummies and they win a lot of money. Just think how much you could rake in.' " He chose the latter. "I thought I was smarter than the dice." He won, but he also lost, sometimes big. "I've always thought that gambling is not a problem unless you begin spending your future. I knew guys who blew every paycheck and went deep into debt. I never did that, but back in those days I did lose more than my share." Each month, Uptain put his rent money in an envelope and then stuffed the rest of his cash into a cigar box. Whenever it got full, he hit the craps tables. "I would take a couple of hundred and tell myself that was all I was going to spend. Then I'd lose it and drive home and take a couple more hundred, and another hundred to make up for the cash that I'd already lost, and I'd head back to the tables." Often, he didn't stop playing until the box was empty. "I wasted a lot of gasoline making those trips back and forth during the night to that cigar box."

He noticed that he gambled the most after he had been drinking. There was a reason casinos always gave away free drinks to people gambling. "After I lost big, I would go home feeling sick to my stomach. I couldn't sleep, and the next morning I'd feel bad all day because I blew four thousand or five thousand dollars and I was only making twenty-five dollars in wages, plus my tips, of course. But I didn't always lose, and some nights after I had won five thousand, I'd rush home and get a half hour's worth of sleep and then scramble back to work and think the world was just wonderful."

One night Uptain lost all his cash shooting craps at

the Silver Slipper. In the 1960s, downtown casinos would give dealers a $100 marker simply on their signature, so Uptain signed one and immediately lost a $100 bet. He walked over to the Mint, and signed one there, and lost, so he marched over to the Golden Nugget, signed a marker, and lost that too. The same thing happened at the Four Queens casino. On his way home, he stopped at the Thunderbird and signed his fifth $100 marker of the night. He bet the entire amount in a single hand at a blackjack table—and won. He let it ride and won again. An hour later, he had won $2,000.

He hurried downtown to pay off his five markers and then returned to the Thunderbird with $1,500. "Oh, hell," he told a friend at the bar, "I was shit broke when I walked in here so I might as well go out in a splash." He went to the craps table and called out, "Fifteen hundred across the board," which meant Uptain was betting $300 on each of the numbers on the craps table except what is called the "point." Another gambler already had control of the dice, and he threw winning combinations for the next twenty minutes. Uptain won $15,000 and immediately drove downtown to a Cadillac dealership. Strutting inside, he asked a salesman the price of an El Dorado convertible sparkling before him on the showroom floor. The salesman glanced at his baby face and smelled the alcohol on his breath. "Son, now how would you ever pay for an expensive car like that?" he asked.

Uptain pulled a thick wad of bills from his pocket. "Is cash good enough for you?"

He kept the car for two months before he sold it because he needed money. "I think for me it was the thrill of gambling, the rush that came from the risk."

One year after he went to work at the Dunes, the culinary union went on strike. He didn't like crossing the picket line, so he decided to move back to Lake

Tahoe. He had fallen in love with another dealer on the Strip and she had recently moved to Lake Tahoe. His stepfather rehired him and Uptain stopped gambling as soon as he got married. He knew he couldn't keep losing paychecks if he had a family. Much to his surprise, he didn't miss it.

A look at Uptain's career during the next twenty years reveals how important friendships were in the gambling business during the seventies and eighties. He worked at four different casinos as he moved up the ranks, and in each case every job was arranged by a friend. "Some people complain about 'juice' and how you have to know someone to get a job in this business," Uptain said, "but there is a reason why this is done. You hire people who are your friends because you know you can trust them. No one trusts a stranger when it comes to handling money. So it really isn't favoritism, it's about hiring people who are not going to cheat you."

Uptain had begun gambling again two years ago, after he and his wife went through a painful divorce. Now, however, his philosophy differed from when he was twenty-two and thought he knew enough about craps to beat the game. "The reason why casinos have enough cash to build giant pyramids is because of fools who think they can beat all the odds against them." Why, then, did he start gambling again? "Because," he replied, "I like the excitement and sometimes even a fool wins."

Tom Carilli and the two high rollers returned to the casino from dinner shortly before midnight to play blackjack. The taller man asked Uptain if he had a cigar clipper. There was none to be found, so Uptain hurried into one of the Luxor's sundry shops and bought one. The two gamblers sucked on their stogies and began betting $400 per hand as Uptain watched. A few minutes later, a black man dressed in a salmon-colored polo shirt, dirty khaki shorts, black socks, and black wing-tips sat down at the same table as the high rollers. He began betting $50 per hand. The two high rollers had been laughing loudly as they played but they were quiet now. They also began to lose. After several hands, the taller one called the cocktail waitress over and asked her to bring him some bottled water. The new arrival asked if she had any cigarettes. She didn't, but offered to get him some. She walked over to the same sundry shop where Uptain had been. He had simply gone to the front of the line at the cash register, but the waitress walked to the end to wait.

Back at the blackjack table, the taller gambler began complaining about how long it was taking to get a drink of water. Five minutes passed. "Tom," he grumbled, "what the hell does a man have to do around here to get a drink?" Carilli glanced at Uptain, who decided to fetch a bottle himself. He started toward the Sports Bar. Usually, the high-limit gaming area had its own cocktail waitress, but this was her night off and the supervisor in charge of scheduling was trying to save money by having a cocktail waitress from another pit cover the high-roller area as well as her own pit. The taller gambler lost another $500 hand. He was furious.

"Jesus Christ, I've lost two grand here and I can't even get a fucking drink!" he thundered. "I'm never playing here again!" He ordered the dealer to cash him out. Carilli tried fruitlessly to calm him. It was at this point that the cocktail waitress returned with the cigarettes. She handed them to the black man, he gave her a $1 tip, and she suddenly realized that she had forgotten the bottle of water.

"Goddamn," the high roller bellowed at Carilli. "I gave your waitress a hundred dollars earlier for bringing me one drink and she gets this guy cigarettes and forgets my water." He stormed out of the pit with Carilli following behind, apologizing as they crossed the casino floor. "Tom, I like you, but this place has a long way to go before I'll play here again," the man could be overheard saying.

Uptain felt frustrated. Tom Robinson was not going to be pleased when he returned from Asia.

CHAPTER TWENTY-FIVE

....

Kelly Jo Steinfort, Showgirl

The auditions for *Imagine* drew 125 women and 50 men. Dick and Lynne Foster, along with their director, David Gravatt, rated each by using a secret code so they were the only ones who could tell by glancing at the scoring sheets who had done the best. They needed only 14 women and 6 men to complete the 52-member cast. The others had already been hired and were performers, like Kelly Jo Steinfort, from the original show. Nonetheless, the Fosters let everyone audition who showed up, because they thought it was cruel not to give them a chance. Rehearsals were set to begin July 25 and the show's opening was scheduled for August 30, in time for the Labor Day weekend when the last crowds of summer swarmed into town.

Not long after the show was cast, the Fosters learned that Circus Circus executives were looking for a headliner to open their new theater with a splashy one-night show. They immediately objected to the Luxor's entertainment director, Michael Hartzell. "Putting a star in for opening night will hurt us," Dick Foster warned.

All the stage lighting would have to be changed, the sound system adjusted, the scenery moved. "Besides," he complained, "it sends a lousy message to our cast and the public that our show isn't good enough for opening night." Hartzell promised to pass along the complaint, but the Fosters went directly to Tony Alamo. A few days later, they were told that the theater would open with *Imagine*.

The Fosters breathed a sigh of relief, but it was brief. Construction crews were weeks behind schedule finishing the theater. How could the cast begin rehearsals when the stage was filled with scaffolding? Bill Richardson, the chief executive in charge of construction, was unsympathetic. After a series of pointed exchanges, a compromise was reached. No sooner had that dispute been settled than another problem surfaced. The Fosters wanted a professional stage craftsman to install a trapdoor for the show's magician, but Richardson argued that the $2,300 expense was unnecessary and insisted his carpenters could do the job. After three failed attempts to get the trapdoor to work properly, Richardson brought in the professional.

And so it went through much of the summer.

When Steinfort reported to the first rehearsal inside the new theater, sparks from welders' torches were flying near the entrance and electricians were installing wires overhead, but those distractions were quickly forgotten as Gravatt and the show's choreographer began putting the dancers and acrobats through their moves. Steinfort wore no makeup and kept her hair cut short, so it was easy to slip on the curly blond wig and headpieces she wore during the show. She rehearsed in black leotards. Because she was a gymnast as well as a dancer, she was given a role that required both skills. The Fosters paid everyone the same basic salary so there would be no bickering. Dancers got $600 a week. Steinfort earned an extra $50 because she did gymnastics too. There was no nudity in the show, but if there had been, the going rate for a dancer to appear topless in a Strip show was an additional $50 a week.

Imagine had a lot of dance numbers, and Steinfort and the others raced from one number to the next. Each had an exotic name: "Native Expressions," "Tribal Gathering," "The Ritual." It was difficult to perform. The first week, one dancer sprained her ankle and was forced to drop out. Steinfort developed tendinitis. Rehearsals began at 10 A.M. and lasted late into the night. The cast would do a dance combination again and again and again as Gravatt reviewed each step. Steinfort was exhausted by the time she went home. She loved it. Slowly, the show began to jell.

A pantomimist and twin Chinese contortionists were the first performers the audience would see when the show opened. Their role was to warm up the crowd. There were no speaking roles in *Imagine*: instead, a short recorded narration was broadcast over the sound system during each act. The first act was called "The Lost World," and when the curtain rose, dancers and acrobats in primitive costumes bolted forward to the beat of tribal drums. With a puff of smoke and a thunderclap, a wizard appeared and made one of the dancers float high above the stage in full view of the audience. As she neared the rafters, she simply faded away. The trick was an illusion that Dick Foster had created exclusively for the show, and while other magic tricks would follow, none was as dramatic. Midway through Act One, a specialty act called "Dimensions in Flight" took the stage. Specialty acts were done by independent performers who put together their own routines. Often they moved from one Strip show to another. The Fosters had incorporated five specialty acts, the show's magician among them, into *Imagine* to give the production variety. These acts could be replaced over time by other specialty routines to keep the show fresh. Steinfort's gym partner, Phillip Millaudon, was the strong man in "Dimensions in Flight." His two partners used his chest, knees, back, and shoulders as their base when they did handstands and other feats that required tremendous balance and strength. They were followed by the Chinese contortionists and the wizard, who vanished from a bamboo box that had been pierced by burning torches as the act ended.

Act Two, "Neptune's Playground," was supposed to take place in an imaginary ocean. A net of ropes was lowered at the rear of the stage and Steinfort and other showgirls in glittering sequined costumes climbed the web and swayed back and forth as if they were sea creatures. The wizard floated a dancer on jets of water that spouted from a fountain in the center of the stage. But the most sensational moment in this act came when two showgirls in skinhugging mermaid costumes emerged from hidden panels on each side of the auditorium and "swam" out over the heads of the audience. As they hung from invisible metal cables, they did flips and waved their tails, with the theater's spotlights capturing them frolicking as if they were in a black sea. The narrator's voice explained that water had cleansed "The Lost World" of Act One and prepared it for Act Three, "Cyber World." Once again, the wizard performed and Steinfort and her colleagues did a series of demanding dances. But the most startling performance of all came near the end of the show, when an acrobatic troupe from mainland China leaped from a platform above the stage and did somersaults, flips, and other acrobatic twists while careering toward the floor. Just as it looked as if they were about to slam into it, bungee cords attached to their waists snapped them back to safety.

Because Millaudon was part of a specialty act, he wasn't required to attend the same rehearsals as Steinfort. Nor did she have time to continue their morning workouts in the gym. She missed talking to him, but

she didn't make any effort to stay in touch. Paul
Morgan had apologized over the telephone for not writing to her more while she was in Japan. He had agreed
to give up his jazz career in New York City and move to
Las Vegas, and was coming to see her next month so
they could find an apartment. Morgan had become jealous when Steinfort mentioned that she and Millaudon
had been working out in the gym regularly. Although
Millaudon had never said or done anything suggesting
that he wanted to be more than a platonic friend,
Steinfort had started backing away from him out of respect for Morgan, and there was another reason why
she had stopped meeting him at the gym. One day, he
had told her about his plan to help stage a production
of *The Nutcracker* for disadvantaged children through
a local charity. She sensed his excitement and was
moved when he talked passionately of the help his gym-
nastic instructors had given him when he was young.
He wanted to do the same thing himself now, and
Steinfort had promised to help him. Then her work at
the Luxor had taken over and she never followed
through. She felt guilty.

It soon became obvious to the Fosters and their cast
that the new theater was not going to be ready on time.
Rows of theater seats, wrapped in clear plastic, were
waiting to be bolted onto the still-uncarpeted floor. The
top of the stage was still an exposed skeleton of steel
beams, gray wires, and silver ductwork, lacking the ceiling that would cover it. As opening night drew closer,
the Fosters and Richardson ended their ongoing bickering and scrambled to get the theater ready. There was
no finger-pointing when the $45,000 stage curtain was
unpacked and found to be the wrong shade of blue.
Nor was there any time for petty squabbles among the
cast members. The dancers and acrobats began working
fourteen hours a day for fourteen days straight without

taking a break, readying themselves for opening night. "If this were a job in an office," Steinfort said, "I would hate it and feel awful because we had to put in such long, long hours. But I love coming in to rehearsals even though we're all exhausted."

In between dance numbers, the cast commiserated together. "We have become our own little world inside this theater," Steinfort explained one afternoon, sitting cross-legged on the floor of the stage. "We have worked together so closely that we've gotten to know everything there is to know about each other—bodily functions, sex lives—it's all out there. I'm not talking about our pasts, because the other cast members really don't need to know my life history in order to know who I am. They have learned me inside and out because of what we've been through these past weeks."

Regardless of how long they worked, at least once each week the cast met for drinks at a local bar to blow off steam. Every conversation swirled around the show. Every bit of gossip was about the show. "It has consumed my life," Steinfort said. Much of the talk was about whether Circus Circus executives would like what they saw. Everyone knew the three previous Luxor shows had failed and that Michael Hartzell's job was riding on *Imagine*. Although he was a suit, the cast felt he was one of them. He had as much at stake as they did.

Late one afternoon the Fosters announced they were putting on two nights of shows exclusively for Luxor employees before the official August 30 opening. These would be dress rehearsals. The performances went very well. Exit surveys that Hartzell commissioned confirmed that *Imagine* looked like a hit. Now it was up to the public.

On opening night, Hartzell paused while leaving his office for the theater. "Get ready for anything," he told his longtime secretary. He meant it as a joke but both knew he wasn't really kidding. Hartzell had been certain that *King Arthur's Tournament* was going to be a colossal flop because the dress rehearsals had been a disaster, yet the public had adored it. The reverse could be true at the Luxor.

The theater was filled on opening night, but only about half were paying guests. The others had received comps from Circus Circus executives, casino hosts, or the cast. Then, ten minutes before the show was scheduled to begin, David Gravatt called everyone together in the dressing room to announce that the computer controls that raised and lowered the $140,000 bungee platform used by the Chinese acrobats were not working. There was no backup system. The acrobats were not going to be able to perform. As Gravatt talked, the show's interpreter translated. Steinfort watched the acrobats' faces become distraught.

"How about the curtain call?" someone asked. Would the acrobats be allowed to take a bow with everyone else at the end of the show if they weren't performing? The question set off a chorus of support for the acrobats, who had no idea what was being said until their interpreter told them. Although they were a specialty act, they had been to every rehearsal and had tried to befriend the other dancers and acrobats. "Of course they can take a bow," said Gravatt.

Steinfort was excited and scared. "The curtain rises and here are these people who have come to see you," she said. "They've come because they want to be entertained and escape for an hour or two from their cares and concerns and their routines. Something magical can happen between an audience and a show when everything clicks. It doesn't happen all the time, but when it does, you get chills because you know what you are doing matters and is special."

The first performance went off without a hitch even

without the acrobats. The second show was just as good as the first. Hartzell passed word to the Fosters, who let the cast know that the corporate suits seemed happy. The next big test was media night, when the Luxor invited reporters, theater critics, and a varied assortment of others—including cab drivers, whose word of mouth could help a new show or cripple it—to watch the performance.

Steinfort was more nervous about this show than opening night. Moments before it was scheduled to begin, Dick Foster received a panicky call from his stage manager. The curtain was stuck. The controls that raised it weren't working. Foster and Hartzell scrambled backstage in their tuxedos to check them. The Luxor would be the butt of acid jokes if the curtain couldn't be raised. Foster called the manufacturer of the controls and relayed instructions to his stage crew. Minutes passed, five, ten, fifteen. The audience was beginning to grumble. Another ten minutes crept by.

"I got it!" a stagehand cried. He had found two burned-out $1.35 fuses. The show started thirty minutes late. "This is why live performances are so exciting," Hartzell deadpanned.

After the performance, Steinfort joined the other cast members in the lobby for a brief party. She noticed Millaudon glaring at her. It was *The Nutcracker,* she assumed. She started toward him, but he moved away. The next morning she read the local critics' enthusiastic reviews and then called Millaudon. "Okay," she told him as soon as he picked up the receiver. "I'll say the word: Nutcracker. There. I said it."

"What the hell are you talking about?"

"You're mad at me because I never followed through with my promise to help you stage *The Nutcracker,* right?" she asked.

"Is that what you think?"

"Yeah. What else could it be?"

Millaudon said he was so angry he had to hang up. That night, he confronted her outside her dressing room at the theater. "Tell me that I'm not crazy," he said, jerking open a grocery bag. She peered inside and was stunned. He had kept every letter she had written to him from Japan. "Tell me that I am not the only one who is feeling the way that I feel about us? I want you to tell me that you don't look at me onstage and see the same thing that I see in your eyes when I look at you." He didn't wait for a reply. Shortly after they had met in Lake Tahoe two years before, he told her, he had been walking to his car with his best friend when they spotted Steinfort leaving the casino's theater. Millaudon had turned to his friend and whispered, "That is the woman I am going to marry."

Steinfort looked at him, numb. "Don't you know that I am in love with you?" Millaudon asked.

She didn't.

Paul Morgan was arriving in Las Vegas in a week to be with her.

"I don't know what to say," she mumbled.

Millaudon closed the bag.

CHAPTER TWENTY-SIX

....

Shawna Gray, Whore

The first sign that Ginger was having problems surfaced when the second month's rent was due. She couldn't pay her share. Shawna Gray didn't understand why. Ginger was earning at least $375 a week from the four local customers who came to their apartment for sex, and her beeper was always going off with calls from the "entertainment" service. Added to her locals, Gray figured Ginger was earning as much as $1,000 a week turning tricks. Where was it all going? Gray knew lots of hookers who had drug problems, but she didn't think Ginger was one of them. She decided to confront her about the rent money.

"I have a problem," Ginger admitted, "with video poker machines."

Gray laughed. "Those things are harmless," she replied.

Ginger quickly corrected her. The day before she had gone into a neighborhood bar to play one of her favorite quarter machines. You could wager five coins at once, which meant that she was actually betting $1.25

per poker hand. She played a hand about every fifteen seconds. In other words, the machine was costing her $5 a minute to play, or as much as $300 an hour. She had won dozens of hands that day, but then she went on a binge and played for twelve hours straight. She had lost $1,352 of her own money and another $1,000 she had won while playing. Total losses: $2,352—all in a quarter video poker machine. "I am not a stupid woman," Ginger explained later, "but when I sit down in front of one of those machines, it's like the entire world gets blocked out. It's just me and my machine and nothing else matters. I ignore my beeper. I forget to eat. I'm not even tired. I could play for days without stopping if I had enough coins."

It had not always been that way. Ginger had rarely gambled when she first moved to Las Vegas in the 1980s. Back then she had worked as a nurse in a hospital emergency room and was dating a doctor. "ER terrifies some nurses, but I loved the excitement of never knowing what sort of trauma would be coming through the door." Ginger and her boyfriend liked to eat in the city's better restaurants, and those were usually in Strip casinos. "I'd play the slots, but I never really had too much interest in gambling. I thought it was boring." Years later, she could still recall the exact moment when that changed. She had been waiting for her boyfriend at Caesars Palace. "He was delayed. I was standing by a video poker machine and I dropped a few quarters in it just to kill time. On my first hand, I hit four aces and a two of spades and won seven hundred bucks! That was a tremendous amount of money for me back then. It was more than what I was earning in a week as a nurse. That night I paid for our dinner. The next morning, I left for work an hour early so I could stop at Caesars. I wanted to play the same machine because I felt lucky and I couldn't get over how easy it had been to win all that cash."

Someone was playing "her" machine when she got there. "I stood there waiting until I only had about twenty minutes before I had to be at work. I decided to ask this woman to leave, but before I could do that, she hits a jackpot—one thousand dollars. I was so angry. I felt like it was *my* jackpot. That was my lucky machine." The next day, Ginger arrived at the casino two hours before she was due at work. "I knew about how some people can become addicted to gambling, but I also knew that wouldn't happen to me. I was just having fun, relaxing before work. I had a stressful job and this was my way of blowing off steam."

During the coming months, Ginger lost steadily but she also won enough to feel as if she was breaking even, and several times she hit jackpots that paid more than $1,000. "Because I was a nurse, I'd work long shifts and then be off for several days. That's when I would play. I started playing for a few hours and then I went to twelve and even sixteen hours. Once I hit two royal flushes in one fourteen-hour period. I won close to four thousand dollars." Several casinos offer local players incentives if they cash their paychecks at their places. Ginger began cashing hers in a neighborhood bar that had video poker machines. "The first time I blew my entire paycheck, I got scared. I couldn't believe it. I felt so—so *stupid*. I don't think people understand how totally humiliated you feel after you do something like that. I decided I was the most worthless human being alive. I vowed never to play another video machine again and I stopped."

Ginger didn't play for a month. Then her boyfriend got called away on an emergency when they were supposed to be going out. She drove to Caesars. "I decided I had been overreacting. I kept telling myself, 'I drink and I'm not an alcoholic. I've smoked weed and I'm not a drug addict.' I honestly didn't feel I had an addictive personality." Just to be sure, she read several books

about compulsive gambling. They made her feel better.
Although the experts disagreed about some points, the
books said that only 2 to 6 percent of all gamblers become addicted. Those same experts offered a list of potential reasons why some gamblers couldn't control
themselves:

- Growing up in a family with an extremely
  critical, rejecting, or emotionally unavailable
  parent.
- Having a family history of alcoholism or
  compulsive gambling.
- Growing up in a family with an emphasis on
  status where money is overvalued.
- Being extremely competitive.
- Hyperactivity.
- Exposure to gambling at an early age in a way
  that made it particularly appealing.

Ginger found all this reassuring. None of those factors
applied to her. But over time, Ginger started to lose
more money than she was earning as a nurse. She
exhausted her savings and charged the maximum
amounts on her credit cards. Her boyfriend noticed.
"We would be eating dinner in a casino and I would excuse myself to go to the ladies' room, but as soon as I
got out of sight, I would hurry to play a video poker
machine. At first he thought it was funny, but then he
realized I was losing control. He begged me to get into
Gamblers Anonymous, but I kept telling him I was
fine."

Ginger borrowed money from her boyfriend and
her parents. It wasn't enough. After nearly a year of
steady losses, she was $20,000 in debt. "I kept think-
ing, 'If I can just hit one big jackpot everything will be
okay.' "

Then she met a man who offered to pay her for

prescription drugs. She began stealing them from the emergency room and was caught. The hospital didn't prosecute, but she was forced to resign. She broke up with her boyfriend and became depressed. "That made me want to play video poker even more, because when I played I didn't think about how screwed up my life was."

Ginger had applied for several nursing jobs, but didn't get them. She suspected word had spread about why she had resigned. She took a part-time job at a local elementary school as a nurse and was bored. She owed everyone, it seemed. She hit bottom one afternoon after a thirteen-hour video poker binge. "I had given the casino a hot check for two hundred dollars and then had lost all of it playing the machines. It pissed me off because I actually had had a fantastic run. I mean, I'd played thirteen hours on that two-hundred-dollar bad check, which is damn good playing. If I had only stopped when I was ahead." She went into the casino bar. "I'd lost my job, my boyfriend, all my savings. I was way in debt and didn't have money for groceries, bills, my rent. Now I was going to go to jail for passing a hot check. This guy at the bar notices how I'm starting to tear up, and he asks me what's wrong. That's when I just unleashed all my frustration. I told him how stupid I was and how I had written a hot check. He listens to my story and says, 'I will buy that check back from the casino for you on one condition—you have dinner with me.' He was a nice-looking guy and I thought about it, and it was like I suddenly understood what I needed to do. I was already feeling like a worthless piece of crap. I said, 'How about if we skip dinner and just have sex?' That's how I got started being a hooker."

Not long after that, Ginger went to work full-time for the telephone out-call service. "Once I started hooking, I was able to get rid of my bills. Funny, the hooking didn't bother me. What bothered me was how stupid I felt about the video machines. I am not a stupid person, okay? But when I lost, I'd really tell myself off. I'd say, 'You stupid bitch! When are you going to get control of your life? You are so disgusting. You deserve to be a whore.'" Ginger went to a GA meeting, and for several months she floated between GA and video poker. "I'd stay straight for a week or ten days and then I'd go on a binge and play sixteen hours."

Ginger promised Gray that she would start putting her share of the rent money aside so she would be sure to have it. "I'm doing better now, really." Gray was skeptical. She mentioned Ginger's problem to David, the sixty-two-year-old Las Vegas widower who was paying her twice a week for sex. He had spent forty years working in casinos before he retired. "I've seen hundreds of compulsive gamblers," he said. "Ginger is going to end up stealing from you and lying to your face. Find a new roommate."

Despite the forty-six-year difference in their ages, Gray liked being with David, and she knew he was falling in love with her. By this time, they had been "dating" for three months. He brought her a bottle of Dom Pérignon champagne on their third-month "anniversary" and a cake on her birthday. She had turned eighteen but told him that she was twenty-two. He cosigned a car loan for her so that she could buy a red Firebird.

"David is sweet but I'm not in love with him," she explained one afternoon. "Look, I get lonely. I mean, most girls who are eighteen are still living at home getting ready for the prom, right? I'm out here fucking married men my father's age for money. The only guys I meet are tricks or pimps, and even if I met a guy, I doubt if he could handle what I do. I mean, okay, like one day I was sunning myself at the pool in our apartment complex and this nice-looking guy my age starts hitting on me. First, he starts telling me how he plays high school football or track or something and then he asks me where I go to school. The whole time, I'm thinking, 'Why should I go out with this kid and spread my legs if he isn't going to pay me for it? That's what he's after but he's got nothing to offer.' "

Gray began letting David spend Thursday nights with her in her apartment. It was the first time in her life that she had slept with a man next to her all night. "David is different. He doesn't act like an old man. He's funny, you know. We both like to go on picnics at Lake Mead. He's got a boat and we do water-skiing. We even had sex in his boat on the lake once. He says I keep him young. I started taking Thursday afternoons off so we could do stuff, but I still charge him a hundred bucks if we have sex."

In June 1997, Gray got a frantic call from Ginger. She had been beaten up and raped. Gray called David and they went to get her. Both of her eyes were swollen, two teeth had been knocked out, she had several broken ribs, and she was covered with dirt. David wanted to take her to a hospital, but she refused.

Back in the apartment, Ginger told them that she had been at the Sunset Station, a new casino that was attracting crowds of local players, when she had run out of cash and started looking for a trick. It hadn't taken her long to find a man who agreed to pay her $75 for sex in his truck. When they got inside, he pulled a knife and drove her into the desert, where he raped her, beat her with his fists until she blacked out, and pushed her out on the ground. David urged Ginger to call the police, but she refused. Gray took care of her during the next few days. She also had sex with Ginger's regular clients. One night, Gray discovered Ginger wasn't at home. She found her playing video poker in a neighborhood bar. "Leave me alone!" Ginger snapped. "Just leave me alone."

Things went downhill after that. Gray came back to the apartment one afternoon and discovered her television and stereo missing. Ginger claimed someone had broken in, but Gray knew better. They started avoiding each other and David helped Gray find a place of her own near his house. A week later, one of Ginger's steadies called her. Ginger had been missing their dates, and he wanted to know if Gray was interested in having sex. She invited him over. That night, Ginger phoned. "You bitch!" she screamed. "Stay away from my clients."

Unlike Ginger, Gray was doing fine financially. "I've always been a saver. I don't have gambling problems either," she explained one afternoon at lunch. "I think video poker machines are boring. The only real problem in my life is David. Why is it men think they can tell you what to do as soon as they have sex with you?" David wanted her to stop being a hooker. He had been pushing her to enroll in a dealers school. "I got David paying me two hundred a week and two other steadies who used to date Ginger. I met this other guy at McDonald's who calls me twice a month. I'm earning about three hundred a week just from them, plus, I'm making two hundred per night on weekends working for the out-call service. I don't want to be a whore forever, you know, but I'm only eighteen, okay?"

Gray turned pensive. "Someday, I want to meet the right guy and have kids, but right now I have my own apartment. I'm buying my own car, and I'm even saving money so my kid brother can come live with me. I might even buy a house. How many eighteen-year-olds are doing that?" Two weeks earlier, Gray had telephoned her mother on her birthday. She told her that she was working as a cocktail waitress, but her mom hadn't believed her and they had gotten into a terrible fight.

It was mid-October when Gray finally heard from Ginger again. They hadn't spoken for three months.

Security guards at the Boulder Station casino had caught Ginger soliciting a trick and banned her from the casino. She needed a ride and help. Gray went to see her and was shocked by what she saw. Ginger was ghostly thin, pale, and disheveled. She had been evicted from her apartment, she said, and her car had just stopped running. She thought it needed a new battery but wasn't sure. It was parked a few blocks away and Ginger had been sleeping in it at night. Gray drove her to a McDonald's and bought her two Big Macs. She gobbled down both and asked for more. As they were leaving, Ginger began to cry.

"I got the AIDS virus," she said. Gray was stunned. For godsakes, she thought, Ginger had been a registered nurse! "It was the bastard who raped me," Ginger said. "He told me that he had gotten AIDS from fucking a whore and now he was getting even by giving it back to whores."

Ginger was scared. "I called my brother in San Diego and he and his wife said I could live with them for a while. Maybe I can get my life straightened out," she said. Her brother had sent her money for an airplane ticket, but she had gambled it away. She was afraid to call him again because he would be angry and tell her not to come.

"Can you give me a loan?" she asked.

Gray wondered if Ginger was lying. "I didn't want to believe her," she recalled later. "Nothing—the story about AIDS, her brother—all of it could have been a big lie. But I also had a sad feeling it was true."

Gray called David and they helped Ginger collect her belongings. A few hours later, they drove her to the bus station, bought her a one-way ticket to San Diego, and waited with her for the bus. David held onto the ticket. He wasn't going to give it to Ginger until she boarded. As they waited, Ginger began to cry.

"When you're little, you think you are going to

grow up, fall in love, and live happily ever after, but it just doesn't happen that way sometimes, does it?"

"Most times it doesn't," Gray replied.

"I don't know why what I had wasn't enough, you know?" Ginger said. At one time, she had had a good job, a boyfriend. "It wasn't enough and I can't tell you why. I just know it wasn't enough."

The three of them hugged when Ginger left. Afterward, Gray talked about how she felt. "Ginger was like a mom to me when we first met, you know, then she was like my best friend, and then I ended up being like a mom to her. It's weird. You know, that guy who did this to Ginger, he was mean."

Inside the Casino:
Kiddie Land

My uncle is in the black book—the one that identifies mobsters who are banned from entering casinos. A lot of my relatives are "connected." When I was sixteen, my dad took me into this back room in a Chicago bar and there was a casino there. Anyway, my dad liked to gamble and I would go with him and run errands for the guy who ran the joint. One day he needed help running the roulette game and so he taught me. If a guy threw down a $100 bill folded in half, that meant he was betting fifty. If the corner was bent, it was twenty-five. The owner tells me, "Never lose sight of the fact that you are sixteen and don't know what you are doing and the guys who come here to gamble have been doing it for twenty years. You got to expect that they will try to cheat you."

One night, this fellow from Vegas shows up. Babe. His daughter is a dealer here at the Luxor now. He tells the owner, "You got a sixteen-year-old kid running the wheel—are you nuts?" The owner says, "The kid is okay. You watch this kid for five minutes and if you don't like what you see, we'll toss him out." I had two guys at the table and I knew they were going to try to past-post me. When they tried it, I caught them and the boss had them taken outside and they got their asses kicked. Babe comes over and says, "Kid, whatever he's paying you, you tell him to give you five percent more from the rake from now on." I didn't know this guy, but I knew he was important in Vegas.

In 1967, the Vietnam War really began heat-
ing up. I was eighteen and my dad says to me, "I
don't love you any less than your two younger
brothers, but I want you to enlist because of the
three of you, I think you got the best chance to
survive over there." I was really angry, but I
joined the army. I got wounded three times. My
chopper was shot down, and everyone but me was
killed. For a while, I was missing in action and the
army sent an officer to tell my folks I was dead.
My dad was the only one home and when the
guy handed him a folded American flag, my dad
dropped dead on the spot from a heart attack.

After the war, I went by the old backroom
casino but it was closed. I called my uncle and
told him I needed a job and he called me back an
hour later and told me to move to Vegas. He'd
gotten me a job at the Four Queens. When I got to
town, I found Babe and the guy who had run the
back room. It was like a reunion.

Vegas was different back then. You knew
everyone who was important and they knew you.
Now that the corporations are in charge, it's like
kiddie land. Christ, you never saw a kid in a
casino back then. The bosses took care of you.
My younger brother had to have heart surgery
and I told my boss that I needed to go home to
help him. When I got there, my mother was holding a bag of money from the casino for my
brother.

Back in those days, you would see stars like
Elvis just hanging around Las Vegas because this
is where they came to party. I became a "clerk"—
a dealer who was so good he could do whatever
needed to be done. They used to call me when

they had some guy beating the house really bad and I would clean him out. I made more money back then than I do now twenty years later. Okay, every once in a while, someone ended up in the desert dead. You figured he just got greedy. But for the rest of us, the clerks, those old days were the best of times.

—*Pit boss, Luxor*

Fall: Crapped Out

....

"Why am I really such an irresponsible infant? Can't I see that I am a doomed man? . . . But wait. Remember what happened to me seven months ago . . . before I lost everything. Oh, it was . . . beautiful . . . I lost everything I had then I walked out of the casino and suddenly discovered I still had one gulden in my waistcoat pocket. Well, that'll pay for my dinner at least, I said to myself. But after I had taken a hundred steps or so, I changed my mind and went back to the roulette table . . . I won, and twenty minutes later I left the casino with one hundred and seventy gulden in my pocket. It's the absolute truth! That's what your very last gulden can sometimes do for you! But suppose I had lost heart then? What if I hadn't dared to risk?"

—Fyodor Dostoyevsky, *The Gambler*

....

CHAPTER TWENTY-SEVEN

Don Archer, Poker Room

A sea of tourists swept in and out of the Luxor. Half of the hotel's 4,407 rooms changed occupants in an average day. If these guests were remembered at all, and most were not, it was for some freak reason. Perhaps a tourist won a big jackpot, like the older couple from Georgia who hit all eight numbers on a keno card and pocketed $40,000; perhaps they wore some outlandish outfit, such as the four-hundred-pound Hawaiian dressed in an orange sherbet T-shirt and electric lime-green polka-dotted shorts; perhaps they did something outrageous, such as the drunken player who tried to urinate on a dealer. But even if a tourist was remembered, it was rarely for long. There were too many of them. It was the local players who were recognized. The dealers, cocktail waitresses, and other Luxor employees who came into contact with these regulars got to know them well and the locals ended up learning nearly as much about the workers whose shifts they frequented. In casino terminology, the regulars were called "rocks." Their everyday lives were played out in an ongoing soap opera inside the pyramid.

The rocks inside the Luxor's poker room were mostly retirees in their sixties or older. Mary was a grandmother who often got angry when she lost. Don was a former Los Angeles police detective. No one knew for certain what Larry had done before settling in Las Vegas. And then there were Philip and Camille Friedman, the only couple. Phil always wore a navy blue cap, and liked to sit in the chair to the immediate right of the dealer so he got the last cards dealt. Camille didn't play poker, but she always sat directly behind her husband of fifty years. Four years earlier, she had been diagnosed with Alzheimer's disease, although Phil never called it that in front of her. He referred to it as "memory loss." On her good days, Camille recognized the dealers, but lately she seemed more confused. One afternoon, she had wandered away from her seat without Phil's seeing her. Richie Tucci, who worked as a "shill" in the poker room, had escorted her back. Tucci's job was to keep a game going whenever there were only two or three players at a poker table.

The poker room contained eight tables big enough to seat seven players and a dealer. It was located in the southwestern corner of the pyramid in an open area, fenced in by a waist-high brass rail. A sign listed the two games dealt: Texas hold'em and seven-card stud. The Luxor limited the amount of betting in order to keep the pots to about $50 to $80. This was low by most Strip standards, but was exactly what the Luxor wanted in its poker area. High-stakes games drew professional players and cheats, who could easily pick a tourist clean. In poker, players compete against each other, so the only way the casino makes money is by charging a "rake"—10 percent of every pot, with a maximum of $4.

The poker room was Don Archer's domain, and at age seventy-two, he was the oldest department head. Archer had worked in poker rooms for more than fifty years. He had been one of the original casino employees whom Angel Naves had brought with him to the Strip to help revive the failing Circus Circus casino, and he had stayed until 1986 when he retired. Seven years later, he returned to the Strip when Tony Alamo asked him to design the poker room in the MGM Grand. He then moved with Alamo to the Monte Carlo casino poker room, and then followed him to the Luxor. Now he was responsible for all eight poker rooms that Circus Circus ran in its biggest casinos.

Archer's appearance was deceiving. He liked to wear cardigan sweaters rather than suit jackets, and his pure-white hair and grandfatherly manner made him seem sedate. Actually, he was an avid roller skater, former championship rodeo rider, and skilled water-skier. In 1989, he had won the team roping championship for cowboys age fifty and older at the National Rodeo Finals. At the time, he was sixty-four. Not long afterward, his horse stumbled and rolled over him, breaking several of his ribs and a collarbone. His doctors ordered him to quit team roping, so he began competitive roller-skating, entering events with a partner ten years his junior that were not much different from the ice-skating competitions seen on television.

Archer enjoyed mingling with customers, but on this particular morning he was preoccupied as he strolled through the Luxor's poker room on his way to lunch. He slipped through a back entrance of the Pyramid Café and chose a booth away from Alamo and Michael Starr, who were dining in a nearby corner. He wanted to be alone. Today was the anniversary of his only son's murder.

Don Archer had always wanted a son, partly because

of the close relationship that he had shared with his own father, Bob Archer. The senior Archer was a scoundrel by society's standards. He made his living during the Depression hustling pool. "My father would always lose the first game and then toss a dollar bill onto the table. When his opponent asked what the money was for, my dad would say, 'Why, you always play for something, don't you?' " Most of his opponents took the bait. "The real skill in hustling pool is not winning," Bob Archer had lectured his son. "It's easy to beat someone. The trick is making it look as if you are going to lose up until that final shot."

After a stint in the navy during World War II, Don Archer returned to Portland, Oregon, to work in a downtown billiards hall, the Rialto, that his father owned. Although gambling was illegal, there was always a card game going on in its back room. Because the Archers didn't trust anyone to handle their money, the senior Archer would work from noon until midnight and his son from midnight until noon.

At first, gambling fascinated Archer. "There was a thrill to betting, especially at poker. I had a knack for it and always wanted to see the next card." But the fascination ended when a woman came to the pool hall to complain because her husband had lost his paycheck playing poker that weekend. She had two small children and no money for groceries. Archer gave her some cash and barred her husband from the Rialto. By this time, he was married and had a son and daughter of his own. "I quit playing cards—just like that."

For the next two decades, Archer lived a double life. At work, he encountered pimps, prostitutes, cardsharps, and con men. At home, he led a quiet suburban life. "No one in my children's public schools or in our neighborhood knew how I made my living." But he didn't think there was anything immoral about his job. "I always felt justified doing what I did because my father and I were very honest people. People were going to play, so why not give them an honest place to play in?"

When the Portland police began a crackdown on gambling in 1965, Archer learned a grand jury was about to indict him, so he fled to Lake Tahoe and five days later went to work in a poker room at the Sahara Tahoe casino. One of the first customers was the Portland city official behind the crackdown. "He wanted to put me in jail for doing in Portland what he had come to Lake Tahoe to enjoy." Archer's wife, Grace, joined him in Nevada and during the next year, he worked out a deal through his attorney that led to the dropping of charges against him.

It was at about this same time that Archer's son, Dennis, surprised his parents by announcing his engagement to a stunning Bolivian, Maria Elena, age eighteen, who was a classmate of his at Oregon State University. Dennis was twenty-two, and shortly after he graduated and joined the navy as a pilot, they were married. Archer would later recall that he and Grace had welcomed their new daughter-in-law, but their feelings quickly soured. For the next eleven years, their relationship with Maria was so strained that the only time they got in touch with their son was when he was at sea away from her. Even after Maria gave birth to a daughter and son, the Archers stayed away.

On the Fourth of July in 1980, Archer decided to call Dennis at the Whidbey Island Naval Station in Oak Harbor, Washington, where he was stationed. "Dennis, Maria, and the kids were having a backyard barbecue," he remembered, "and I spoke to my son for a few minutes and then he said, 'Dad, Maria is all upset about us talking. I really have to go.'"

That was the last time that Archer would ever hear his son's voice.

Twelve days later, a naval officer called the Archers in Las Vegas. "I'm sorry to inform you that your son is dead," the officer said. Don Archer asked if Dennis, who was then thirty-three, had been killed during a naval flying exercise.

"No sir," the caller replied. "He was murdered."

Dennis had been shot by a gun-wielding intruder who had burst into his home at the naval station at night while he was playing with his children, ages seven and nine. Maria was not at home. In the months that followed, the Archers and police investigators became convinced that Maria had arranged the murder in order to collect a $50,000 life insurance policy. The police investigation showed that she had been having a sexual affair with Roland Pietre, a former martial arts instructor at the naval station, and detectives claimed that Maria and Pietre had hired a hit man for $5,000 to do the actual killing. Maria was put on trial and the Archers attended every day of the highly publicized hearing. The case against her was based almost entirely on her former lover's testimony. He had turned on her and was cooperating with state prosecutors in return for a twenty-year prison sentence rather than a life term. After several days of sensational testimony, the jury found Maria innocent. It decided a jealous Pietre had hired the hit man entirely on his own. The Archers were dumbfounded. Before the trial, they had filed legal papers to take custody of their grandchildren, but after Maria was released, their petition was dismissed. She and the children left town without telling the Archers where they were moving. The Archers had not only lost their son, but their grandchildren.

Disheartened, Archer and Grace moved to a ranch in Oregon, and Archer took up riding in rodeos. But coincidence intervened. A friend recognized the Archers' granddaughter and tipped them off. It turned out that Maria and the children lived less than an hour away.

Archer tried to talk to his granddaughter after school one day, but she would have no part of it. "She told me I needed to apologize to her mother. She knew we still believed her mother was guilty," he said. He had better luck with his grandson. The boy played on a high school basketball team, and Archer attended every one of his practices and games, nodding or calling hello to him from the bleachers. When he finally worked up enough courage to introduce himself, his grandson agreed to a hot dog and soft drink after a game and they became friends.

Six years after the murder trial, Archer learned that Maria's former lover, Roland Pietre, was being paroled from prison, and he decided to track him down. He confronted him in a seedy Seattle neighborhood. "I wanted to ask him if he had held back anything at the trial," he said. "I was scared, but I needed to have some sort of closure." He didn't get it. Pietre told him a wild story about how Dennis had been murdered because he was about to expose a drug ring at the naval station. A short time later, Archer heard that Pietre was back in prison for violating his parole and was a prime suspect in the murder of his girlfriend, whose body had been found in the trunk of her car.

Over the years, the Archers had kept in touch with their grandson, and just two months before, they had proudly attended his college graduation. They had taken him, his sister, and Maria out for dinner afterward to celebrate. It was the first time the Archers had been in the same room with Maria since the trial and they still thought she was guilty.

Now, it was the anniversary of his son's murder and Archer was eating alone in the Pyramid Café. "There isn't a day that goes by when I don't think about my dead son," he said. "He would have been fifty years old this year, and what I think about a lot is how it would have been if he were alive. I think about how he and I used to throw the baseball around. I think about how he and I and his son could have done things like that together—the three of us."

After lunch Archer returned to the poker room and noticed all of the locals were still playing. Phil Friedman waved him over. Four of them had each drawn hands that had four of a kind, the second-best poker hand possible! What were the odds of this happening? Archer admitted that he couldn't ever remember seeing that before.

Although Philip Friedman enjoyed socializing with other locals, he preferred playing poker with tourists. This was because he knew the "tells" of his fellow rocks. Mary wet her lips if she had more than three of a kind. Larry would peek at his cards on the table over and over again whenever he had a good hand. Knowing their tells gave Phil an edge, but he didn't really enjoy beating them. "Sometimes I feel bad if I take a pot from someone who I know needs the money or gets angry every time they lose," he explained. Only a few weeks earlier, he had been playing when another rock sat down and began tossing chips into the pot. Phil could tell from the four cards that had been dealt faceup on the table that his friend had a flush. Phil had four of a kind, which beats a flush, so he whispered: "Hey, don't keep getting into this one." His friend had ignored him and raised the bet. After he won, Phil turned to his friend. "I warned you not to get in there," he said. His buddy had bristled: "Don't you ever tell me how to play!" A few days later, Phil was playing when the same friend joined the game. This time Phil drew another winning hand but folded so that his friend could win. That's just how he was.

Phil enjoyed talking to tourists and he liked playing with them because they bet more. If his first three cards weren't any good, Phil folded. But tourists rarely gave up until they had been dealt all seven cards. They would just keep throwing money into the pot. Phil couldn't afford to play that way because he spent at least four hours every day of the year playing poker. "If the cards don't come, I just fold and sit back because I know there's always tomorrow."

When he and Camille moved to Las Vegas back in 1985, Phil had deposited $10,000 into a checking account for gambling. Eight years later, he had $21,500. He'd won $10,500 of it in one hand at the Luxor when he drew four of a kind and won a special progressive jackpot. Don Archer had offered to have a security guard escort Phil and Camille to their car, but Phil figured this would attract attention. They just walked out to the parking lot the way they normally did and drove to the bank.

Phil and Camille had first visited the Strip with friends from Los Angeles in the early 1960s, crammed into the backseat of a Volkswagen Beetle. Phil had been a car mechanic back then, brakes and front-end alignments mostly. He had learned to repair cars during World War II. Ironically, he hadn't even known how to drive until the army decided to teach him auto mechanics. In Brooklyn, New York, where he came from, there was no need for a car. As a kid, he had gotten around on roller skates and once held his street's record for jumping over wooden milk bottle cases.

Phil and Camille lived less than thirty minutes from each other when they were youngsters, but they had been reared in completely different worlds. She was Italian and a Roman Catholic. Phil was German and Jewish. They met at a movie theater when they both were nineteen. He spotted her at the concession stand, thought she was cute, and offered her some candy. Camille was self-conscious. When she was a baby, someone had tossed a firecracker into her carriage on the Fourth of July and the explosion had blown out an eye. She had had a glass eye ever since and didn't think anyone would want to marry her because of it. Phil hadn't even noticed. When she mentioned it, he stared at her and said: "Which eye is glass? You look perfect to me."

Her parents didn't object when she brought him home. They used to sit on the stoop in front of her house and talk until her father would come outside and say, "Hey, it only takes five minutes to get into trouble, so why are you taking so long?" But Phil's parents felt differently about his dating a Roman Catholic and his mother refused to speak to Camille. In 1942, Phil enlisted and was sent to Guadalcanal. On his first day there, a soldier called him a "dirty Jew." Phil socked him in the face.

Camille wrote him every day. As soon as he was discharged, he asked her to marry him. They were wed on March 31, 1946. Phil went to work at his parents' fruit store in Brooklyn and Camille converted to Judaism and tried to fit in. Her mother-in-law renamed her Judy because Camille sounded "too Italian." But as the years passed, relations between them grew strained, so in 1956, Phil and Camille moved to California. By this time, their two daughters, Paula and Diane, were eight and ten, and every morning during the cross-country trip Phil woke them at 5 A.M. by saying, "Westward ho!"

They bought a new $12,000 house in Covina, a suburb of Los Angeles, putting $5 down as a down payment. It was the Tinkerbell model in Peter Pan Village. Their monthly house payment was $52. For the next twenty years, Phil worked as a mechanic at Sears Roebuck and Camille was a classified-ad taker at the San Gabriel Valley *Tribune*. In remembering her childhood, Diane Friedman, whom everyone called DeeDee, described her father as a "happy-go-lucky, hear-no-evil, speak-no-evil guy who didn't like problems and saw life very simply." In contrast, Camille was a "worrier" who often felt insecure and, in her daughter's opinion, was often too demanding and too strict.

Phil and Camille adored each other. "My parents have something special," DeeDee Friedman said. "My father is a hopeless romantic and my mother worships him." Phil kept a photograph of his wedding picture in his wallet. When he turned fifty, Camille described him in a letter to the local newspaper as "a man of warmth, a good husband and fine father . . . who has worked to provide for us to the best of his ability, and his efforts are more than all riches to us." Phil framed the clipping and hung it in his den.

When they retired to Las Vegas, they lived off their pensions and Social Security checks. It wasn't much, but they made it last. On many a morning, Phil would wake up and tell Camille: "Darling, we have it made! Forget about yesterday, it's gone. Don't worry about to-morrow. It might never come. Let's just enjoy today. We can smell the air, see the birds, hear and taste and feel. Most of all, we've got each other. What more could we want?"

But in 1992, Phil noted that Camille was becoming absent-minded. She left the water running in the bath-room sink several times and couldn't remember where she had left a cigarette she had been smoking. When she went in for a routine physical exam, the doctors diagnosed Alzheimer's. Phil didn't believe it. He told her that she was just forgetful. After all, they were both in their seventies, and all older people forgot things some-times. Camille liked to play the slots while Phil played poker; she would curse at them in Italian. But she began losing interest shortly after the diagnosis. The machines seemed to confuse her, and after the afternoon when she became disoriented and couldn't find the poker room where Phil was playing, she stayed close to him. Phil liked the Luxor poker room because it wasn't walled in. Camille could sit behind him and watch the people go by. Phil became so friendly with the dealers that he began inviting them to his house on Wednesday nights to shoot pool. Camille fixed them snacks. From 1992 until late 1996, Camille held her own, showing few further signs of Alzheimer's, and Phil decided she had been misdiagnosed. But in the summer of 1997 that began to change. By the fall, Camille was having real problems coping.

"What's wrong with me?" she asked Phil one morning in September when they were getting ready to drive to the Luxor.

"Nothing, darling. We're both just getting older," he replied.

The next morning he noticed that some of Camille's hair had been pulled out and she had chewed her fingernails to the quick. "I'm scared," she said. "I'm really, really scared. Why is this happening to me? I've been a good girl all my life."

When it was time for them to leave for the Luxor, Camille said she didn't want to go. "I'm scared," she kept repeating. They went nonetheless; Phil thought she would be fine once she was in the familiar poker area. But she was on edge the entire time he was playing. "Who are all these people?" she kept asking. That night, she wouldn't get into bed. She sat in a chair the entire night chanting: "I'm scared, Phil. I'm scared, Phil. I'm scared, Phil." In the morning, he drove her to DeeDee's house. He thought this might reassure her, but she began looking for him as soon as he left to play poker. When he came back later in the day, she made him promise never to leave her again. DeeDee, who had read a great deal about Alzheimer's, told her father that he was going to have to put Camille into a nursing home at some point. He was adamant. "I'll never do that," he said. "This is your mother. I can take care of her."

DeeDee didn't argue. "When I was a child, I never thought my father had much patience," she said, "but he certainly learned how to be patient with my mom."

By November, Camille had become so frightened whenever anyone visited them that Phil stopped having the Luxor dealers come over to shoot pool. Then came spells when she was hysterical and incoherent.

One night she telephoned DeeDee. "I have to go."

"Where?" DeeDee asked.

"I have to get away. I'm scared."

"Of what?"

"Everything."

Her dementia grew still worse in December. "Why is she going downhill so fast?" Phil asked her doctors. "She was fine for years."

It was simply the way it was with Alzheimer's, they told him. What made it all seem so unreal was that Camille would snap out of it for brief moments. She would suddenly talk to Phil as she used to, then lapse into her terrible chant: "I'm scared, Phil." The new year was a disaster. Camille was now so disoriented that Phil had to dress her, feed her, and take her to the bathroom. The worst part was watching the woman he loved turn into an infant. He missed his wife.

He gave up his card games and felt like a prisoner in his own house. "I think I'm going nuts," he told DeeDee, but he still resisted a nursing home. "I can't abandon her."

After several more weeks full of what DeeDee later called "insane moments," an exhausted Phil relented. DeeDee already had made arrangements with the Miriam Miller Alzheimer's Center. They told Camille they were going to visit friends, drove to the center, sat down together for coffee and doughnuts, and then left the room without her. She began screaming. The nurses had told them to wait three days before coming back to visit. When DeeDee called that night, a nurse said that Camille had been sobbing nonstop. DeeDee cried all night too. Three days later, Phil was afraid to visit. He thought she would hate him.

Phil and DeeDee soon fell into a routine. Both visited Camille every day. After Phil saw her, he would drive to the Luxor poker room. Everyone asked about her. "I don't tell them how she really is," he said one afternoon. "She was always so proud. I don't want them to think of her like she is now. She's in her own world." Phil would play poker all afternoon and then drive home, but he rarely stayed there more than an hour. "What is there for me at home now that Camille isn't there?" he asked. He began playing poker at night at the Sunset Station, a casino close to his house. He had never realized how many other elderly people went to casinos because they didn't want to be alone. Now he was one of them.

DeeDee knew that her father couldn't afford to keep Camille in a home without help from Medicaid, but the lawyer she saw gave her troubling news. Under federal law, her mother's share of her parents' assets had to be depleted before she qualified for assistance. Once those assets were spent, DeeDee realized Phil was going to be hard-pressed to continue supporting himself. She told her father that they had to take steps to protect his resources. One of the first was to move Camille into a different nursing home, even though they knew the care there wouldn't be as good. Phil broke into tears. He made DeeDee her mother's legal guardian because he no longer could stand making decisions about her future.

As Camille's health deteriorated, nurses asked DeeDee

if she wanted her mother attached to any life-saving devices. Alzheimer's itself is not fatal; patients suffering from it usually die from pneumonia, heart disease, cancer, or a stroke. "I only want comfort measures taken for my mother," said DeeDee. "No life-support machines." She told her father why. "There are elderly people in this home who have been vegetables for ten years because their loved ones have decided to keep them alive at all costs. I don't want to do that to Mom." She also was concerned about her father's finances and the emotional toll of prolonging Camille's life. Her mother was in such bad shape now that she didn't recognize either of them.

Phil kept up his visits nonetheless. "I think a lot about how it was when I first met Camille," Phil explained one morning at the Pyramid Café. "I like to think of her like she was then, not now. I bought her peppermint candy at the movies. Some men would have been afraid to marry a woman with only one eye because she might go blind and you'd have to care for her. I never thought anything about it. You know, some people in that nursing home haven't gotten any visitors for years. I couldn't leave Camille alone like that. I miss her. Sometimes at night, I wake up and reach for her and then I think I'm going crazy because I know she isn't there. People say that when you're old, you're in your 'golden years.' Ha. Look at me. My 'golden years' were when I was in high school and when I first met Camille. I talk about those days to her now but I don't know if she hears me or if she even is capable of remembering those days. That's what hurts. Even the memories are gone now. All those years together and she doesn't even remember them or know how much I love her."

DeeDee took her mother candy, put her in a wheelchair, pushed her outside for a change of scene, but

Camille never spoke. And then one afternoon, after
DeeDee kissed her good-bye and started for the door,
she heard a voice.

"My darling DeeDee," Camille said. "Don't worry.
It's okay."

DeeDee spun around. Her mother's face was un-
changed and for a moment, DeeDee wondered if she
had imagined it. "Mother? Mother? Can you hear
me?" she asked. Camille stared blankly ahead.

DeeDee was getting ready to take a shower a few
days later when her husband handed her the telephone.
"Your mother is dead," a nurse said. "We found her
when we went in this morning." DeeDee hadn't wanted
Camille to die alone. She had asked the nurses to warn
her if they thought she was dying. She called her father.
He couldn't talk. He started to cry. DeeDee made all the
funeral arrangements but wasn't sure her father would
even attend because he hated funerals. He was there. "I
never felt we were a close family," DeeDee said later.
"My mom and dad were close—so close my sister and
I felt left out at times. But I feel close to my dad now.
As strange as it sounds, I'd go through everything that
we went through again—all the insanity and pain—
without giving it a second thought because it brought
my dad and me together."

The day after the funeral, Phil drove to the Luxor at
his usual time to play cards. All of the dealers and the
rocks had heard that Camille had died. "People can say
what they want about Las Vegas being a wicked place,"
Phil said, "but I know that this poker room kept me
sane during all this. If I couldn't have come here, I
wouldn't have survived because this is where I could relax. You know, it is really my home now."

During a break in the game, Don Archer told Phil
how sad he was to hear about Camille.

"Thanks," Phil said.

Archer wanted him to know that he understood

what it was like to lose someone you love. They talked privately for a few minutes and then Phil took his regular seat at the seven-card stud table. The first two cards were threes. He got another three dealt to him faceup. He wondered if he had any tells that the other rocks noticed whenever he got good cards. It was a question he would have liked to have asked Camille.

CHAPTER TWENTY-EIGHT

....

Kelly Jo Steinfort, Showgirl

Kelly Jo Steinfort didn't mention her encounter with
Phillip Millaudon when Paul Morgan visited in October. He was to be there for three weeks, and they
quickly fell into the same routine they had developed
when they lived together in Manhattan and Atlantic
City. He enjoyed sleeping in, getting bagels for lunch,
and staying up late to watch videotaped movies after
her last show. She didn't say anything, but she missed
working out in the gym and hanging around with the
other cast members. Most nights, the cast met at the
Luxor's Sports Bar after their final show to drink beer
and critique their performances. One night Steinfort introduced Morgan to the cast, but he was an outsider
who didn't understand the inside jokes and wasn't
much interested in hearing the cast drone on endlessly
about missed cues. Luckily, Millaudon hadn't been
around on that night. If he had been, Steinfort would
have felt even more awkward.

She and Morgan made love only three times during
his visit. She thought that odd. A spark was missing,

but she brushed off her misgivings by telling herself that everything would be fine once they actually moved in together. They made a pact to get together every two weeks until he was able to move to Las Vegas.

Dick and Lynne Foster were pleased with *Imagine*. It was averaging six hundred ticket sales per show, which was good, but not extraordinary. Not everyone at Circus Circus was pleased, however. At one point, Michael Hartzell suggested they cut back to one show a night because the twelve-hundred-seat theater looked empty when it was only half full. But the Fosters insisted the audiences would grow once the show established its reputation. Besides, they were still tinkering with it. The magician wasn't dynamic enough, so they hired a drama coach to give him pointers. They also asked Steinfort if she would learn how to play one of the mermaid roles in the second act. The next day she began practicing somersaults while dangling fifty feet above the theater's seats on metal cables attached to a leather waist harness.

In November, Steinfort used her contacts to get Morgan's jazz group a job playing in a lounge at Caesars Palace during Comdex, a computer show that attracted as many as a hundred thousand self-proclaimed "computer geeks" to the Strip each year. Las Vegas welcomed them by jacking up room prices and doubling the number of raunchy girlie shows. "Guys who come to Comdex bring a twenty-dollar bill and one white shirt and don't change either one," said a Luxor casino host. "They do not gamble, but they'll hit every tittie bar in town as long as they can charge it on their expense account."

Steinfort also got herself an afternoon job working at a Comdex booth for a company that made a floppy disk system. The night before the computer show opened, she was given a thick packet of information to memorize that described why this floppy disk was better than its competitors. She had taken her assignment seriously, and she reported to work the next afternoon with her head buzzing with computer terms. She handed out pamphlets and offered to answer questions from conventioneers. It was fun at first, but then a group of men came into her booth and one of them starting asking her technical questions. She could tell he was showing off for his friends.

"You definitely have gone beyond my level of knowledge," she told him. "Let me find you someone who can answer those for you."

But when another customer did the same thing, her confidence was shaken and by the end of the day, she felt like a total failure. At least a dozen men had asked her technical questions that she couldn't answer. The next day, a Las Vegas modeling agency sent her to read a script for a local television commercial and she was tongue-tied trying to say "jewelry." After several embarrassing attempts, she was dismissed. After that, she was sent to audition for a job as a runway model for a fashion show in a glitzy mall. She knew it was a mistake the moment she walked in and noticed that all the other women were thinner, taller, and younger. She had a muscular build. She wasn't hired.

Morgan had never been sympathetic to her insecurities and he brushed them off now. "Those jobs aren't worth worrying about anyhow." They had agreed that he would move to town in January, and they spent much of his visit looking for an apartment. One afternoon, Steinfort drove Morgan to the University of Nevada in Las Vegas because he wanted to enroll once he settled in and earn his master's degree in music. On the way back to her apartment, he badgered her about when she was going to quit dancing and study physical therapy.

"You aren't going to be able to dance forever," he warned. Someday she would have to get a "real" job. She kept quiet.

"It's like I'm cheating on him," she told a friend in the cast that night. "Not in the traditional way, because I'm not seeing anyone else, but I'm cheating in our relationship because I've not told him the truth."

"What truth is that?" the friend asked.

"That I am quite happy living *without* him."

The night before Morgan was scheduled to return to New York, Steinfort mustered her courage and announced that she was having misgivings about their relationship. But as soon as he got upset, she backpedaled. He left three days before her birthday without having a clue that she wanted out.

The cast threw a birthday party for Steinfort at Tommy Rockers, a local bar, on a Monday night. It lasted well into the next morning and nearly everyone attended except Millaudon. Shortly after 4 A.M., he finally sauntered in.

"Where's Paul?" he asked her.

"He had to go home because he had some gigs," she replied. Steinfort knew he didn't care. He was really pointing out that her birthday hadn't mattered enough for Morgan to stick around for three more days. Then, after everyone else was gone, Millaudon walked Steinfort to her car. When they reached it, he kissed her. "I let it happen," she said later, "and it completely bowled me over."

Steinfort drove home and tried to sleep but she felt so guilty that she telephoned Morgan and told him what had happened.

"What do you want me to say?" he asked. "Do you want me to say that it's over? I love you but this is ridiculous. You've got to make up your mind."

She did. He called her every night for ten nights, but he couldn't sway her. She told him it was over.

Rumors that Michael Hartzell was about to be fired as entertainment director swept through the cast shortly before Christmas. What did it mean? Were the suits in the corporate offices disappointed in the show? Was the show going to be canceled? The Fosters insisted everything was fine but a few weeks later, Circus Circus announced it was restructuring its entertainment offices. An outsider was being hired to oversee the running of the new twelve-thousand-seat amphitheater being built at Mandalay Bay and to head up the corporation's overall entertainment program. Hartzell was being transferred to a new job where he would book acts, primarily for the Circus Circus casino. The change sparked more rumors. "My whole life is subject to change at a moment's notice," Steinfort recognized. "Who knows what is going to happen? They could shut down the show. I could stumble and hurt my leg. There are no guarantees when you're a Las Vegas dancer so you have to enjoy your life as much as you can and enjoy the moment."

She and Millaudon tried to keep their romance secret, but everyone in the cast soon knew about it. "We have definitely hit some bumps," Steinfort said, shortly after New Year's Eve of 1998, "but I'm truly happy. Phillip really respects what I do." She didn't think many people did. The term "showgirl" conjured up images of ex–high school cheerleaders trying to hang on to their glory days. "That word—'showgirl'—really is outdated," she said. "Nearly all of us are professional dancers and acrobats, not sexy women who waltz around onstage with our tops off, looking beautiful. It's taken me a while to understand this, but what I do matters. It really does. I'm proud of who I am."

Eight months later, Millaudon asked her to marry him.

She said yes.

CHAPTER TWENTY-NINE

....

Keith Uptain, Casino Shift Manager

By Christmas, the construction of the high-limit gaming area was finally complete and casino host Tom Carilli was busy bringing in high rollers to see the "new" Luxor. Keith Uptain wasn't much of a schmoozer, so he didn't volunteer to come in on his day off to play in a golf tournament that Carilli had arranged, but the other two casino shift managers, Dave Maturino and Stewart Madden, both did. It was the first golf tournament ever sponsored by the Luxor, and Carilli predicted the casino would easily recoup the $22,000 that it cost to treat the twenty-five elite gamblers to an all-expenses-paid weekend. One of them had a million-dollar credit line, the highest Circus Circus had ever given. Less than a year earlier, casino officials had gotten excited whenever they won $15,000 from a player. During the golf tournament, one gambler lost almost $100,000 playing craps and another dropped $65,000 at blackjack. "We've never had action this big at any Circus Circus properties," said a pleased Maturino, who at age forty had worked at Circus Circus his entire career. "Word is definitely getting around that we are becoming an up-scale resort."

The high stakes also attracted more card counters and thieves. The day after the golf tournament, a dealer discovered thirteen checks (chips) worth $1,000 each missing from the roulette table where she was working. It had happened on Maturino's shift, so he called the surveillance crew and asked it to review all the tapes recorded by cameras in the ceiling above the table. They revealed that an hour earlier a man had reached over the two-foot-high Plexiglas barrier that was supposed to protect the dealer's checks and scooped up a handful. Had he grabbed $100 checks, his crime might never have been noticed, but $13,000 was too much for any-one to overlook.

Maturino quickly determined that the only $1,000 checks that were unaccounted for in the entire casino were the ones that had been stolen, so he came up with a plan. He collected all the teal-colored $1,000 checks in the casino, replaced them with new $1,000 checks of a different color, and told the tellers in the casino cage to call security if anyone came into the Luxor and tried to cash in a teal-colored one. Three days later, an older Asian woman handed a teller four teal checks.

"Excuse me, ma'am," Maturino said to the woman. "Can you tell me where you got these?"

The woman glanced around nervously. "I won them yesterday," she replied.

"I'm afraid that isn't possible," Maturino said. When he told her that the checks had been stolen, she ran out of the Luxor, leaving them behind. That left nine unaccounted for.

Two days later, a man dressed in a suit and tie strolled up to the cashier's cage and slapped six teal checks onto the counter. Maturino and casino manager Tom Robinson confronted him.

"I don't have to tell you where I got these," he

declared. "But I will. I am an attorney and they were given to me by a client as partial payment for his defense. Now I would like you to pay me."

"We believe they were stolen," Maturino said.

"Well, that's your problem, not mine," the lawyer replied. "I certainly didn't steal them, but they were paid to me for my services, and I expect the Luxor to give me cash for them."

When Robinson told him that they were not going to redeem the checks, the lawyer began to get loud, so Robinson turned tough. The Luxor was prepared to call the police and accuse him of trying to fence stolen property, he said. The lawyer backed down. "I have three more in my car," he volunteered. "I'll get them for you." Robinson sent a security guard with him to bring them back.

"Is your client the one who stole these from us?" Robinson asked.

"I have no way of knowing," the attorney replied. "He told me he won them and simply wanted to pay me with them because he didn't have any cash, so I agreed."

As the attorney turned to leave, Robinson asked: "Can you tell me what your client was arrested for— why you were hired to defend him?"

"He's been accused of stealing casino chips from the Golden Nugget downtown," the lawyer replied.

"Well, didn't it dawn on you that your client might be giving you stolen chips to pay his legal bills?"

"My client has assured me that he is not guilty," the attorney replied.

Robinson laughed out loud.

While Tom Carilli kept busy recruiting U.S. high rollers, Robinson and his overseas casino hosts put together travel packages for Asian players, and when they began arriving in the fall the amount that they bet quickly overshadowed that bet even by Carilli's elite gamblers. The Asian players' game of choice was baccarat, and the Luxor suspended its normal table limits when they came to town and let them bet as much as 5 percent of their personal credit lines. For most, that was between $15,000 and $30,000 per hand.

Baccarat is an easy game to play, because a gambler has to make only one decision, but it is extremely difficult to understand because of its complicated rules. In order to play, a gambler takes a seat at a baccarat table. The seats are numbered one through fifteen but there are actually only fourteen spots. That's because the number thirteen is always omitted. Seven players can sit at each end of the peanut-shaped table and there are usually three dealers—one who handles the shoe and two who collect and pay off bets. Only two hands are dealt in baccarat. One is called the Player's hand, the other is the Banker's hand. Gamblers try to predict which hand is going to win. They can also bet that the two hands will tie. There are three squares on the table in front of each gambler with the words "PLAYER," "BANKER," and "TIE" printed on them. All a gambler has to do is decide where to put his bet. That's it.

After the bets are made, the dealer slides a card from a shoe that contains eight decks. "Card for the Player," he announces, placing the card facedown in the center of the table. He says, "Card for the Banker," and slips out another card, which he tucks facedown under the corner of the shoe. Out comes a second facedown card for the Player's hand, followed by another for the Banker's hand. The dealer gives the Player's hand to the gambler who has made the largest bet on the table. He gets to turn it over for everyone else to see. Many Asians make turning over these cards a great ceremony. They peek under one corner of the first card, then rub the second card for several seconds for luck before looking at it. The goal is to end up with nine points. The ace counts as one. The two through the nine cards are worth their face value. The ten and the face cards— the jack, queen, and king—are worth zero. A jack and a four, for instance, mean the hand is worth four points. If a hand contains cards that add up to more than ten points, the digit in the left column is dropped. For example, if a hand consists of a seven and an eight, the cards add up to fifteen points. Taking away the number on the left means the actual value of the hand is five.

After the Player's hand is revealed, the dealer turns over the Banker's hand, and the hand that is closest to nine points wins. The casino takes all the bets that are incorrect.

While this may sound simple, it actually isn't, because the Player's and Banker's hands often tie or are worth only a few points. Whenever this happens, the rules dictate when and if a third card can be drawn, and here is where the game gets tricky, because nearly every casino follows its own set of rules. In some, for instance, the Player's hand might not be able to receive a third card if it already has a total of six or seven points. But the Banker's hand might be allowed to receive a third card even when it has six or seven points.

One of the first Asians to play at the Luxor arrived from the airport at about three in the morning during Dave Maturino's graveyard shift. He began betting $5,000 per hand and after seven hours was $200,000 in debt. Because he had a sizable credit line, he was allowed to sign markers. The gambler went to his suite to sleep, reappearing the following midnight to play again. This time, he picked winning hands five times in a row. He lost a couple and then picked another seven consecutive hands correctly, which was incredibly lucky. He continued winning and by 5 A.M., he had $380,000 in baccarat chips in front of him and was ready to take a break. He called Maturino over to the baccarat table

and asked for a favor. He still owed the $200,000 in
IOUs, so he counted out $100,000 in chips and asked
Maturino if he would take them to the casino cage and
pay off half of his markers. The Luxor usually required
gamblers to pay off their markers in person but
Maturino didn't want to offend the man, so he picked
up the chips and hurried over to the casino cage. The
teller there deposited the $100,000 into the gambler's
personal account and then handed Maturino five markers. Maturino returned to the baccarat table and gave
the gambler a $100,000 deposit slip plus the markers.
The gambler looked puzzled for a moment, but didn't
say anything. Instead, he tore up the markers and left
the table. When Maturino's shift ended, he went home
without realizing that he had just made a $100,000
error.

Tom Robinson called Maturino the next morning
and asked him to come back. The teller in the casino
cage had misunderstood Maturino's instructions. The
$100,000 in chips he gave her should have been de-
posited into the Luxor's account—not into the gambler's personal account—because they were supposed to
be used to pay off the man's IOUs. Instead, the teller
had deposited the $100,000 into the gambler's account
and given Maturino the $100,000 worth of markers
that the gambler still owed. Simply put, the Luxor was
out $100,000.

Robinson and Maturino met with the gambler and
explained what had happened. They took along an
interpreter so there would be no misunderstanding,
but the man refused to cooperate. "If I owe you one
hundred thousand dollars, then you show me the markers," he said coolly. There was nothing Robinson or
Maturino could do because the Asian had already destroyed the markers.

An hour later, Robinson asked Maturino to resign.
The shift supervisor had worked for Circus Circus for

eighteen years and was well liked. The gambler, meanwhile, continued playing baccarat as if nothing had ever happened. When he checked out the next day, he paid off his remaining $100,000 in IOUs and returned home with $150,000 in winnings.

Not long after that incident, a dealer in the high-limit gaming area made a mistake in the baccarat pit that cost the Luxor $45,000. Robinson decided it was time to bring in an expert to run the baccarat tables. He hired Brian Folger from the Tropicana, a resort that had collected $145 million in baccarat revenues the previous year. Folger added a third baccarat table to the high-stakes pit, ordered tuxedos for the dealers who worked there, issued a thick book of regulations for them to follow, and assigned two supervisors to watch over every game to eliminate mistakes. He also had tangerine and kumquat trees brought into the pit because in China they are considered good luck signs.

All this flurry sparked an ongoing debate among veteran employees. The question they were asking: Does Circus Circus really have enough backbone to compete in the high-stakes world of baccarat? "Everyone's excited right now because we're finally getting players in here with more than just chump change," one dealer explained. "But what happens when one of these Asians walks in and wins a million dollars? I mean, you got Tony Alamo running around laying people off because we're pinching pennies. How is he going to square that with a million-dollar baccarat loss?"

Shortly after New Year's Day, Brian Folger received a telephone call from a friend at Caesars Palace just before three o'clock in the afternoon. A whale had just won $2.6 million playing baccarat, and was now on his way to the Luxor in a Caesars Palace limousine. Folger called one of the Luxor's Asian hosts, who was upstairs in a hotel room asleep because she had been up all night making sure the credit needs of several Asian high rollers had been met. She scrambled downstairs to greet the whale, who was waiting for her outside in the limousine. He did not want to enter the Luxor without a formal welcome. The hostess apologized profusely for not being there when his limousine arrived and immediately escorted him inside to the high-limit gaming area, where Tom Robinson was waiting to greet him. Tony Alamo had been alerted and was downstairs watching the gambler on a big-screen television. The surveillance crew was patching the picture through from the casino's ceiling cameras. Robinson told the whale that he would be permitted to bet a maximum of $60,000 per hand, but only after he deposited the $2.6 million check from Caesars Palace into the Luxor's casino cage. He agreed and was taken to a table readied just for him. He was accompanied by three young women whose job was to provide him with cigarettes and to order drinks if he wished them.

Folger posted a security guard near the table to keep gawkers and other baccarat players away, and the whale sat down in seat number eight for luck and signed a marker for $100,000. His first bet was $50,000 and he bet it on the Banker's hand. Because of the rules of the game, the mathematical probability of baccarat dictates that the Banker will win more hands than a player— about fifty-four hands out of every eighty that are dealt. To keep gamblers from always betting with the Banker, casinos charge a commission every time the Banker wins a hand. The fee varies. The dealer pulled four cards from the shoe. Even though the whale had bet on the Banker's hand, under the rules, it was his job to turn over the Player's hand. Leaning his face as close as possible to the table, he peeked under the right corner of the first card, bending it back so much that it cracked. He took a puff of his cigarette and looked at the next card, slowly turning over its corner too. "Ummp!" he grunted, flipping up both cards. The Player had a three and four, which totaled seven points—a good hand. The dealer turned over the Banker's hand. It contained a face card and nine, which totaled nine—a perfect score. Because the Banker's hand won, the dealer paid the whale $50,000 minus a commission.

The gambler put his next $50,000 wager in the Player's square. He won again and the dealer gave him another $50,000. In just two hands—less than five minutes—he had made close to $100,000. During the next three hours, he picked the winning hand with uncanny frequency. By the time he stopped for dinner, he had won $900,000, and there were so many people gathered around the perimeter of the high-limit gaming area watching him that a second security guard was called to keep the crowd from spilling inside. The Luxor had never lost so much money to a single gambler.

The whale announced that he was tired, so a security guard escorted him and the three women with him to one of the Luxor's luxury suites. As soon as he left the baccarat pit, Alamo hurried upstairs.

"Is he playing fairly?" Alamo asked Folger.

"Yes," Folger replied. "He's just on a winning streak."

"Okay," said Alamo. "Then let's hope his luck changes."

Folger nodded. "He's trying to win a million bucks. He's not going to stop until he does, so we should have a chance at winning back our money."

About an hour later, the whale returned with his entourage. This time, however, luck was against him. He lost eight straight hands for a total of $400,000. Without flinching, he continued betting $50,000 per hand.

"That's more than I make in a year," said someone watching the action from outside the pit.

The Asian guessed correctly on the next hand and the next one too. During the coming hour, he seesawed back and forth, winning $100,000, then losing $100,000. Shortly before nine o'clock, he announced that he wanted to play at two different tables simultaneously. Folger checked with Robinson, who okayed the request, and another team of dealers was sent in to deal to him. The whale moved back and forth between the two tables, betting $50,000 at each. For the next hour, his wins and losses seemed to cancel each other out and then he won several hands in a row at both tables. His winnings now totaled $950,000. He announced that he now wanted to play at only one table, and he raised his bet there to $60,000. If he won, he would pass the $1 million mark.

The whale slid his bet onto the square marked PLAYER and was dealt two cards. He peeked under the corner of the first card, then reached over and picked up the second one. When he peeked under it, he threw both cards down, cursing softly. They were a two and an ace, for a total of only three points. It seemed certain he would lose. But the Banker's cards were two queens. This meant the Banker had drawn a zero. The Asian grinned. Under the rules, both hands would get another card. He peeked at the Player's new card, then turned it over triumphantly. It was a five, giving him eight points. Some of the crowd watching from outside the pit applauded. The dealer turned over the Banker's third card. It was a five. The whale had won the hand. The dealer paid him and the gambler paused for a moment. Then he pushed $60,000 worth of chips into the Banker's square.

Downstairs, Alamo suddenly realized he wasn't quitting. As he watched, the whale continued beating the mathematical odds. He correctly guessed another six hands in a row. Finally, he announced that he was finished. The dealers calculated that he owed $70,000 in commissions from his bets with the Banker's hand and when that was deducted, he was told that his winnings came to nearly $1.3 million. He also was told that he had earned $18,000 worth of airfare comps and $30,000 worth of hotel room and restaurant comps, based on the time that he had gambled and his average bet.

The whale shook hands with Folger and Robinson, then gave the six dealers at the two tables a tip of only $85 to split between them. His limousine from Caesars Palace was still waiting and when he climbed inside, he was carrying a check for nearly $4 million, which represented his combined winnings from the Luxor and Caesars Palace. He was overheard telling the driver that he felt like playing baccarat at the International Hilton. Folger called the baccarat pit manager there to warn him. The Luxor would later learn that the whale had won another $1.4 million there. He left Las Vegas with checks totaling $5.5 million.

Everyone in the baccarat pit was waiting to see Tony Alamo's reaction when he came upstairs. Some speculated that Folger would be fired. Circus Circus had never lost $1.3 million under Bill Bennett and Bill Pennington. A few dealers wondered if Alamo would close down the baccarat tables. A somber Alamo arrived a few seconds later and immediately went to talk to the dealers.

"Thank you for doing such a professional job," he told them. "You all handled yourselves well."

Turning, he nodded to Folger and said, "Good night."

That was it.

"I guess we'll have to start calling you Lucky," Robinson said to Folger after Alamo left.

About an hour later, when all the executives were gone, Uptain walked over to chat with Folger. Even though everyone had seemed accepting of the $1.3 million loss, both knew that the chief executives at Circus Circus were not going to be happy about it. "I guess," said Uptain, "that tonight should prove to those people out there who think Circus Circus isn't serious about baccarat that they are wrong."

Folger nodded.

The Bill Bennett grind days at Circus Circus were definitely over.

CHAPTER THIRTY

....

Glenn Schaeffer, Corporate Headquarters

By the close of 1997, there was much unrest in the Circus Circus boardroom and the snail's pace and rising cost of renovating the Luxor were not the only reasons why. There were other irritants. As soon as Bill Bennett was ousted, Clyde Turner started refurbishing the company's older hotels and casinos. If the board wouldn't let him get rid of them, at least he could upgrade them. He added a thousand-room hotel tower, fancier restaurants, and a new lobby to the Las Vegas Circus Circus casino, and then turned his attention to the casinos in Laughlin and Reno. Nearly all of these renovations were completed in 1996 and it now became clear that none of them had led to an increase in profits. In fact, revenues at the refurbished casinos and hotels were down. "Clyde Turner was used to dealing with upper-middle-class guests and upscale customers at the Mirage," said one manager. "He simply didn't understand the blue-collar working stiffs whom Bill Bennett had understood so well. They didn't spend more in a casino simply because it had new drapes and someone turned down their bed at night and left a mint on their pillow." The cost of remodeling the original Circus Circus casino had been budgeted at $60 million, but had actually cost $128 million. The general managers at the Las Vegas Circus Circus casino and the Colorado Belle casino in Laughlin were told to resign.

There were other miscues. The pink-and-white Circus Circus theme wasn't going over well in Tunica County, Mississippi, so the company was spending $125 million to expand and renovate its resort there, which it was renaming Gold Strike. Meanwhile, Circus Circus was giving the Excalibur a costly face-lift, expanding its Reno operations, and building Mandalay Bay—its new super casino. Glenn Schaeffer was still trying to win a gaming license in Detroit, and was moving forward with the company's plans to expand into Atlantic City. He was also busy getting the company's new Mississippi Gulf Coast casino under way. Circus Circus was involved in so many expensive projects that it had doubled its long-term debt in a single year. It now owed a record $1.4 billion. Wall Street analysts knew Circus Circus was profitable enough to handle its debts, so they weren't worried about its financial soundness. What bothered them was its management. There didn't seem to be much forethought in the company's helter-skelter projects. In their advisory reports to clients, the analysts characterized Circus Circus as a house badly divided. "Who," one analyst asked, "is in charge? And where is this company going?"

Turner was the company's chairman and chief executive, but Schaeffer was its most visible officer, its financial guru, and its point man. Yet it was the reclusive Ensign who controlled the most stock and made all of the final decisions. And it was becoming increasingly obvious that the three didn't agree on much. For instance, after the renovations flop and missteps in Tunica, Turner wanted to hire a national marketing director to do more customer research. Schaeffer was convinced that the company needed to spend more on national advertising, including television commercials and slick layouts in magazines. But Ensign and Alamo wanted to pour more into Mandalay Bay and the Luxor. Their squabbling leaked out publicly when the *Las Vegas Review-Journal* declared in late August that "Circus Circus Enterprises is a ship adrift." Philosophically, Turner was still seen by analysts as a Steve Wynn mimic. Ensign was from the Bill Bennett school and, as the newspaper put it, "still using the old Circus Circus playbook." Schaeffer was caught between them.

The company's vast holdings seemed as disjointed as its executives, so much so that one analyst suggested in the *Las Vegas Review-Journal* that Circus Circus needed to divide itself into two different companies: one that operated grind joints, the other super casinos.

All of this criticism hit like a bomb in the boardroom. Each of the executives denied talking to reporters, but clearly someone was leaking information. Already frustrated, Turner, Ensign, Schaeffer, and Alamo became even more annoyed with one another. These tensions flared in late 1997 when the four executives sat down with officials from R & R Advertising, a Las Vegas firm hired to come up with promotional ideas for the "new" Luxor. By this point, Circus Circus had spent close to $450 million renovating the pyramid—$200 million more than initially budgeted and $50 million more than the original resort cost to build. Schaeffer began the meeting by saying that he was in favor of spending as much as 5 percent of the $450 million on a national advertising campaign to "reintroduce" the Luxor to the public.

Ensign disagreed. Surveys showed that 80 percent of Las Vegas visitors picked a casino based on word of mouth or a previous visit, not because of advertising.

The two men began to argue and their comments quickly developed an edge. The four executives in the room were responsible for the biggest stock drop in Circus Circus's history. The price of a share would soon hit $15.50 and continue to slide. That was only 50¢ more than what it sold for in 1983 when Bill Bennett and Bill Pennington had taken the company public. On paper, all of the executives had lost huge sums, and none more than Ensign. His six and a half million shares had been worth $286 million in June. Now, they were worth $101 million, a loss of $185 million in less than six months.

Schaeffer took a verbal jab at Ensign. "I'd rather spend money on image advertising than dumping more marble into the Luxor," he said, referring to a disagreement that they had had months earlier about how much marble Alamo was buying. Ensign didn't reply, but Alamo did. He knew that Clyde Turner wanted him fired, so Alamo looked directly at Turner and then said that he would be happy to listen to anyone's suggestions about how he could do a better job getting guests into the Luxor. He'd rather have it said to his face than behind his back.

Turner didn't respond, but Alamo's comment irked Ensign. He told Alamo that he was out of line and they began arguing.

"What do you want me to do?" an exasperated Alamo finally snapped, jumping up from the table. "If you want me to resign, then I'll resign! I'll resign right now, right here, this very moment."

Alamo and Ensign had been close friends for more than thirty years, dating back to when they had started out working at a craps table together. No one had ever seen them argue like this.

"Sit down and be quiet," Ensign ordered. "No one is resigning."

The meeting was over.

Turner decided it was time for him to make his move. He met privately with Ensign and urged him to replace Alamo. A few days later, Circus Circus announced that Turner was the one leaving. Ensign had sided with his longtime friend. Turner did not want to go, but a hefty $5.5 million severance package helped smooth his departure and ensured that he left without bad-mouthing the company.

A new rumor soon was making the rounds. Michael Ensign was weary of running Circus Circus and ready to turn over the reins to Glenn Schaeffer. It seemed fitting since Schaeffer had once been Bennett's heir apparent and had spent most of his career training for the job. Two months later, however, Ensign squelched the speculation by announcing that he was staying put.

Schaeffer took the news in stride. Without complaint, he delved into a series of new projects. In a speech before the World Gaming Congress and Exposition, Schaeffer predicted that the next step for super casinos was the combining of entertainment with education. Just as he had used the phrase "entertainment architecture" to describe the outlandishly shaped buildings on the Strip, he now used the word "edutainment" to describe his idea of making museums and art exhibits a part of super casinos. He revealed that he wanted to add a museum at the Luxor called the House of History, where traveling exhibits, such as the popular "Treasures of King Tutankhamen," could be displayed. He was not the only proponent of combining culture and gaming. Steve Wynn was buying fine artwork for display in his Bellagio resort. "I once heard a tourist standing in front of the medieval Excalibur resort who said, 'Well, I don't have to go to England now—I've seen it all right here in Las Vegas,' " Schaeffer declared.

As a teenager, Schaeffer had dreamed of becoming rich. He was now forty-four, was worth $25 million, and was highly respected on Wall Street. Yet, he still worked long hours and traveled on grueling business trips that took him away from his wife and young children. Like Alamo, Schaeffer had missed birthdays, anniversaries, and vacations because he always put Circus Circus first. "The money isn't what drives you," he told his friends. "Money is simply a way to keep score." It was the competition—the game—that kept him going. He still woke up many mornings feeling that he had to push himself to do better and worried that he might already have passed his peak. The insecurities that had driven him as a child to get straight A's continued to prod him as an adult. "As you get older, you realize time is limited," he said. "It is your real enemy. Your chance to make your name, or your fame, or your money, whether in the business world or other walks, counts on speed. Most of us only get one chance to play in the big leagues, and when that time comes, you don't run and hide, you pay the price and step up to bat—and you don't quit in the middle of the third inning."

Shortly after New Year's Day 1998, Steve Wynn announced that he was voiding the contract he had signed with Circus Circus and Boyd Gaming to jointly develop the 181-acre tract in Atlantic City. Wynn claimed that his partners were unwilling to cough up their shares of development costs, which were much higher than anyone expected. "You just can't nullify a deal because you want to," thundered a livid Schaeffer. Circus Circus and the Boyd Group filed separate, bitterly worded lawsuits against Wynn. Several Wall Street analysts also commented. "To invite in two highly respected, high-profile gaming companies, have them as your partners as you're shepherded through the regulatory, political, and legal process, and then decide you don't need them anymore," one stock analyst told reporters, "is a sign of corporate arrogance." Schaeffer took up his company's fight with Wynn.

A few weeks later, Hilton Hotels announced that it wanted to merge with Circus Circus. Schaeffer was sent to handle those talks. When both sides decided to bow out of the deal, a real estate investment trust revealed that it wanted to buy Circus Circus. Again, Schaeffer was sent in to negotiate. Those meetings also ended up with Circus Circus deciding to stay on its own.

In the midst of all this frenzy, Detroit chose Circus Circus, MGM Grand, and a local company as the winners of its three gaming licenses. Steve Wynn's and Donald Trump's bids were rejected.

Schaeffer was still not chairman of Circus Circus—a job that he had always wanted—but he was clearly a major player in gambling and Wall Street's big leagues. And as he flew back and forth across the country discussing billion-dollar mergers, the Detroit project, and the company's ongoing dispute in Atlantic City, another fact became very clear. He was having the time of his life.

CHAPTER THIRTY-ONE

....

Shawna Gray, Whore

David called Shawna Gray at her apartment on October 18. "Have you read today's newspaper?" She hadn't. She rarely did. He brought her a copy of the *Las Vegas Review-Journal*. A prostitute had been murdered at the Luxor. She had picked up a john in the Nile River bar and agreed to have sex with him in his room for $300. Midway through the act, he had choked her to death and then engaged in numerous sexual acts with her corpse. Initially the police had thought she was twenty-one, but it turned out she was a sixteen-year-old runaway with a fake ID.

Gray read the story without comment.

"How many times have you picked up tricks in the Luxor bar?" David asked. "That could have been you! You've got to stop being a prostitute."

"Working girl," Gray said, correcting him. She hated the term "prostitute," and while she frequently referred to herself as a whore, she bristled if anyone else used that word.

David offered her a deal. He would pay her tuition

if she would enroll in a dealers school and stop working as a hooker. He'd also pay the rent on her apartment as long as she stayed in school. "Okay," she said. "I'll quit, but not my steadies." She was having sex with three local men, as well as David, which earned her $375 a week. David called a dealers school and made the arrangements. He drove her to the first class. The course was supposed to last six to eight weeks, depending on how fast a student caught on. It turned out that Gray had a knack for blackjack and craps. "I didn't think I would, but I was always good with numbers and it's fun." David would pick her up after class and they'd go to her apartment so she could practice dealing to him. When she completed her first week of classes, he took her to celebrate at a popular Italian restaurant on Sahara Avenue. Gray always sat beside him in a booth, not across, and after they ordered, he held her hand and told her how proud of her he was. She was talking about her class when he suddenly pushed her hand away. An older couple was coming toward them.

"David!" the woman said. "How wonderful to see you!"

He stood up and embraced the woman, and then shook hands with her husband. He didn't introduce Gray. The three of them chatted.

"This must be one of your granddaughters," the woman said at last, offering her hand to Gray.

"No," David stammered. "She's—ah—just a friend."

There was an awkward silence and then the couple followed the headwaiter to an empty booth. David did not take Gray's hand again during dinner, nor did he say much. When he drove her to her apartment, he said he was tired and wanted to go home. Gray knew how embarrassed he had been. After all, he was now sixty-three years old and she was eighteen.

There were six other students in Gray's blackjack

class. Of the two single men in the group, one was clearly gay, and the other was a newcomer to town named Charlie. During the second week of classes, Charlie asked Gray if she would like to practice dealing blackjack together after class. She knew he had been watching her and she thought he was cute, but she begged off since David was coming to give her a ride home. She told him that she was free the following night, however. During the drive back to her apartment, Gray told David that she would be driving herself to class the following night because she was going over to a classmate's apartment to practice dealing.

"Is it a woman or man?" he asked.

The question irritated her. "A man, but I'm not going to fuck him," she said. "Unless I want to." They finished the ride home in silence.

Gray had fun with Charlie. She had thought he might make a move on her but he didn't. She got back to her apartment at 3 A.M. and the phone rang. David said he had been worried because she had been gone so long. He asked her if she had had sex with Charlie and she hung up on him. "I know David's in love with me, or he thinks he is," she said later, "but he has a son and a daughter who are older than I am. He thinks I'm in my twenties because I never told him my real age, and I know it bugs him because I'm, like, his granddaughter's age. But this was his choice, you know." She was still angry about his embarrassment at being seen with her in the restaurant. "David is getting too possessive. He doesn't like me having sex with anyone else, even my steadies, which is like, really stupid, because I mean, I was doing this when he met me, right? So it's not like he didn't know what I did."

The next night, Charlie asked Gray if she wanted to practice dealing at his apartment again and order in a pizza. Gray knew it would irritate David so she said no, but told him the next night would be fine. When she got home, David called. She said she was going to be busy tomorrow night.

"That's Thursday," he said.

It took her a moment to realize what he meant. Thursdays were when he came to her apartment and spent the night with her. She asked him if he wanted to come over now, but he hung up. On Thursday night, Gray and Charlie practiced dealing and then watched a video over pizza. "I couldn't believe the video—it was *Pretty Woman*!" Gray said later, referring to the movie that starred Richard Gere as a rich playboy who becomes smitten with Julia Roberts, a good-hearted hooker. When the video ended, Charlie kissed her.

"It was so innocent," Gray said later, "and that was strange, because I was used to having sex with guys who paid me but I didn't let tricks kiss me on the lips. I let David, but no one else. Ever. With Charlie, I didn't have sex but I was letting him kiss me."

When she got home, David called. "Did you have sex with him?" he demanded. Gray lied. "Yes," she said. "It was great. He's so much younger than you."

David slammed down the receiver.

In the following weeks, Charlie and Gray practiced at his apartment almost every night after school and he told her about himself. He worked in a Las Vegas auto parts store during the day to pay his bills. He had moved to Las Vegas after barely getting through junior college in California, where he had spent most of his time drinking beer with his buddies. He had decided to become a dealer because he loved playing blackjack and figured being a dealer was one of the last well-paying jobs in America for someone without a college education. When he asked her about her past, Gray told him that she had graduated from high school in Sacramento and was being supported by her grandfather, who was named David and lived in Las Vegas, until she finished dealers school. Charlie said he had seen an older man dropping her off at dealers school and she said that was her grandfather. That night, she and Charlie made love.

"He wasn't, like, real experienced," Gray said later, "and I had to be careful. I almost took him over to the sink to wash off his dick the first time because that's what I always did with tricks." It was the first time in three years that Gray had sex with a man without charging him.

Her relationship with David was deteriorating. "I used to look forward to seeing him and I sorta feel guilty now because he really has done a lot for me, you know, but when he calls, I'm always disappointed it isn't Charlie." David showed up at Gray's apartment one afternoon unannounced and told her he wanted to have sex. He took out a $100 bill and slapped it on the table. She led him into her bedroom and he calmed down and tried to kiss her. She turned her head. If he was going to treat her like a whore, she was going to treat him like a trick. He left angry.

Just before Christmas, the instructor at the dealers school told Gray and Charlie that they knew enough to begin going to auditions. He had heard that the El Cortez, a downtown grind joint, was hiring. Each put on the standard white shirt and black slacks, but went to try out at different times. Charlie did fine, but Gray was nervous and made several mistakes. Neither was hired, but both felt it was good experience, and they decided to audition at other casinos. Charlie would go in first and give Gray tips when he was done. Two weeks later, he landed a job at a downtown casino dealing blackjack, but Gray hadn't found anything, even though she had worked an eight-hour shift at one lowbrow club. "They had this dealer who didn't show up and I happened to be there, so they put me on her table. I worked the whole time and then they told me that they didn't need anyone and said they weren't going to pay me because I had been auditioning, which was bullshit. I told them to go fuck themselves."

Gray decided to audition at the Luxor. "It was funny walking by the bar there, knowing that this is where I used to hang out looking for johns." She was sent to see Richard Woods, Keith Uptain's assistant, and he watched her deal blackjack for about ten minutes. "I was nervous the entire time but I kept telling myself, 'You can do this. You can do this,' " she said afterward. Woods gave her a mediocre rating in his written evaluation. But two days later, one of the smaller hotel casinos off the Strip offered her a job. "I'm not making as much money as I did being a whore, but I am a dealer. I mean, can you believe it? I'm actually a Las Vegas dealer." Her goal was to become good enough to be hired at the Luxor or the Mirage. "Charlie wants to work on the Strip too," she said. "Wouldn't that be great if both of us got jobs dealing there?"

Now that Gray had a full-time job, she stopped having sex with her steadies. "It was getting awkward anyhow because of Charlie." She didn't want him to find out. She also stopped seeing David. "I was worried at first because I thought he would maybe tell Charlie and try to mess things up for me, but he said it was okay. He stopped calling me. I didn't know what to say or do, but I was really relieved."

Charlie and Gray both worked on Christmas Day, but they were off the next day and Charlie invited her to go to Los Angeles with him to meet his parents. His family had waited to celebrate Christmas with them. She met Charlie's three younger brothers and his parents, who were Italian and devout Catholics. "We had pasta for our Christmas dinner and they even had a present for me," she recalled.

On the ride back, Charlie told Gray that he had once been engaged to his high school sweetheart, but she broke it off because she had met someone else. "He told me he felt really betrayed because he hadn't had a clue his girlfriend was going out with someone else," she said. "He went on this big kick about how honesty was like, really, really important in a relationship." Gray worried all the way home about how she was going to tell him about her past. "I decided I wouldn't, you know, tell him. I mean, how would he ever find out? But then I knew someday he would and he'd be resentful."

She decided to call David for advice. They had been through so much together and she trusted him. He told her never to tell Charlie and warned her that he wouldn't understand. "I didn't know what to do, and then Charlie gave me this card and it had this beautiful poem on it about how we were soul mates and could share our innermost thoughts and feelings and would love each other no matter what happened to us."

They both worked New Year's Eve and were exhausted by the time they met at his apartment. Charlie had bought champagne, and after they toasted each other, he told her that he loved her. She decided it was time. She began by talking about her mother and how she had been a cocaine addict. She started from the beginning and didn't skip much. He was devastated and furious. "How could you do this to me?" he kept saying. He told her that his mother would never accept her. She began crying, "I love you," she said, "but you got to deal with this or we're through." The next day, Gray called him to see if they were going to have dinner together.

"I'm busy," he said.

"Well, when won't you be busy?" she asked.

"I'm busy for the rest of my life," he said.

She still thought Charlie would call and apologize, but he didn't. Ten days later, she finally called him and he told her he wanted to be left alone.

"I was angry at him and at me because I wanted to believe love could conquer everything, but I guess when you find out someone has slept with a couple of hundred men for money, that's a lot for a guy to handle. I mean, I am a whore, or I was a whore, okay. But I'm not anymore. Doesn't that count?"

In February, Gray called David for help. She had decided to leave Las Vegas and she wanted to use him as a job reference. She knew he would lie about her past. He gave her the name of an assistant shift manager who worked at a casino in Laughlin. She drove down for an audition and was offered a job dealing.

"I don't know how long I'll last because I've heard Laughlin has nothing but old farts living and playing there, and there isn't much to do, but David and I talked a lot about it and he said it would be good for me to go somewhere where I could get a fresh start. There isn't much prostitution down there so I shouldn't be, like, tempted, you know, if times get tough. We talked about how we felt about each other and he told me he loved me but because of his kids and his age and everything, it really wasn't right. I thought he was sweet, because he knew me when I was turning tricks and he still stuck with me, not like Charlie. I mean, David paid for me to become a dealer and that was important to me. We both cried—he did too—and I told him I'd send him a postcard."

On her way out of town, Gray decided to drive along the Strip one last time even though it was out of the way for her. "I guess the Strip means different things to people. I remember having quickies for fifty bucks in the parking garage at Caesars Palace, but I think the Luxor is the place I will remember the best, and not because I used to hang out there turning tricks. I never got a job dealing there, but I remember what it was like to walk into that audition. I was wearing my white blouse and pressed slacks and they took me seriously and let me deal. I only did it for ten minutes, okay, and they never called me back, but for those ten minutes, I was a professional blackjack dealer. I wasn't a whore. I was a dealer. I know lots of people will judge me when they read about my life, but I'd like to know how many of them could have done what I did. I came to this town with less than a hundred bucks and the clothes I was wearing and I was only seventeen, and I'm leaving with money in my pocket. I got my own car and I'm a blackjack dealer now and I am a hell of a lot smarter than most girls my age. I know most people are selfish and mean and all they care about is using you. I've learned that telling the truth isn't always what's best in life. Believe me, I'm lying about my past from now on. But it's not been all bad. I've learned some people are pretty good, too, and they are the ones you remember."

She glanced back as she drove by the Luxor.

"I'll be back someday," she said.

CHAPTER THIRTY-TWO

....

Tony Alamo, the Boss

On New Year's Eve the year before, Tony Alamo had stood in a VIP tent and watched while the doomed Hacienda was imploded to clear the way for Mandalay Bay. On this New Year's Eve, he was standing in front of RA, the Luxor's new nightclub, watching a line of two hundred eager partygoers hoping to get inside. They were willing to pay $75 each, but their chances weren't good because the club was already packed. Alamo felt content. The nightclub, which was named after the Egyptian sun god Ra, was his final project at the Luxor. The work was over at last. "We can now compete with the Mirage, MGM, and Caesars Palace," he said proudly.

Inside RA, green and gold laser beams shot from the eyes of a huge statue of a winged creature, half man, half bird, hanging behind the bar as bartenders mixed cocktails, pausing occasionally to entertain customers by eating fire and then blowing it from their mouths. Inside steel cages in front of the stage, two women in black-studded bras and skin-tight shorts slithered to the deafening beat of the band. Security guards dressed entirely in black checked IDs at the door. RA had a dark Gotham feel to it, as if it were a scene in a Tim Burton Batman movie. It was the new hot spot on the Strip.

Everywhere Alamo looked inside the Luxor, he saw improvements. The steak house was jammed; ticket sales to *Imagine* were increasing; nine retail shops lined the Giza Galleria. The entire place felt new. Alamo knew that many of the Luxor's employees had not liked him when he had taken charge. He had come into the job with a reputation for cutting jobs and budgets. When he had first walked through the pyramid, he had often noticed employees averting their eyes. It was virtually a tradition on the Strip that every new casino boss cleaned house and installed his own people. Alamo had made cuts, but he had purposely not brought in his own people, nor had he played favorites. He had kept many of Bill Bennett's loyal managers in place even though he knew they had been critical of him. Still, for a long time he had not been well liked. The turning point had come when he reinstated the enraged supervisor who had threatened to kill him; it won him newfound respect. Now he was greeted with a steady chorus of "Hello, Mr. Alamo" as he watched the crowd outside RA. When a cocktail waitress stopped to chat, Alamo called her by her first name and asked if she was still working two jobs. "Yes," she replied, "but I almost got enough to go back home to Tennessee." Alamo explained later that the waitress was trying to save enough to move back to Nashville and buy a house. She had come to Las Vegas after a nasty divorce, and she wanted to go back now and fight for custody of her son. A waiter from the Pyramid Café paused to brag to Alamo that his son had just passed the bar exam.

"He's a lawyer," the waiter said.

"Doesn't that make two?" Alamo asked.

The waiter was thrilled that Alamo remembered

that the man's daughter had also become a lawyer a few years earlier. "That guy put both of his kids through law school with tips he earned while working for Circus Circus," Alamo explained afterward.

A Hispanic dealer waved at him and he waved back. He recalled that a pit boss had wanted to fire the dealer during his first six months on the job because he had such poor math skills.

"Is there a problem with him coming to work on time?" Alamo had asked.

"No," the pit boss had replied. "In fact, he comes in an hour early every day because he wants to watch other dealers and learn how to better himself."

"Is he respectful?"

"Oh, yes. He does everything he's told and sometimes he stays after to help out."

"Is he friendly to customers?"

"Always. But he is terribly slow. He makes mistakes and it takes him a long time to count out chips."

Alamo had taken the time to watch the employee at a craps table. "He is ninety percent there," he told the pit boss afterward. "Give him six more months to try."

The dealer had mastered the math and excelled ever since. "Math you can teach," Alamo said. "You can't teach attitude."

As he looked around, Alamo said, "You know, building one of these places is really not a lot of fun. You worry at night about what you're missing—the mistakes you're making—and worry about the decisions that you've already made. You think: 'Should I have done something different?' You're dealing with an eight-hundred-million-dollar property. That's eight hundred million dollars! Four thousand employees. Hundreds of decisions must be made each day. It's not fun, especially when things aren't going in the right direction in terms of return on our investment, and that's what the whole game is about: the bottom line.

Producing a profit. Maybe some people in my position worry at night about being fired, but that's not why I worry at night. It's your professional pride that makes you worry. You want everything to be perfect. You want people to be proud of you."

Alamo was bitter about Clyde Turner's efforts to oust him. "I am certain I've made plenty of mistakes here," he said, "and if Mike Ensign thinks he could find someone better to do this job, he should hire him. That's the nature of business. But I also know there is not a person alive who would have put more effort into doing this job. I can honestly say I gave it my best."

By the time Alamo stepped outside, the desert air had cooled. "There is more to all of this than just making a profit," Alamo said. "Look at this place. These are magical places. Look inside. The Luxor is a building made of glass and steel, but it's more. It's a place where people come to forget their problems. It's a place that provides a job for the waiter to pay for his children to go to law school. It's a place where a Hispanic kid who isn't good with math can learn a profession and support himself. I do not believe gambling is evil or wrong or immoral. Yes, some people get addicted to it and I'm sorry about that. But people get addicted to everything nowadays. Some people are addicted to eating. Do we close down food stores to protect them? What we have created here is a place for people to amuse people. People come here to eat things that they don't normally eat at home. They come here to drink more than they do at home. They come here to see shows that they can't see at home, and yes, they come to gamble. They come here and they sit in front of a slot machine or they play blackjack and some of them lose and some of them win and go home with cash. Either way, they all have a story to tell. They have a memory. The Luxor can be a million different things to a million different people. No one forces anyone to come to Las Vegas and stay at the Luxor. They come because they want to come and each one of them leaves with a little different experience and memory. This is what makes a place like this so special to me."

CHAPTER THIRTY-THREE

....

Leaving Las Vegas

Delta flight 1776 was scheduled to depart at 6:40 A.M. and the passengers waiting to board were a sleepy, somber group. Janice and Terry Clark, two sisters, were sipping coffee and trying to recover from hangovers brought on by an all-night binge at Harrah's when a man in his early twenties wearing tight black jeans, rattlesnake-skin boots, and a black T-shirt with a box of cigarettes rolled up in one of its short sleeves walked into the gate area searching for a friend. He wore his hair like the movie star James Dean and he paused in front of the women.

"Wow, you have a nice body!" Janice blurted.

Terry punched her in the ribs with her elbow.

"Thanks," he said, barely giving her a glance. As he walked away, Terry berated her sister. "I can't believe you said that. You don't have a clue who he is."

"So what?" replied Janice. 'I'm just having fun."

"Well, you'd better knock it off before we get home. Jesus!"

Sitting by themselves near a corner of the gate area,

Andy Montoya offered his bride, Maria, a container of orange juice and a Danish for breakfast. She was crying softly. They were on the last morning of their four-day honeymoon. "The wedding was beautiful," Maria recalled. "We had a big Roman Catholic wedding and afterward invited two hundred guests to a sit-down dinner and dancing to a band." Maria had carried a silk purse at the reception and well-wishers had deposited cash in it. When they added it up that night, it totaled nearly $4,000. They'd talked about all of the things they could buy with it, but both of them had gotten carried away gambling and lost it all. They'd also run up another $300 on their credit cards. Maria was afraid her parents would find out and Andy was badly embarrassed. "I repair copying machines," he said. "It's a good job, but, whew, we really could have used that money and now it's gone. I don't know, we just started drinking and partying and pretty soon, boom, we were broke."

Dorie Alvers preferred Diet Coke to coffee in the morning. At age fifty-three, she was a big woman who had never married, although she once had been engaged. She worked at an East Coast travel agency and had come on a weekend junket to see the New York New York casino. She was putting away her change from buying her morning soda when she decided to try her luck at a slot machine. She really hadn't gambled much that weekend. She dropped three quarters into a machine and hit the button marked "spin." A seven appeared, then the second wheel stopped on seven and so did the third. Before Alvers could react, a bell started ringing and the yellow light on top of the slot machine began flashing. Everyone waiting in the gate glanced at her. A few walked over to see what she had done. Alvers had played a progressive machine, and the neon bulbs on the electronic billboard above it were frozen on $685,987.50. An attendant in a brown uniform hurried over.

"My God!" Alvers said. "Is this really how much I won?" The attendant assured her it was. By this time a crowd had formed. Some congratulated her, others simply stared at the figures on the billboard. A few minutes later, a Delta flight attendant announced the jet was ready to board. Passengers in the gate area fell into line.

"Oh my gosh," said Alvers, "I'm supposed to be in a meeting tonight. That's my flight. I really can't miss that meeting." The attendant told her that it would be at least an hour before a representative from the slot company could complete all of the necessary paperwork. Alvers began to fret, then looked up at the electronic billboard and the number: $685,987.50.

"What am I thinking?" she said, laughing. "Depending on how they pay me, I'm probably going to have enough to retire. My boss can find someone else to send to that meeting." She smiled. "My head is spinning thinking about everything." She'd been putting off buying a pair of shoes even though her feet hurt. Now, she was $685,987.50 richer.

"Nothing like this has ever happened to me in my entire life," she said. Her eyes became wet. "I mean," she said softly, "just think of what I can do now with all this money."

Inside the Casino:
Real Gamblers

People come to Las Vegas and they lose $300 or maybe even $1,000 and they go home and really feel like they're big gamblers. Well, they aren't. They are playing at gambling. Let me tell you what real gambling is all about. Real gambling is standing at a craps table and shooting the dice with your entire paycheck spread out on the numbers, okay? It's knowing if the dice hit, you are going to win two or three or maybe five times your weekly salary, and if they don't hit, then you will be broke for the entire week—I mean, not even have enough to buy a can of dog food.

What I'm saying is that unless you have really put enough out there to hurt you if you lose or make a substantial difference if you win, then you aren't really playing the game. You see, it's not really about money. It's about risk. It's about pushing the envelope, taking chances that have real and immediate consequences. Let's keep it simple. You ever go to the circus? I used to love watching guys on the trapeze. I remember as a kid watching a guy do all sorts of flips and twirls and turns, and he was really, really good. The next week, my old man took me to another circus and this guy came out and he couldn't do half the acrobatic stuff the other guy had done, but it was much, much more exciting and you want to know why? Because he didn't have a net. You knew if he missed that bar, he was going to fall and die. That guy was risking everything to entertain you and it kept you on the edge of your seat! It gave you an adrenaline rush.

I have felt that same rush gambling, and you want to know the really weird part of it all? When I'm gambling, I am having the best time of my life and I am having the absolute worst time too. I'm talking about those nanoseconds when you are waiting for that card to fall or the white ball to drop into the red or the black or the dice to stop rolling. It can be absolutely terrifying and absolutely beautiful. You are standing there wishing like hell that you hadn't put down your complete paycheck. You are thinking: "Am I nuts? What am I going to do if I lose?" You are terrified and you are also totally alive. Your every sense is primed and as you stand there, you suddenly begin believing, "I'm going to do it!" You tell yourself, "I'm going to hit it big!" That's when you are pushing the edge, baby! Pushing the envelope as far as you can! And then that card falls or the ball stops or the dice quit rolling and you see the results and you either have won more than you dreamed possible or you have lost everything. People will tell you that they gamble to win, but I don't believe them. It's those brief seconds before you know the outcome that really turn you on. Those are the moments when you learn if you are a player or a real gambler, a winner or a loser. Those are the moments that really count because you are up there flying without a net.

—*Casino assistant shift manager*

EPILOGUE

....

The first super casinos on the Strip—the Mirage, the Excalibur, Treasure Island, and the Luxor—were surpassed in size and grandeur in the late 1990s by a second generation of even more colossal resorts. As before, Steve Wynn and Circus Circus led the way. Wynn's Italian-themed Bellagio earned gross revenues of $244 million, equal to more than $3 million per day, during its first seventy-seven days of operation. Those were the highest earnings ever recorded by a Nevada casino. Circus Circus followed with Mandalay Bay.

Tony Alamo was in charge of getting the $950 million Mandalay Bay ready and he faced a swarm of problems during 1998, including thin layers of rock and silty soil on the building site that caused the forty-three-story hotel to sink sixteen inches before an engineering firm found a way to shore up the structure. The South Seas–themed resort—Alamo's fourth super casino project—impressed even its harshest critics when it opened on schedule in May 1999. Alamo had filled it with imaginative sights. In a four-story wine cellar, acrobatic waitresses in black bodysuits floated up and down the racks on elastic cords in search of just the right bottle. A gentle rain fell in the indoor mock sugar refinery that housed a microbrewery. A wave machine kept a steady surf rolling across the eleven-acre lake outside.

In keeping with his view that the entertainment market in America is much larger than the gambling one, Glenn Schaeffer said he expected only 40 percent of Mandalay Bay's revenues to come from its casino. The rest would be earned by food and beverage sales, hotel room rentals, and high-end concerts and musical stage shows—a testament to the claims of Las Vegas promoters who have declared the city the world's new entertainment capital. On opening night, the Tony award–winning musical *Chicago* was performed at Mandalay Bay, followed by a midnight concert by legendary singer Bob Dylan. Opera tenor Luciano Pavarotti was scheduled to appear in the resort's twelve-thousand-seat entertainment complex.

Mandalay Bay was targeted at the "age forty-something" generation, Schaeffer said. "Somebody turns forty-nine years old every seven and a half seconds. This resort will bring in the rock 'n' roll generation looking for a high-class experience."

The opening of Bellagio and Mandalay Bay came at an opportune time. During 1998, gambling stocks fell into a slump, largely for two reasons: Financial turmoil in Asia reduced the number of whales flying into the United States, and Wall Street analysts lowered their expectations because they were convinced Las Vegas was overbuilt. Because Circus Circus operates more rooms on the Strip than any other company, its stock had been hit the hardest, dropping to a low of $7.12 a share by year end. But in 1999, Circus Circus stunned Wall Street by revealing that its earnings during its final quarter in 1998 were much better than analysts had predicted. The company reported earnings of $14.5 million, compared with only $708,000 in earnings during the prior year's fourth quarter. Glenn Schaeffer credited the Luxor for the increase. The company had spent close to $20 million marketing the remodeled Luxor and those efforts had helped bring in throngs of customers. More importantly, the Luxor's repeat business had climbed from the low teens to nearly 50 percent. Tony Alamo's efforts were finally paying off.

Overall, the Luxor earned $97.6 million during 1998, making it the company's largest money earner. Although that was less than the $120 million cash flow mark that Schaeffer had originally promised investors, the Luxor was well on the way to finally hitting or exceeding that mark by the start of 1999.

The company's surprise earnings caused analysts to reevaluate Circus Circus, sending its stock upward. The dramatic opening of Mandalay Bay propelled the stock even higher. It jumped up five dollars a share in a single day—a move that was later credited with energizing other lackluster gambling stocks. Within the first five months of 1999, Circus Circus stock had more than tripled in value, closing at $25½ a share. While that was still not close to the price that its shares commanded during Bill Bennett's glory days, Schaeffer insisted it was proof that the company had been smart in making its properties more upscale. "1997 proved to be the worst year in this company's history," Schaeffer said, "but without the trauma of our remodeling at Luxor and our decision to put this company on a new course, today's results could never have happened. The Boys of the Las Vegas Boom are back in business." In June, the company took another step to shed its ties with its grind-joint past and its Bill Bennett legacy. It changed its name from Circus Circus to Mandalay Resort Group.

Other companies were undergoing major changes

on the Strip, too. In 1998, Hilton Hotels rid itself of its gambling properties by spinning them off into a new company called Park Place Entertainment. Its president, Arthur M. Goldberg, took advantage of the slump in the gaming industry to buy Bally Entertainment, the Mississippi casinos owned by Grand Casinos, and the biggest plum of all—Caesars World, owners of Caesars Palace. These acquisitions made Park Place Entertainment the largest gaming company in the world, with casinos in Las Vegas, Reno, Atlantic City, Australia, and Uruguay. Goldberg also entered the super casino competition by opening Paris–Las Vegas, a Strip resort patterned after the French capital, complete with its own miniature Eiffel Tower. The Strip gained another flamboyant player in 1999, when Sheldon Adelson, the former owner of the Comdex computer show, opened the Venetian, a super casino that featured waterways and gondolas. By the turn of the century, there were twelve super casinos on the Strip, four of which cost in excess of $1 billion each. The number of hotel rooms had jumped from 100,000 to more than 120,000.

When will it end? With increased competition from Indian casinos in California, some doomsayers are predicting the 1990s Las Vegas boom will bust in 2000. They say the super casinos will be unable to draw the crowds necessary to support their billion-dollar buildings and will become modern-day monuments to excess, decaying in the desert sand.

But Schaeffer dismisses such talk, noting that he has heard such dire predictions before. Mandalay Resort Group still has enough land within its masterplan mile to build another 3,000-room super casino, this one tentatively called Project Z. If there is a lesson to be learned by studying the history of Las Vegas, Schaeffer says, it is this: There is only one boundary that limits a dreamer, and that is the boundary that he imposes on himself.

ACKNOWLEDGMENTS

....

This book could not have been written without the co-operation of the management at Circus Circus Enterprises, especially Glenn Schaeffer and Tony Alamo. Schaeffer was the first to agree to give me unlimited access to the Luxor and Alamo encouraged employees there to speak to me without fear of retribution. The period of late 1996 to early 1998 proved to be a difficult time for the company but Schaeffer and Alamo never limited my access or tried to sugarcoat what was happening. I know there are incidents reported in this book that both of them wish had not been noted by me, but they have not tried to censor my material. I know of few executives in major corporations who would have risked letting an outsider observe their operations without some prearranged editorial control. Both men deserve my deepest thanks for letting me inside Circus Circus without any such requirements.

I also wish to thank Brian Folger, Stewart Madden, Dave Maturino, Tom Robinson, and Richard Woods for answering questions about casino operations. I owe a special thanks to Keith Uptain for the countless hours that he spent with me inside the Luxor casino. He always took time to explain what was happening and his years of experience proved invaluable to the writing of this book. The same is true of Don Archer in the Luxor poker room. Circus Circus public relations director Sarah Ralston is also owed a special thank-you, as is Diane Spataro, who helped me understand what Las Vegas was like before the birth of its super casinos.

Others whom I would like to thank by name include: Terrance Alden, Richard Banis, Robin Bayley, Sonja Beaton, William G. Bennett, Racquel Bridgewater, John Bjorklum, Bud Boor, Alan Buchholz, Michael Caffrey, Katherine Caffrey, Tom Carilli, Jay Connor, Marti Crain, Linda Dennis, Sandy Dobritch, Terry Dowgall, Kirk Dougan, Ron Edwards, Alan Feldman, Gloria Ford, Dick Foster, Lynne Foster, David Fowler, DeeDee Friedman, Phil Friedman, Linda Gillen, Don Givens, Mike Hartzell, Peter Harms, Patti Harms, Clifford Hay, Marie Heffelfinger, Melissa Heffelfinger, Robert E. Hunter, Susan Infeld, Susie Isaacs, Susan Jarvis, Brian Jentzen, Adele L. Johansen, David Johnston, Marshal Kaplan, Bill Keeton, Scott Kent, Joyce Sarno Keys, Yvette Landau, Mel Larson, Robert Leidenheimer, Vicki LePore, Yvonne Lewis, Betty Archer Liddington, Stanley Mallin, Richard Marino, Emmett Michaels, Richard Miles, Phillip Millaudon, Angel Naves, Rick Ninomiya, Carole Parker, Bill Paulos, Tom Peacock, William N. Pennington, Myriam Pennington, Jack Pickett, Nanci Pileggi, Jon Ralston, and Jake Rice.

I also want to thank September Joy Sarno, Thomas Schmitz, C. T. Shades, Paulla Shaw, Thomas Silverstein, Mike Sion, Steve Sless, Michael Sloan, Arthur Smith Jr., Gary J. Smith, Lynn Smith, Lou Ann Smith, Sally Smith, Michael Starr, Kelly Jo Steinfort, Heidi Sarno Straus, Leon Symanski, Suzanne "Maria" Tamayo-Soto, John Thacker, Richard Tucci, Clyde Turner, Vera

Turner, Andy Vanyo, Stephanie Wilson, Melinda Winn, and Steve Wynn.

I am indebted to my literary agent, Robert Gottlieb, at the William Morris Literary Agency, and his assistant, Lauren Sheftell, for their help. At Bantam Books, I wish to thank my editor, Ann Harris, for her thoughtful suggestions and skillful handling of the manuscript. I also thank Jean Lynch for her keen eye in copyediting the manuscript, attorney Matthew Martin, and my publisher, Irwyn Applebaum. Although all of the characters in this book are actual people, several pseudonyms were used. Usually, I have identified pseudonyms by using only first names to identify characters. The only major players who were given pseudonyms were Dorie Alvers, Gary Brown, Malcolm Fry, Shawna Gray, Andy and Maria Montoya, Paul Morgan, Jack and Martha Wallace, and Travis Westfield. Much of the dialogue in this book is based on personal observation. Other conversations were re-created based on the recollections of the participants. I did not pay anyone for their cooperation.

I also wish to thank Bill and Rosemary Luzi, Billy Luzi, Jeff Luzi, Charles and Donna Stackhouse, and Gary and Beverly Zell.

Finally, I wish to thank my parents, Elmer and Jean Earley, who proofread the manuscript, offered me advice, and provided me with moral support. I also am indebted to fellow writers Nelson DeMille, Walter Harrington, and Michael Sager for their longtime friendship. In addition, I wish to thank Ellen Brown, Gloria Brown, James Brown, LeRue Brown, Phillip Corn, Joanne Corn, Donnie Davis, Dana Davis, Matthew Davis, George Earley, Linda Earley, Elsie Strine, and Jay Strine. Most of all, I want to thank my wife, Patti, for her unwavering encouragement, wisdom, and love, and our children, Stephen, Kevin, Tony, Kathy, Kyle, Evan, and Traci, for the blessings that they bring into both of our lives every day.

INDEX

About the Author

....

Pete Earley, a former reporter for *The Washington Post,* is the author of five previous books: *Family of Spies: Inside the John Walker Spy Ring; Prophet of Death: The Mormon Blood-Atonement Killings; The Hot House: Life Inside Leavenworth Prison; Circumstantial Evidence: Death, Life, and Justice in a Southern Town;* and *Confessions of a Spy: The Real Story of Aldrich Ames.* He lives in Virginia with his family.

For more information, visit the author's website at www.peteearley.com.